Flyfisher's Guide to™

Northern New England

Vermont, New Hampshire, and Maine

TITLES AVAILABLE IN THIS SERIES

Flyfisher's Guide to Colorado

Flyfisher's Guide to Idaho

Flyfisher's Guide to Montana

Flyfisher's Guide to Northern California

Flyfisher's Guide to Washington

Flyfisher's Guide to Oregon

Flyfisher's Guide to Wyoming

Flyfisher's Guide to Pennsylvania

Flyfisher's Guide to Michigan

Flyfisher's Guide to™

Northern New England

Vermont, New Hampshire, and Maine

Steve Hickoff and Rhey Plumley

Wilderness
Adventures
Press™

Belgrade, Montana

Published by Wilderness Adventures Press
45 Buckskin Road
Belgrade, MT 59714
800-925-3339
Website: www.wildadv.com
email. books@wildadv.com

10 9 8 7 6 5 4 3 2

Printed in the United States of America

Library of Congress Cataloging-in-Publication Data:

Hickoff, Steve, 1958–
    Flyfisher's guide to Northern New England : Vermont, New Hampshire, and Maine / Steve Hickoff and Rhey Plumley.
        p.   cm.
    Includes index.
    ISBN 1-885106-47-5
    1. Fly fishing–Vermont–Guidebooks.   2. Fly fishing–New Hampshire–Guidebooks.   3. Fly fishing–Maine–Guidebooks.   4. Vermont–Guidebooks. 5. New Hampshire–Guidebooks.   6. Maine–Guidebooks.   I. Plumley, Rhey, 1947– II. Title.   III. Title : Fly fisher's guide to Northern New England.
    SH555.H53   1999
    799.1'24'0974 – –dc21   99-19498
                                                                                                    CIP

Table of Contents

Acknowledgments

I've included flyfishing opportunities based on my personal experiences and insights provided by regional experts without whose gracious help there would be no book. These good people include state fisheries biologists, information and education specialists, Chambers of Commerce personnel, fly shop contacts, sales associates, established outfitters, individual angling guides, and ardent flyfishers like you.

My appreciation also goes out to all publishers, editors, and writers who have encouraged, assigned, and accepted my work as a freelancer over the years.

Finally, but certainly foremost, thanks to Elizabeth: angler, wife, and friend.

—Steve Hickoff

It has been enjoyable sharing some of northern New England's flyfishing waters with you. There were many who helped with and supported this effort: Erin Garcia, typist; Sue and Tom Haney, photos; John and Mary Austin, editors; Bill Weber, who rode shotgun; as well as Roger Ranz, Jim Lavigne, the staff of Wilderness Adventures Press, and the staffs of the state fish and wildlife agencies and fly shops of northern New England. Thank you.

—Rhey Plumley

Introduction

Opening day of fishing season in northern New England features icy blue water, tumbling around snowcapped boulders. Trees are black against snowcovered streambanks, and as first light breaks, a path of boot prints is already leading the way to the jump pool below the falls. Fisherman are lined up on both sides of the stream, standing in the frigid water up to the ankles of their hip boots, casting in cadence and letting their offerings drift slowly in the current near the rocky bottom. This opening day ritual repeats itself year after year on the Willoughby River and Lewis Creek in Vermont, on New Hampshire's Merrymeeting and Newfound Rivers, and Maine's Crooked River and Grand Lake Stream, where rainbow trout migrate from the downstream lakes to spawn upriver, or landlocked salmon forage for smelt.

Sooner or later, the ice breaks up on inland lakes and "ice-out" anglers launch boats and canoes to troll their beautiful feather and hair smelt imitations hoping to catch landlocked salmon, brook trout, or lake trout. New Hampshire offers this early-season fishing in Lake Winnipesaukee or the Connecticut Lakes. In Maine, Rangeley, Moosehead, and Sebago Lakes are among dozens of clear, cold stillwaters known for early-season salmon and trout. Vermont shares this wealth with Lake Champlain and Lake Memphremagog, among others.

As the sun reaches higher over northern New England and the days lengthen, warming waters entice mayfly nymphs and caddis larva to stir and swim about the rocks and gravel of streambeds. Hendricksons begin their nuptial flights as the dogwoods bloom on the Battenkill in Vermont; alderflies appear for their short dance number on New Hampshire's upper Androscoggin River; and in Maine, brookies sip on emerging caddisflies.

In Maine's Down East waters, sea-run Atlantic salmon begin to appear in the pools below Veazie Dam on the Penobscot River, and stripers chase bait in Great Bay near Portsmouth, New Hampshire. I guess you could say fishing season in northern New England is in full swing.

This book is offered to the reader, not so much as a how-to or where-to guide but rather as a resource for discovering flyfishing in northern New England. Please feel welcome on our rivers, streams, and stillwaters. Come hike the trails to remote ponds or stay with outfitters in their camps and lodges. Share with us the quiet pleasures of flyfishing in lovely northern New England.

—Rhey Plumley

Northern New England

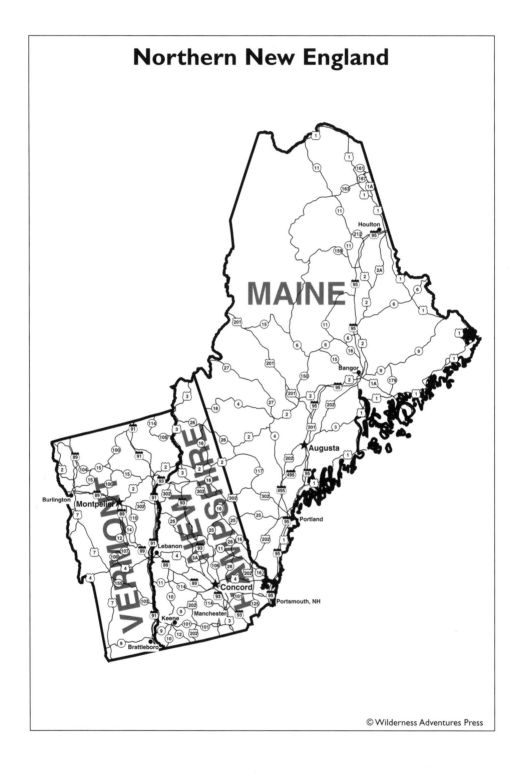

© Wilderness Adventures Press

Tips on Using this Book

For each northern New England state, major river systems, lakes, and ponds, as well as the wild haunts and waters sustained by annual plantings have been highlighted. Flyfish these places alone or arrange time with a professional guide. Outfitters can help you plan trips. This book should assist you in arranging a flyfishing trip by phone, by mail, or by simply driving to a particular location. Contacting a local fly shop can often help improve the quality of your fishing experience.

This book is divided into three sections: Vermont, New Hampshire, and Maine. To assist you in contacting local services, area codes for these states are: Vermont, 802; New Hampshire, 603; and Maine, 207.

Although the information in this guidebook is accurate at the time of printing, be aware that information about accommodations, restaurants, fly shops, and other businesses may change. The quality of services provided also varies. In this regard, fishery conditions, available flyfishing, and management approaches can fluctuate from season to season. Always check the current sport fishing regulations for each state.

Motel Cost Key

$ — up to $60
$$ — $61–$80
$$$ — $81–95
$$$$ — $96–$125
$$$$$ — $125 and up

Maps and accounts of proven flyfishing haunts are included, as well as fly patterns, techniques, and major hatches. Salmon fishing on many waters is dependent on the spring smelt run and autumnal spawning urges.

Come flyfish this region. Let the buyer beware, however—you may not want to go home.

—*Steve Hickoff*

Major Roads and Rivers of Vermont

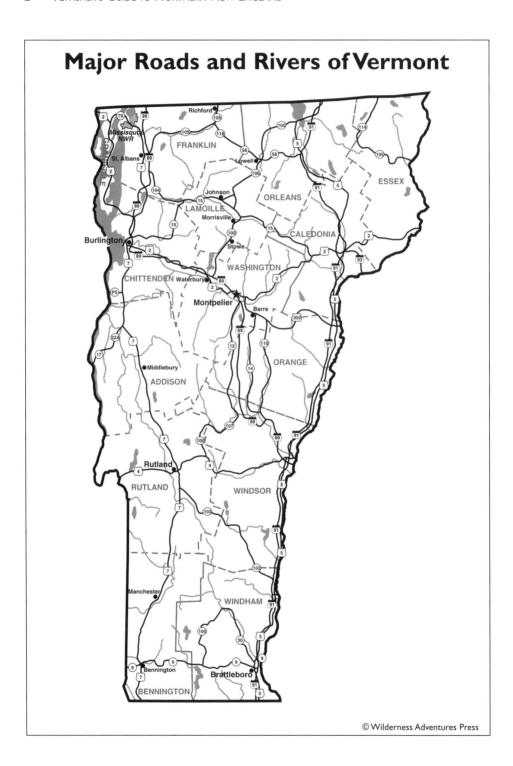

© Wilderness Adventures Press

Vermont Facts

45th largest state in the union
9,615 square miles

Elevation: Averages 1,000 feet
Counties: 14
Population: 588,654

    50   State Parks
    36   State Forests
    33   State Natural Areas
     1   National Forest (Green Mountain)

State Motto: Freedom and Unity
State Song: "Hail, Vermont," written by Josephine Hovey Perry
State Flower: Red Clover
State Animal: Morgan Horse
State Tree: Sugar Maple
State Bird: Hermit Thrush
State Fossil: Charlotte, the fossil whale
State Rocks: Granite, Marble, and Slate
State Mineral: Talc
State Gem: Grossular Garnet
State Warmwater Fish: Walleye
State Coldwater Fish: Brook Trout

Vermont Flyfishing

The ancient and quiet Green Mountains offer a framework for Vermont's streams and lakes. The streams drain the mountains to the west into Lake Champlain, and to the east into the valley of the Connecticut River. Wild brook trout still swim in the stream headwaters and beaver ponds of Vermont. Landlocked salmon and lake trout inhabit the deeper lakes and ponds. Rivers, such as the Battenkill, Winooski, White, Lamoille, and Missisquoi, are home to rainbow and brown trout. And there are stillwaters and warmwater sections of rivers that provide rich habitat for large and smallmouth bass, northern pike, pickerel, and panfish.

The Vermont Department of Fish and Wildlife manages an aggressive trout and salmon-stocking program throughout the state. As a result, several rivers now have special regulations that limit catches and restrict sizes. In 1997, an extended catch-and-release season was started that opened up fishing in some rivers during the winter months.

There are six rivers that the Department of Fish and Wildlife has designated as wild trout fisheries and manages without stocking. They are the Battenkill, Castleton, Dog, Poultney, and Mettawee Rivers, and Furnace Brook. Other river systems, such as the Barton and Willoughby, the Johns and Black, and sections of the Winooski, support trout reproduction and hold wild fish.

Most of Vermont's rivers are freestone streams and are subject to high flows during spring runoff and spate conditions from summertime rains. Dams that interrupt flows and cause frequent changes in water levels restrict spawning activity and aquatic insect life in many of the state's rivers. Local clubs and groups, such as Trout Unlimited, the New Haven River Anglers Association, the Lamoille River Anglers Association, and the Orleans County Rod and Gun Club, are working with state agencies and private groups to restore historical fish runs, improve stream habitat and water quality, and manage the recreational use of the state's rivers.

In general, Vermont's rivers and stillwaters are open to trout fishing from the second Saturday in April through the last Sunday in October. The bass season runs from the second Saturday in June through November 30. There is a special, artificial-lures-only, catch-and-release season for bass from the second Saturday in April to the Friday before the second Saturday in June. Resident and nonresident fishing licenses are available at town clerk's offices, license outlets, and tackle shops throughout the state. Nonresident licenses are available for one-day, three-day, seven-day, and full season. Current rates are from $11.00 to $38.00. There are no other stamps or permits required.

Tourism is a major Vermont industry-each region offers a full array of excellent facilities and services to make visitors comfortable and happy. There are hotels and motels, country inns, and bed and breakfasts. Restaurants for every taste are nearby. Local fly and tackle shops can give you up-to-date conditions, hatch information, and referrals for area guides.

Wild brook trout are found in many Vermont rivers and streams.
(Photo by Elizabeth Edwards)

In this beautiful state, you'll find a quiet pace and old New England friendliness among the people. Likewise, the rivers flow gently out of the hills, through forests and farmlands. Insects hop and skip on the surface of quiet pools in the summer sun. A small, wild brookie, adorned like a jewel, glides to the surface to feed. In another river, an aggressive silver-sided landlocked salmon turns wildly with your streamer in its mouth and leaps into the cool, autumn air. You're welcome to visit Vermont and share some its beauty and flyfishing opportunities.

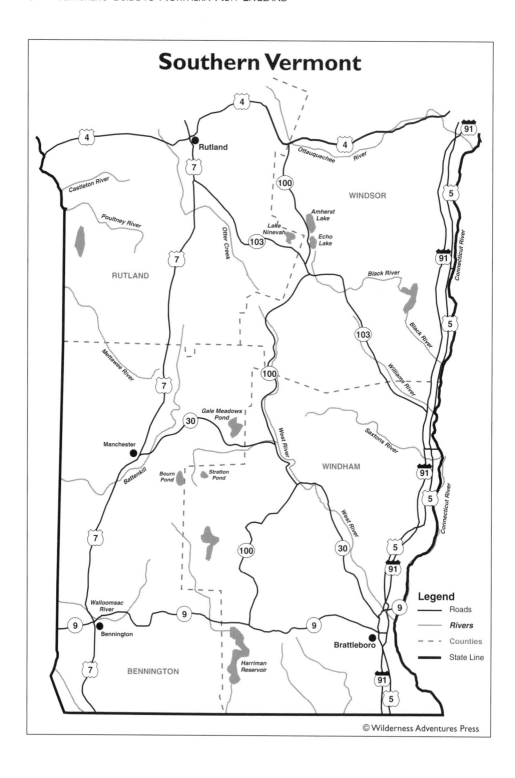

Southern Vermont

WINDSOR

Ottauquechee River

Castleton River

Poultney River

Otter Creek

RUTLAND

Amherst Lake

Lake Ninevah

Echo Lake

Black River

Black River

Williams River

Mettawee River

Gale Meadows Pond

Manchester

Battenkill

Bourn Pond

Stratton Pond

West River

Saxtons River

WINDHAM

West River

Walloomsac River

Bennington

Harriman Reservoir

Brattleboro

BENNINGTON

Rutland

Connecticut River

Connecticut River

Legend

—— Roads

—— *Rivers*

- - - Counties

—— State Line

© Wilderness Adventures Press

Southern Vermont

You'll discover old New England as you cross the Massachusetts or New York border and enter the southwest corner of Vermont. The mills and factories of North Bennington operate with eternal rhythm. Narrow streets lined by the look-alike homes of the workers parallel railroads and river passages.

On the outskirts of town, you'll pass the massive, groomed lawns bearing the pillared homes of the "old families." Stone-framed entrances, long driveways, and lanes replace the streets. The landscape is entirely manicured and groomed. Many of these impressive homes have Revolutionary War era construction dates. Roadside historical markers describe such things as, "George Washington slept here in...," or "Daniel Webster spoke..." There is a deep sense of history as you gaze upon the hills and lawns of southern Vermont.

Rivers and streams wander lazily through the valleys and farmlands of southwestern Vermont: the Walloomsac near North Bennington; the "most holy" Battenkill passing through Manchester and Arlington; the beautiful Mettawee; the Poultney and Castleton Rivers; and the headwaters of Otter Creek share their history with the landscape.

In southeastern Vermont, the east-facing slopes of the Green Mountains have their own history. The transportation offered by the Connecticut River encouraged industrial and commercial development from Brattleboro north to Springfield. The healing spring waters near Brattleboro and Woodstock attracted wealthy patrons from around the country as tourists and settlers. Mills, once hydropowered, and factories mix with the federal and Greek revival residential styles in southwest Vermont's villages.

The most popular Vermont tourist area lies in the state's southeast corner. From the city of Brattleboro, near the Massachusetts border, north to White River Junction, the Connecticut River forms the border that Vermont shares with New Hampshire. Five beautiful trout streams, the Ottauquechee, the Black, the West, the Saxtons, and the Williams Rivers, flow out of the Green Mountains into the Connecticut River, sharing their beauty with the landscape, covered bridges, inns, and antique shops that attract visitors from all over.

Flyfishers coming to southeastern Vermont will find rivers holding warmwater species, mostly bass and pike, near their mouths at the Connecticut River. Upstream are found brown trout, rainbows, and wild brook trout.

SOUTHERN VERMONT MAJOR HATCHES

Insect/Bait	J	F	M	A	M	J	J	A	S	O	N	D	Patterns
Quill Gordon			▮										Quill Gordon or Adams #12
Caddis				▮	▮	▮	▮	▮					Black Elk Hair Caddis #16–20 (early and late season); Tan Elk Hair Caddis #14–18; Soft Hackles and Emergers #14–18; Hare's Ear Nymph and Beadhead Pupae #14–18
Blue-winged Olives				▮					▮				Parachute Adams #14–20; Thorax Blue–winged Olive #14–18; Pheasant Tail Nymph #14–20
Hendricksons				▮	▮								Dark Hendrickson or Red Quill #12–14; Hendrickson Nymph #12–14; Rusty Spinner #14
March Brown					▮								March Brown Dun #12; Hare's Ear Nymph
Sulphurs						▮							Sulphur Duns and Hare's Ear Nymphs #16–18
Light Cahill						▮	▮						Cahill Dun or Parachute #16
Stoneflies					▮	▮	▮	▮					Black Stonefly Nymph #8–14; Yellow Stonefly Nymph #8–10; Yellow Sally #14
Tiny Mayflies *Tricorythodes stygiatus*							▮	▮	▮				Trico Spinner #18–20
Terrestrials							▮	▮	▮				Hoppers #6–12; Ants #14–18
Midges						▮	▮	▮					Griffith's Gnat #18; Parachute Adams #18–22
Minnows and Leeches	▮	▮	▮	▮	▮	▮	▮	▮	▮	▮	▮	▮	Woolly Buggers and Streamers

SOUTHWESTERN VERMONT
Walloomsac River

From the mountains east of Bennington, the Walloomsac River flows for 25 miles within Vermont before it enters New York state, where it joins the Hoosic River. Access is gained from Routes 7A and 67A that parallel the river between Bennington and North Bennington. (If you park near a local business, first ask permission from the owner.) This section of river is quite fertile, supporting a healthy base for regularly stocked (as well as holdover) brown trout, rainbows, and brookies. Caddis and stoneflies are the dominant aquatic insects, with regular mayfly hatches occurring throughout the summer.

The upper reaches of the Walloomsac are largely unproductive as trout waters. Tributaries, including Furnace Brook and Paran Creek, however, are good nursery habitat and hold healthy numbers of wild trout. Downstream the river broadens and flows over gravel bars, through cutbanks under low-hanging trees, and into many deep pools. Three covered bridges cross the Walloomsac in the 7 miles between the villages of Bennington and North Bennington.

The Walloomsac's season runs from the second Saturday in April through the last Sunday in October, with no special regulations.

Annual stockings of 1,000 each of brook trout, brown trout, and rainbow trout supplement the wild and holdover fish that are abundant in this river. Average length is 8 to 14 inches, with many over 18 inches caught every year.

The Battenkill

The promise of fishing over selective brown trout on the legendary Battenkill draws flyfishers each season from all over the world. They come to fish the one-time homewaters of Charles Orvis, John Atherton, and Lee Wulff. The Battenkill is the most famous of Vermont rivers and, until recently, the most heavily fished.

Maintained and managed for decades as a wild fishery without stocking, the Battenkill has had a reputation as one of the top trout rivers in the East. The East and West Branches join in Manchester to form the main stem. From there, it slowly flows through the concealed back side of the exclusive country clubs and estates of Manchester's lower village, through brushy pastures and farmland along Route 7A through the town of Sunderland and on to the village of Arlington, where it turns sharply to the west for a 9-mile journey to the New York border.

Access may be gained in the lower village of Manchester by turning east on Union Street off Route 7A by the mall of the Equinox Inn. There are several unmarked pull-off areas near the two bridges and along Richville Road and River Road, which eventually return to Route 7A. Through this area, the Battenkill is mostly pocketwater of medium depth with some undercut banks and pools. As you continue south, the river deepens and meanders lazily through fields with good cover. The banks are steep and holes, undercutting the sides, are deep. There is a marked Vermont Fish

Walloomsac River

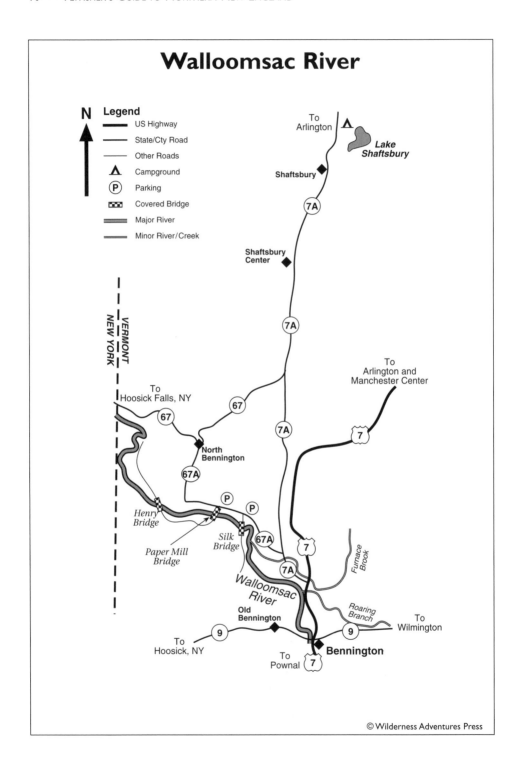

© Wilderness Adventures Press

and Wildlife public access at the river crossing in the town of Sunderland on Route 7A. A quarter-mile down the road, turn east on Dunham Road and backtrack upriver to Sunderland Station. There are a couple of good pull-offs with river access near the railroad tracks along this dirt road.

Access to the Battenkill is limited as it continues south behind a very conveniently located campground on the river, named "Camping on the Battenkill." It continues behind a residential area and golf course before entering Arlington, where it turns abruptly west toward New York state. There are both marked and unmarked access points along Route 313 and on River Road, which parallels the Battenkill to the south. The easy access and water quality have made this section of river one of the most popular fishing areas in Vermont. It is also a very popular recreational float for canoeists and tubers. The state fish and wildlife department previously managed the stretch of river from the West Mountain Bridge in Arlington downstream to Benedict Crossing for artificial lures only, with a slot limit for fish between 10 and 14 inches. It is becoming apparent that additional rules

The Battenkill holds self-sustaining populations of brook and brown trout. (Photo by Steve Hickoff)

The Battenkill

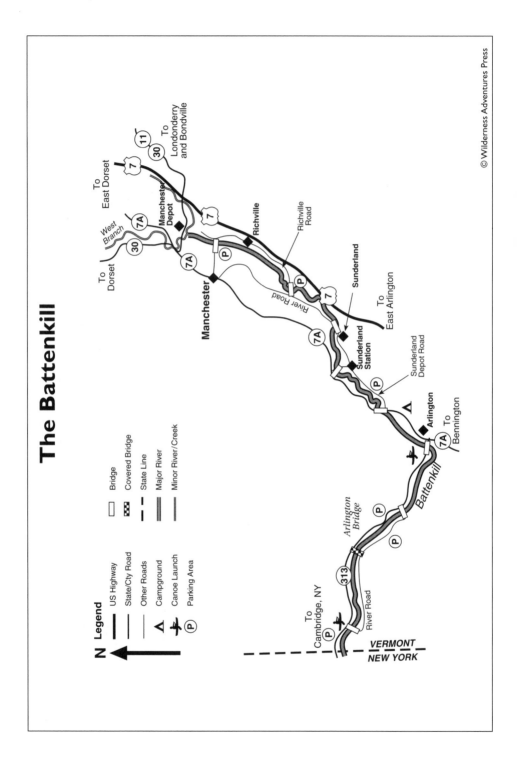

Legend

N

US Highway	
State/Cty Road	
Other Roads	
Campground	△
Canoe Launch	
Parking Area	Ⓟ

Bridge	▯
Covered Bridge	▦
State Line	
Major River	
Minor River/Creek	

Flyfish too early and you'll find yourself staring at the cold, brawling, discolored version of the Battenkill. (Photo by Steve Hickoff)

are necessary to address the issues of competing recreational interests among canoeists, tubers, and anglers. New regulations have taken effect in April 2000, limiting all fishing on the Vermont section of the Battenkill to catch and release while further studies are made.

In general, the Battenkill may be classified as a spring creek, receiving much of its icy waters from beneath the riverbed. It offers a rich habitat for wild trout. Consequently, Vermont has managed the river without stocking since the 1970s. Wild brook trout can average from 8 to 11 inches, and brown trout may range up to 16 or 17 inches.

Unfortunately, the Battenkill has become more of a memory of its former days when prolific hatches brought scores of wild trout to the surface. Merwin, in his book, *The Battenkill*, puts it this way, "It's a lovely river that's now more rich with angling tradition than with trout." Recent state studies indicate real trouble. Fish catches have dropped from 12,400 in 1988 to 2,000 last year, according to an editorial in the *Burlington Free Press* dated May 15, 1998. Further, the same editorial states, "the quantity of fish larger than 10 inches is down 89 percent in some stretches."

Local newspaper headlines, such as these, tell a grim tale: "Battenkill Shadow of Its Former Self," "Conservation Group Wants Battenkill Rules," and "Killing the Kill."

In recent years, development and heavy use by canoeists, tubers, and anglers have brought dramatic changes to the Battenkill and the fish that inhabit its cool waters. The situation is critical, and local and state officials need to take the lead to correct abuses and help return this river to a more natural condition.

In spite of these troubles, the Battenkill still draws devotees to its challenging currents and trout. Brown trout and brookies in this river are wild and sophisticated. The riverbanks are steep and undercut, making an approach to a fish rising close to shore almost impossible. Hatches are legendary: Mayflies, from quill Gordons, blue quills, and Hendricksons, pop from the river's surface film and float downstream like miniature sailboats during early spring afternoons. Later in the day, evening caddis, sulphurs, and drakes appear. In the heat of summer, waters remain cool and trout feed on various terrestrials that stumble into the water from the riverbanks and proceed to struggle, enticing the waiting predator. During August and September on the Battenkill, tiny mayflies, Tricos, and blue-winged olives make their way to the fishes' table.

The Manchester-Arlington area is one of Vermont's major tourist centers. Inns, historical sites, shops, museums, and breathtaking scenery bring visitors from all over the world. Manchester is the home of the Orvis Company and where Orvis fly rods are built. The American Museum of Fly Fishing has treasures to share and will stir your imagination of bygone eras of flyfishing. Arlington was the home of Norman Rockwell, and the area's splendor and character of local life inspired his work. The Battenkill itself remains a treasure and an attraction. If we continue to show an interest by visiting this once-great river and contributing to organizations such as Trout Unlimited, the Battenkill may once again be the jewel of flyfishing streams in northern New England.

The Battenkill's season runs from the second Saturday in April through the last Sunday in October. New regulations have just taken effect as of April 8, 2000, limiting all fishing to catch and release only on the Vermont portion of the Battenkill from the base of Dufresne Pond Dam in Manchester to the New York state line. This regulation is in response to the marked decline in wild brown trout over the last decade.

The Mettawee River

Four of the six Vermont rivers that are managed as wild trout streams (no stocking) are in the southwestern part of the state: the Battenkill, Mettawee, Poultney, and Castleton Rivers support wild brook trout, brown trout, and in the Mettawee, rainbow trout. The waters of these streams have a high dissolved mineral content and are nurtured by many underground springs. Trout thrive in this habitat, and there is significant reproduction in the upper reaches and tributaries.

Mettawee River

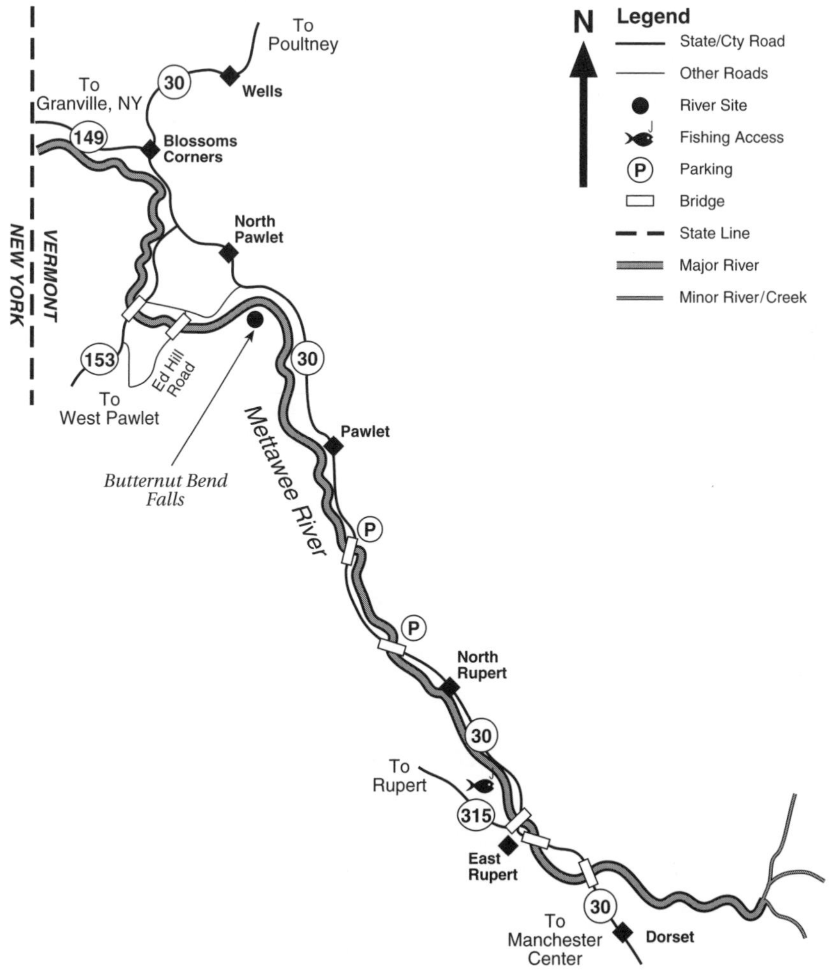

N

Legend

——————	State/Cty Road
————	Other Roads
●	River Site
✦	Fishing Access
Ⓟ	Parking
▭	Bridge
– – –	State Line
▨▨▨	Major River
═══	Minor River/Creek

To Poultney

To Granville, NY

To (30) Wells

(149) Blossoms Corners

NEW YORK

VERMONT

North Pawlet

(153)

Ed Hill Road

To West Pawlet

Butternut Bend Falls

Mettawee River

(30)

Pawlet

Ⓟ

Ⓟ

North Rupert

(30)

To Rupert

(315)

East Rupert

To Manchester Center

(30)

Dorset

© Wilderness Adventures Press

The Mettawee flows 17 miles within the borders of Vermont, from the hills in the town of Dorset to the New York state line west of Granville. One of the loveliest of Vermont trout streams, it slowly meanders through fields and woods, paralleling Route 30. Between the village of East Rupert and North Rupert, there is a Vermont state fish and wildlife public access. As you continue north along Route 30, several bridges cross the Mettawee, creating unmarked access points. The water is crystal clear, and there is good stream cover keeping water temperatures cool on even the hottest of summer days.

The West Pawlet cutoff joins Route 153 where the river bears away from Route 30. There is a natural waterfall creating a local swimming hole. Much of the area around the falls is posted. Downstream and as the river continues to twist and turn, there are some fine runs and deep holes.

Early season caddisflies give way to Hendricksons, stoneflies, and cahills as temperatures warm in May, June, and into July. The cahill and *Potamanthus* hatches of midsummer can bring even the most selective trout to the surface. The old-faithful cream variant has been a most successful pattern.

Early mornings in August bring out Tricos, and as fall begins to color the valley, blue-winged olives make an appearance. Each river's unique character comes from the hatches, particularly the Trico hatch, which is timed differently on each river. A favorite memory of fishing southwestern Vermont was finding the Tricos hatching around 5:30 am on the Castleton. When they were finished there, we moved to the Mettawee, where there was good activity around 7:30 or 8:00 am, and on to the Battenkill, where fish were rising around 11:00 am. When you stop at a bridge to check out the river, don't forget to inspect resident spider webs for the insect du jour.

The Mettawee's season consists of the second Saturday in April through the last Sunday in October with no special regulations.

Favorite Pattern	Trico (male)
Hook	Dry fly, size 20–24
Thread	Black
Tail	Three light dun micro fibetts
Body	Black and olive thread, wound together
Thorax	One strand of peacock herl
Wings	White hackle, divided and shaped as spent wing

Poultney River

The west-facing slope of Tinmouth Mountain near the village of Middletown spawns the headwaters of the Poultney River. The river runs approximately 40 miles west and then north through the towns of Poultney and Fair Haven. It defines the New York/Vermont border for several miles and eventually flows into the Lake

Poultney River

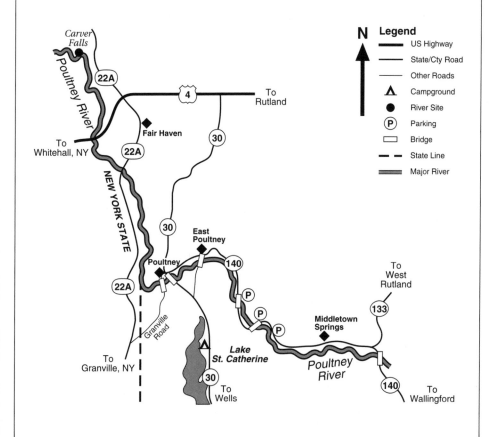

© Wilderness Adventures Press

Champlain Canal near Whitehall, New York. New York state has river jurisdiction along the border. Residents of Vermont with current fishing licenses are able to fish this stretch of the Poultney. Nonresidents are required to purchase a New York state fishing license.

The Poultney is a wild trout stream, and its upper flow contains high quality spawning and nursery habitat for brook and brown trout. Downstream from the village of Poultney, the cover is sparse and flow diminishes. This section of river, except for the area just below Carver's Falls, 3 miles east of Fair Haven, holds no significant population of trout. The brook trout are wild and small—a good one is 12 inches. Browns average 10 to 14 inches, with the occasional one of 18 inches or more caught each year below Carver's Falls.

According to Tom St. John of St. John's Sporting Goods, "Not many people flyfish the Poultney because it has too much cover." The river flows flat, and its banks are steep and muddy.

There is a 3-mile section of quality water between the villages of Poultney and East Poultney. It begins near the falls just west of Poultney at the New York state line off the bypass on Route 22A where Vermont Route 140 begins. Access is made near the bridge by the falls and at several unmarked pull-offs as you continue upstream along Route 140. Pocketwater, tumbling from narrow gorges and fertile tributaries, make this section of the Poultney excellent wild brook trout water.

The best flies are small beadheads fished up into pockets and dries, such as Hornbergs and bivisibles. The deeper pools hold brown trout averaging 10 to 14 inches. Early in the season, fish woolly buggers deep and slow through pools. Later, watch for caddis and fish beadheads and emergers.

In general, the season runs from the second Saturday in April through the last Sunday in October. From Lake Champlain to Carver's Falls in the town of West Haven, angling for brook trout, rainbows, and brown trout is open all year. The limit is 3 fish in total.

Castleton River

Castleton River is a tributary of the Poultney and flows from the marshes in Whipple Hollow in the town of West Rutland for 20 miles until it joins the Poultney west of Fair Haven. The waters of the Castleton are cooled by springs welling up in the riverbed along its length, from the headwaters to the outflow of Lake Bomoseen. The constant cool temperatures and rich mineral content of its waters have made this an important wild trout resource.

Flyfishing on the Castleton River has always been a challenge. Access is limited due to posted land. In the small village of Hydeville on Route 4A, turn south to a bridge and small pull-off area. The land on the south bank is posted, but access can be made on the opposite side. Once you've gained access, the fun really begins. The river is slow moving and the bottom deep with mud. Alders and brush canopy the river as it twists and turns. Access can also be made east of Castleton Corners where

Castleton River

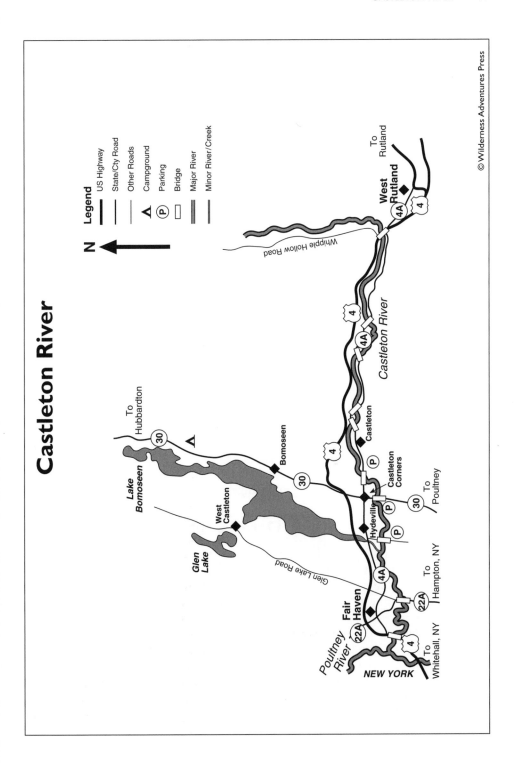

Legend

US Highway	
State/Cty Road	
Other Roads	
Campground	
Parking	
Bridge	
Major River	
Minor River/Creek	

N

To Hubbardton

Lake Bomoseen

30

Bomoseen

30

Glen Lake

West Castleton

Glen Lake Road

Castleton Corners

Castleton

Hydeville

30 To Poultney

Castleton River

4

4A

4

Whipple Hollow Road

West Rutland

4A

4

To Rutland

Poultney River

Fair Haven

22A

4A

22A

To Hampton, NY

4

To Whitehall, NY

NEW YORK

© Wilderness Adventures Press

the train tracks cross the river and Route 4A. Be patient-a hike through the brush and mud can pay off with the sight of a rising 16-inch wild brown trout.

Early in the season, the Castleton River plays host to a strong population of Hendrickson mayflies. As the season continues, other mayflies, such as March browns, sulphurs, Tricos, and blue-winged olives, make their presence known. Midges seem to be around constantly, and there is some caddis activity.

This is a wild trout fishery managed by the state of Vermont without stocking. It has a strong population of brook trout in the upper stretch of the river between the villages of West Rutland and Hydeville. Brook trout of 12 inches aren't uncommon, and browns reach 17 or 18 inches. Below the outflow of Lake Bomoseen in Hydeville, the water is generally unsuitable for trout, as warmer waters skimmed off the surface of the lake enter the river, making water temperatures uncomfortable for trout. Downstream from the village of Castleton, the river bottom is covered with silt and mud. Upstream, the current runs more swiftly, and there is good spawning habitat.

The second Saturday in April through the last Sunday in October comprises the season on Castleton River.

Favorite Pattern	Quigley Cripple (Hendrickson)
Hook	Dry fly, size 12–14
Thread	Gray
Tail	Dun spade hackle, clipped blunt
Body	Gray or light rust turkey biot
Thorax	Gray dubbing
Wing	Natural deer hair, set forward
Wingcase	Clipped butt of deer hair wing over thorax
Hackle	Dun hackle wound between wing and wingcase

Upper Otter Creek

Otter Creek is a 100-mile long river flowing north from its source in Emerald Lake near the village of East Dorset to Lake Champlain, east of Vergennes. The nature of the river ranges from cold brook trout water to slow, warm water that holds smallmouth bass and some good-sized northern pike.

The upper portion of Otter Creek has productive trout waters as it parallels Route 7 from the villages of Danby to Rutland. The area known as Danby swamp has a history of better-than-average brook trout numbers. Fishing the swamp area is best done by canoe. Access is gained by a short carry from pull-offs along the highway. This swampy area is loaded with insect life. Swimming nymph patterns, large Hornbergs on summer evenings, and caddis imitations are flies of choice.

From the Railroad Bridge in the village of Danby to the #10 Bridge on Forest Road in Mt. Tabor, the state allows a 2-fish limit for brook trout, rainbows, and brown trout.

Upper Otter Creek

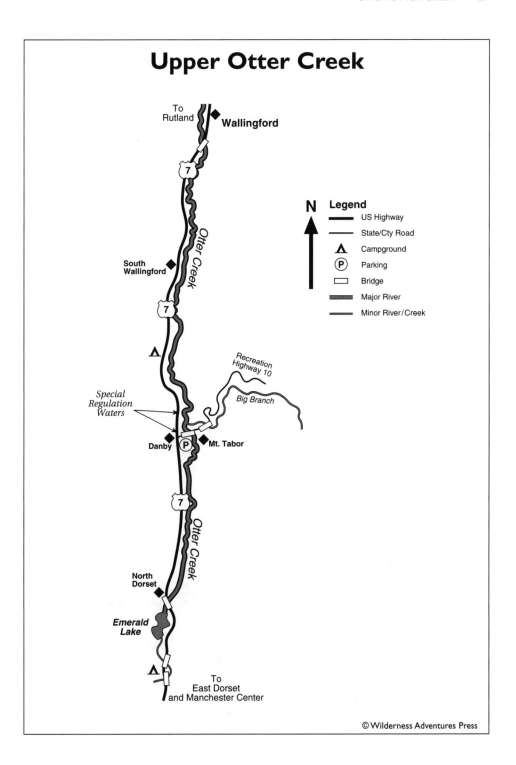

To
Rutland
Wallingford

7

Otter Creek

South
Wallingford

7

N

Legend

US Highway
State/Cty Road
△ Campground
Ⓟ Parking
▭ Bridge
Major River
Minor River/Creek

Recreation
Highway 10

Big Branch

*Special
Regulation
Waters*

Danby Ⓟ **Mt. Tabor**

7

Otter Creek

North
Dorset

*Emerald
Lake*

To
East Dorset
and Manchester Center

© Wilderness Adventures Press

Otter Creek is refreshed at this point by the Big Branch. This is a beautiful little tributary holding brook trout in its tumbling upper waters and rainbows, browns, and brookies below the Long Trail crossing. Where Big Branch joins the Otter, brown trout gather in the deeper holes that are shaded by the deep banks and streamside cover. This is a challenging stretch of water with access limited to pull-offs near bridges and thickly covered, deep cutbanks. But, as with many quality waters, the effort can be worthwhile.

Farther north, two tributaries, Mill River in Clarendon and Cold River in the village of North Clarendon, enter Otter Creek. The mouths of these rivers create a small but suitable habitat for trout. Mill River's headwaters offer excellent wild brookie fishing. Try fishing soft hackle patterns into the pockets as you work upstream.

Otter Creek receives regular stockings of brook and brown trout. Fish average 8 to 14 inches, with numbers supplemented by the state with the occasional introduction of trophy-sized fish. As the Otter proceeds north of Darby, the flow slows and heats up as it passes through open fields and pastures. There is some cooling provided by tributaries, but trout fishing becomes less productive as you travel north. There are good numbers of warmwater species, such as smallmouth bass and northern pike, throughout the lower section.

Upper Otter Creek's season extends from the second Saturday in April through the last Sunday in October. From the railroad bridge in the village of Danby to Forest Road #10 bridge in Mt. Tabor, the total creel limit of brook, brown, and rainbow trout is 2.

Bill Weber in Manchester, Vermont, home of The American Museum of Fly Fishing. (Photo by Rhey Plumley)

SOUTHWESTERN VERMONT HUB CITIES
Manchester/Bennington
Manchester Elevation–700 • Population–3,622
Bennington Elevation–750 • Population–16,451

ACCOMMODATIONS
Best Western New Englander Motor Inn, Historic Route 7A (Bennington 05201) /
802-442-6311 / $$–$$$

Emerald Lake Motel & Chalet, Route 7 (North Dorset 05251) / 802-362-3946

Equinox Hotel & Resort, Historic Route 7A (Manchester 05254) / 802-362-4700 /
$$$$$

Four Winds Country Motel, Route 7A North (Manchester 05254) / 802-362-1105 /
$$–$$$$

Marble West Inn Bed & Breakfast, West Dorset Road (Dorset 05251) /
802-867-4155 / $$$$

River Meadow Farm Bed & Breakfast, P.O. Box 822 (Manchester Center 05255) /
802-362-1602 / $

The Battenkill Inn, P.O. Box 948 (Manchester Village 05254) / 800-441-1628;
802-362-4231 / $$$$

CAMPGROUNDS
Camping on the Battenkill, RD 2, Box 3310 (Arlington 05250) / 802-275-6663

Dorset RV Park, RR1, Box 180 (Dorset 05251) / 802-867-5754

Emerald Lake State Park, RD Box 485 (East Dorset 05253) / 802-362-1655

Lake Shaftsbury State Park, RD#1, Box 266 (Shaftsbury 05262) / 802-375-9978

RESTAURANTS
Chanteclear, Route 7A (East Dorset 05253) / 802-362-1616

Four Chimneys Restaurant, 21 West Road (Bennington 05201) / 802-447-3500

Mulligan's, Route 7A (Manchester Village 05254) / 802-362-3663

Sirloin Saloon, Routes 11 & 30 (Manchester Center 05254) / 802-362-2600

FLY SHOPS AND GUIDES
Orvis Manchester, Historic Route 7A (Manchester 05254) / 802-362-3750 / Full
service flyfishing and fly tying / Instruction and guide service / Call for current
area stream conditions

Gray Hackle Fly Shop, Route 7 (Pownal 05261) / 802-823-4003 / Full service fly-
fishing, fly tying, and tackle / Instruction and guide service / Rocky Harrington
or Redge Galvin

The Battenkill Angler's Nook, Route 313 (Shushan, NY 12873) / 3 miles west of the
Vermont/New York border / Access to the Battenkill's lower stretch / Specialty
trout flies and hackle / George Schlotter, owner

MEDICAL

Southwestern Vermont Medical Center, 100 Hospital Drive (Bennington 05201) / 802-442-6361

FOR MORE INFORMATION

Manchester Chamber of Commerce
2 Main Street
Manchester, VT 05254
802-362-2100

Bennington Chamber of Commerce
Veterans Memorial Drive
Bennington, VT 05201
802-447-3311

STILLWATERS OF SOUTHERN VERMONT

There are two beautiful brook trout ponds east of Arlington, known as **Stratton Pond** and **Bourn Pond**. The road that leads to the foot trails is unpaved and can be impassible during wet seasons. It is called the Kelly Stand Road and intersects the Appalachian and Long Trails near a memorial to Daniel Webster. There is a parking area for about four to five cars, and the trail to the ponds is well marked. Both of these remote mountain ponds are shallow and the banks are densely vegetated. They are best fished from shore. Good flies include dragonfly and damselfly imitations.

Gale Meadows Pond is off of Route 30 near the village of Bondville, east of Manchester. It is regularly stocked with rainbow trout. There is good public access and a boat ramp.

Amherst Lake and **Echo Lake** are right along Route 100 north of the village of Ludlow. Amherst holds rainbow and lake trout. Echo is stocked with rainbows. Both have state fish and wildlife public access areas and boat launches. They're busy lakes during the summer months, so you might want to schedule yourself for the early or late season. There are good midge hatches during the fall that can produce large rainbows. Camp Plymouth State Park is close by and offers convenient camping facilities.

Lake Ninevah is reached from Dublin Road, which runs west from the south end of Echo Lake. It is stocked with rainbow trout and has a public boat ramp.

Harriman Reservoir is a large coldwater impoundment that hosts rainbow trout, large brown trout, and lake trout. Its north shore is near the village of Wilmington, along Route 9, convenient to two public boat launches. There is a third public access area at the south end of the reservoir, near the village Whitingham, on Route 100.

Panfish are plentiful in many northern New England stillwaters. Fish deer hair bugs, poppers, and terrestrials. (Photo by Elizabeth Edwards)

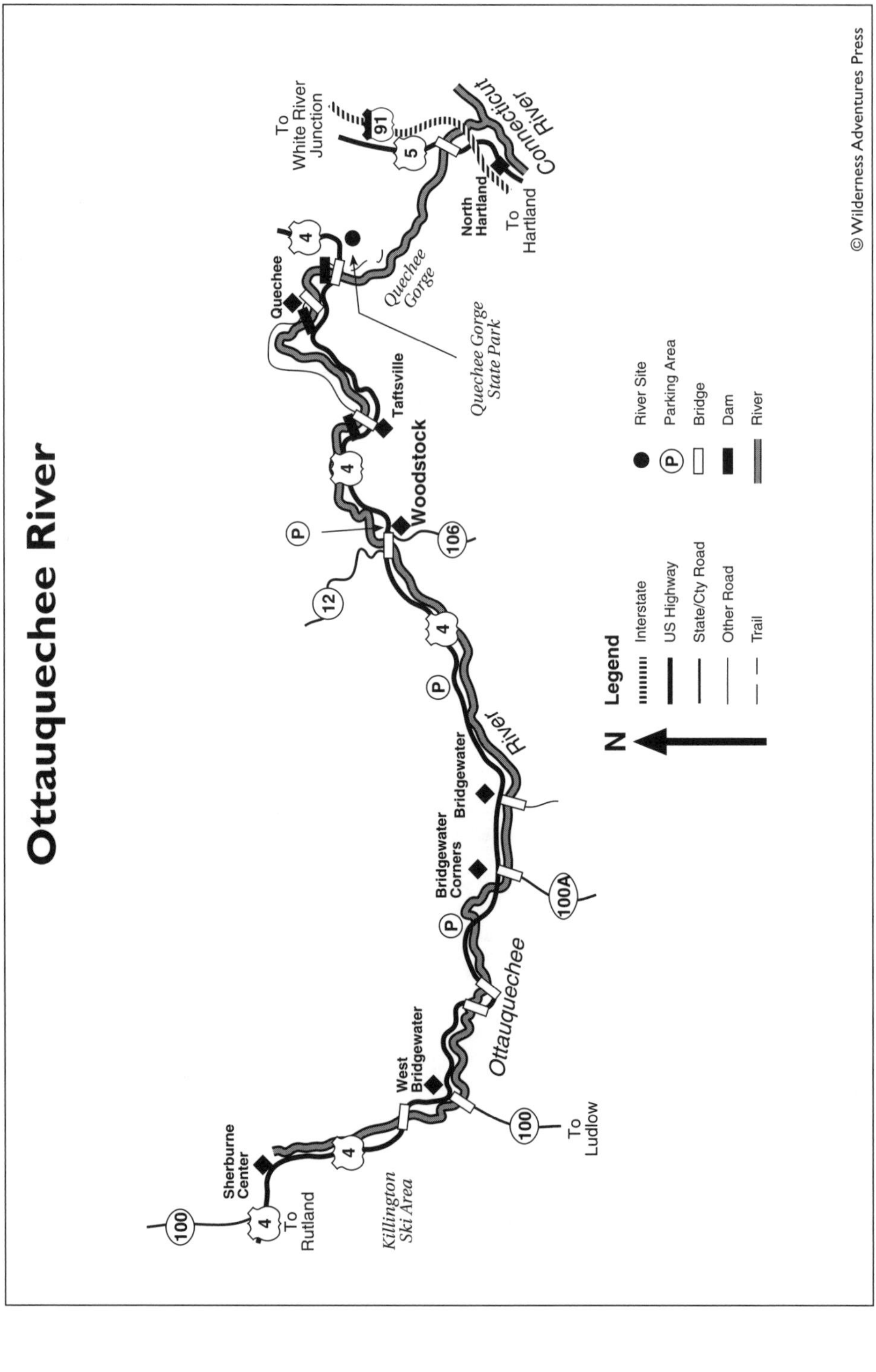

Ottauquechee River

To White River Junction

91

5

Connecticut River

North Hartland

To Hartland

Quechee Gorge

Quechee Gorge State Park

Quechee

4

Taftsville

Woodstock

4

12

P

106

4

P

River

Bridgewater

Bridgewater Corners

Bridgewater

100A

P

West Bridgewater

Ottauquechee

To Ludlow

100

Sherburne Center

4

To Rutland

100

Killington Ski Area

N

Legend

▥▥▥	Interstate
▬▬	US Highway
—	State/Cty Road
—	Other Road
– –	Trail

●	River Site
Ⓟ	Parking Area
▭	Bridge
▮	Dam
▬	River

© Wilderness Adventures Press

SOUTHEASTERN VERMONT
Ottauquechee River

The Ottauquechee, from its mountain headwaters in the town of Sherburne, flows southeast for 38 miles toward the Connecticut River. Its journey begins as a tiny brook trout stream studded with boulders and jump pools that are shaded and cooled by an awning of overhanging tree branches. Fishing access is good along Route 4 at the several unmarked pull-off areas and side road river crossings. Along with brook trout, the upper stretch of the Ottauquechee offers good flyfishing for wild and stocked rainbows.

Near the village of West Bridgewater, the Ottauquechee bends more to the east, passing the "mill-turned-mall" in the village of Bridgewater, and then through the quaint and lovely village of Woodstock. Access continues to be good along Route 4. The river is fed by several small streams and widens and deepens into waters that favor brown trout as well as rainbows.

There is less cover along the river through this stretch. It's best to fish before and after the high sun. As water temperatures rise in the summer, look for active fish near the mouths of tributaries. Elk hair caddis and stonefly patterns, along with attractors like Adams and Wulffs, work well.

Below Woodstock, three dams control the power of the river before it charges through Quechee Gorge. The shear rock walls of the gorge drop 165 feet down to the river. There are two trails that start at the highway bridge on Route 4 spanning Quechee Gorge. The trail along the west rim goes upstream about a half-mile and provides access to the Ottauquechee where it enters the canyon. From the bridge, the trail on the east rim slopes down, again about a half-mile, meeting the river at the lower end of the gorge. Anglers should be cautious when fishing in and around the gorge. The dam, upstream at Deweys Mills, regulates the flow of the river through the gorge, and at the sound of an alarm, the water can rise rapidly. The river passes through some deep pools that can hold large brown trout. Stonefly nymphs and weighted woolly buggers work well here.

The Ottauquechee below the gorge, to the river's fourth dam in the village of North Hartland, is not trout water. There are, however, some opportunities to fish for rainbows coming out of the Connecticut River in the spring and fall below the North Hartland dam, but this is very unpredictable.

Tourists gather in the area around Quechee Gorge and Woodstock throughout the summer season. There are inns, campgrounds, restaurants, and shops all along Route 4. Visitors find this to be one of the most scenic and popular parts of Vermont. A good share of this region's beauty comes from the Ottauquechee River as it passes under covered bridges and carves out farm valleys and deep canyons along its way. The flyfishing is good and deserves a try on your next visit.

The season on the Ottauquechee run from the second Saturday in April through the last Sunday in October. From the river mouth upstream to the first highway bridge crossing the river, please refer to Connecticut River Regulations. Wild trout

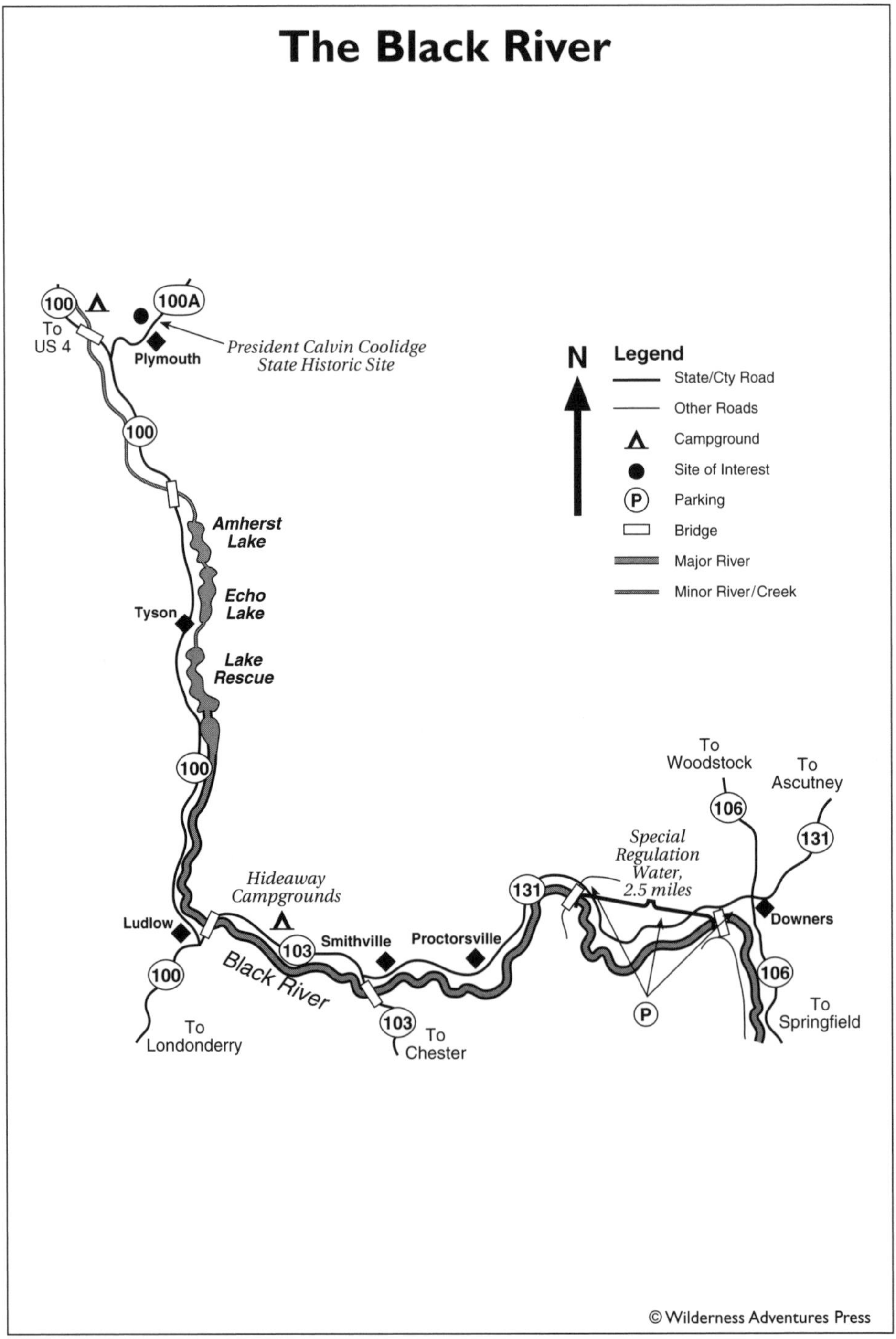

The Black River

N

Legend
— State/Cty Road
— Other Roads
▲ Campground
● Site of Interest
ⓟ Parking
▭ Bridge
▨ Major River
▨ Minor River/Creek

100
To
US 4

100A

President Calvin Coolidge
State Historic Site

Plymouth

100

Amherst
Lake

Echo
Lake

Tyson

Lake
Rescue

100

To
Woodstock

To
Ascutney

106

131

Special
Regulation
Water,
2.5 miles

Hideaway
Campgrounds
▲

131

Ludlow

103

Smithville

Proctorsville

Downers

100

Black River

106

To
Londonderry

103

To
Chester

ⓟ

To
Springfield

© Wilderness Adventures Press

Created by the Ottauquechee River, the Quechee Gorge has several runs and pools that hold trout. (Photo by Steve Hickoff)

populations are reinforced with regular stockings of brook trout, rainbows, and brown trout throughout the river.

The Black River

The upper reaches and tributaries of the Black River as it comes out of Coolidge State Forest above the village of Plymouth are beautiful brook trout waters. Route 100 follows the river south through the village of Plymouth Union. There are pull-offs along the main highway and several hiking trails in the state forest that provide access to small feeder streams. As the Black continues on its 40-mile journey to the Connecticut River, several dams, including those at Amherst and Echo Lakes and Lake Rescue, stifle and warm its flow. Amherst and Echo offer fishing for lake trout and pretty good-sized rainbows. Each has a public boat access. Lake Rescue is primarily a warmwater fishery.

*Downers Covered Bridge
on the Black River.
(Photo by Rhey Plumley)*

Near the village of Ludlow, the Black swings east and passes below Okemo Mountain, parallel to Route 131. Some of the best fishing is found downstream from the village of Cavendish to Amsden, a section of river the state regularly stocks with brown trout, rainbows, and brookies. The 4-mile stretch in the town of Weathersfield, between Howard Hill Bridge and the covered bridge in the village of Downers, is restricted by special regulations with a creel limit of 2 fish of either species. There are good access areas along Route 131. The river still has an unpredictable flow caused by the demands of the upriver power dams, but overall, the trout habitat is stable.

Caddis and stonefly imitations work well throughout the season. Fluctuating water levels limit regular hatches of mayflies. Attractor patterns, such as small royal Wulffs and Adams, do work well, however. In warmer months, the downstream banks of the small tributaries hold active trout. Last year in late fall, the state fish and wildlife department provided a bonus stocking of large brook trout in the Black River.

The Black River's season extends from the second Saturday in April through the last Sunday in October. From the river mouth upstream to the Interstate 91 bridge, please refer to Connecticut River regulations. From the Interstate 91 bridge upstream to Gould's Mill Site in the town of Springfield, there is an artificials only, catch-and-release winter season from the last Sunday in October to the Friday before the second Saturday in April. The 4-mile stretch between Downers Covered Bridge and the Howard Hill Bridge has a 2-fish creel limit.

The upper Black holds some wild and stocked brook trout. The river receives regular stockings of brook trout, rainbows, and brown trout. While there is little spawning habitat in the river below the village of Ludlow, there are some holdover fish that can reach 14 to 16 inches.

The Williams River

The Middle Branch of the Williams River runs along Route 11, and the South Branch rises and tumbles out of Williams River State Forest. The two branches meet to form the main stem of the Williams River near the village of Chester. These streams and their smaller tributaries offer good, small-water brook trout fishing. Access is good off Route 11 and the back roads and trails of the state forest.

The Williams is a freestone stream with rocky runs and some deeper pools. It flows parallel to Route 103 and the Green Mountain Railroad tracks all the way to its mouth at the Connecticut River. Green Mountain and Pleasant Valley Roads follow the river on the north side to the covered bridge in the village of Bartonsville. There is good access on either side of the river. The state has maintained stockings of brook, brown, and rainbow trout in the river branches and main stem. In the Williams, below Chester, water temperatures can get quite high in the summer, making it tough on the fish. Brown trout seem to have adapted best, although you will find some wild rainbows and brookies in the deep gorge above the power dam at Brockway Mills. The best flies to fish are small beadhead nymphs, caddis dries, and terrestrials.

Below the dam at Bartonsville, the fast water holds some trout and a lot of small-mouth bass. The backwaters of Herrick's Cove, where the Williams joins the Connecticut River, provide excellent smallmouth fishing from a canoe or boat. Access is near the junction of Routes 5 and 103 at the picnic area.

Seasons for the Williams River are: second Saturday in April through the last Sunday in October; from the Route 5 Bridge to Brockway Mills Falls, refer to Connecticut River regulations.

The Saxtons River

The Saxtons River begins its 20-mile journey in the town of Windham. Route 121 follows the river as it twists and turns through a picturesque valley of woods, rocky fields, and old stone walls to where it joins the Connecticut River near the village of Bellows Falls. The upper river and small tributaries, upstream from the village of

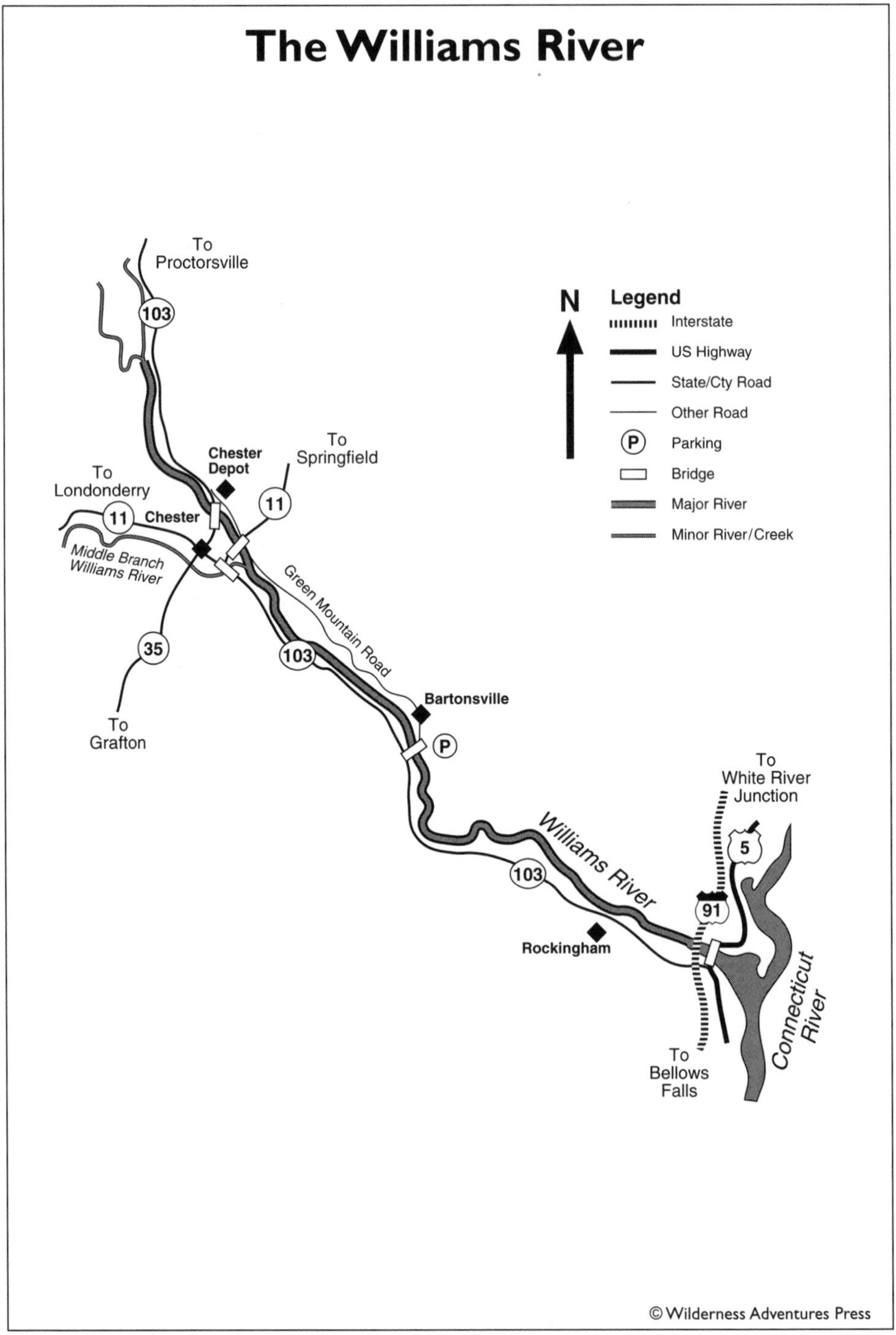

The Williams River

To
Proctorsville

103

N

Legend
|||||||| Interstate
— US Highway
— State/Cty Road
— Other Road
ⓅParking
▭ Bridge
▬▬ Major River
▬▬ Minor River/Creek

Chester
Depot

To
Springfield

To
Londonderry

11 Chester

11

Middle Branch
Williams River

Green Mountain Road

35

103

To
Grafton

Bartonsville

Ⓟ

To
White River
Junction

5

Williams River

103

91

Rockingham

Connecticut River

To
Bellows
Falls

© Wilderness Adventures Press

The Saxtons River

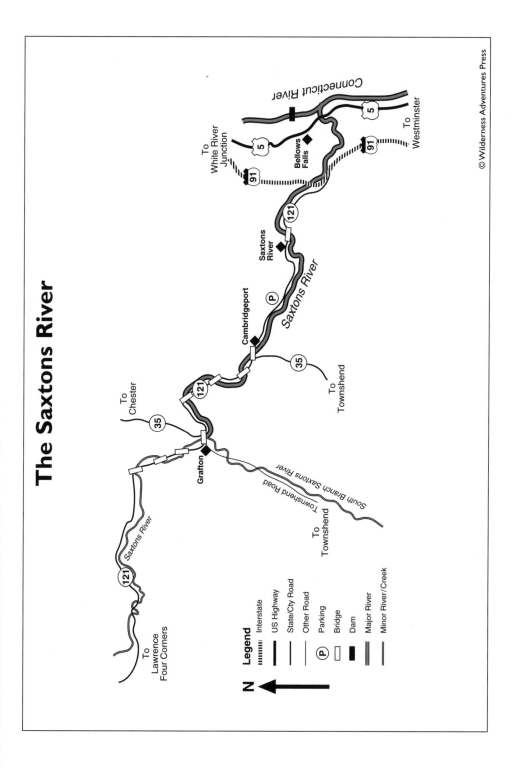

Legend

- ▪▪▪▪▪ Interstate
- ▬▬ US Highway
- ▬▬ State/City Road
- ▬ Other Road
- Ⓟ Parking
- ▭ Bridge
- ■ Dam
- ▬ Major River
- ▬ Minor River/Creek

N

© Wilderness Adventures Press

Lemon and white English setter pup, Midge, points a trout.
(Photo by Elizabeth Edwards)

Grafton, offer good fishing for small brown trout and brookies. These cool waters from the Green Mountains provide some spawning and nursery habitat.

As you proceed downstream from Grafton toward the village of Saxtons River, streamside cover diminishes and the river warms significantly, causing trout populations to dwindle. This portion of river is limited pretty much to an early-season, put-and-take fishery for browns and brookies. The river's broken rock and ledge bottom forms some deeper pools as it passes downstream from Saxtons River village. These pools hold some nicer browns.

The downstream passage of the Saxtons River is blocked, not far from its mouth, by a falls and dam in the village of North Westminster. Some Connecticut River rainbow trout move in and out of the Saxtons in the spring and fall.

The season on Saxtons River is the second Saturday in April through the last Sunday in October. The short stretch from the Route 5 bridge, south of the village of Bellows Falls to the mouth is covered under Connecticut River regulations.

The West River

A tremendous amount of water flows through the West River drainage. Springs and small mountain tributaries feed the main stem of the West from its headwaters, above the village of Weston, throughout its entire 46-mile length. Ironically, the main stem of the West River is predominantly a warmwater fishery. Springtime floods annually scour the riverbed, depositing silt and gravel and filling in the downstream pools. Summertime water temperatures regularly reach in excess of 80 degrees in the main river. A flood control project dam at Ball Mountain and one forming Townsend Lake have limited flooding and created two, short tailwater fisheries. The river stretch just below both dams stays cooler and more aerated, providing some good flyfishing for brown trout throughout the season.

The main stem of the river parallels Route 100 South from the village of Weston. Route 100 joins Route 30 in the village of Ransomville and escorts the West all the way to the river's mouth in Brattleboro. It is the upper reaches of the West River's tributaries and small feeder brooks that offer the best flyfishing opportunities. You'll find some lovely wild brook trout in the headwaters of some of these brooks and in the lower sections some nice, small browns. It's a way to enjoy some solitude and maybe catch a few fish. You can reach these somewhat more remote areas from either Routes 100 or 30 on the several maintained and unimproved back roads that follow the brooks back up into the Green Mountains. There are some excellent hiking trails in Jamaica State Park and Townsend State Park that give access to some of these smaller streams as well as to the two tailwater sections of the West.

A short distance downstream of the dam at Townsend, the West River broadens and becomes a slower moving, warmwater river. This section is wide open, with gravelly runs and long, slow glides. There is good fishing for smallmouth bass in this lower stretch of river. Access is easy along the highway, making it a popular area for canoeists and tubers.

Insect hatches on the main river are sporadic, probably because of the severe scouring the riverbed experiences during spates and runoff. There are caddis and stoneflies throughout the river system. In the smaller brooks, fish small attractor patterns, such as Adams, Wulffs, and Humpys. Also try small, weighted hare's ears fished up into the pockets. The tailwater areas are popular. Fish them early and late in the day. Brown trout of up to 15 inches might be fooled by a small midge pattern drifted in the right feeding lane. Otherwise, try beadhead nymphs, caddis emergers, and woolly buggers.

Like many of the Connecticut River's major arteries, the West River once shared the run of Atlantic salmon. The Atlantic Salmon Restoration Project continues to provide smolt and fry stockings throughout this watershed.

Regulations allow fishing from the second Saturday in April through the last Sunday in October. From the Route 5 bridge at Brattleboro to the river mouth, refer to Connecticut River regulations. From the Route 5 Bridge upstream to Townsend Dam, Townsend, there is a winter, artificials only, catch-and-release season from the Monday after the last Sunday in October to the Friday before the second Saturday in April.

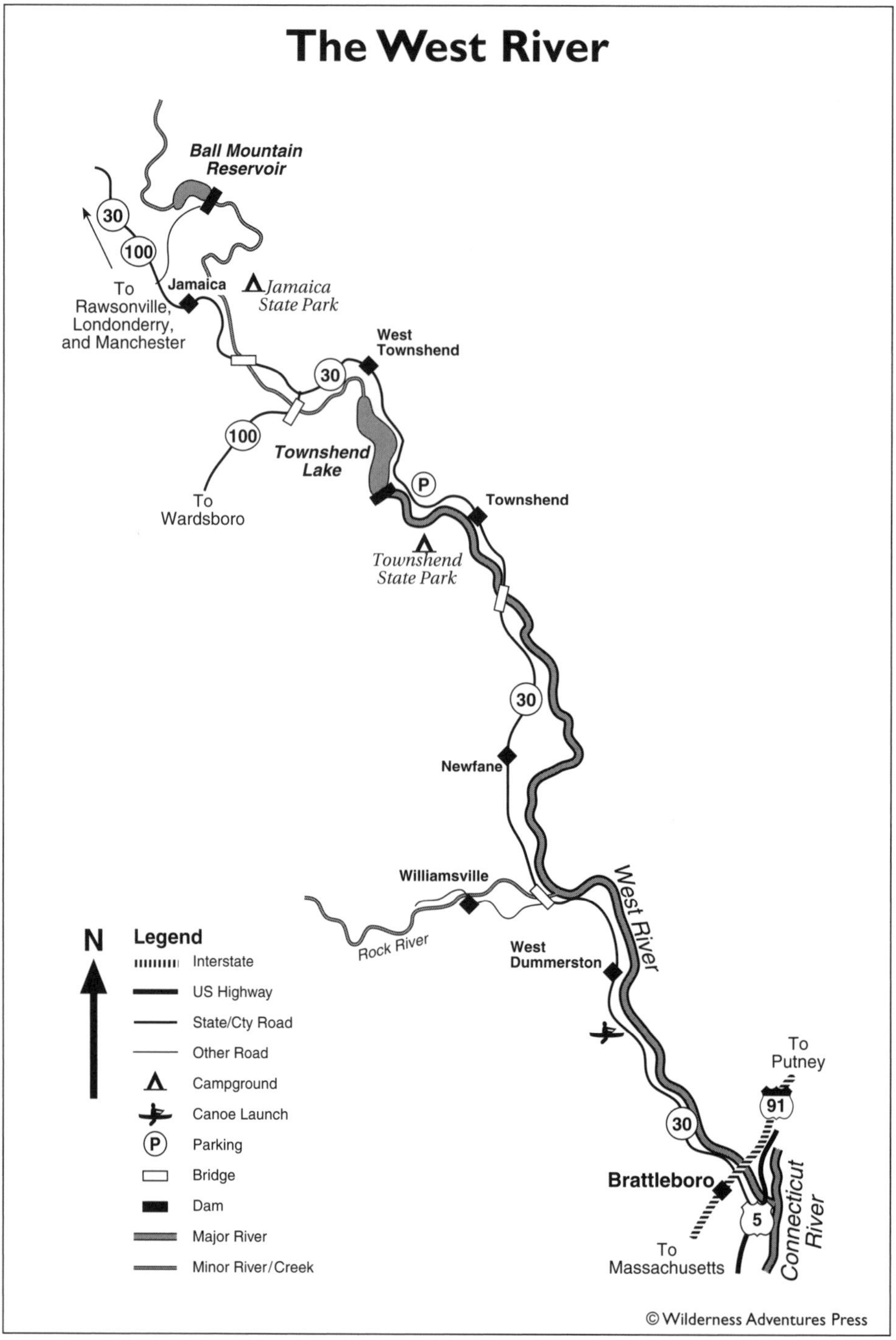

The West River

Ball Mountain Reservoir

30

100

To
Rawsonville,
Londonderry,
and Manchester

Jamaica

▲ *Jamaica State Park*

West Townshend

30

100

Townshend Lake

To
Wardsboro

(P)

Townshend

▲ *Townshend State Park*

30

Newfane

Williamsville

Rock River

West
Dummerston

West River

To
Putney

91

30

Brattleboro

Connecticut River

5

To
Massachusetts

Legend

N

⊪⊪⊪⊪	Interstate
▬▬▬	US Highway
——	State/Cty Road
——	Other Road
▲	Campground
✈	Canoe Launch
(P)	Parking
▭	Bridge
▬	Dam
▬▬▬	Major River
——	Minor River/Creek

© Wilderness Adventures Press

SOUTHEASTERN VERMONT HUB CITIES
Brattleboro/Wilmington
Brattleboro Elevation–310 • Population–12,241
Wilmington Elevation–1,580 • Population–1,968

ACCOMMODATIONS
Days Inn, Putney Road (Brattleboro 05301) / 800-329-7466; 802-254-4583 / $$–$$$
Colonial Motel & Spa, Putney Road (Brattleboro 05301) / 800-239-0032; 802-257-7733 / $$
Hermitage Inn, Coldbrook Road (Wilmington 05363) / 802-464-3531 / Sporting clays range

CAMPGROUND
Townsend State Park, RR1, Box 2650 (Townsend 05353) / 802-365-7500 / Camping on the West River

RESTAURANTS
Chelsea Royal Diner, Route 9 West (Brattleboro 05301) / 802-254-8399
Max's, 414 Western Avenue (Brattleboro 05301) / 802-254-7747
Tavern Restaurant, Putney Road (Brattleboro 05301) / 802-254-9675
Townshend Dam Diner, Route 30 (Townshend 05353) / 802-864-4107

FLY SHOPS AND GUIDES
Taddingers, Route 100 North (Wilmington 05363) / 800-528-3961; 802-464-1223 / Full service fly shop / Orvis dealer / Guide service and instruction / Jim Gnabe, owner

MEDICAL
Brattleboro Memorial Hospital, 9 Belmont Avenue in Brattleboro / 802-257-0341

FOR MORE INFORMATION
Brattleboro Chamber of Commerce
180 Main Street
Brattleboro, VT 05301
802-254-4565

Wilmington Chamber of Commerce
West Main Street
Wilmington, VT 05363
802-464-8092

Central Vermont

CALEDONIA

7

Cedar Lake

Winona Lake

22A

Otter Creek

New Haven River

17

116

Middlebury

ADDISON

Middlebury River

Pleiad Lake

30

7

125

Sugar Hill Reservoir

Silver Lake

Lake Dunmore

22A

Neshobe River

RUTLAND

Sunset Lake

North Pond

144

22A

Glen Lake

Lake Bomoseen

4

Otter Creek

Furnace Brook

Chittenden Reservoir

South Pond

Colton Pond

Kent Pond

7

Rutland

4

100

White River

Rood Pond

14

Sunset Lake

12

89

ORANGE

302

Waits River

91

5

Connecticut River

110

Waits River

91

5

Ompompanoosuc River

5

107

89

WINDSOR

White River

89

91

5

Connecticut River

Connecticut River

Legend

—— Roads

—— *Rivers*

- - - Counties

▬▬ State Line

CENTRAL VERMONT

The rivers of central Vermont flow west from the Green Mountains into Otter Creek and east into the Connecticut River. Visitors seeking the home of poet Robert Frost or the spectacular autumn colors on display through the mountains of central Vermont can also take advantage of some of Vermont's finest trout streams. Otter Creek finishes its 100-mile journey north to Lake Champlain by picking up four major tributaries: Furnace Brook, the Neshobe River, the Middlebury River, and the New Haven River. From the eastern slope of the Green Mountains, the Wells and Waits Rivers, the Ompompanoosuc River, and White River flow to meet their fate in the mighty Connecticut River.

CENTRAL VERMONT MAJOR HATCHES

Insect/Bait	J	F	M	A	M	J	J	A	S	O	N	D	Patterns
Caddis					■	■							Black Elk Hair Caddis #16-20 (early and late season); Tan Elk Hair Caddis or Vermont Hare's Ear Caddis #14-18; Soft Hackles and Emergers #14-18; Hare's Ear Nymph and Beadhead Pupae #14-18
Blue-winged Olives				■	■				■	■			Parachute Adams #14-20; Thorax Blue-winged Olive #14-18; Pheasant Tail Nymphs #14-20
Hendricksons				■	■								Dark Hendrickson or Red Quill #12-14; Hendrickson Nymph #12-14; Rusty Spinner #14
March Brown					■	■							March Brown Dun #12; Hare's Ear Nymph
Sulphurs						■	■						Sulphur Duns and Hare's Ear Nymphs #16-18
Light Cahill						■	■						Cahill Dun or Parachute #16
Stoneflies					■	■	■	■					Black Stonefly Nymph #8-14; Yellow Stonefly Nymph #8-10; Yellow Sally #14
Golden Drake *Potamanthus distinctus*							■						Paradrake #8
Tiny Mayflies *Tricorythodes stygiatus*							■	■					Trico Spinner #18-24
Terrestrials								■	■				Hoppers #6-12; Ants #14-18
Midges								■	■				Griffith's Gnat #18
White Mayfly *Ephoron leukon*								■					Cream Variant #10
Minnows and Leeches	■	■	■	■	■	■	■	■	■	■	■	■	Woolly Buggers and Streamers

WEST CENTRAL VERMONT
Furnace Brook

High above the village of Pittsford, Furnace Brook tumbles down through boulders and gorges, abruptly flattening out through farmland and floodplain to where it enters Otter Creek. It is managed by the Department of Fish and Wildlife as a wild trout fishery without supplemental stocking and is home to brook trout, rainbows, and browns. The natural spawning areas and nursery waters have been enhanced by habitat improvement programs through modest grants and the volunteer labors of the Green Mountain Fly Tyers Club, which is located in Rutland.

There is a federal fish hatchery on Furnace Brook in the small crossroads town of Holden. Brown trout escaping from this hatchery in the 1950s helped establish a population in the lower section of the river. Now, the hatchery raises landlocked salmon for Lake Champlain and Atlantic salmon fry for the Connecticut River Restoration Project.

Furnace Brook crosses Route 7 on the south side of the village of Pittsford, about 8 miles north of Rutland. Furnace Brook Road follows the river upstream crossing the river in Grangerville. Between this crossing and the hatchery, a hike into the gorge from one of the unmarked roadside pull-offs offers the flyfisher challenging pocketwater fishing for rainbows and brook trout. The water stays cool and aerated

"Wishful thinking" or "whatever it takes." (Photo by Steve Hickoff/ Elizabeth Edwards)

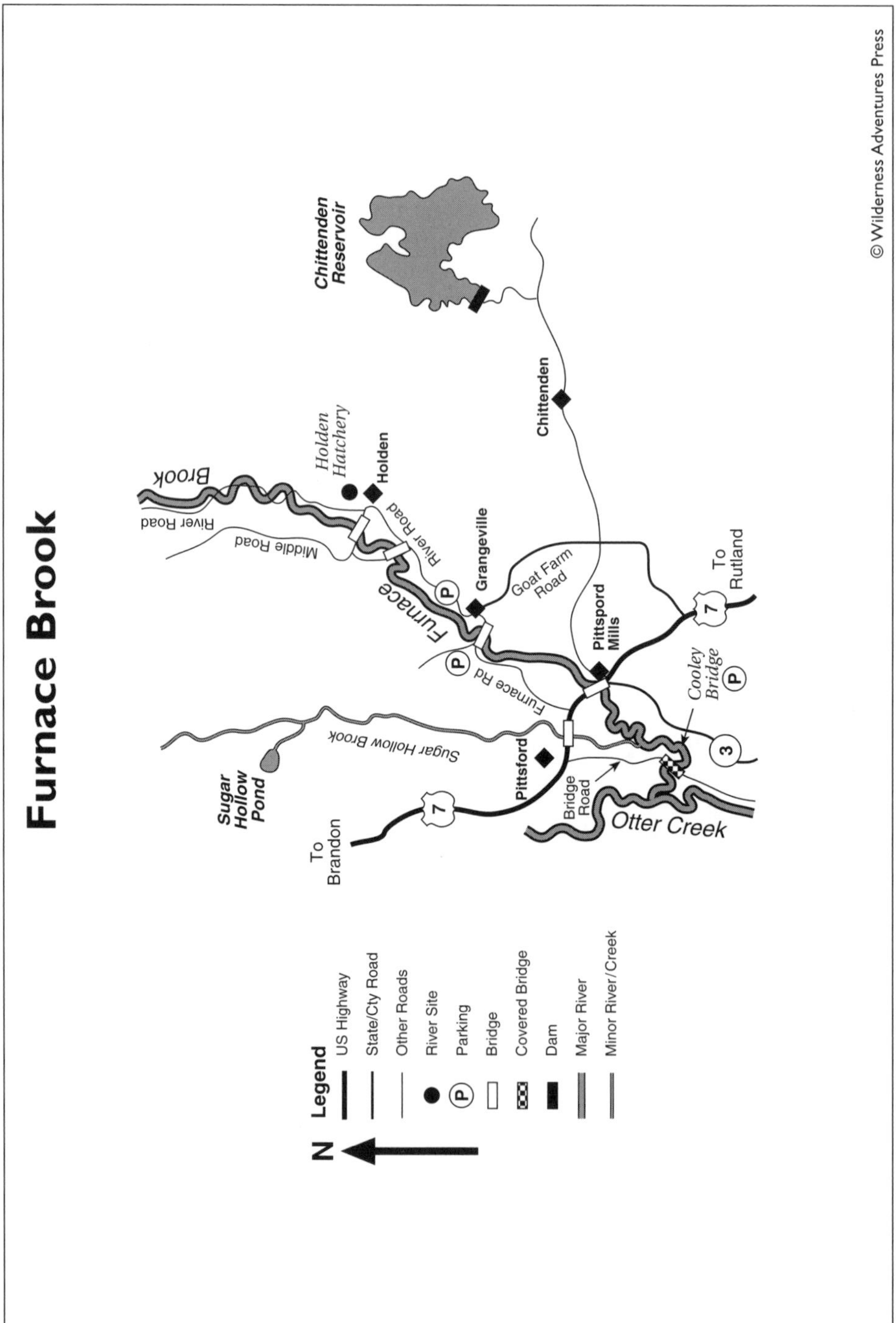

Furnace Brook

© Wilderness Adventures Press

Legend

	US Highway
	State/Cty Road
	Other Roads
●	River Site
Ⓟ	Parking
▢	Bridge
▨	Covered Bridge
▰	Dam
	Major River
	Minor River/Creek

N

Chittenden Reservoir

Chittenden

Holden Hatchery

Holden

Brook

River Road

Middle Road

River Road

Furnace

Grangeville

Goat Farm Road

To Rutland

7

Pittsford Mills

Cooley Bridge

Ⓟ

Ⓟ

Furnace Rd

3

Sugar Hollow Pond

Sugar Hollow Brook

Pittsford

To Brandon

7

Bridge Road

Otter Creek

Case-building caddis can be found in many northern New England waters.
(Photo by Steve Hickoff)

throughout the summer. Beadhead nymphs and stonefly patterns fished up into the pools work well. Dries, such as small caddis and Wulff patterns, will often catch a wild, 12-inch rainbow off guard.

Downstream from Pittsford, Elm Street follows Furnace Brook and crosses it with a lovely covered bridge near the confluence with Otter Creek. This stretch of river is dominated by brown trout and offers good spring and early summer hatches. Here also is the mouth of Sugar Hollow Brook, a small tributary of Furnace Brook. At one time, the alder-covered waters of Sugar Hollow held a wealth of the most beautiful wild brook trout in the state. Sadly, development along this little stream over the past 25 years has taken its toll and used up a great deal of the resources available to the fish. Many people miss this brook.

The Neshobe River

The Neshobe rises out of the foothills of the Green Mountains in the town of Goshen. It follows Route 73, eventually crossing Route 7 in the village of Brandon and finally enters Otter Creek. It is a healthy stream, supporting three varieties of trout. Rainbows and brook trout populate the stretch of river above Brandon. The waters below hold more brown trout. Much of the land near the upper river is private and

Neshobe River

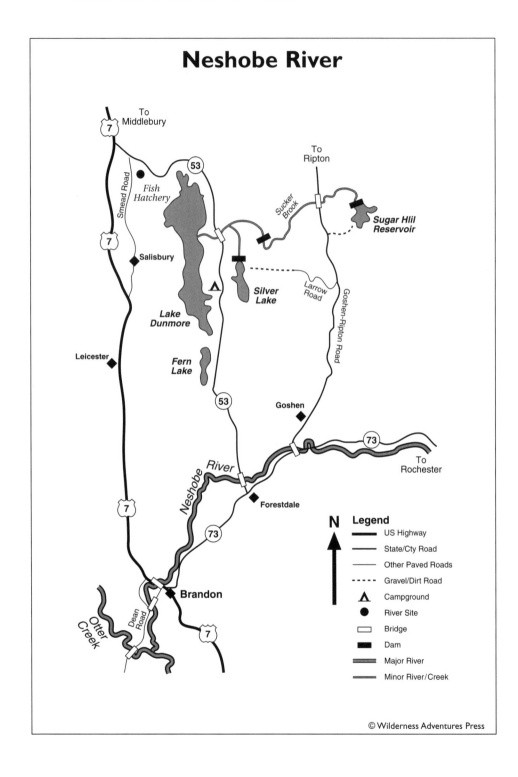

© Wilderness Adventures Press

posted against trespassing, making access difficult. There are a few unmarked pull-offs along Route 73 near the golf course that afford modest access.

The swift moving, cold waters of the upper Neshobe are perfect breeding areas for caddis and stoneflies. Fish move in and out of Otter Creek into the lower Neshobe to feed. Here, you might try swimming nymphs and streamers fished in the slower waters and deeper pools.

The Middlebury River

Just a stone's throw from the Long Trail where it passes Middlebury Gap, you'll find Pleiad Lake, the source of the South Branch of the Middlebury River. The title of this lake is somewhat misleading. Pleiad is not much more than 5 acres, but it does hold brook trout. The South Branch runs parallel to Route 125 toward the village of Ripton, where it joins the Middle Branch and forms the Middlebury River. A third stream, the North Branch, joins the river 2 miles farther down.

The Middlebury River is a lovely mountain stream that sings through gorges, running cold and clear toward Otter Creek in the valley below. Its cold waters make it a real treasure in midsummer when other rivers warm to uncomfortable temperatures. Wild brook trout are found throughout the upper stretches and tributaries. Although the trout are generally small, if you like fishing little, pristine waters, these fish are a worthy reward.

The river enters a deep gorge that extends 2 miles downstream from the village of Ripton. Sheer rock walls, boulders, and bottomless pools make this area safe water for rainbow and brook trout from 10 to 16 inches. Although a safe haven for trout, the gorge is treacherous wading for anglers. The gorge is about 150 feet deep, making access very difficult. There is a bridge just east of the village of East Middlebury. This is the easiest and safest point to enter the gorge. There is not much room to cast. Roll casting dries or quick-sinking nymphs cast up into the pocketwater is the best approach. Use attractor patterns, such as Wulffs and hare's ear nymphs.

West of East Middlebury, particularly after the Middlebury River crosses Route 7, the flow slows and holds more brown trout. Access is possible from several unmarked pull-offs along Three Mile Bridge Road that runs east from Route 7. Although unmarked, these pulloffs are obvious and easily located.

Middlebury River

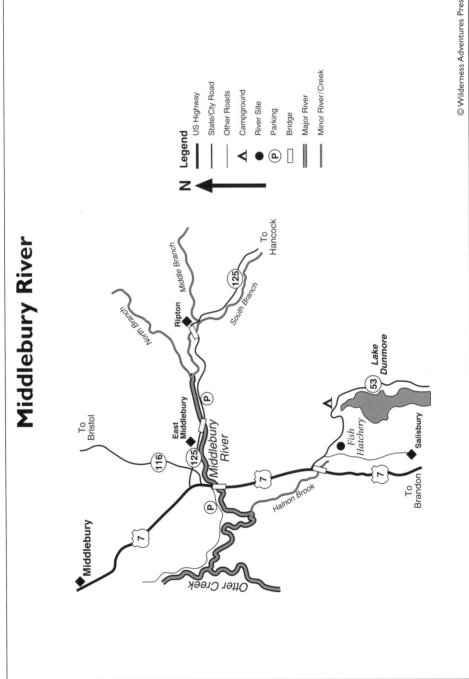

Legend

	US Highway
	State/Cty Road
	Other Roads
	Campground
	River Site
	Parking
	Bridge
	Major River
	Minor River/Creek

New Haven River. (Photo by Tom Haney)

The New Haven River

The New Haven River is a lovely trout stream that flows off the western slope of central Vermont. From its headwaters in South Lincoln, the New Haven travels almost 30 miles to where it joins Otter Creek just north of the village of Middlebury. The upper river and its main tributary, Baldwin Creek, are classic brook trout waters. Downstream from Bartlett's Falls in Bristol, you'll find browns, rainbows, and brookies, particularly browns.

Lincoln Gap Road follows the New Haven as it twists and turns around boulders, creating swift runs and deep pools. There are some unmarked parking areas, but be prepared to hike and climb over some boulders to get to the river. The trout aren't very selective in the upper section. Hornbergs, Adams and other attractor dries, and small nymphs will be all you'll need. The river becomes larger as it approaches Bartlett's Falls. This is a popular summer swimming and sunning area, and there are a number of roadside pull-offs.

Baldwin Creek joins the New Haven River where the Lincoln Gap Road meets Routes 17 and 116. There is good access to the river along the highway and as you leave the village of Bristol on Lower Notch and Carlstrom Roads. The river becomes

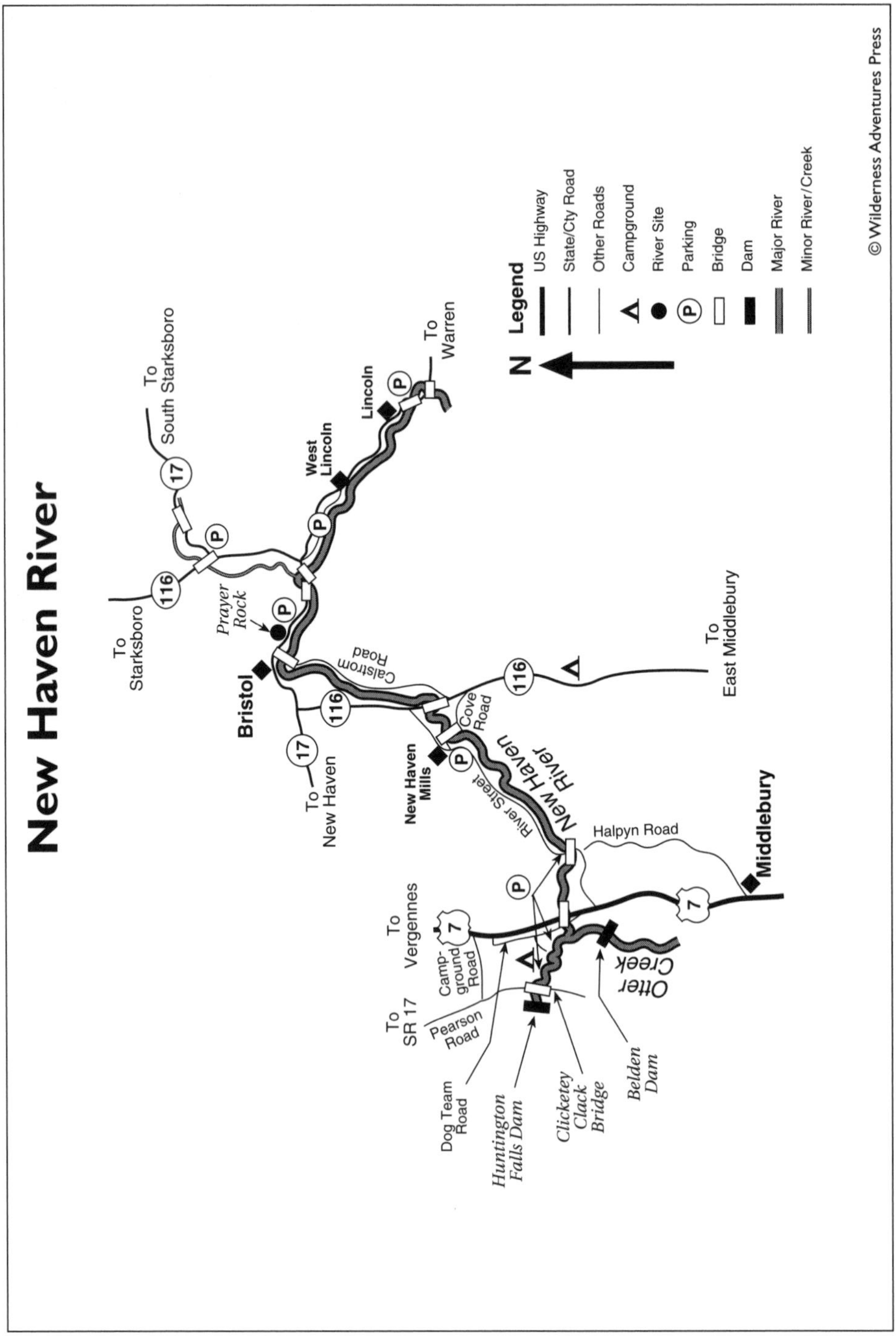

New Haven River
To Starksboro
116
17
To South Starksboro
Prayer Rock
Bristol
Calstrom Road
West Lincoln
Lincoln
To Warren
17
To New Haven
Cove Road
116
To East Middlebury
New Haven Mills
River Street
New Haven River
Halpyn Road
Middlebury
7
To Vergennes
Camp-ground Road
To SR 17
Pearson Road
Otter Creek
Dog Team Road
Huntington Falls Dam
Clicketey Clack Bridge
Belden Dam
N
Legend
US Highway
State/Cty Road
Other Roads
Campground
River Site
Parking
Bridge
Dam
Major River
Minor River/Creek
© Wilderness Adventures Press

*Netting a trout
on the New Haven River.
(Photo by Tom Haney)*

somewhat more remote through this section and receives less angling pressure. Recent flooding has made some changes to the stream through this section. However, it is still a productive area to fish.

River Road joins Route 116 near a bridge and follows the New Haven to Route 7. The mouth of the New Haven where it joins Otter Creek is less than a mile downstream and is accessible near the Dog Team Tavern or the River Bend Campground. There is a small parking fee at the campground.

Favorite Pattern	Someone's Favorite Nymph
Hook	Mustad 3906B, size 12-14
Thread	Pale yellow
Tail	A few white hackle barbules, short
Abdomen	A blend of cream fur and clear antron, picked out
Rib	Fine copper wire or brown thread
Thorax	Same as abdomen
Throat	The lightest, almost white, partridge barbules
Wing case	A jungle cock feather, tied in flat over the thorax and lacquered

Lower Otter Creek

Lower Otter Creek crawls for nearly 70 miles from the city of Rutland to the river mouth at Lake Champlain near Vergennes. There is little cover through the farmland and low swampy areas of the Otter Creek Valley. The only relief the river gets is the aeration from the five dams that interrupt the flow and the refreshing waters of its four coldwater tributaries.

The most productive trout water available in the lower section of Otter Creek, from the city of Rutland to its mouth at Lake Champlain, is between the two dams near the mouth of the New Haven. This short section of river holds rainbow and brown trout in the more aerated waters below Beldens' Dam. From the confluence of the New Haven, the water warms and becomes an excellent smallmouth bass fishery. You can reach this section of Otter Creek by turning west off Route 7 on the Beldens' Dam Road or from River Bend Campground. There is an area to launch a canoe by the "Clickety-clack" Bridge near the Huntington Falls Dam downstream. It's an easy paddle upstream, and the smallmouth fishing can be exciting.

Otter Creek is a very fertile piece of water. Caddisflies in all sizes and colors hatch near Beldens' Dam and the campground through May and June. As the summer warms up, you'll find sulphurs and cahills. August and September bring *Isonychia* and blue-winged olives. Fishing a woolly bugger or a streamer could result in the tackle-shattering strike of a 3-pound smallmouth.

From here, Otter Creek makes slow, winding progress over another two dams through the city of Vergennes and on to Lake Champlain. There are stories of some landlocked salmon and steelhead running from the lake in the spring and fall as far as the dam in Vergennes. All in all, the run of salmonids from the lake seems insignificant.

The physical characteristics of the four lower Otter Creek tributaries (Furnace Brook, Neshobe River, Middlebury River, and New Haven River) are quite similar. All flow west out of the Green Mountains. Their headwaters are steep and rocky and hold good populations of wild and stocked brook trout. As these rivers descend, the flows slow down and become a series of riffles and deep corner pools holding rainbow and brown trout. Brookies in these streams are generally small, averaging 7 or 8 inches. Rainbows and browns average 8 to 12 inches. Occasionally, a fish in excess of 16 inches is caught.

The season for these tributaries is the second Saturday in April through the last Sunday in October, with no special regulations.

Seasons and regulations for Lower Otter Creek are as follows:
- Second Saturday in April through the last Sunday in October.
- Largemouth and smallmouth bass, all year.
- From the falls in the center of Rutland to the falls in Vergennes, there is a catch-and-release season for trout from the Monday after the last Sunday in October to the Friday before the second Saturday in April.
- From the falls in Vergennes to Lake Champlain, regulations for Lake Champlain are in effect.
- No special regulations are in effect for Lower Otter Creek.

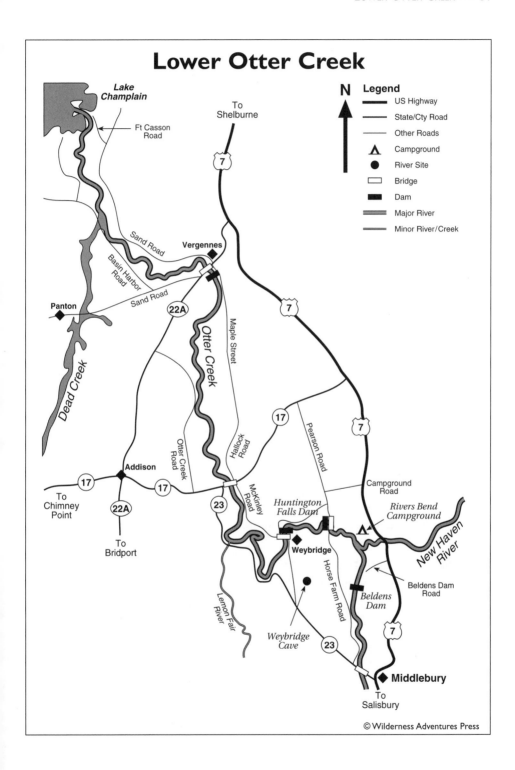

Lower Otter Creek

N

Legend

▬▬▬	US Highway
────	State/Cty Road
────	Other Roads
▲	Campground
●	River Site
▭	Bridge
▬	Dam
▬▬▬	Major River
────	Minor River/Creek

Lake Champlain

To Shelburne

Ft Casson Road

7

Sand Road

Vergennes

Basin Harbor Road

Sand Road

22A

Panton

7

Maple Street

Otter Creek

Dead Creek

Otter Creek Road

Hallock Road

17

Pearson Road

7

Addison

17

17

23

McKinley Road

Campground Road

Huntington Falls Dam

Rivers Bend Campground

New Haven River

22A

To Chimney Point

To Bridport

Weybridge

Horse Farm Road

Beldens Dam Road

Lemon Fair River

Weybridge Cave

Beldens Dam

7

23

Middlebury

To Salisbury

© Wilderness Adventures Press

WEST CENTRAL VERMONT HUB CITIES
Rutland / Middlebury

Rutland Elevation–540 • Population–18,320
Middlebury Elevation–370 • Population–8,034

ACCOMMODATIONS

Green Mountain Motel, 138 North Main Street (Rutland 05701) / 800-774-2575;
802-775-2575 / $

Brandon Motor Lodge, Box 130, Route 7 South (Brandon 05733) / 800-675-7614;
802-247-9594 / $$

Sugar House Motor Inn, Route 7 North (Middlebury 05753) / 802-388-2770 / $$

The Brandon Inn, 20 Park Street (Brandon 05733) / 802-247-5766 / $$$$

Waybury Inn, Route 125 (East Middlebury 05740) / 800-348-1810 / $$$$

By the Way Bed and Breakfast, Route 125, P.O. Box 264 (East Middlebury 05740) /
802-388-6291 / Next to Middlebury River / $$-$$$

CAMPGROUNDS

Branbury State Park, RR 2, Box 242 (Brandon 05743) / 802-247-5925 / Located
on the eastern shore of Lake Dunmore

River Bend Campground, P.O. Box 9, Dog Team Road off Route 7 (New Haven
05472) / 802-388-9092 / Located at the confluence of the New Haven River
and Otter Creek

RESTAURANTS

Casa Bianca, 76 Grove Street (Rutland 05701) / 802-772-7401

Dog Team Tavern, Dog Team Road off Route 7 North (Middlebury 05753) /
802-388-7651

Rosie's, Route 7 South (Middlebury 05753) / 802-388-7052 / The owner, Kevin
Cummings, is an avid flyfisher

Fire and Ice Restaurant, 26 Seymour (Middlebury 05753) / 802-388-7166

Mary's of Baldwin Creek, Junction of Route 1, 16 and 17 (Bristol 05443) /
802-453-2432

FLY SHOPS AND SPORTING GOODS

Vermont Field Sports, Wolcott Shopping Center, Route 7 South (Middlebury
05753) / 800-734-3572; 802-388-3572 / Full service tackle and flyfishing, local
information and guide referral / Peter Burton, one of the best, ties flies for this
shop

Lindholm Sport Center, 2 South Main Street (Rutland 05701) / 802-773-6000

Adventure Guides of Vermont, P.O. Box 3 (Ferrisburg 05473) / 800-425-TRIP;
802-425-6211 / Located in central Vermont, an excellent resource and guide
referral service

MEDICAL

Rutland Regional Medical Center, 160 Alien Street (Rutland 05701) / 802-775-7111
Porter Hospital, South Street (Middlebury 05753) / 802-388-4701

FOR MORE INFORMATION

Rutland Regional Chamber of Commerce
256 North Maine Street
Rutland, VT 05701
802-773-2772

Middlebury Chamber of Commerce
2 Court Street
Middlebury, VT 05753
802-388-7951

Lake Dunmore and Silver Lake

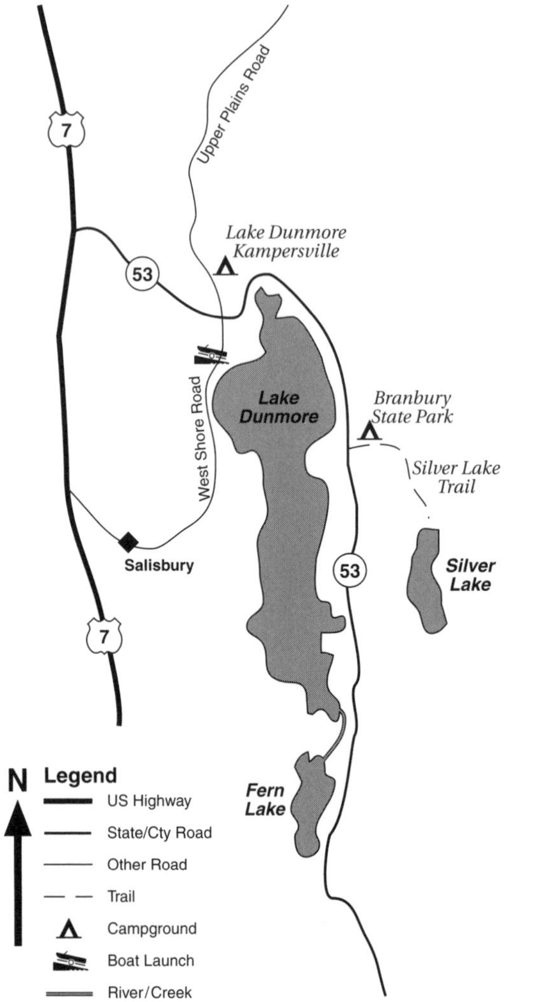

7

Upper Plains Road

Lake Dunmore
Kampersville

53

West Shore Road

**Lake
Dunmore**

*Branbury
State Park*

*Silver Lake
Trail*

Salisbury

53

**Silver
Lake**

7

N Legend

US Highway

State/Cty Road

Other Road

Trail

Campground

Boat Launch

River/Creek

**Fern
Lake**

STILLWATERS OF CENTRAL VERMONT

Cedar Lake, some know it as **Monkton Pond**, and **Winona Lake**, alias **Bristol Pond**, are two excellent warmwater ponds less than 20 miles from the city of Burlington. From Burlington, Route 116 south passes through Hinesburg and on Silver Street, to Monkton Ridge and Cedar Lake. The lake supports smallmouth as well as largemouth bass and panfish. There is state fish and wildlife public boat access on the north shore.

Winona Lake, just north of the village of Bristol on Route 1 16, has a good reputation for bass as well as some good-sized northern pike. There is a public access and boat ramp at the north end of the lake. Winona is a fairly shallow lake with a healthy population of aquatic plant life, making it difficult if not impossible for your float tube.

Pleiad Lake is a small brook trout pond near the Long Trail, where it passes over Middlebury Gap, near the village of Ripton. Access to the pond is a short hike south from Route 125. There is primitive camping available nearby on the Long Trail.

South of Middlebury, off Route 7 near the village of Salisbury, is **Lake Dunmore**. It is a good-sized lake with a mixed cold and warmwater habitat that supports bass and northern pike, as well as lake trout, rainbows, and landlocked salmon. There is a boat launch on the west shore, and on the east shore, there is an excellent campground at Branbury State Park.

Silver Lake is on a high ridge east of Lake Dunmore. It is a beautiful lake that receives regular stockings of rainbows and brown trout. The north end is shallow, having a silt-covered bottom that gives rise to good insect hatches in May and June. Silver Lake is accessible by foot on a trail that starts just across the road from Branbury State Park. The trail is about a mile long and uphill all the way. Primitive camping is available at the lake.

Sugar Hill Reservoir is located at Goshen Dam, east of Silver Lake. Access to this brook trout pond is by a foot trail off the Goshen-Ripton Road, which runs south from the village of Ripton.

Several years ago, *Outdoor Life* published an article on the outstanding northern pike fishing available in eastern Vermont. In addition to the southernmost end of Lake Champlain, Lakes Bomoseen and Hortonia were named in this article as top northern pike waters. Both still deserve that recognition.

In recent years **Lake Bomoseen** has gained a reputation as a coldwater fishery, producing some very large brown trout weighing up to 8 pounds. Both Lake Bomoseen and Lake Hortonia are easily accessible from Route 30 south of the village of Middlebury.

Sunset Lake is a deep, coldwater lake, supporting rainbows and lake trout. It is part of a flood control project and, although water levels fluctuate, its average maximum depth is in excess of 100 feet. Sunset Lake is located east of the village of Benson off Route 144.

Glen Lake lies near the western shore of Lake Bomoseen not far from Bomoseen State Park. It is a cold, clear lake that supports rainbow trout.

Chittenden Reservoir is an impoundment, reclaimed in the mid-1970s, that supports brook trout, rainbows, brown trout, and landlocked salmon. It is located in the Green Mountain National Forest, near the village of Chittenden, about 8 miles north of the city of Rutland. There is public fishing access and a boat launch on the south end adjacent to the spillway.

There are footpaths that lead to the Long Trail, about a mile east of Chittenden Reservoir. From Long Trail, it is a short hike to the two brook trout ponds, **North Pond** and **South Pond**. There is primitive camping on the trail.

East of the city of Rutland and not far from the Killington Mountain Ski Resort are **Colton Pond** and **Kent Pond**. Kent Pond is north on Route 100, less than a mile from the bottom of the Killington access road. The pond supports brook trout and rainbows and has a public fishing access area and boat launch. Excellent camping facilities can be found nearby at Gifford Woods State Park. Colton Pond is a brook trout pond and is located just 2 miles farther up Route 100.

The famous "Floating Bridge" that spans the narrows of a second **Sunset Lake** (this one located in the village of Brookfield) is worth a visit. It is located south of the village of Northfield on Route 65. As you pass over the bridge, the weight of your vehicle will sink the bridge a few inches into the lake and water will lap at the boots of pedestrians. Sunset Lake holds rainbow trout and can be fished from shore or from a canoe or float tube.

Rood Pond is located north of the village of Brookfield by continuing up the dirt main street of the village, bearing east until you intersect with Rood Pond Road. From the north, Rood Pond Road intersects with Route 64, 2 miles west of the village of Williamstown. This pond receives regular stockings of brook trout and has a reputation for nice evening hatches of insects. There is a well-maintained public access and boat launch.

EAST CENTRAL VERMONT
The White River

In the heart of the Green Mountains above Granville Gulf, the White River has its humble beginnings. Rising as a small brook trout stream, it gathers water from dozens of brooks and other larger tributaries to become one of the finest trout rivers in northern New England. Uninhibited by dams, the White River flows 57 miles southeast from the town of Granville through the villages of Hancock, Rochester, and Bethel to the villages of Royalton, Sharon, and Hartford, where it finally joins the Connecticut River near White River Junction.

Historically, the White River was a major spawning area for Atlantic salmon. The series of dams built on the Connecticut River during the latter part of the nineteenth century terminated the salmon migration by blocking access to upstream spawning water. The White, however, was spared and has remained healthy and vital. Today, it is an important part of the Atlantic Salmon Restoration Project being carried out by the U.S. Fish and Wildlife Service and Vermont Department of Fish and Wildlife. The White River National Fish Hatchery is located near the junction of Routes 107 and 12, about 2 miles east of the village of Bethel. It is worth a visit to the hatchery to take a tour of the facility and learn more about the Salmon Restoration Project.

The White River is a freestone stream, and its headwaters and cold tributaries provide steady flows of clean, cold water to the main stem, offering excellent spawning and nursery habitat. Wild brook trout can be found in the upper stretches of the river where the water passes under the cover of green forests, tumbling over rocks into small pools and riffles. The Hancock and West Branches join the White near the village of Rochester. Here, wild and stocked rainbows, which make up the bulk of the river's trout population, some brown trout, and planted Atlantic salmon fry begin to share water.

There are several unmarked highway public access areas along Route 100 as the White River winds south of Rochester. Route 100 curves sharply west and crosses the river in the village of Stockbridge. After the bridge, turn north to enter the Peavine National Travelway Site. This area provides excellent access. Other access sites include an area near the mouth of the Tweed River on Route 100 and on Blackmer Boulevard, a small road between Routes 100 and 107.

Near the junction of Routes 100 and 107, the Tweed River meets the White as it bends sharply to the east. The river, from the mouth of the Tweed to the village of Bethel where the Third Branch enters, offers some quality flyfishing opportunities. The trout habitat in this area is a combination of classic freestone and deep ledge pools. Access is readily available along route 107 at marked and unmarked public access areas. The Vermont Department of Fish and Wildlife has designated a 3.3-mile section of river in this stretch as a special regulation test area. From Lillieville Brook, which enters the White on the north bank near Gaysville, downstream to just below the junction of Cleveland Brook, fishing is with artificial flies and lures only, and all trout under 18 inches must be released. The daily limit is 1 fish.

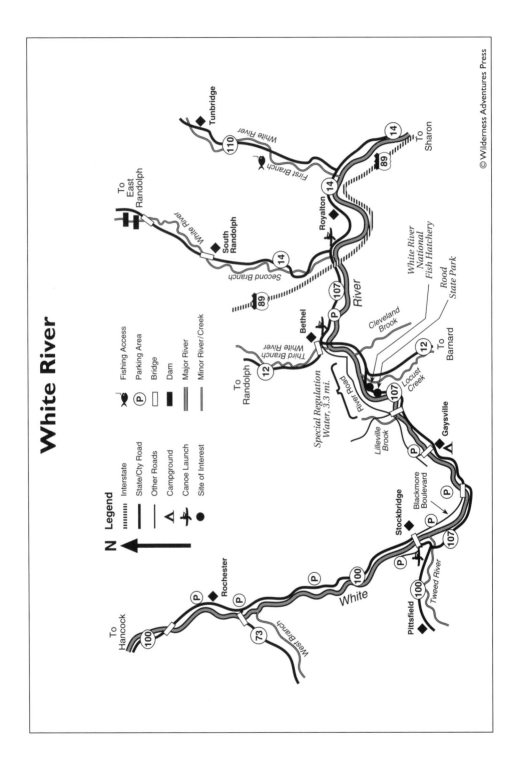

Headwaters of the White River at Granville Gulf. (Photo by Rhey Plumley)

Spring on the White River brings large hatches of caddisflies. Stonefly nymph patterns work throughout the season, and as the weather warms in July and August, there are hatches of stoneflies at dusk. The mayfly hatches of mid- and late summer are the most anticipated by flyfishers. The *Potamanthus* bring many good fish to the surface in the slower pools just before and after dark during July and August. If you're an early riser, you'll find Tricos emerging between 6:30 and 7:30 am from July through the month of September. The White also gives rise to *Isonychia* bicolor during the late season. Patterns with peacock herl as the major body ingredient, such as the zug bug, Prince nymph, and leadwing coachman, are effective wet flies. Dry patterns include the gray Wulff and dun variant. Autumn is also time to enjoy some good blue-winged olive fishing.

There's a gentleman for whom I tie flies who every year requests a half-dozen, size 8, Henryville specials. He told me he uses it as a small hopper imitation. There is a little green stonefly that you'll see sporadically hatching in the late afternoon in pocketwater on the White during the summer. A larger-than-usual Henryville special can sometimes be just the ticket.

From the village of Bethel, the White River flows south to the Second and First Branches as it runs along Route 14 and Interstate 89. The flow is slower through this section making it popular with canoeists and patient anglers seeking larger browns and rainbows. There are significant summer hatches of midges throughout this stretch of river, particularly where it flows from the village of Royalton to the village of South Royalton. In fact, the observant angler may see larger browns and rainbows sipping on midges in the many ledge pools between Royalton and the village of Sharon. There is a canoe launch near Sharon and downstream about 5 miles at a picnic area on Route 14 near the village of West Hartford. Other access areas are dispersed along the highway, so an angler should plan on some hiking. This is a popular area for swimmers and tubers. The best fishing times in the summer are early morning and late evening. As you continue down the White, you'll also have the opportunity to cast flies for some very nice smallmouth bass.

Favorite Pattern	Golden Comparadrake
Hook	Dry fly, size 12- 14
Thread	Tan
Tail	Three Moose body hairs
Body	Light yellow fur, over which is a small bunch of light brown deer hair. The tips of the hair are trimmed and tied in forming an extended body back to about midway up the moose hair tail. Spiral the thread back and forward to bind the hair d own and create a rib.
Wing	Fine, natural coastal deer hair tied in a 180-degree arc on top.
Head	Dubbing, same as underbody, in front of the wing.

The branches of the White River are noteworthy. The cool waters of the Hancock and West Branches offer the angler some opportunities to catch small, wild rainbows and brook trout. The Hancock Branch tumbles down the mountain from Texas Fall near Middlebury Gap on Route 125. The West Branch picks up Brandon Brook, a good brook trout stream in its own right, and flows along Route 73 from Brandon Gap to the village of Rochester. Both of these tributaries have good cover and cool temperatures throughout the season. The Tweed River, which follows Route 100 north from above the village of Pittsfield, is known to have excellent spawning habitat for rainbows. It is a cool, fast flowing stream with many shallow riffles and pockets. The Third Branch runs parallel to Route 12 from the village of East Granville through Randolph and into the village of Bethel. The best fishing is for brook trout in the upper reaches. The lower section can offer some brown trout fishing in the slower, deeper runs.

The Second Branch runs south along Route 14 from above the village of Braintree to where it meets the White River in the village of Randolph. Access is limited in the upper stretch, and there has been significant streambank erosion. There is some good fishing for rainbows and browns near the mouth of the Second Branch.

The First Branch offers the best fishing of all the branches. As it crisscrosses Route 110 from the village of Chelsea to the village of Tunbridge, there are several bridges. This section offers good fishing for rainbows and browns in its long riffles and deep ledge pools. As the river approaches the mouth near the village of South Royalton, the water warms and trout fishing becomes more limited.

The White River and its relatively large tributaries drain a huge area of central Vermont. The headwaters are fast flowing and well-covered brook trout waters. Downstream, the river deepens and carves out deep corner pools and runs. The river flows over large gravel and broken ledge rock as it turns east. From the village of Bethel, downstream, the gradient decreases and the water temperatures begin to rise. Ledges are now more pronounced and the bottom more silty. The White River is one of the most beautiful rivers in the Northeast. It shares the character and the moods of a wild and free Atlantic salmon river.

Seasons and special regulations for the White River include:
- Second Saturday in April through the last Sunday in October.
- From the river mouth upstream to the Route 5, Bridge Street bridge in the town of Hartford, refer to Connecticut River Regulations.
- From the Route 5, Bridge Street bridge, town of Hartford, upstream to the Route 107 bridge, village of Bethel, there is a winter, artificials-only, catch-and-release season from the Monday after the last Sunday in October to the Friday before the second Saturday in April.
- From Cleveland Brook, in the town of Bethel, upstream to Lillieville Brook in the town of Stockbridge, angling is restricted to artificials; there is a length limit of 18 inches and a creel limit of 1 fish.

Ompompanoosuc River

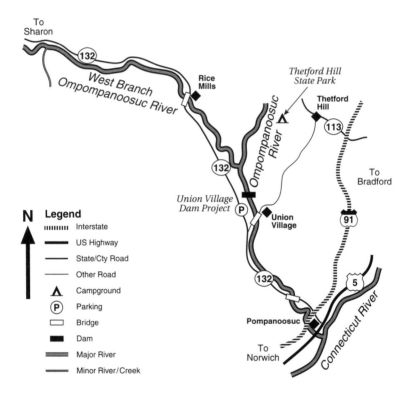

Ompompanoosuc River

The Ompompanoosuc River has its headwaters in the hills above the village of Vershire. The river runs south along Route 113, picking up water from a tributary flowing out of Lake Fairlee, and from its main source, the West Branch, which joins the river about 2 miles south of the village of Thetford Center. There is a large, flood-control dam at Union village from which the Ompompanoosuc makes a short run to its mouth at the Connecticut River.

High water temperatures limit fishing in the upper river in summer. The West Branch, which flows from South Strafford along Route 132, does offer some wild and stocked brook trout fishing. Above the Union Village Dam, where the river flows through the Federal Forest Management Area, the state of Vermont regularly stocks brown trout and rainbows. Fish, holding over in the deeper pools, can average 13 or 14 inches. There is excellent access to this stretch of river from the recreation and picnic area just outside Union Village.

At Union Village a dam blocks the flow, creating slower runs and deeper pools for stocked as well as holdover trout. The lower river quickly turns into a warmwater fishery. The river setback and backwaters near the mouth are best fished from a boat or canoe. As with all the rivers that flow into the Connecticut River, the Ompompanoosuc offers excellent flyfishing for smallmouth bass near the river mouth.

Fish ants and beetles as northern New England waters warm up. (Photo by Steve Hickoff and Elizabeth Edwards)

There are no special regulations for the Ompompanoosuc River, and its seasons are:

- Second Saturday in April through the last Sunday in October.
- From the river mouth upstream to the Route 5 bridge in the town of Norwich, refer to Connecticut River regulations.
- From the Route 5 bridge in Norwich upstream to the dam in Union Village, there is a winter, artificials-only, catch-and-release season from the Monday after the last Sunday in October to the Friday before the second Saturday in April.

Waits River

The Waits River begins as a small brook trout stream in the high mountains of Groton State Forest. The river flows southeast through the town of Orange, picking up Route 25 near the village of West Topsham. The trees, which most years begin to show autumn colors in late August, provide a protective canopy over the river. This upper stretch of river holds a good population of wild and stocked brown trout and rainbow trout, as well as some brookies. A short walk through the woods provides access from roadside pull-offs.

As you follow the Waits downstream along Route 25 toward the village of East Corinth, water temperatures rise and trout fishing diminishes. The river becomes broad and shallow with a gravel-covered bed, especially from where the South Branch joins the Waits to the high dam in the village of Bradford.

No special regulations apply to the Waits River. Its seasons are as follows:

- Second Saturday in April through the last Sunday in October.
- From the river mouth upstream to Route 5 in the village of Bradford, refer to Connecticut River regulations.

Wells River

The Wells River rises out of the hills and ponds of Groton State Forest. The upper reaches are generally warm and unremarkable as trout waters. Its main artery, the South Branch, which flows out of Noyes Pond, is a fine little brook trout stream. Its shaded waters remain cool all season long, and the steep runs and pockets provide good trout habitat.

The South Branch meets the main stem of the Wells a few hundred yards east of the intersection of Routes 232 and 302. Route 302 follows the river the rest of its 20-mile course to its mouth at the Connecticut River in the village of Wells River.

From the mouth of the South Branch, downstream to the village of South Rygate, the Wells River is home to both brown trout and brookies. The banks are undercut and the runs are deep and cool. River access is along Route 302 and off the side roads and river crossings.

Waits River

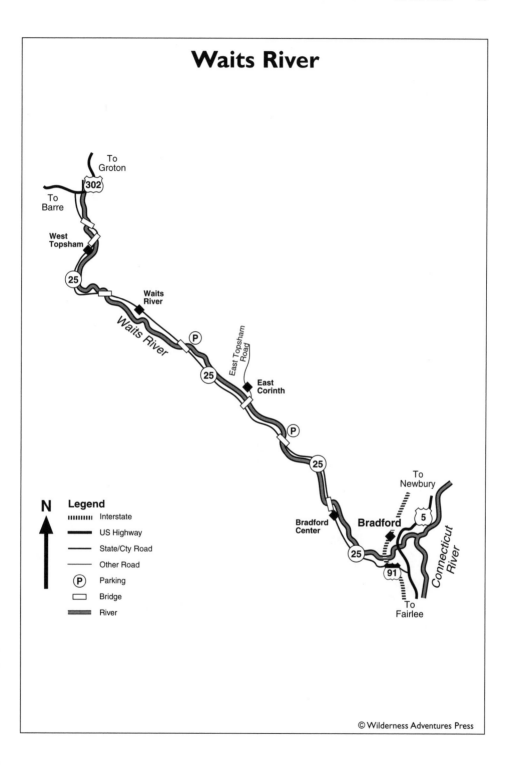

Wells River

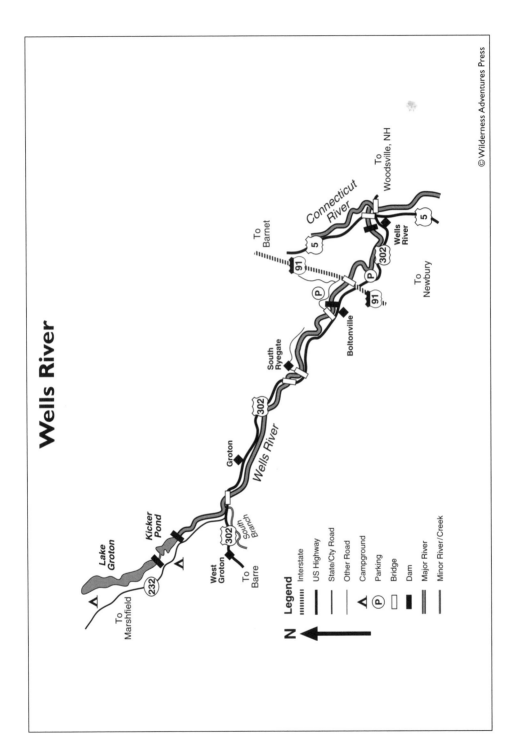

Legend

Interstate	
US Highway	
State/Cty Road	
Other Road	
Campground	
Parking	
Bridge	
Dam	
Major River	
Minor River/Creek	

N

The Wells is not a large river. Light tackle and a quiet approach are the best tools. The most productive flies are small, weighted nymphs, caddis imitations, and terrestrials. The river continues in graceful meanders through valley fields and then over some steep ledges to a dam in the village of Boltonville. There is good river access to the water below the dam from the north bank of the river from a dirt road after you cross the dam. Downstream from the overpass of Interstate 91 there is a state fish and wildlife access area near a very nice stretch of water.

With no special regulations, Wells River seasons include:

- Second Saturday in April through the last Sunday in October.
- From the river mouth upstream to the Route 302 bridge in the village of Wells River, refer to Connecticut River regulations.

East Central Vermont Hub Cities
White River Junction/Woodstock/Bethel

White River Junction Elevation–367 • Population–2,375
Woodstock Elevation–705 • Population–3,212
Bethel Elevation–573 • Population–1,866

Accommodations

Best Western at the Junction (White River Junction 05001) / 802-295-3015 / $$$

Columns Motor Inn (Sharon 05065) / 802-763-7040 / $

Quality Inn at Quechee Gorge, Route 4 (Quechee 05059) / 802-295-7600 / $$

Woodstock Motel, Taftsville Road (Woodstock 05091) / 802-457-2500 / $-$$$

The Quechee Inn at Marshland Farm Bed & Breakfast, Clubhouse Road (Quechee 05059) / 800-253-3133; 802-295-3133 / Flyfishing school / $$-$$$$$

Campgrounds

Quechee Gorge State Park, 190 Dewey Mills Road (White River Junction 05001) / 802-295-2990 / Located off Route 4 in Quechee

White River Valley Campground, Route 107 (Gaysville 05746) / 802-234-9115 / Camping on the White River

Restaurants

Bentley's Cafe, 7 Elm Street (Woodstock 05091) / 802-457-3400 / Breakfast

Spooner's Steak House, Route 4 East (Woodstock 05091) / 802-457-4022

Fire Stones, Route 4 Waterman Park (Quechee 05059) / 802-295-1600

Gillam's Restaurant, Sykes Avenue (White River Junction 05001) / 802-296-3071

Fly Shops and Guides

Briggs, Ltd., 12 North Main Street (White River Junction 05001) / 802-295-7100 / Flyfishing equipment, flies and tying supplies, guide referrals

Complete Fly Fishing Supplies, Route 4 West (Woodstock 05404) / New and used rods and reels, fly tying materials, books / 802-457-2073

Locust Creek Outfitters (Bethel 05032) / 802-234-5884

Trout on a Fly Guide Service (East Randolph 05041) / 802-728-6599

Medical

Mary Hitchcock Memorial Hospital, 1 Medical Center Drive (Lebanon 03766) / 603-650-5000

FOR MORE INFORMATION
Upper Valley Chamber of Commerce
61 Old River Road
White River Junction, VT 05001
802-295-6200

Northern Vermont

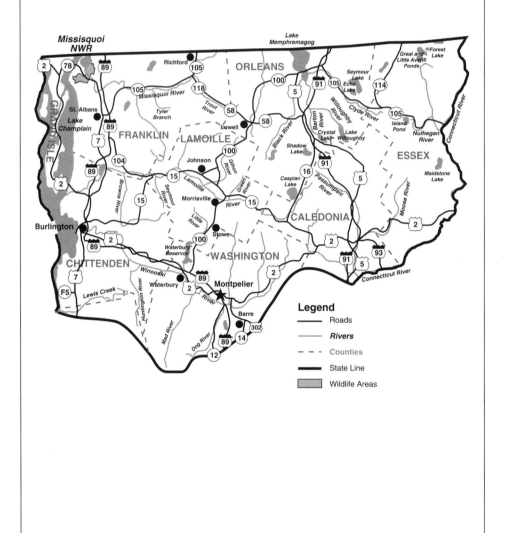

Legend

—— Roads

〜〜 *Rivers*

- - - Counties

━━ State Line

▨ Wildlife Areas

© Wilderness Adventures Press

NORTHERN VERMONT

Northern Vermont is a world of extremes. Northwest Vermont is the population and development center of the state. To the east are the forests, small farms, and towns with dirt for their main roads. Tourists seeking remote places to ski, hike, camp, or just "to peep" come to the Green Mountain State throughout the year. Some come to fish. The large lake trout of Lakes Seymour and Willoughby, the historic spring run of rainbow trout in the Willoughby River, and the competition of Lake Champlain International Fishing Derbies and BASS Top 100 Tournaments bring those who fish from other parts of New England, New York, and Canada.

Once the Battenkill in southern Vermont was the flyfishers' jewel. Now, those seeking a quality flyfishing experience are discovering other treasures: the beautiful Winooski, the Lamoille, and Missisquoi Rivers and their tributaries. On the west side of the Green Mountains are the more secluded Barton, Clyde, and Nulhegan Rivers, and the trophy trout water the state of New Hampshire shares, the upper Connecticut River.

With the success of the program to control the sea lamprey in Lake Champlain and the opening of the Ed Weed Fish Hatchery in Grand Isle, state stocking programs have been more aggressive. The result is a stronger run of landlocked salmon and steelhead, more trophy-sized brown and rainbow trout in waters available to the public, and healthier brook trout populations in the streams and ponds.

Maintaining and improving fish habitat in Vermont's rivers and streams is an ongoing challenge for the state, local Trout Unlimited chapters, and other grassroots conservation organizations. Streambank planting, the installation of flow diversions, and the creation of lunker structures are providing richer and more protected aquatic environments. Laws that regulate water removal, streambed graveling, and agricultural runoff are having a positive impact. The decision to remove the hydroelectric dam on the Clyde River in Newport has been a giant step toward the restoration of that landlocked salmon fishery. Now wild salmon are returning from Lake Memphremagog to their historic spawning areas, and sport fishers once again have the opportunity to fish over these spectacular leapers.

There are three main river systems that drain the northwest slope of Vermont into Lake Champlain—the Winooski, the Lamoille, and the Missisquoi. The business and population centers of Burlington and St. Albans make these rivers and their tributaries very accessible to visiting flyfishers. Everything is here, from wild brook trout, trophy brown trout, and rainbow trout to landlocked salmon and steelhead. For the warmwater flyfishing enthusiast, there are largemouth and smallmouth bass and great northern pike.

In the northeast, the lack of nutrients in many streams and the harshness of winter greatly limit the amount of aquatic insects available to fish. The Green Mountains are geologically old, and minerals are all but spent. In the winter, anchor ice chokes the rivers and just as quickly turns into spate that can scour the streambed of most life. Caddis and stoneflies have hardened themselves to these conditions and are the predominant food source in the northern streams. You will find the more delicate mayflies (Hendricksons, cahills, sulphurs, and blue-winged olives) scattered in their cycles throughout the season. May, June, and July are the prime months to flyfish the hatches. Terrestrials, particularly flying ant patterns, small nymphs, and streamers, work well in the late summer and as the season comes to a close.

NORTHERN VERMONT MAJOR HATCHES

Insect/Bait	J	F	M	A	M	J	J	A	S	O	N	D	Patterns
Caddis				▮	▮	▮	▮	▮	▮	▮			Black Elk Hair Caddis #16-20 (early and late season); Tan Elk Hair Caddis or X-Cadds #14-18; Soft Hackles and Emergers #14-18; Hare's Ear Nymph and Beadhead Pupae #14-18
Blue-winged Olives					▮				▮				Parachute Adams #14-20; Thorax Blue-winged Olive #14-18; Pheasant Tail Nymphs #14-20
Hendricksons				▮	▮								Dark Hendrickson or Red Quill #12-14; Hendrickson Nymph #12-14; Rusty Spinner #14
Sulphurs						▮							Sulphur Duns and Hare's Ear Nymphs #16-18
Light Cahill						▮	▮						Cahill Dun #14
Giant Mayfly *Hexagenia limbata*							▮						Comparadun #8
Minnows and Leeches	▮	▮									▮	▮	Woolly Buggers and Streamers
Fish roe		▮	▮	▮									Egg Patterns

NORTHERN VERMONT HATCHES (cont.)

Insect/Bait	J	F	M	A	M	J	J	A	S	O	N	D	Patterns
Golden Drake *Potamanthus distinctus*							▮						Paradrake #8
Stoneflies				▮	▮	▮	▮	▮					Black Stonefly Nymph #8-14; Yellow Stonefly Nymph #8-10; Black Woolly Buggers #6-10
White Mayfly *Ephoron leukon*								▮					Cream Variant #10
Tiny Mayflies *Tricorythodes stygiatus*									▮				Trico Spinner #18-24
Leadwing Coachman *Isonychia bicolor*								▮	▮				Leadwing Coachman Wet Fly #10-12; Zug Bug and Prince Nymph #10-14; Gray Wulff and Adams #10-14
Midges					▮	▮	▮	▮	▮				Griffith's Gnat #18; Parachute Adams #18-22
Terrestrials						▮	▮	▮	▮				Hoppers #6-12; Flying Ants #16

NORTHWESTERN VERMONT
The Winooski River

The Winooski River flows west and north from the hills of Cabot to its mouth near the city of Burlington at Lake Champlain. For 90 miles, the Winooski carries the waters of more than 1,000 square miles of watershed. Its varied habitat is home to wild brook, rainbow, and brown trout. Smallmouth bass, salmon, and steelhead reside in the lower river where they migrate from Lake Champlain.

Montpelier, the state's capital city, is the portal to the upper Winooski. The river's beginnings are fragile. Water temperatures run extremely high for trout species and beaver activity has choked the river's flow, making life pretty tough for the brookies and small browns in this section of river. Consequently, the fish are weary and fishing can be a challenge. Access is along Route 2, where pulloffs come close to the river or off side roads that cross the river away from the highway. You'll find a freestone stream with pocketwater and many twists and turns. The best way to fish this stretch is to cover some ground. Do some walking and explore the runs and pools. Popular waters are those near the Twin Field School and Onion River Campground—both easily recognized by their signs along U.S. Route 2. Spring (mid-May through June) is beautiful in this area. Mayfly hatches are somewhat sparse, but caddis and stoneflies maintain a strong presence.

Local Pattern	VT Hare's Ear Caddis
Hook	Dry fly, size 14 - 20
Thread	Brown
Body	Hare's ear dubbing, picked out
Hackle	Short brown/ grizzly mixed

Branches of the Winooski

The **North Branch Winooski** follows Route 12 from above Worcester to its mouth near Montpelier. Brown trout are predominant below the Wrightsville Dam. Above Wrightsville Reservoir, one is more likely to encounter brook trout.

Stevens Branch and **Jailhouse Branch** (where legend has it that Elvis fished) are in the Barre area running along Routes 62 and 302. These are good brook trout waters and are stocked liberally each year by the Vermont Department of Fish and Wildlife. Just about 17 miles east of Barre is **Noyes (Seyon) Pond**. This is the only "flyfishing-only" water regulated by the state, and it is truly a jewel. Lodging and boat rental are available. It is a large pond full of brook trout and surrounded by remote public land. It is not uncommon to share the company of loons or a large bull moose. Don't pass this up on your visit.

The lower Winooski, flowing north from Montpelier to Burlington, is the most heavily fished water in the area. Following Route 2 from the dam at Middlesex into the village of Waterbury, there are several unmarked pull-off areas giving good river access. For 7 miles the river receives the cooling effects of the dam and Mad River, which enters the Winooski just downstream from Middlesex. The river is larger through this section and has boulders that break up the river flow. Runs and pools are more rapid and deep. This is good holding water for browns and larger rainbows throughout the season.

The state manages a specially stocked stretch of river that runs from the Route 2 bridge in Waterbury to the railroad bridge just north of town. Access can be made either from behind the state hospital in town or from River Road, which parallels the river along the southwest bank. Here, the Winooski is flatter and its bottom is made up of small gravel, silt, and cut ledge. Fishing pressure is heavy at times, and there are no restrictions on bait or other angling techniques. Early morning and evening hours tend to be the best times to fish this stretch of river, where there is a chance for a large brown or rainbow.

The Winooski River gets another cool drink from the outflow of the Waterbury Reservoir dam through the Little River in the town of Waterbury and from the Bolton Dam in the town of Bolton. The river from Bolton Dam to the village of Richmond is very productive. River Road follows the Winooski closely, giving anglers good access to its many runs and deep pools. You find River Road where the bridge crosses the river in Jonesville, just east of Richmond on Route 2, or from the east side of town in Waterbury off Route 100 south. The banks are steep but wading is fairly forgiving. Pay attention to changes in flow—water can be released from the dams without warning, creating strong currents.

Caddis and stonefly imitations work consistently throughout the season. The first really important mayfly hatches on this portion of the river are the sulphurs and cahills in late May. You will probably see some blue quills and Hendricksons earlier, but the water's usually so cold the fish show little interest. In midsummer at dusk, a large, yellow mayfly, the golden drake (*Potamanthus*) emerges. The first indication that this hatch is occurring is the watchful cedar waxwings taking flight and diving for this mouthful of an insect. There is little chance for the trout to get at the adult after the birds have had their way, so the hatch is best fished with swimming nymph (sizes 8 and 10) or emerger patterns. Fall can provide some good blue-winged olive (sizes 16 to 20) fishing.

In the village of Winooski at the site of the old falls is the Salmon Hole. For many years, the dam that replaced the falls was a barrier to fish migrating from Lake Champlain to spawn. In 1993, as a result of licensing conditions negotiated by members of the Central Vermont Chapter of Trout Unlimited and the Vermont Department of Fish and Wildlife, a trap truck facility with a fish elevator was constructed at the dam. Supervised jointly by hydroelectric personnel and state and federal fish and wildlife biologists, this facility allows spawning steelhead and landlocked salmon to be captured and trucked upstream above the dams, where they have access to tributaries and native waters. The farthest upstream access for these migrant species is the Bolton Dam in the town of Bolton.

Fishing in the Salmon Hole area is closed from mid-March through the first of June to protect spawning walleyes that also arrive from the lake. After this period,

Winooski River

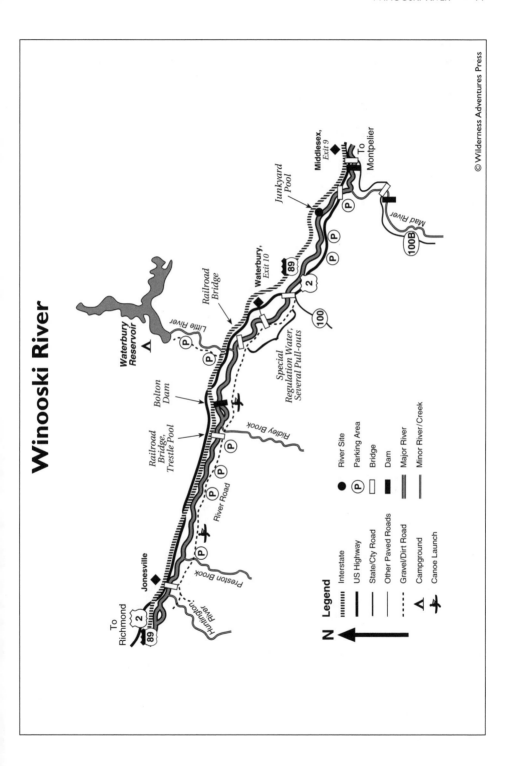

© Wilderness Adventures Press

Legend

N

Interstate
US Highway
State/City Road
Other Paved Roads
Gravel/Dirt Road
▲ Campground
✈ Canoe Launch

● River Site
Ⓟ Parking Area
▢ Bridge
■ Dam
Major River
Minor River/Creek

Salmon Hole on the Winooski River. (Photo by Rhey Plumley)

and especially in autumn, fishing for lake-run salmon and steelhead can be exciting. Streamer patterns that represent smelt or small nymphs, fished on the swing or dead-drifted deep, are the most effective methods of fishing Salmon Hole. Fish all the water. During the day, salmon will move out of the fast water and into the depths.

Access to Salmon Hole is gained from either the Burlington side off Riverside Avenue or in Winooski by the fish trap or at the canoe access on West Canal Street. Wading can be challenging because the river bottom is typical of areas below city dams. Rocks and concrete blocks with rebar protruding are a hazard to wading but make good flow diversions for holding fish. Also, watch out for unannounced changes in flow levels.

There are other varieties of fish that reside in and around Salmon Hole, such as smallmouth bass, the occasional lake trout, perch, pike and pickerel. So if you're in the Burlington area with a little time to kill, cast a fly in the Winooski River at Salmon Hole.

Seasons for the Winooski River are:

- Second Saturday in April through the last Sunday in October.
- From Bolton Dam to ledges west of Route 7 in Winooski, there is a catch-and-release season from the last Sunday in October to the Friday before the second Saturday in April that is artificial fly or lure only.

- From Lake Champlain to the blue railroad bridge in Winooski, the river is open all year (Lake Champlain regulations).
- The section from Blue Bridge to ledges west of Route 7 in Winooski is open all year except from March 16 through June 1.

Special regulations for the Winooski River include:

- From Bolton Dam to ledges west of route 7 in Winooski, the minimum length for rainbow trout is 10 inches and a creel limit of no more than 2.
- From railroad bridge to the Route 2 bridge in Waterbury, a total of brook, brown, and rainbow trout is no more than 2; designated as "trophy trout waters" by Vermont Department of Fish and Wildlife due to annual stocking of large (14- to 18-inch) browns and rainbows.

Brown trout are stocked regularly and average 8 to 14 inches with larger fish in the range of 4 to 5 pounds caught each year. Rainbow trout in the area downstream from Bolton Dam are wild and average 6 to 13 inches with many in the 18-inch range. Brook trout are found in the upper section of the river.

The Winooski River is a freestone stream with its flow interrupted by seven dams. Levels fluctuate without warning, and the water can color up after a summer storm. Water temperatures fluctuate quite dramatically from a springtime temperature at runoff of the middle 30s and 40s to summertime temperatures of as much as 85 degrees. Although temperatures approach dangerous limits for trout, enough cooling waters enter the main stem to provide habitat throughout the river's length. Caddisflies are the predominant aquatic insect, with a fair representation of mayflies, as well.

Favorite Pattern	Sulphur Wulff (Berry)
Hook	Dry fly, size 14 - 18
Thread	Primrose
Tail	Light elk hair
Body	Fine sulphur-yellow dubbing
Wing	Light elk hair
Hackle	Ginger

From its headwaters in Roxbury north to its confluence with the Winooski River in Montpelier, the **Dog River** slowly winds its way through valley fields and farmland. The Dog has a good population of wild brook, brown, and rainbow trout managed by the state without stocking as a wild trout fishery. Access is along Route 12 and 12A. There is quite a bit of posted land, so please be courteous and ask permission—most landowners are very willing to allow anglers access to the river as long as they ask first. As with most wild trout fisheries, a slow, cautious approach is advised. There can be a good Hendrickson hatch on the Dog River early in the season. Later, small nymphs, midge patterns, and terrestrials do well. In mid-August, there is a Trico hatch just at dawn.

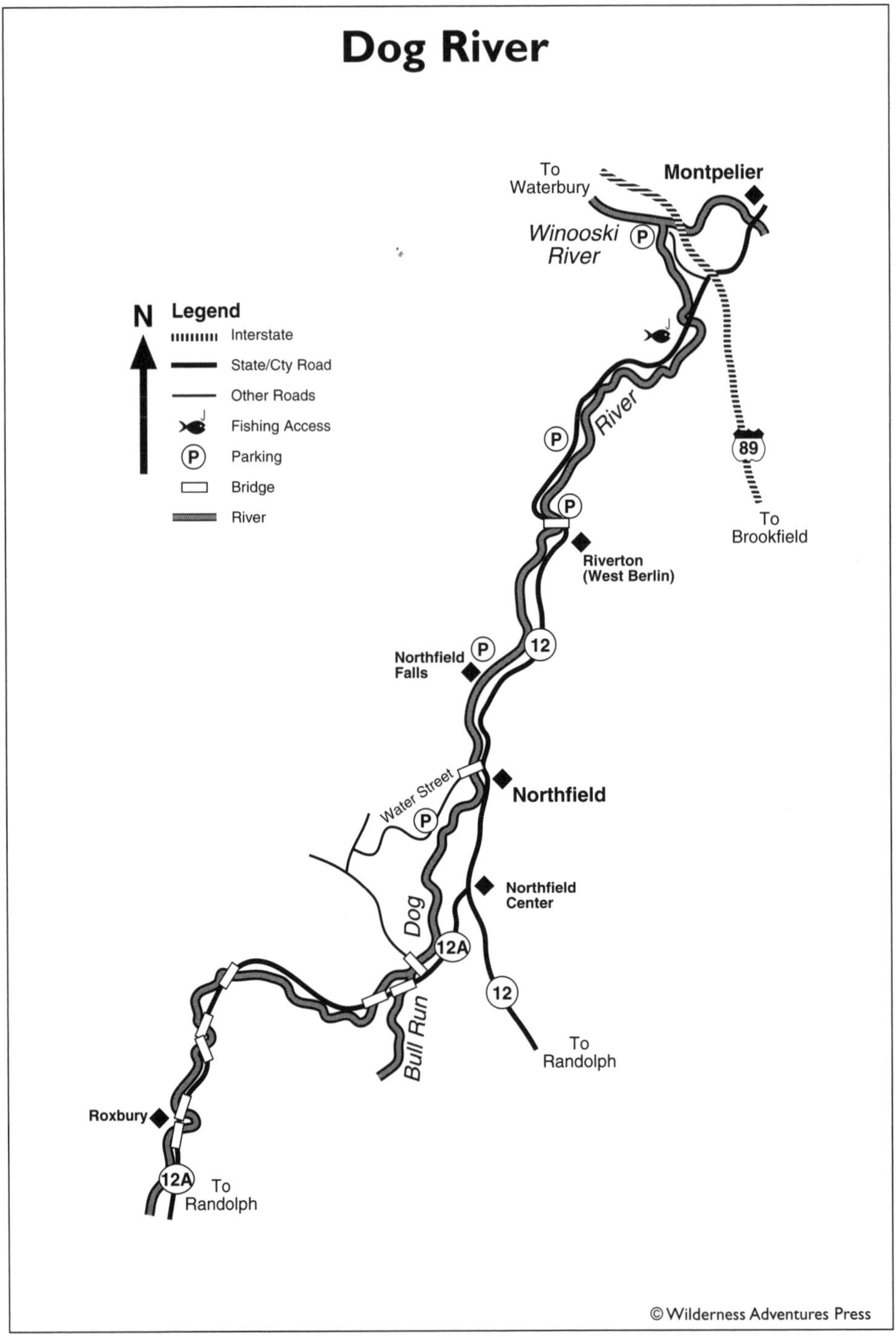

Dog River

N

Legend
ⅢⅢⅢⅢ	Interstate
▬▬▬	State/Cty Road
▬▬	Other Roads
✕	Fishing Access
Ⓟ	Parking
▭	Bridge
▰▰▰	River

To Waterbury

Montpelier

Winooski River Ⓟ

River

Ⓟ

Ⓟ

89

To Brookfield

Riverton (West Berlin)

Ⓟ 12

Northfield Falls

Water Street

Ⓟ

Northfield

Northfield Center

Dog

12A

12

To Randolph

Bull Run

Roxbury

12A To Randolph

© Wilderness Adventures Press

The next major tributary of the lower Winooski is the **Mad River**. The Mad's head-waters are found to the south in Granville Gulf. The river flows north along Route 100 for about 25 miles through the scenic ski area villages of Warren and Waitsfield. Mad River is a classic beauty. Its course makes deep cuts in ledge rock, creating waterfalls and deep, cold pools. The upper reaches hold wild brook trout in tumbling pocket-water, while below, in the more defined runs and pools, there are rainbows and browns. This is a river that deserves a visit, so take the time to check it out.

Below the village of Waterbury, the **Little River** enters the Winooski. As an out-flow of the Waterbury Reservoir, it is the cooling source of the Winooski where it flows past the village of Richmond. In summer heat, browns and rainbows will seek shel-ter in and around the Little River, providing good fishing opportunities. The Little River runs quite high at times due to power release surging and cutting through the clay and ledge that line its bottom. When generating stops, so does the river, holding trout in its now quiet pools.

You should not overlook the waters of **Waterbury Reservoir**. They hold small-mouth bass, brown trout, and rainbows, and even some brookies. Trolling with flies in spring after ice-out and casting at the mouth of Stevenson Brook, one of the reser-voir's tributaries, could produce a lively, fat rainbow. Waterbury Reservoir is consid-ered a trophy smallmouth bass fishery. It offers great summer and autumn fly casting action from a canoe along the shore. The campground at Little River State Park is excellent and provides access to much of the area.

The **Huntington River** enters the Winooski at Jonesville. It is a beautiful trout stream, flowing out of the foothills near Camel's Hump through farm fields and meadows until it crashes into a gorge three-quarters of a mile from its mouth. The Huntington is a popular river, particularly in the area around the gorge. It is home to large browns and rainbows coming in and out of the Winooski. The Huntington River Gorge is best fished early in the season or later, and early in the day before swimmers and picnickers gather. Large stonefly patterns, woolly buggers, and streamers fished with patience can pay off with a large brown or rainbow on your line. Upriver, small brown trout and brookies are found.

The last major tributary of the Winooski River is **Mill Brook**. It is accessible off Route 117 east of the village of Essex Junction. A good deal of the brook is posted. The upper portions of Mill Brook offer good brook trout pocketwater with plenty of cover, while the lower section has brown trout and some rainbows that migrate out of the Winooski in spring. The mouth of Mill Brook fishes well at low water.

Lewis Creek

This small stream runs virtually uninhibited for 20 miles from its source in the foothills above Starksboro and into Lake Champlain. At its origin, the creek drops fast and is good brook trout water. Stocking programs to introduce steelhead have had a varied degree of success. The run of steelhead that everyone anticipates each year can occur anytime during the months of March and April, if at all. A few years ago, we had a very dramatic thaw in January that coincided with the mouth not being totally frozen. The resulting heavy runoff caused an influx of steelhead that

Mad River

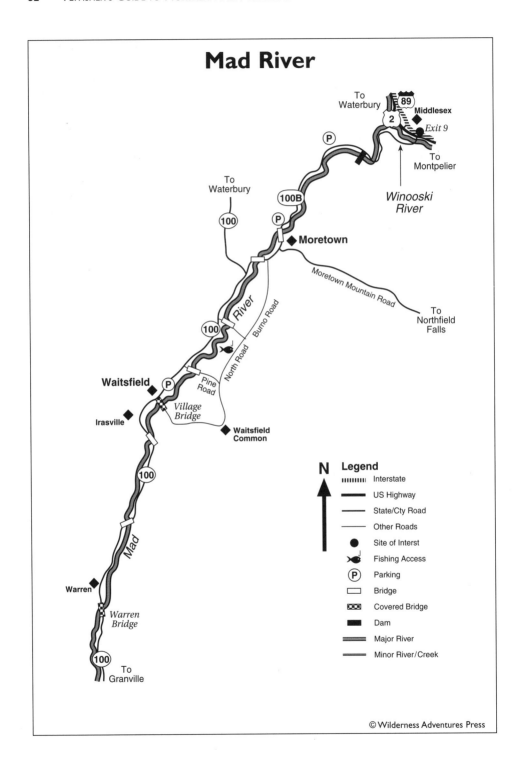

To
Waterbury

89

Middlesex ◆

2

Exit 9

To
Montpelier

P

100B

To
Waterbury

100

P

*Winooski
River*

◆ **Moretown**

Moretown Mountain Road

To
Northfield
Falls

River

100

Burno Road

North Road

Waitsfield ◆ **P**

Pine
Road

*Village
Bridge*

Irasville ◆

◆ **Waitsfield
Common**

100

Mad

Warren ◆

*Warren
Bridge*

100

To
Granville

N

Legend

ⅢⅢⅢ	Interstate
▬	US Highway
—	State/Cty Road
—	Other Roads
●	Site of Interst
🐟	Fishing Access
Ⓟ	Parking
▢	Bridge
▨	Covered Bridge
▬	Dam
▬	Major River
▬	Minor River/Creek

© Wilderness Adventures Press

Andrew Plumley and his father, Bob, with Andrew's first fly-caught rainbow trout at Lewis Creek. (Photo by Rhey Plumley)

is still talked about. Flies for steelhead include egg patterns and small nymphs. Fish them deep and slow.

Access is from Route 7, where Lewis Creek passes under the highway in North Ferrisburg, about 15 miles south of Burlington. Hollow Road follows the creek upstream for a way, or you can find access from Starksboro. Lewis Creek below North Ferrisburg is good smallmouth water in May and June. Flycasting woolly buggers or yellow marabou streamers can reward an angler with a fat, leaping smallmouth bass in heavy current. Be ready to bend at the knees and dig in your heels.

The Lamoille River

Near Caspian Lake in the town of Greensboro, the Lamoille River receives its first waters from the mountains. As it begins its 85-mile journey toward Lake Champlain, the upper Lamoille to Hardwick is a classic brook trout stream, covered by alders, and contains a series of bends and pocketwater. As the river turns toward the west, it widens and courses through pastures and farms. Recent flooding has silted many of

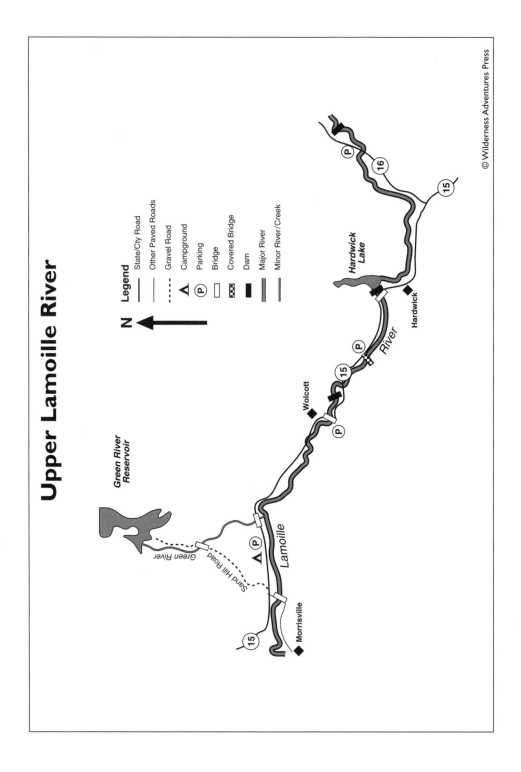

© Wilderness Adventures Press

Middle Lamoille River

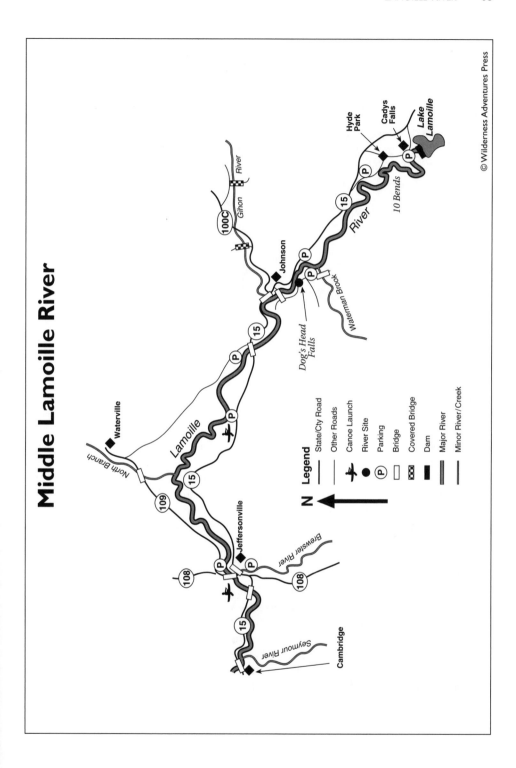

Legend

N

State/Cty Road
Other Roads
Canoe Launch
River Site
Parking
Bridge
Covered Bridge
Dam
Major River
Minor River/Creek

An angler nets a trout on the Lamoille River. (Photo by Tom Haney)

the pools and straightened out runs. Water temperatures run dangerously high in the summer. However, the colder waters of the tributaries make the main river tolerable to trout throughout most the season. Silt has taken its toll on the insects, and hatches have been sparse in recent years. There is good caddis activity throughout the season, and it was encouraging to see a good blue-winged olive hatch this past fall. The stretch from Greensboro Bend downstream along Route 16 to Hardwick is accessible by several unmarked pull-off areas. With a little hiking and bushwhacking, an angler can have a quiet, enjoyable day stalking brook trout. Small nymphs fished upstream into the pockets and searching patterns, such as bivisibles and Hornbergs, are good bets.

The river broadens along Route 15 as it flows between Hardwick and Morrisville. Brown trout and rainbows begin to dominate the river in this area. The Green River's cooling waters where it enters the Lamoille have a great influence on the quality of water, making this a productive stretch of river to fish. In general, however, this part of the river has taken a beating in recent years—floods and decreased flows from development have caused a downturn in the numbers of fish available. Sue Haney and her husband, Tom, wildlife photographers and flyfishing enthusiasts from Hyde Park, have fished this area of the Lamoille as much as anybody over the years. Sue says she's seen a lot of changes. "Overall, there is less volume of water. The fish have stacked up in the pools. More homes and general development in the hills have lowered the amount of groundwater. When the big storms of summer come, the water rises in a quick spate and almost immediately recedes."

On the other hand, groups such as the Lamoille River Anglers Association and their work to reinforce stream bands and aggressive state stocking programs are aiding the Lamoille's recovery. Sue was encouraged by the increase in the amount of smaller fish caught last summer. "This is a sign that things are improving. Next year the fishing should be much better," she says.

Sue's favorite flies are small beadhead nymph patterns, especially the hare's ear. Hatches are limited, but searching patterns like brown bivisibles can bring up a curious trout. Fishing slowly through the big holes with woolly buggers and crayfish patters is also effective. "Last fall there was a good blue-winged olive hatch," according to Sue.

The Lower Lamoille begins below the impoundment called Lake Lamoille in Morrisville at Caddy's Falls. A privately managed catch-and-release area, known as "Ten Bends," starts there and winds slowly through Hyde Park to just upstream from the village of Johnson. Access to Ten Bends is at the farmhouse on a side road off Route 15 near the high school to the west of Hyde Park. You're asked to register there and to report your catch at the end of the day. This is good dry-fly water throughout the season. The water does heat up during the summer, making early mornings and evenings the best times to fish. The river bottom is silty and provides habitat for drake mayflies and other burrowing aquatic life forms. Swimming nymphs and large mayfly patterns should be tried just at dark on hot summer nights. Blue-winged olives are the best bet in the fall, and caddis appear consistently throughout the season.

Downstream from Ten Bends, the Lamoille picks up speed as it rounds a bend near Waterman Branch, a small tributary. For three miles, the river becomes a real quality fishery for rainbows and browns. The flow cuts under the ledge rock creating deep, swirling pools. As the river approaches the village of Johnson, it courses through a small canyon and eventually receives a cool drink from the water of the Gihon River that enters from the north bank. All in all, this is a beautiful area and deserves a day or two of your flyfishing time.

Access can be gained on either side of the river. From Route 15, there is an obvious pull-off close to the riverbank just to the west of Johnson. In Johnson, turn south by the bank, cross the river, and head east near the lumberyard on Patch Road. This brings you to where Waterman Brook enters the Lamoille. There are several pulloffs providing access to the south side of the river. Wading is easy here—you can cross with care in many areas above and below the big holes in this stretch of river. I think this is a particularly nice piece of water for the less experienced angler to have an enjoyable day of fishing. It's also a section of river from which, with a little patience and persistence, a large, yellow-bellied brown trout might be coaxed.

Beadhead nymphs, such as hare's ears and zug bugs, are effective. Early in the morning, try running a big, weighted woolly bugger or crayfish pattern slowly through a big back eddy, such as the one below Dog's Head Falls. There are caddisflies throughout the season, and in autumn look for blue-winged olives.

The river from Johnson to Cambridge along Route 15 and via Hogback Road on the north side can be fished either on foot or by canoe. The North Branch Lamoille, Brewster, and Seymour Rivers cool off the main stem of the Lamoille and provide good trout holding water. The river warms as it passes from Cambridge to Fairfax along Route 104. Below the falls at Fairfax Dam, the state stocks large rainbows and browns, usually ranging from 13 to 18 inches, for a regulated put-and-take fishery. There is good smallmouth fishing below this run, where the river eventually dumps into an impoundment known as Arrowhead Lake.

At West Milton, the outflow of Peterson Dam is the lowest stretch of the Lamoille River where it passes into Lake Champlain. As in the Winooski River to the south, runs of landlocked salmon and steelhead have made this section of river important. Access is limited to the area below the dam and a couple of pull-offs on West Milton Road. The season is closed to fishing in the spring until the first of June. After that and in the fall, you should try your luck with streamers and small nymphs.

Seasons on the Lamoille River are as follows:
- Second Saturday in April through last Sunday in October.
- From Route 104 bridge in Fairfax Falls Dam: catch-and-release season from Monday after the last Sunday in October to Friday before second Saturday in April.
- From Lake Champlain to West Milton Bridge open all year (Lake Champlain regulations).
- From West Milton Bridge to Peterson Dam open all year except closed to fishing March 16 to June 1.

From the Route 104 bridge in Fairfax to Fairfax Falls Dam, the total of brook, brown, and rainbow trout is no more than 2.

Brown and rainbow trout are stocked throughout the river and average 8 to 13 inches. There is some natural rainbow reproduction and a limited population of wild fish, especially in the Johnson area. Larger browns and rainbows are stocked in the special regulation section in Fairfax.

Lamoille River Branches

Between Wolcott and Morrisville is the first of the Lamoille River's main tributaries, the **Green River**. Coming out of Green River Reservoir, this alder-covered canyon is a coldwater sanctuary for some nice-sized brown trout. Rainbows and brook trout also call the Green their home, especially in the heat of summer when temperatures in the Lamoille often reach the uncomfortable mid-70s. Access on this 2 1/2-mile river is limited to walking from Route 15 near the mouth. The going is tough and the fish are skittish. For the more adventurous flyfisher, the Green River can be a fun day.

The **Gihon River**, a tributary that enters in the village of Johnson, is a lovely stream with wild brookies as well as colorful brown trout. Covered bridges cross the river in classic Vermont style following its course out of Lake Eden along Routes 100 and 100C for about 14 miles. There are several pull-offs and side roads making the Gihon relatively accessible. Temperatures remain cool and cover is good. Fish with small nymphs or attractor dries, such as bivisibles or small Wulffs.

The **North Branch Lamoille** is a major tributary that extends from Belvidere Pond and running beside Route 109 to where it enters the main river in Jeffersonville.

Tributary of the Lamoille River. (Photo by Tom Haney)

In the last few years, the North Branch has become a pretty good fishery due, in part, to increased stocking. There is little streamside cover overall, but deep holding pools for brown trout can be found in the lower stretch. Rainbows and brookies can be found all along the upper flows. There are unmarked pulloffs providing access along Route 109.

On the south side of the Lamoille in Jeffersonville, the **Brewster River** joins the main river after its run off Sterling Mountain along Route 108. Wild brook trout can be found in this lovely little stream. In its lower reaches, one will find spawning browns and rainbows in the fall and spring. Don't forget to pack your float tube and make the mile hike north on the Long Trail at Smuggler's Notch off Route 108 to Sterling Pond, Vermont's highest brook trout pond. Wading is possible from the west end, but you can't beat a lazy float in a high Eastern mountain pond while casting dry flies for sipping brook trout.

Favorite Pattern	Rhey's Mistake
Hook	Dry fly, size 12–16
Thread	Red
Tail	Mixed brown and grizzly hackle barbs
Body	Stripped brown hackle quill
Hackle:	Mixed brown and grizzly

An angler casts on a tributary of the Lamoille River. (Photo by Tom Haney)

The **Seymour River** flows into the Lamoille in the village of Cambridge. This small stream, which tends to have low summer flows, can hold browns in the 8- to 15-inch range. There's been a lot of residential development in this area, and unfortunately, access is limited.

Finally, the **Browns River** joins the Lamoille just a short distance below the town of Fairfax. The best trout waters on this river are in Underhill along Route 15 and near where the Lee River enters in the village of Jericho. The upper portion of the river holds some brookies, but in general, it has been the unfortunate victim of development and gravel removal for commercial development. The lower stretch runs very warm. Efforts by local groups to restore the river are continuing.

The Missisquoi River

The visiting fly angler seeking trout in the most northeastern part of Vermont should consider the Missisquoi River. Its headwaters drain the Lowell Mountains as Burgess and East Branch join to form the main river in the village of Lowell. From here, the Missisquoi winds north for 15 miles, where it makes a sudden 14-mile tour

Upper Missisquoi River

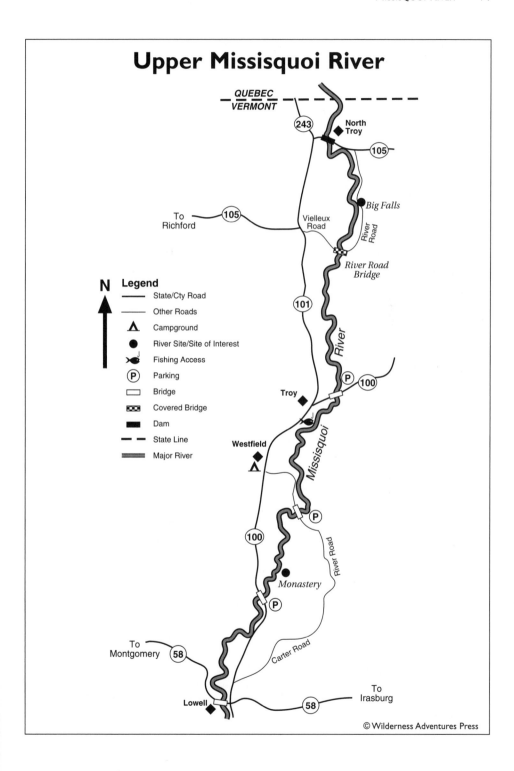

QUEBEC
VERMONT

243

North
Troy

105

Big Falls

To
Richford

105

Vielleux
Road

River
Road

River Road
Bridge

101

River

P

100

Troy

Missisquoi

P

Westfield

River Road

100

Monastery

P

To
Montgomery

58

Carter Road

To
Irasburg

Lowell

58

Legend

N

— State/Cty Road
— Other Roads
▲ Campground
● River Site/Site of Interest
🐟 Fishing Access
Ⓟ Parking
▭ Bridge
▦ Covered Bridge
▬ Dam
– – State Line
━ Major River

© Wilderness Adventures Press

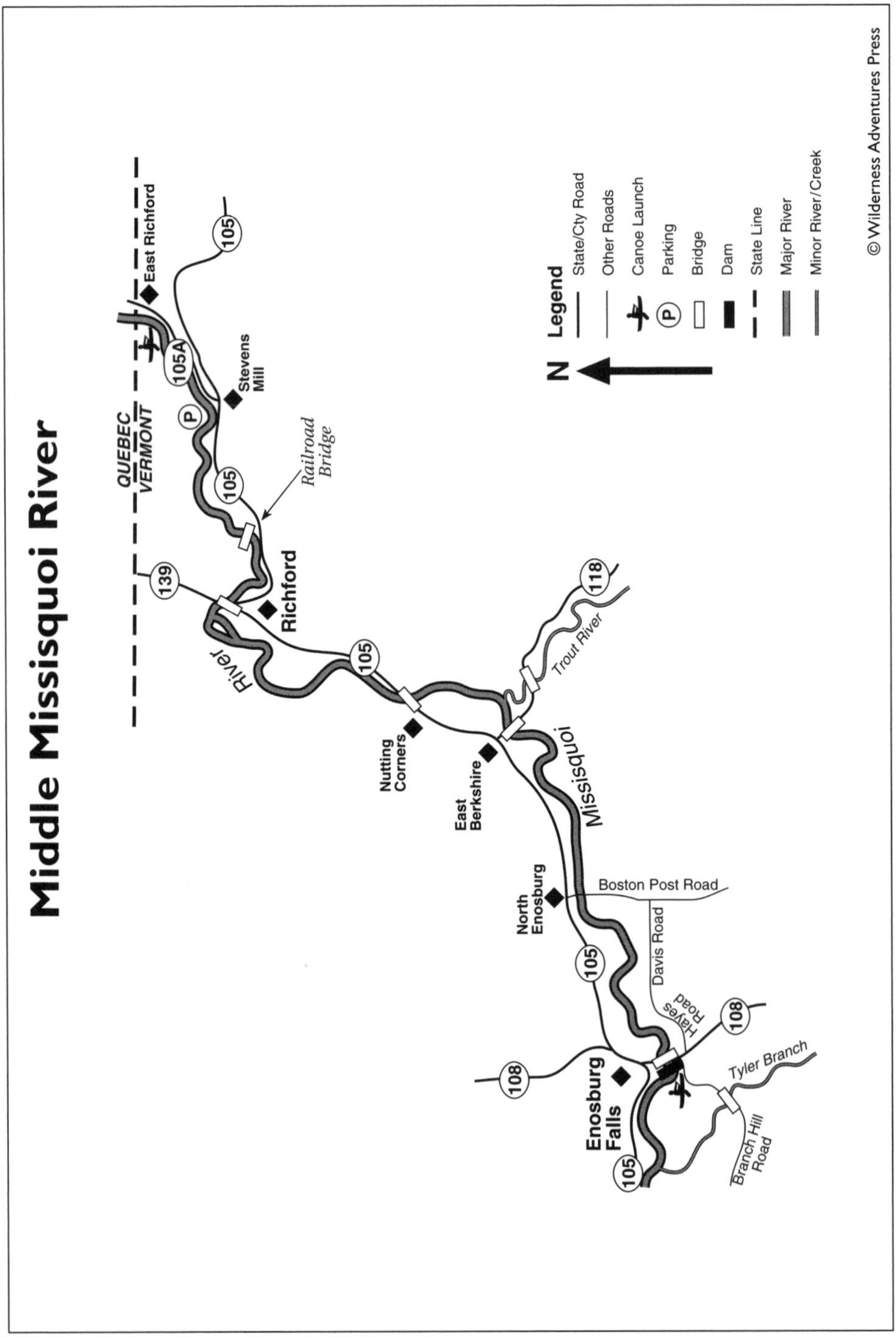

Middle Missisquoi River

East Richford

105

QUEBEC
VERMONT

105A

Stevens
Mill

P

105

Railroad
Bridge

139

Richford

River

105

118

Trout River

Nutting
Corners

East
Berkshire

Missisquoi

North
Enosburg

Boston Post Road

Davis Road

105

Hayes
Road

108

108

Tyler Branch

Enosburg
Falls

Branch Hill
Road

105

N

Legend

——	State/Cty Road
----	Other Roads
✈	Canoe Launch
Ⓟ	Parking
☐	Bridge
■	Dam
– –	State Line
——	Major River
——	Minor River/Creek

Runoff on the Upper Missisquoi and covered bridge. (Photo by Rhey Plumley)

through Sutton, Quebec. The river returns to its natal Vermont at East Richford and journeys south and east for another 45 miles to its confluence with Lake Champlain in Swanton.

The upper section of river, from Lowell to Westfield and paralleling Route 100, is good brook trout habitat. As it winds through fields and farms, the banks are undercut and the riverbed tends to be made up of medium-sized gravel. Small feeder streams are good brook trout nurseries. From Westfield upstream, the Missisquoi becomes a mixed brook trout and brown trout fishery. There is good brown trout fishing from Big Falls to North Troy. Large browns are reported to come from the base of the falls each year.

Access to the river can be gained where it crosses at the town line on the north edge of Lowell. The river sweeps back from the road about a quarter of a mile, and the hike can be worth the effort. Just east of the intersection of Routes 100 and 101 in Troy, a secondary road follows the Missisquoi downstream past a covered bridge and on to Big Falls.

Spring comes late in the northern part of Vermont. The waters are cold and snow will be in the woods into May. Brook trout chase small streamers and nymphs fished slowly early in the season. As temperatures warm, caddis will become active as well as small midges and terrestrials. Try big, weighted woolly buggers and crayfish patterns for browns.

Summer evenings are pleasant times to flyfish on the upper Missisquoi. The Hornberg is my favorite pattern for this part of the river. Fished in all sizes, it can represent a caddis on the surface or a large, struggling mayfly. Fished as a wet fly, the Hornberg looks like a small, tempting minnow.

Favorite Pattern	The Hornberg
Hook	Mustad 9671 or long shank dry-fly hook, size 8 to 18
Thread	Brown
Body	Flat silver tinsel
Wing	Golden pheasant crest, enveloped of a mallard flank feather on each side
Cheek	Jungle cock eye (Ron Alcott, salmon fly dresser, suggests substituting a small black and orange section of golden Pheasant tippet, and says, "Brook trout can't resist it.")
Hackle	Mixed brown and grizzly

The middle stretch of the Missisquoi begins where the river returns to Vermont at East Richford and continues on to below the village of Enosberg Falls, where the Tyler Branch enters. It is an open river, coursing through farmlands and pastures. Agricultural runoff and lack of cover cause the temperatures to rise the farther you go downstream. The cooling waters of the two main tributaries, the Trout River in East Berkshire and the Tyler Branch in Enosberg Falls, help maintain good conditions for brown trout throughout this section.

There are several pull-offs from Route 105 as it parallels the river and the old bed of the Central Vermont Railroad. The river's flow is a good blend of runs and deep pools, gravel bottom in the rapids, and more silt in the long, deeper glides. This produces fairly abundant aquatic insect life, and where the stream touches pastures, good terrestrial activity.

My old friend, Charlie, often told the story of the day he decided to fish his Orvis One-Ounce. Somewhere near Richford, he never told us where, he tied on a woolly bugger. He said he wanted to feel how this rod behaved with a small trout. Well, you guessed it. Charlie hooked and landed the biggest brown trout of a lifetime of Vermont flyfishing. After he released the fish and got his strength back, he returned home and hung the rod in the garage behind a pile of boxes so he'd never again fish with it.

The lowest section of the Missisquoi River doesn't really hold much interest for flyfishers pursuing trout. The waters below North Sheldon, however, have a good population of smallmouth bass. Salmon restoration efforts from Lake Champlain to the dam in Swanton have had little return.

Missisquoi River Branches

From its small beginnings on the towering Jay Peak and Hazon's Notch, the **Trout River** flows from Montgomery Center for 7 miles along Route 118 to East Berkshire. This area has been devastated by major floods in recent years, and many of the river-bends have been straightened and pools filled in with silt. The Trout River has a good reputation as a brown trout nursery, and large fish come up out of the Missisquoi in the autumn to spawn. This is a river to keep an eye on in the years to come. Mother Nature has a way of healing her injured.

The **Tyler Branch** is the second important tributary that nurtures the Missisquoi. Its cold waters enter the main stem downstream about 2 miles from the falls in Enosberg Falls. This area holds the only significant amount of rainbow trout in the whole river system. Also, in its upper waters, the Tyler Branch has some nice brook trout fishing. Access is off the back road to East Sheldon on the south side of the Missisquoi.

The Missisquoi's seasons are as follows:
- Second Saturday in April to last Sunday in October.
- From Lake Champlain to 850 feet below Swanton Dam in Swanton: open all year (Lake Champlain regulations).
- From 850 feet below dam to Swanton Dam: open all year except closed to fishing March 16 to June 1.

The upper section of the Missisquoi holds brook trout. Wild fish are supplemented with stockings. The small upper tributaries are good breeding areas for natives. Brookies run from 6 to 10 inches. It's not uncommon for the cautious fly caster to break the 12-inch barrier.

Below Westfield there is a mix of brown and brook trout. Browns average 8 to 14 inches. Larger ones are caught each year below Big Falls and farther down near Richford and the tributaries, Trout River in East Berkshire, and Tyler Branch in Enosburg Falls. The waters of the Missisquoi warm up quite a bit as the season progresses, however, there are pockets of cold water all the way down to Sheldon springs where, while casting for smallmouths, you might pick up a big brown.

Rainbow trout have a small showing around the Tyler Branch downstream from Enosberg Falls and in the Tyler Branch itself.

The Missisquoi River runs a course of 80 miles. The river winds through fields and farmland and has been subject to agricultural runoff and severe floods. The temperatures warm dramatically in the summer, and, were it not for the major tributaries, Trout River and Tyler Branch, trout wouldn't stand a chance. You'll find some mayfly activity, sulphurs, and blue-winged olives. Fish terrestrials where there are fields by the river. Fishing poppers on summer evenings amidst the big boulders between Sheldon Springs and Enosburg for smallmouths can really pay off.

NORTHWESTERN VERMONT HUB CITIES
Burlington
Elevation–201 • Population–39,435

ACCOMMODATIONS
Best Western, 1076 Williston Road (South Burlington 05403) / 800-371-1125; 802-863-1125 / $$$

The Inn at Essex, 70 Essex Way (Essex 05452) / 800-727-4295 or 802-878-1100 / $$

Raddison Hotel Burlington, 60 Battery Street / 800-333-3333 or 802-658-6500 / $$$$$

The Clarion, 1117 Williston Road (South Burlington 05403) / 802-658-0250 / $$$-$$$$

Sheraton Burlington Hotel, 870 Williston Road / 800-325-3535 or 802-865-6600 / $$$$$

By the Old Mill Stream Bed & Breakfast, RR 2, Box 543 (Hinesburg 05461) / 802-482-3613 / Michelle and Steve Fischer, who is an avid flyfisher / $$

CAMPGROUNDS
Apple Tree Bay Resort, 71 Route 2, P.O. Box 183 (South Hero 05486) / 802-372-3962

Lone Pine Campsites, 104 Bay Road (Colchester 05446) / 802-878-5447

RESTAURANTS
Libby's Blue Line Diner, 1 Roosevelt Hwy (Colchester 05446) / 802-655-0343 / Breakfast

Rusty Scuffer, 148 Church Street / 802-864-9451 / A local favorite serving steak and seafood

Shanty on the Shore, 181 Battery Street / 802-864-0238 / Fresh seafood

Sirloin Saloon, Route 7 (Shelburne 05482) / 802-985-2200 / Steakhouse

The Vermont Pub & Brewery, 144 College Street / 802-865-0500 / British fare

Waterworks, Champlain Mill (Winooski 05404) / 802-655-2044 / Creative American

The Windjammer Restaurant, 1076 Williston Road (South Burlington 05403) / 802-862-6585 / Steak and seafood

FLY SHOPS AND GUIDES
The Classic Outfitters, 861 Williston Road (South Burlington 05403) / 802-860-7375 or 800-353-3963 / Orvis dealer / Full service flyfishing and tying, tackle, luggage and clothing, and qualified instruction / Roger Ranz, owner; Rhey Plumley, manager

Schirmer's Fly Shop, 34 Mills Avenue (South Burlington 05403) / 802-863-6105 / Flyfishing shop and guide service

Great Scot Charters, RR 1 Box 545 (Hinesburg 50461) / 802-482-4286 / Captain Scot Keefe / Bass fishing on Lake Champlain / Flyflshers welcome

Sure Strike Charters, 218 River Road (Essex Junction 05452) / Captain Rich Greenough / Lake Champlain lake trout and landlocked salmon

Uncle Jammer's Guide Service, RR 1, Box 6910 (Underhill 05489) / 802-899-5019 or 800-805-6495 / Stream trout fishing

Adventure Guides of Vermont, PO. Box 3 (Ferrisburg 05473) / 800-425-TRIP; 802-425-6211 / An excellent statewide guide referral service

AUTO REPAIR

Spillane's Service Centers, 811 Williston Road (South Burlington 05403) / 802-863-2896

AUTO RENTAL

Located at airport:

Avis / 802-864-0411

Budget / 802-658-1211

Hertz / 802-864-7409

National / 802-864-7441

Thrifty / 802-863-5500

LOCKSMITH

All Secure Locksmith and Safe Service / 802-658-1848 or 800-658-1848

MEDICAL

Fletcher Allen Health Care, 111 Colchester Avenue / 802-656-2345

FOR MORE INFORMATION

Lake Champlain Regional Chamber of Commerce
60 Main Street
Burlington, VT 05401
802-863-3489

Stowe/Waterbury/Montpelier/Barre

Stowe Elevation–723 • Population–3,433
Waterbury Elevation–425 • Population–937
Montpelier Elevation-523 • Population–8,247
Barre Elevation–609 • Population–9,482

ACCOMMODATIONS

Holiday Inn of "Ben and Jerryville," Waterbury-Stowe, Exit 10, I-89 (Waterbury 05676) / 802-244-7822 or 800-621-7822 / $$$$

Topnotch at Stowe Resort & Spa, Mountain Road (Stowe 05672) / 802-253-8585 / $$$$$

Town & Country Motor Lodge, Mountain Road (Stowe 05672) / 802-253-7595 / $$–$$$

Beaver Pond Farm Inn B & B, Golf Course Road (Warren 05674) / 802-583-2861

CAMPGROUNDS

Little River State Park (Waterbury 05675) / 802-244-7103

Gold Brook Campground (Stowe 05672) / 802-253-7683 / Open year-round

RESTAURANTS

The Common Man, German Flats Road (Warren 05674) / 802-583-2800 / French

Horn of the Moon Cafe, 8 Langdon (Montpelier 05601) / 802-223-2895) / Vegetarian

McCarthy's Restaurant, Mountain Road (Stowe 05672) / 802-253-8626 / Breakfast

Shed Restaurant & Brewery, Mountain Road (Stowe 05672) / 802-253-4364

FLY SHOPS AND GUIDES

Fly Rod Shop, Route 100 (Stowe 05672) / 800-535-9763; 802-253-7346 / Full service fly shop and guide service / Call Sumner Stowe for current stream conditions

Fly Fish Vermont (Stowe 05672) / 802-253-3964 / Retail shop and guide service / Owner is Bob Shannon

R&L Archery, 131 South Main Street (Barre 05641) / 800-269-9151 / Complete line of flyfishing and tying materials, managed by Bob Skowronski / Open 7 days a week / Local fishing information and guides

MEDICAL

Central Vermont Hospital (Berlin 05602) / 802-371-4100

FOR MORE INFORMATION

Stowe Area Association
PO. Box 1320 / Main Street
Stowe, VT 05672
802-253-7321 / 800-24-STOWE
Fax: 802-863-1538

Central Vermont Chamber of Commerce
PO. Box 336 / Beaulieu Place, Stewart Road
Barre, VT 05641
802-229-5711 / Fax: 802-229-5713

Waterbury Tourism Council
PO. Box 468
Waterbury VT 05676
802-244-7822
Fax: 802-244-7822

Johnson/Morrisville
Johnson Elevation–516 • Population–3,194

ACCOMMODATIONS

Ten Bends, RD 2, Box 4099 (Hyde Park 05655) / 802-888-2827 / Restored flyfishing lodge with easy access to the Lamoille River

CAMPGROUNDS

Brewster River Campground, RR 2, Box 4970 (Jeffersonville 05464) / 802-644-2126
Mountain View Campground & Cabins, Route 15 (Morrisville 05661) / 802-888-2178

RESTAURANTS

The Charlmont Restaurant, Route 15 (Morrisville 05661) / 802-888-4242

SPORTING GOODS

Woods and Waters, 21 Portland Street (Morrisville 05661) / 802-888-7101
Right Way Sports, Route 15 (Hardwick 05843) / 802-472-5916

MEDICAL

Copely Hospital, Washington Highway (Morrisville 05661) / 802-888-4231

FOR MORE INFORMATION

Lamoille Valley Chamber of Commerce
P.O. Box 445
Morrisville, VT 05661
802-888-7607

St. Albans / Richford / Lowell
St. Albans Elevation–388 • Population–7,339
Richard Elevation–477 • Population–2,178
Lowell Elevation–996 • Population–594

ACCOMMODATIONS
Comfort Inn and Suites, 16 Fairfax Road (St.Albans 05481) / 802-524-3300 / $$
The Missisquoi River Bend Bed & Breakfast, Route 100 (Troy 05868) / 802-744-9991 / $$

CAMPGROUNDS
Barrewood Campground, HCR 13, Box 4 (Westfield 05874) / 802-744-6340
Mill Brook Campground, P.O. Box 133 (Westfield 05874) / 802-744-6673

RESTAURANTS
Jeff's Maine Seafood, 65 North Main Street (St. Albans 05481) / 802-524-6135

SPORTING GOODS
Vermont Outdoor Sports, Inc., 196 Federal Street (St. Albans 05478) / 802-524-3892

MEDICAL
Northwestern Medical Center (Kerb's Unit), Fairport Street (St. Albans 05481) / 802-524-5911

FOR MORE INFORMATION
St. Albans Chamber of Commerce
P.O. Box 327/2 North Main Street
St. Albans, VT 05478
802-524-2444

Stillwaters of Northern Vermont

Lake Champlain

Trolling flies for trout and landlocked salmon in coldwater lakes and ponds is a grand flyfishing tradition in the Northeast. There are still a few who "pull" flies with wire or lead coreline. Many troll flies behind metal dodgers and flashers, using downriggers to reach feeding fish at various water depths. In the spring and fall, changing water temperatures attract baitfish in bays, coves, shallow shoreline areas, and at river mouths. It is not uncommon to see flocks of frantic gulls, diving and picking up injured smelt, driven to the surface by salmon feeding in a frenzy. A streamer, trolled or cast under feeding gulls, can often result in that anticipated interaction between you and a bright, landlocked salmon: a tightening of your line followed by a tightening of all your muscles, climaxed by the fish's silver leap.

In recent years, Lake Champlain has become a main attraction for local and visiting anglers seeking early- and late-season lake trout and landlocked salmon flyfishing opportunities. As a bonus, there are football-sized brown trout and out-of-control steelhead that will take your fly when you least expect it. The U.S. Fish and Wildlife service, along with agencies from New York, Vermont, and the Province of Quebec, continue to work cooperatively to maintain and improve Lake Champlain's water quality. The positive impact of a salmon and lake trout restoration program that began almost 30 years ago and the success of the program to control the sea lamprey infestation in Lake Champlain, has resulted in a coldwater fishery that keeps getting better and better.

Lake Champlain is one of the gems of the Northeast. Last year, it missed the honor of being classified as our nation's sixth Great Lake by a narrow margin. Yet it is very much a great lake. Lake Champlain is 136 miles long and surrounded by mountains: the Green Mountains of Vermont to the east and New York State's Adirondack Mountains to the west. Its jagged shoreline forms almost two-thirds of Vermont's western border and the northeast border of New York. Actually, the official boundary between New York and Vermont is a line that divides the lake essentially in half. In the north, near the lake's outflow, the Richelieu River in the Province of Quebec, Lake Champlain is bejeweled by the Champlain Islands. Causeways and bridges along U.S. Route 2 connect these islands, once home to very productive dairy farms. The body of water between these islands and the mainland of Vermont is known as the Inland Sea. Continuing south toward the city of Burlington, one finds Mallets Bay and Shelburne Bay at the lake's widest point. From here, Lake Champlain begins to narrow as you continue toward the village of Charlotte, where there is a ferry crossing. There are two more ferries that join Vermont and New York, one at Burlington and the other to Plattsburg, New York, from the Champlain Islands. In addition, there is a highway bridge spanning the lake at the village of Port Henry, New York. Many convenient Vermont Department of Fish and Wildlife Access Areas as well as Perkins Pier in Burlington are available, with limited services, as early or late in the season as ice permits.

Lake Champlain

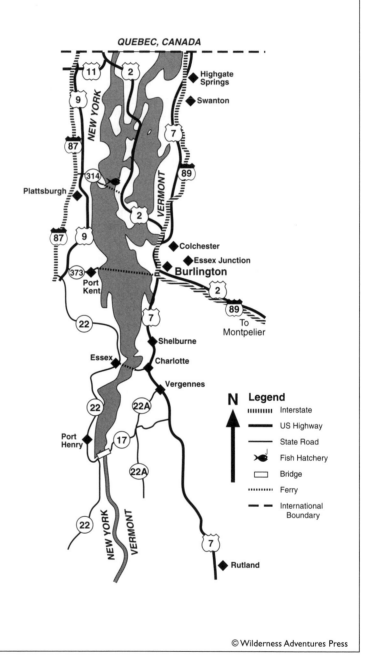

© Wilderness Adventures Press

Trolling for trout and salmon in early spring and late fall is not only rewarding because of the fish you'll catch but for the undisturbed beauty that Lake Champlain offers at those times of year. Techniques and flies vary. To have the most fun trolling, use a fiberglass fly rod, an 81/2-foot, 8-weight, a Pflueger Medalist reel (they don't freeze up in subzero temperatures), and sinking line. The Cortland Line Company makes a 50-foot, level, 8-weight, sinking line just for this type of fishing. The leader need not be tapered, a 10- or 12-foot length of your favorite 8-pound test mono will do nicely. There are dozens of trolling streamer patterns that imitate Lake Champlain's resident smelt and shiners. Excellent resources for patterns are Joseph Bates Jr.'s *Streamers and Bucktails*, Stewart & Leeman's *Trolling Flies for Trout and Salmon*, Donald A Wilson's *Smelt Fly Patterns*, and Mike Martinek's little volume *Streamers: Fly Patterns for Trolling and Casting*.

Local Favorite	Governor Aiken
Hook	Size 2–8 streamer hook, or can be tied as a tandem
Thread	Black
Tail	Section of barred wood duck feather
Body	Flat silver tinsel
Rib	Oval silver tinsel
Throat	Sparse, white bucktail, the length of the hook, and a section of dyed red goose, one-half the length of the bucktail
Wing	A small bunch of lavender-dyed bucktail over which are 5 or 6 strands of peacock herl

There is some shore fishing for landlocks, particularly in the spring. Popular areas include the causeways and bridges on Route 2 through the Champlain Islands. A current builds in these channels, and salmon will chase baitfish and their fly imitations. Coldwater species are not the only draw when it comes to flyfishing in Lake Champlain. There are largemouth and smallmouth bass, northern pike, and an abundance of panfish. In spring, when water temperatures approach the mid-50s, northerns will cruise in the shallows and in the weeds near shore. An angler with a fly can wade and stalk this magnificent game fish as one would fish the flats of some island paradise. The area near Sandbar State Park off Route 2 as you cross into the Champlain Islands is easily accessible by canoe or boat. There are rental boats available at Apple Tree Bay Resort. Also try the shoreline area of Maquam Shore and Missisquoi Bay near the village of Swanton for both bass and pike by wading.

There is no closed fishing season for lake trout, brown trout, rainbows, brook trout, landlocked salmon, northern pike, and panfish in Lake Champlain. The length limit for trout and salmon is 15 inches and 20 inches for northern pike. The creel limit for brook trout, rainbows, and browns totals 3 fish in aggregate. There is a 3-fish limit for lake trout, 2 for salmon, and 5 for northerns. Bass season opens on the second Saturday in June and runs through November 30. The size limit is 10 inches for both largemouth and smallmouth bass. The creel limit is 5 fish total. There is a catch-and-release season for bass from the second Saturday in April to the Friday before the second Saturday in June.

Northern Vermont's Inland Lakes

There are 11 major inland lakes in northern Vermont that offer first-rate fishing for trout and landlocked salmon. Trolling streamers and bucktails is the most popular method of angling in these cold, deep bodies of water. However, the early summer emergence of the large mayflies, *Hexagenia limbata* (referred to as the Hex), in the shallows of several of these lakes brings on a frenzy of feeding fish and provides some excellent fly casting opportunities.

Vermont and Canada share **Lake Memphremagog**, the largest of Vermont's inland lakes. The lake supports rainbow trout, brown trout, and brookies, as well as lake trout and landlocked salmon. Fish have uninhibited access to spawning areas in the lake's tributaries: the Clyde, John's, Barton/Willoughby, and Black Rivers, whose seasonal runs of trout and salmon are legendary. The city of Newport, off Interstate 91, is the lake's port city and offers access and a full array of services to the visiting angler.

The village of Westmore on Route 5A is situated on the eastern shore of **Lake Willoughby**. It is a beautiful alpine lake, and its blue waters fill a long, narrow crack between the Green Mountains. Cliffs that are the backdrop to soaring ravens and peregrine falcons plunge into the lake's western side to a water depth in excess of 300 feet. These cold, deep waters are home to some of the largest and oldest lake trout in the northeast. In addition, Lake Willoughby supports rainbows and brown trout.

Route 111, near the village of Morgan, runs along the north and east shorelines of **Lake Seymour**. For years, Lake Seymour was the destination for anglers from all over New England seeking lake trout, especially during the ice-fishing season. This pressure resulted in the current lake trout limit of 1 fish that is at least 20 inches in length. Lake Seymour also supports brook trout, brown trout, and landlocked salmon. Trolling smelt patterns in spring, soon after ice-out, can be very productive. In early July, the large mayfly hatches and fish will return to the shallows. There is a State Department of Fish and Wildlife Access near the beach area in the village of Morgan Center.

Echo Lake is a small lake connected to Lake Seymour by an outflowing stream. Echo supports brook trout and rainbows as well as lake trout and landlocked salmon. Access is near the village of East Charleston off Route 105.

Crystal Lake is located south of the village of Barton near Route 5. This is another of Northern Vermont's great lake trout fisheries. Each year anglers land lakers weighing in excess of 16 pounds.

Lake Memphremagog

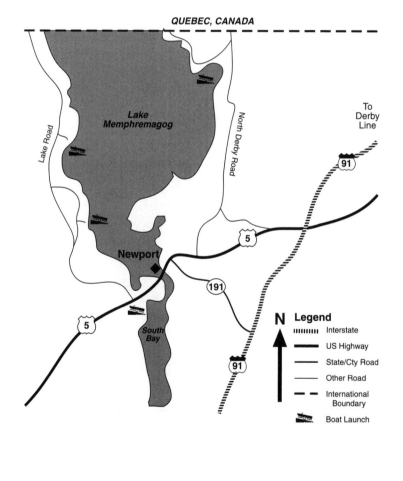

QUEBEC, CANADA

Lake Memphremagog

Lake Road

North Derby Road

To Derby Line

91

5

Newport

191

5

South Bay

91

N Legend
||||||| Interstate
US Highway
State/Cty Road
Other Road
International Boundary
Boat Launch

© Wilderness Adventures Press

Lake Willoughby

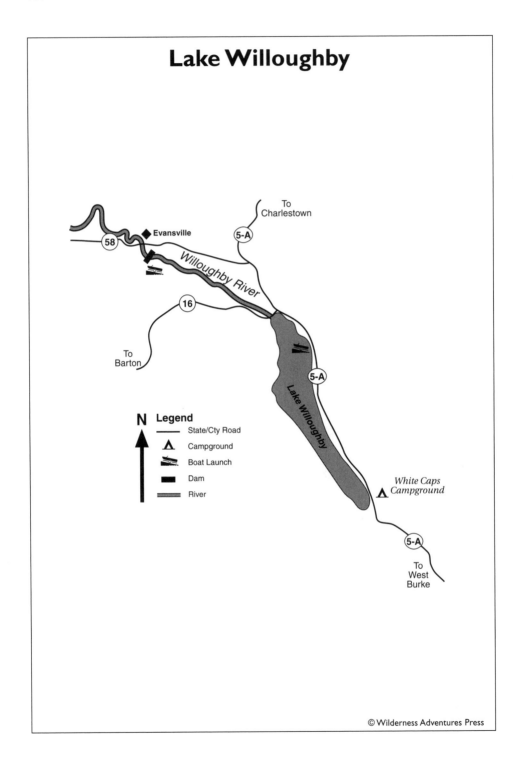

Lake Seymour and Echo Lake

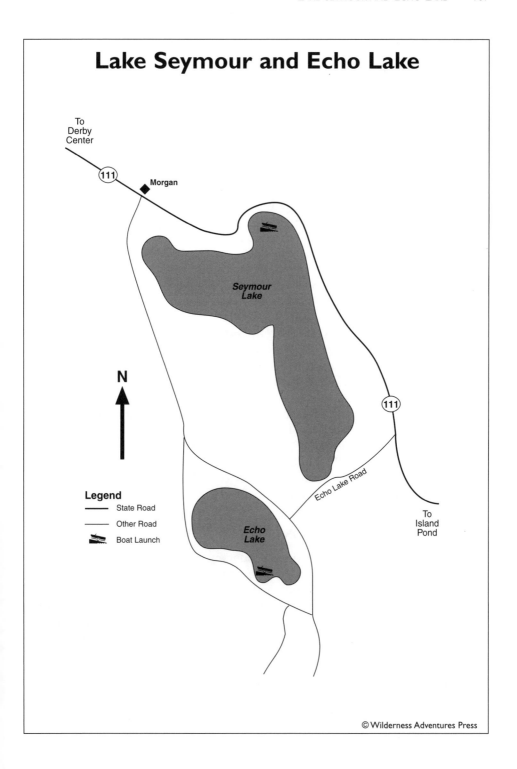

To
Derby
Center

111 — Morgan

Seymour
Lake

N

111

To
Island
Pond

Echo Lake Road

Legend
— State Road
— Other Road
▬ Boat Launch

Echo
Lake

© Wilderness Adventures Press

Off Route 16, about 3 miles south of the village of Glover, is **Shadow Lake**. Dropping off to a water depth of almost 140 feet, Shadow's cold waters support brook trout, browns, and lake trout.

North of the village of Hardwick, off Route 16 near the village of Greensboro, is **Caspian Lake**. The lake's shoreline slopes down from surrounding meadows and is lined with old family cottages and camps. Caspian supports both lake trout and rainbows that are particularly vulnerable to the fly during both ice-out and during the Hex hatch of early summer.

Great Averill Lake lies in the northeast corner of Vermont, less than 2 miles from the Canadian border. It is a small, deep lake offering lake trout and landlocked salmon. In close proximity are two ponds worth mentioning: **Little Averill Pond**, a rainbow and lake trout pond, and **Forest Pond**, which supports browns. All three lakes have good access near the village of Averill.

Island Pond and its close neighbor, **Spectacle Pond**, are located off Route 105 in the village of Island Pond. Brighten State Park, a very convenient camping and recreation area, provides access to both lakes. Island Pond holds large brown trout (the state record came from Island Pond several years ago), rainbows, and brook trout. Spectacle is primarily a brown trout pond.

Maidstone Lake occupies the westernmost ridge before Vermont slips into the Connecticut River Valley. It is a deep-water lake, supporting both lake trout and rainbows. There is good access and a very nice campground at Maidstone State Park a short distance from Route 102, south of the village of Bloomfield.

Waterbury Reservoir is an impoundment formed by a dam on the Little River, a major tributary of the Winooski River. Since the reservoir was drained in 1985, the Vermont Department of Fish and Wildlife has stocked the reservoir with brown trout and rainbows. The smallmouth bass fishing in Waterbury Reservoir is excellent and an added bonus. The nearby Little River State Park is a convenient and excellent campground. Waterbury Reservoir is easily accessible from Interstate 89 at exit 10 near the village of Waterbury, only 26 miles from Burlington.

Ponds of Northern Vermont

Northern Vermont is blessed with an abundance of small lakes and ponds. Some are near highways with well maintained boat ramps, while others are miles back, reached only by traveling over abandoned logging roads or foot trails. The Vermont Fish and Wildlife Department manages the majority of ponds as coldwater fisheries with regular stockings of brown trout, rainbows, brook trout, lake trout, and landlocked salmon. In addition, there are several warmwater ponds in northern Vermont that offer anglers an opportunity to catch large and smallmouth bass, pickerel, or northern pike on a fly. Whatever your choice, northern Vermont has many stillwater flyfishing opportunities.

Shelburne Pond, Colchester Pond, and Indian Brook Reservoir are three ponds within a short drive from Burlington. Shelburne Pond lies to the south, off Route 7, about 3 miles from the village of Shelburne. It is a warmwater fishery, supporting large and smallmouth bass, walleye, and northern pike. Shelburne Pond suffers the eutrophication effects of agricultural runoff and warm summertime temperatures. During some years, weeds choke the water, resulting in fish mortality. It is, however, a lovely pond. The banks are a combination of marsh and woodlands, perfect habitat for waterfowl and wild turkeys. The Vermont Department of Fish and Wildlife's efforts to reclaim and restock the pond have had positive results, and the fishery has been coming back.

Colchester Pond, north of Burlington near the village of Colchester, is managed for the public as a natural area by the Winooski Valley Park District. It is an excellent warmwater fishery with bass and some larger northern pike. There is parking and a canoe access, and for anglers using float tubes, a trail that follows much of the shoreline.

Indian Brook Reservoir is about 2 miles off Route 15 near the village of Essex Center. It is managed by the town of Essex, which charges a modest use fee in the summer. The pond is a mixed warm and coldwater fishery, supporting bass, panfish, and stocked brown trout and rainbows. There is parking and a convenient canoe launch. All power watercraft are prohibited.

High above the Lamoille River Valley and the ski slopes of the resort town of Stowe is beautiful **Sterling Pond**. This is Vermont's highest elevation trout pond and is accessible by foot from the Long Trail. There is a parking area where Route 108 passes through Smuggler's Notch between the village of Jeffersonville and Stowe. Sterling Pond is about an hour's hike north up the well-maintained trail. It is a brook trout pond and receives annual stockings by the State Department of Fish and Wildlife. Flyfishing along the shore is best from the shallow areas on the west and south sides. A float tube gives an angler good access to the entire pond. There is a full-service campsite nearby at Smugglers Notch State Park, and primitive camping is available at the pond.

Green River Reservoir is a recent addition to Vermont's state park program. This impoundment of the Green River, a tributary of the Lamoille, is about 6 miles from Route 15, northeast of the village of Morrisville. It is a warmwater fishery supporting bass, panfish, pickerel, and northern pike. Canoe rentals are available in Morrisville and Stowe.

Zack Woods Pond is one of several small trout ponds near the Green River Reservoir. It is accessible from Garfield Road outside the village of Morrisville on Route 15. Zack Woods is a deep pond, supporting stocked, as well as some very nice, holdover brook trout. Insect hatches are generally infrequent. However, fishing streamers and small wet flies soon after ice-out can be productive.

Anglers gain access to **Lake Elmore** by foot from a trail off Route 12, about 3 miles south of Elmore State Park. The trail is about a half-mile long, making it an easy canoe carry. Lake Elmore receives regular stockings of brook trout.

Long Pond is a deep, coldwater pond that supports brook trout as well as a remnant population of lake trout. There is a boat access on Long Pond Road, 8 miles from its intersection with Route 5A, near the village of Westmore on Lake Willoughby.

To the east are **Newark Pond, Bald Hill Pond**, and **Jobs Pond**. All have convenient boat access areas and receive annual stockings of brook trout.

East of the village of Island Pond on Route 105 there is a railroad crossing, known as Wenlock Crossing. The dirt road immediately on the north side of this crossing is Lewis Pond Road, one of several maintained logging roads that crisscross this remote area of Vermont's Northeast Kingdom. **Lewis Pond** is in about 20 miles, so check your gas gauge before you leave. There is a boat access. It is a lovely brook trout pond in an area rich with wildlife. Chances are good that you'll see a moose before your day's fishing is done.

South American Pond is reached by foot on a trail that begins on a logging road south of Wenlock Crossing. It is a coldwater pond and supports brook trout. As with so many brook trout ponds, the fishing is at its best when the bugs are at their worst.

In recent years, **Norton Pond** has become a warmwater fishery with a reputation for large-sized northern pike and bass. You'll find Norton Pond on Route 114, or Moose Alley, about 8 miles north of Island Pond village. The state maintains a good launch site and public access area.

Holland Pond is only a few miles from the Canadian border north of the village of Morgan near Seymour Lake. It supports brook trout as well as rainbow trout.

There are several beautiful trout ponds in the hills that separate Lake Willoughby and Crystal Lake near the village of Barton. **May Pond**, which offers good brook trout fishing, is easily accessible from May Pond Road that bears south from Route 16 north of Barton. There is a good boat launch, and you'll no doubt see May Pond's resident pair of loons during your visit. South of Barton and Crystal Lake, on Route 5, is **Bean Pond**. The other three ponds, **Vail**, **Marl**, and **Duck**, are reached by foot trails off unimproved logging roads. Vail Pond receives annual stockings of rainbow trout, while the others support brook trout.

Marshfield Dam, whose outflow makes up some of the headwaters of the Winooski River, is located on Route 2, east of Marshfield village. This is a mixed cold and warmwater fishery, supporting bass as well as brown trout. The view of Camel's Hump to the west, clear across the state, is dramatic, as is the undeveloped shoreline.

A road that parallels the reservoir's eastern shore will take you to **Peacham Pond**. This deepwater pond supports brown trout. Try trolling a "Nine-three," tied with a pale blue feather. There is a well-maintained boat launch and public access.

Groton State Forest, which lies about 20 miles east of the Barre/Montpelier area, holds several good flyfishing ponds. This rich wildlife area offers several campgrounds, miles of trails, and access to some of the finest stillwater fishing in Vermont. The south entrance to Groton State Forest is off Route 302, east of Barre near the junction of the south end of Route 232. From the north, follow Route 2 east from Montpelier to where Route 232 joins about 2 miles from the village of Marshfield.

As you enter Groton State Forest from the north, **Osmore Pond** is located adjacent to the New Discovery State Park and Campground. It is a brook trout pond, best fished from a canoe or float tube.

The parking area for the short, foot trail to **Kettle Pond** is about 2 miles farther down Route 232. It is a mixed warm and coldwater pond, supporting smallmouth bass in the shallower east end and rainbows in the deeper sections.

Both **Groton Lake** and **Ricker Pond** are warmwater fisheries supporting bass and panfish. Each offers excellent camping facilities and access to other state forest areas.

Martins and **Levi Ponds** are best reached from the east, from the village of Peacham. Both ponds receive annual stockings of brook trout. Martins Pond has a boat and public access off Green Bay Road, west of Peacham. Levi Pond can be reached by foot on an old logging road south of Martins Pond.

Noyes Pond is perhaps the most well known brook trout pond in northern Vermont. It is located just 20 miles east of Barre on the southern edge of Groton State Forest. The state of Vermont manages Noyes Pond, part of Seyon (Noyes, spelled backwards) Ranch State Park, as flyfishing-only waters. There is a $5.00 per hour fee, and anglers are required to use boats provided by the park. There is an old lodge on the grounds and rooms and meals are available by prior arrangement.

The Vermont Fish and Wildlife Department provides regular stocking of brook trout. Early and late season is the best time to fish Noyes Pond. However, there are early morning and evening caddis hatches all summer long. The emergence of *Hexagenia limbata*, the giant mayfly, in late May and early June can be dramatic and brings many, sometimes large, beautifully-colored brookies to the surface.

The excellent fishing is not the only draw at Noyes Pond. The setting is quietly beautiful. You'll often hear the whistle of a peregrine soaring on the wind currents high overhead. Or you might see a loon dive beneath the surface of the pond, holding its breath for what seems an impossible amount of time, and finally resurfacing far from where it first caught your attention. Or even a moose, wading in the weeds at the shallow west end of the pond, may lift its head to passively observe you, silently drifting on this lovely pond.

Upper Connecticut River

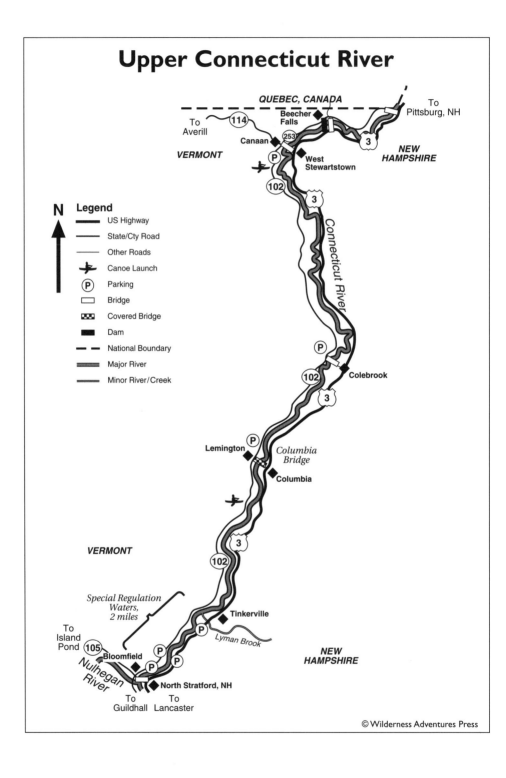

© Wilderness Adventures Press

NORTHEASTERN VERMONT
Upper Connecticut River

The upper Connecticut River, from Beecher Falls, Vermont, near the Canadian border, downstream about 35 miles to the mouth of Paul Stream, in the town of Bloomfield, is one of the finest trout streams in the Northeast. Brook trout, rainbows, and brown trout thrive, often growing to trophy proportions. Early spring can bring hatches of caddisflies that fill the air. Trout feed freely on midges and terrestrials all summer. In autumn, the blue-winged olive fishing can be spectacular.

The river section that forms the Vermont/New Hampshire border belongs to and is managed by the state of New Hampshire. Through an agreement between New Hampshire and Vermont, resident license holders from either state may fish the Connecticut River. Others must purchase a nonresident New Hampshire Fishing License. The state of New Hampshire has established a special regulations area for catch and release from the bridge that spans the Connecticut between the village of Bloomfield, Vermont, and North Stratford, New Hampshire, upstream about 2.5 miles to Lyman Falls.

In Vermont, Route 102 parallels the Connecticut River. There is plenty of access from unmarked pull-off areas and river crossings. There is a bridge near the village of Colebrook, New Hampshire, also the Columbia Covered Bridge near Lemington, Vermont, and the bridge in the village of Bloomfield, Vermont. Floating the Connecticut, either by canoe, drift boat, or inflatable, is a good way to reach the more remote stretches of water. The river, however, is quite easily waded and fishes well from shore.

Cool tributaries and the outflow of Murphy Dam in the town of Pittsburg, New Hampshire, refresh the main stem of the upper Connecticut. Flow levels fluctuate from dam releases, but the changes are not extreme. Healthy water temperatures, in the range of 55 to 65 degrees, and an abundant food supply provide a rich habitat for resident trout.

The water runs fast and clear as the Connecticut enters Vermont. The dam in the village of Beecher Falls briefly interrupts the flow, but the pocketwater below the dam is very fishable. It seems that each spring, the local newspaper features the picture of a young resident proudly holding a huge brown trout caught in the run below Beecher Falls. Pocketwater and deep corner pools alternate with long, slow runs as the river winds through a beautiful valley of farms and woods.

Regulations allow fishing in the Connecticut River and its tributaries up to the first highway crossing from the first of January. Don't get too excited, though. It's pretty cold that time of year, although there can be a mild respite during a "January thaw." If conditions are right and you're sick of jigging for perch through the ice, a winter's day flyfishing on the Connecticut could be just what the doctor ordered. You'll have to run your fly slowly and deeply through the pools. Try woolly buggers and egg patterns, such as the Thor, a known favorite of coldwater brown trout.

Flyfisher Dave O'Brien on the upper Connecticut River.
(Photo by Elizabeth Edwards)

Favorite Pattern	Thor
Hook	Wet fly, size 8
Thread	Black
Tail	Orange hackle barbs
Body	Dark red chenille
Collar	Soft brown hackle
Wing	White calf tail

Spring comes late in northeast Vermont. It is well into the month of May when water levels recede from spring runoff. If spring has been particularly warm, there may be some early dry-fly fishing on the upper Connecticut during an afternoon hatch of small black caddis or Hendricksons. For the most part, though, early fishing is limited to casting sinking or sink-tip lines with streamers and woolly buggers.

June brings warm, sunny days and clouds of caddisflies. Beadhead nymph patterns, deep sparkle pupae, and emergers are effective. During the heat of the day, look carefully for fish sipping midges in the fast water at the head of pools and in the scum lines of back eddies. A tiny, size 18 or 20, peacock herl and partridge soft hackle will work on even the most finicky trout.

*The Connecticut River runs along the southern New Hampshire/Vermont border.
(Photo by Steve Hickoff)*

July and August bring terrestrials. Grasshoppers, ants, beetles, and crickets flitting on the grassy banks of the upper Connecticut are often preoccupied with eating or mating and become careless. This can result in a tumble into the river, a short struggle, and then the overwhelming darkness of the closed jaws of a waiting brown trout.

One day, in mid-August, while watching for rising trout in the big pool upstream from the treatment plant in the village of Canaan, a diaphanous, pale white, cloud appeared in the perfectly blue sky over Van Dyke Mountain to the west. As the cloud neared, it began to break up and I realized it was a swarm of flying ants. When it got near the river, it brought every trout in the area to the surface in a feeding frenzy. Of course, the fish would have nothing to do with my humble imitations of ant life. So I contented myself to sit and watch this wonder of nature.

Fall can be the nicest time to fish the upper Connecticut, when the hardwood leaves are changing color. Golden tamaracks stand out against the evergreens in groves of softwoods. As the river cools, a warm sun will bring on hatches of blue-winged olives. It is also a good time to fish streamers for aggressive brown trout and brookies. Remember: There is no such thing as a streamer that is too large.

The season on the Connecticut River (by agreement between the Vermont Department of Fish and Wildlife and the New Hampshire Fish and Game Department) runs from January 1 through October 15, including all Vermont setbacks and tributaries up to the first upstream highway bridge. This section is specific to the upper Connecticut along the eastern border of Vermont from the Canadian border downstream to the mouth of the Passumpsic River.

From approximately 1,600 feet upstream of the bridge between the villages of North Stratford, New Hampshire, and Bloomfield, Vermont, upriver about 2.5 miles to approximately 250 feet below the Lyman Falls Dam, angling is restricted to artificial lures and flies. All hooks must be barbless or have barbs pinched down. All fish must be immediately released unharmed.

The state of New Hampshire regularly stocks rainbow trout, brown trout, and brookies. Fish generally average 8 to 12 inches. There are resident, holdover browns that frequently reach in excess of 18 inches. And the state of New Hampshire often plants "broodstock" brookies that weigh as much as 3 pounds.

The upper Connecticut River enters Vermont from New Hampshire near the Canadian border as a broad, fast-flowing stream filled with shallow runs and pocketwater. The flow slows down and is interrupted at the low dam in the village of Beecher Falls, Vermont.

From there, it continues first as pocketwater and then as long, slow runs, rapids, and pools. Silt covers the river bottom in some of the runs and pools. Cold water from upriver dam releases and from the minor feeder streams and three larger tributaries, the Nulhegan, Paul Stream, and the Passumpsic River, that enter the main stem, help maintain a healthy habitat for trout and other aquatic life.

Tributaries of the Upper Connecticut River

The **Nulhegan River** and its tannin-stained branches, the North, Yellow, Black, and East Branches, drain a huge area of bogs and woods in the extreme northeast corner of Vermont. This is paper company land where hundreds of miles of logging roads that zigzag through the woods and over the streams providing access. Moose, white-tailed deer, black bear, ruffed grouse, and spruce grouse range freely in this remote wilderness. Brook trout, both wild and stocked, populate the headwaters and upper reaches of the Nulhegan's tributaries. Resident brown trout can be found in the lower river, as well as seasonal migrants from the Connecticut River.

The main stem of the Nulhegan is 15 miles long and parallels Route 105 two miles east of the village of Island Pond to the village of Bloomfield. The upper reach of the Nulhegan, like its tributaries, runs flat and deep with overhanging banks. It passes through a gorge near the junction of the Black Branch and continues as mixed pocketwater, runs, and pools to the mouth.

Wild trout are present but becoming increasingly rare in this river system. The result has been the initiation of a more aggressive stocking program by the state fish and wildlife department.

Paul Stream joins the Connecticut River about 6.5 miles south of the village of Bloomfield. It is primarily a brook trout stream, draining a large area near Ferdinand Bog, northwest of Maidstone Lake. Paul Stream is noteworthy in that, in addition to brook trout and browns in the lower reaches, it hosts a small run of rainbow trout

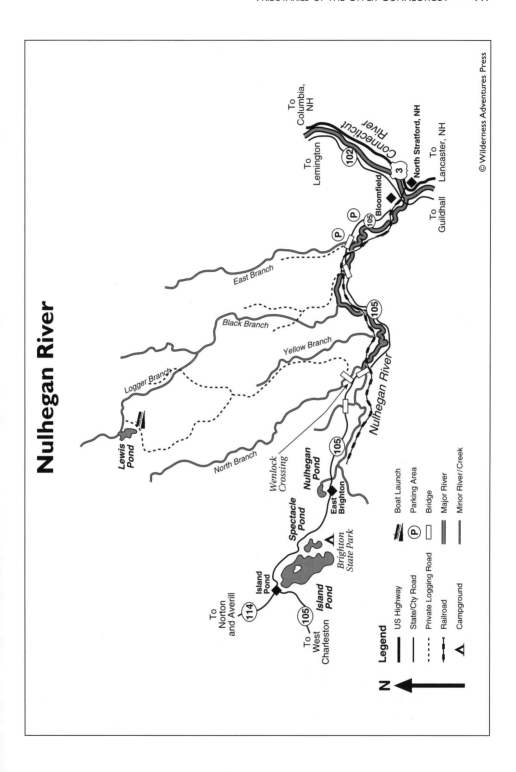

Nulhegan River

© Wilderness Adventures Press

Legend

US Highway	Boat Launch
State/Cty Road	Parking Area
Private Logging Road	Bridge
Railroad	Major River
Campground	Minor River/Creek

N

Passumpsic and Moose Rivers

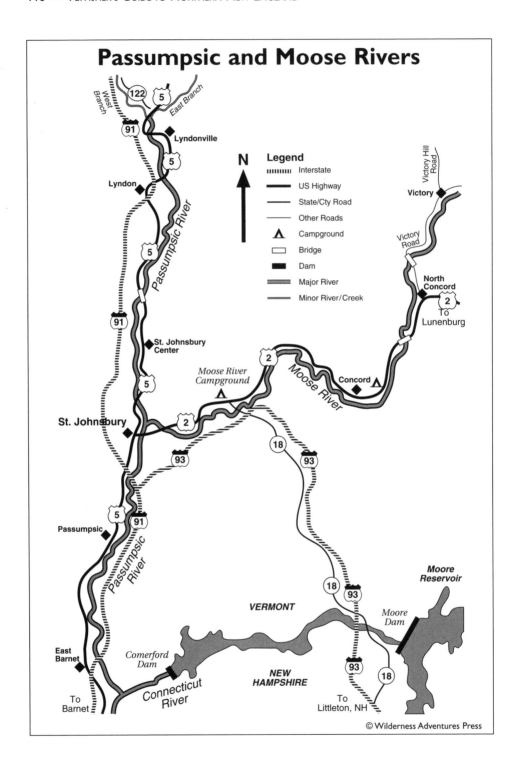

Legend
- ‖‖‖‖‖ Interstate
- ▬▬ US Highway
- ── State/Cty Road
- ── Other Roads
- Λ Campground
- ▭ Bridge
- ▬ Dam
- ▬▬ Major River
- ▬▬ Minor River/Creek

© Wilderness Adventures Press

from the Connecticut River. Access to Paul Stream is along the dirt road that runs parallel to the river toward Maidstone Lake State Park.

The southernmost tributary of the upper Connecticut River is the **Passumpsic River**. The West and East Branches begin in the high, northeast ridges and bogs above the city of St. Johnsbury and join to form the main stem of the Passumpsic a few miles north of the village Lyndonville. The upper reaches run cool and clear and offer good habitat for wild brook trout and browns. Access to the East Branch is from Route 114 between Lyndonville and the village of Island Pond. The West Branch runs parallel to Route 5. Water temperatures in the lower Passumpsic, downstream of Lyndonville, run uncomfortably warm in the summer. You will find some pockets of cold water that hold trout near tributaries.

The **Moose River** is a 25-mile long tributary of the Passumpsic. It rises high in the mountains in the town of East Haven and, with several feeder streams, flows into Victory Bog, which is primarily public land owned by the state. The upper river section and bog area is abundant with wildlife. The waters are deep and dark from the rich forests and soils that surround the river.

Moose River supports both wild and stocked brook trout, and as you proceed downstream below the town of Victory, brown trout share the stream. Access to Moose River, where it passes through the Victory Basin Wildlife Management Area above Route 2, is best gained by canoe. Don't forget to bring your bug dope.

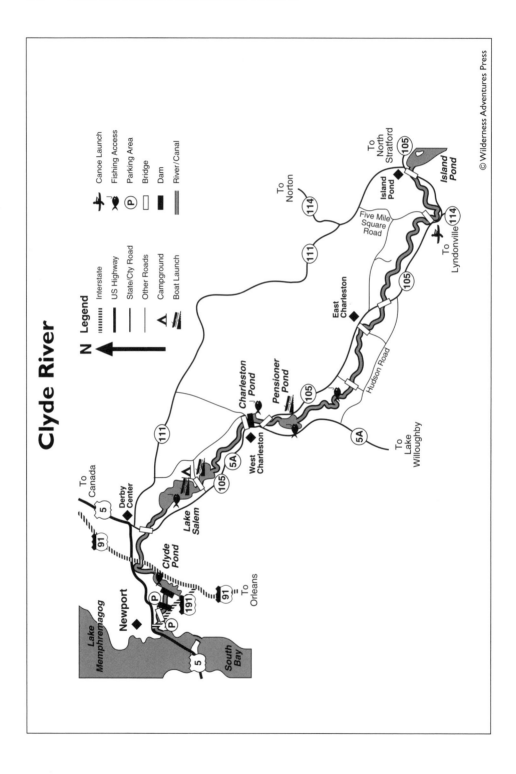

© Wilderness Adventures Press

Other Northeastern Vermont Rivers and Streams

Clyde River offers anglers many pleasant opportunities. It begins as a brook trout stream moving lazily through marshes and alder-crowned channels from its source, the outflow of Island Pond. The upper reaches, between the villages of Island Pond and East Charleston, support brown trout as well as brookies. The river runs slowly, removed from roadways by swamps and marshlands. It is fished easily from a canoe.

Route 105 follows the river on its journey north. Seymour Lake and Echo Lake offer their cold, outflowing water to the Clyde near the village of East Charleston. Much of this stretch of river holds rainbow trout and some landlocked salmon, especially in the run from the dam that forms Charleston Pond to Salem Lake. Below the lake, the waters warm up and you'll find smallmouth bass moving in from Clyde Pond.

The real fish stories come from the lower Clyde. These are the historic spawning waters of the Memphremagog strain of landlocked salmon. Since the 1930s, anglers from near and far have come to the lakeside city of Newport to match wits with the salmon that enter the mouth of the Clyde chasing delicious smelt in the spring and to make their spawning beds in the fall. Tales of tackle breakers weighing in excess of 12 pounds were not uncommon. In season, the hotels and inns were full and the riverbanks would be lined with anglers. In 1957, dams built for generating electric power dealt the salmon runs an almost fatal blow by destroying most of the available spawning areas. Efforts to stock salmon met with limited success through the years that followed, and another glorious chapter of fishing history almost ended.

There were some older anglers, such as Warren "Jersey" Drown, who remembered the bygone days and told the young ones, David and Francis Smith, Gary Ward, Richard Nelson, and other passionate anglers, of the legendary salmon runs. These champions, who became known as the "Heroes of the Clyde," joined forces with Trout Unlimited and went up against the power companies and even against some of their fellow Vermonters who had been tempted by greed and power. The struggle was long and costly. At last, on May 1, 1994, just two days after the combined voices of the state of Vermont, Trout Unlimited, and the U.S. Fish and Wildlife Service called for the removal of the dam, an act of God broke the Newport #11 Dam and set the Clyde River free.

The river is recovering and is once again offering some good landlocked fishing, especially in the fall. From October 1 to the last Sunday in October, angling is restricted to artificial lures and flies only, and all landlocked salmon must be immediately released. Access to the lower Clyde is readily available near the Clyde Street Bridge and upriver along Upper Clyde Street. Streamers, such as the gray ghost and black ghost, as well as nymphs, are effective.

The Clyde River's season is the second Saturday in April through the last Sunday in October. The stretch from the Island Pond outlet in the village of Island Pond downstream one-eighth mile and the stretch from the dam at Citizens #1,2,3 powerhouse to 292 feet below Clyde Street Bridge in Newport are closed to fishing from April 7 to June 1.

Minimum length for landlocked salmon is 17 inches. From the second Saturday in April to May 10, fishing hours are between 5:00 AM and 8:00 PM EST (6:00 AM to 9:00 PM EDST) in the stretch from 292 feet below Clyde Street Bridge to the river mouth.

The river stretch from the dam at Citizens #1; 2; 3; powerhouse to Gardner Park Bridge in Newport is catch and release for landlocked salmon and restricted to the use of artificial lures and flies only from October 1 to the last Sunday in October.

The upper reaches of the Clyde River hold a mix of wild and stocked brown trout and brook trout averaging 8 to 12 inches in length. Rainbows and landlocked salmon are found throughout the river's midsection from about the village of East Charleston to the warmer waters of Clyde Pond. The lower river section, upstream from the mouth, has spring and fall runs of rainbow trout and landlocked salmon from Lake Memphremagog.

The Clyde River is 34 miles in length, flowing north from the outflow of Island Pond to Lake Memphremagog. It begins as a slow-moving, alder-shaded trout stream with steep banks and a silt-covered bottom. The river's gradient increases near the mouth of the outflow of Echo Lake, near the village of East Charleston, and picks up speed, forming pocketwater and more riffles and pools. There are nice sections of pocketwater below the dam that forms Charleston Pond. The lower river mixes pocketwater, plunge pools, and runs over a bottom of broken ledge, boulders, and small gravel.

Barton River is a 22-mile long trout stream flowing north from the marshes above the village of Glover to its mouth in Lake Memphremagog's South Bay, near the city of Newport. The headwaters and small feeder streams upriver from Glover hold wild and hatchery brook trout. The water is cold and crystal clear. There are healthy, reproducing populations of brown trout and rainbows in the reach of river from Glover to the village of Orleans. Although the waters below Orleans are generally too warm to support resident trout, this stretch of river is a passageway for spawning Memphremagog rainbows in the spring and brown trout in the fall.

The flow of the river is relatively slow as it rises but soon quickens into lovely pocketwater. There is good cover on the banks, and water temperatures in the upper reaches stay cool. Downstream, the runs begin to stretch out and pools deepen. The Barton runs slower and warmer from the mouth of the Willoughby to South Bay.

Marked and unmarked river access areas are found along Routes 5 and 16. The Barton is an excellent river, but it is overshadowed by its major tributary, the Willoughby River, one of Vermont's best-known and loved streams.

While the Clyde River has its "heroes," **Willoughby River** has its "guardians." Each year, on opening day of trout season, no matter what the weather, you'll see them standing, shoulder to shoulder, on riverbanks and in the cold water, casting for migratory rainbow trout. For decades, fish and anglers have both stacked up below the falls in Orleans. The anglers are waiting for the fish, and fish are waiting for that inevitable rise in water that will allow them access to the upstream spawning grounds. Each year the fish return. Some years there are more fish and other years, "it's not as good as it was in the good ol' days." It doesn't matter. Each year, before first light on opening day, the "Guardians of the Willoughby" will take their positions on the river.

Barton and Willoughby Rivers

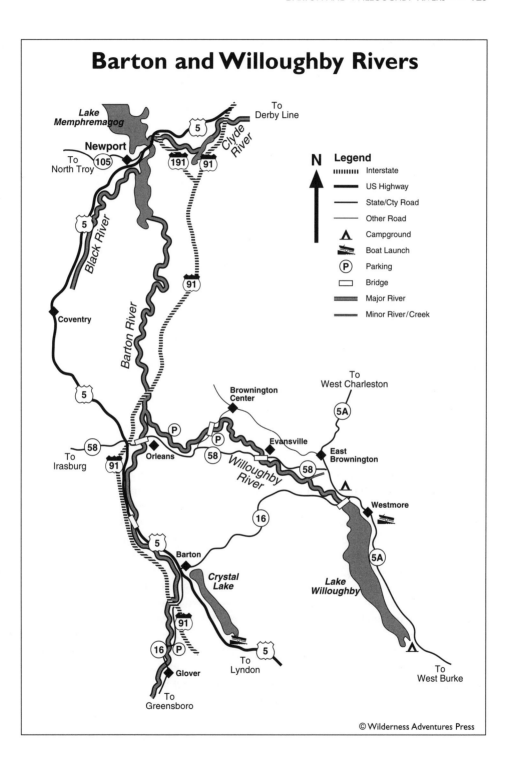

Lake Memphremagog

To Derby Line

5

Clyde River

Newport

To North Troy 105

191 91

5

Black River

91

Coventry

Barton River

5

Brownington Center

To West Charleston

5A

P

P Evansville

58 East Brownington

To Irasburg 58

91 Orleans 58 Willoughby River

16

Westmore

5 Barton

Crystal Lake

Lake Willoughby

5A

91

16 P

To Lyndon 5

Glover

To Greensboro

To West Burke

N

Legend

- Interstate
- US Highway
- State/Cty Road
- Other Road
- ▲ Campground
- Boat Launch
- Ⓟ Parking
- ▭ Bridge
- Major River
- Minor River/Creek

Opening day, Willoughby River rainbow run circa 1960. (Photo by Steve Boyajian)

The rainbow trout that return from Lake Memphremagog to the Willoughby River are big, strong fish averaging 2 to 4 pounds. They enter the river in early April, with the run peaking the first or second week of May. Post-spawn fish return downstream throughout the month of June. This is one of the best opportunities to fish the Willoughby with a fly. Rainbows are hungry after they've completed spawning and greedily chase nymphs and minnows on their way back to the lake. Dead-drifting a streamer through the abundant pocketwater can produce a bone-jarring strike and subsequent loss of all control as a 2- or 3-pound wild rainbow lets loose its full power.

Access to the Willoughby, below the falls in Orleans, is easy. There's a parking lot just across the bridge. Seasoned anglers on the Willoughby know that fully decked out flyfishing gear is not the measure of success when it comes to catching spawning rainbows. All you really need is a 5- or 6-weight Shakespeare Wonder Rod, to which is hung a Pflueger Medalist loaded with monofilament. Terminal tackle consists of a 3-way swivel from which some split shot dangles and a leader section of 2-pound test. The fly of choice for many is Spring's wiggler, a Michigan steelhead pattern, or any of a variety of egg patterns. However, most prefer fresh spawn, night crawler pieces, or yellow sponge on a hook.

Local Pattern	Willoughby Seducer (Christman)
Hook	Fine wire hook, like the Eagle Claw Pattern 59, size 6 or 8
Thread	None
Tail	None
Body	Small piece of the yellowish, under-seat foam from the cushion of a Chevy pickup, pierced by the hook.
Wing	None

Above the falls, the Willoughby flows down from its source, the outflow of one of the most beautiful lakes in the world, Lake Willoughby. Route 53 follows the river all the way to Orleans. Alders shade the upper reach. There are long, protected shallow runs over a fine gravel bottom, providing an excellent spawning area. The midriver section is a mix of pocketwater and corner pools. Below the hills in Orleans, the river slows down and joins the Barton.

There are pull-offs along Route 53 giving access to the river. One needs to be aware of river sections that are posted during spawning times. In addition to rainbows, the Willoughby has a strong population of brook trout in its upper reaches.

The season for both the Barton and Willoughby Rivers is the second Saturday in April through the last Sunday in October; fishing is closed from April 7 to June 1 on the Willoughby from Whetstone in Evansville downstream to the mouth of Brownington Branch and the stretch between the Orleans/Brownington Road bridge to the top of the natural falls.

Both rivers have length limits of 17 inches for landlocked salmon and 10 inches for rainbows, browns, and brookies, and a kill limit of 2 fish. Please note postings on streambanks.

Contributing to the beauty and richness of Vermont's Northeast Kingdom is that beautiful trout stream, the **Black River**. It slowly flows out of the hills and bogs, surrounding the secluded village of Craftsbury Commons. As beautiful as it may be in its gracefully meandering headwaters, the Black begins as only a marginal brook trout stream. Logging near the upper river section has had a negative effect on water quality, and high summer water temperatures are common. As the river continues along Route 14 through the villages of Albany and Irasburg, the water quality improves and so does the fishing. The stream runs cool and is broken up with long stretches of pocketwater and many deep, corner pools. This is good habitat for the wild and hatchery brown trout and brookies that call this section of river home.

Rainbow trout begin to show up in the Black River downstream from the mouth of Lords Creek near Irasburg. Lake-run rainbows in the spring and brown trout in the fall enter the lower Black from Lake Memphremagog. The Black has excellent spawning habitat, and you'll find lovely, little wild rainbows in the river near the village of Coventry, plus you might happen upon large resident, adult brown trout.

Black River

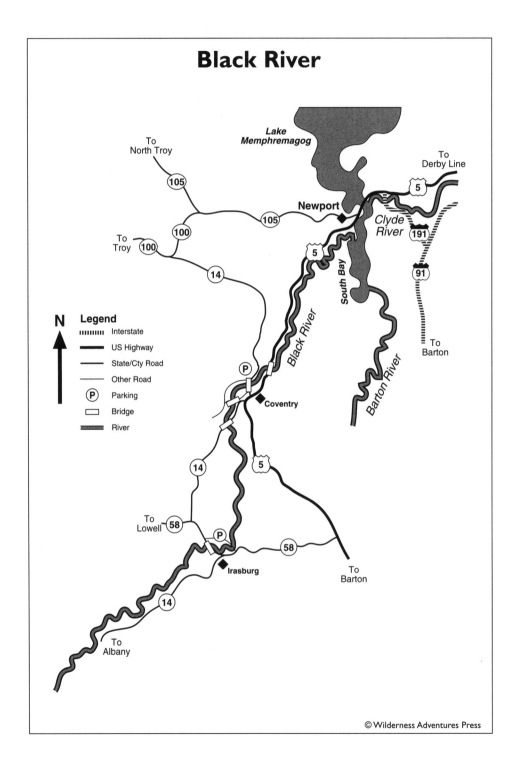

© Wilderness Adventures Press

Stoneflies and caddisflies are the dominant aquatic insects in the Black River. There is access to quality water along Route 14 and in Irasburg off Old Dump Road. In Coventry, the stretch of river below the falls, near the site of the old covered bridge, and downstream fishes well.

The Black River's season runs from the second Saturday in April through the last Sunday in October; a 600-foot section of river from the top of Old Harman Mill Falls in Coventry downstream is closed to fishing from April 7 to June 1.

The length limit for landlocked salmon is 17 inches and 10 inches for rainbows throughout the Black. Limits are generally 2 fish of any species.

NORTHEASTERN VERMONT HUB CITIES
Newport/Derby/Orleans
Newport Elevation–722 • Population–4,432
Derby Elevation–1,011 • Population–855

ACCOMMODATIONS
Bay View Lodge & Motel, 93 Pleasant Street Extension (Newport 05855) /
802-334-6543 / $
Newport City Motel, 974 East Main Street (Newport 05855) / 802-334-6558 / $$
Pinecrest Motel & Cabins, Route 5 North (Barton 05822) / 802-525-3472 /
Convenient to the Barton, Black, and Willoughby Rivers / $$
The Anglin' B & B, Crystal Lake (Barton 05822) / 802-525-4548 / Canoe and boat
rentals / $$
Willough Vale Inn, Route 5A (Westmore 05822) / 800-594-9102 / On beautiful Lake
Willoughby / $$$–$$$$

CAMPGROUNDS
Char-Bo Campground, P.O. Box 54 (Derby 05829) / 802-766-8807 / 3 miles east of
Derby Center on Route 105
Belview Campground, Route 16E (P.O. Box 222, Barton 05822)
Will-O-Wood Campground, RD 2, Box 316 (Orleans 05860) / A mile north of Lake
Willoughby on Route 5A

RESTAURANTS
Parkside Family Restaurant, Clyde Street (Newport 05855) / 802-334-2486
Bay View Lodge Dining Room, 93 Pleasant Street Extension (Newport 05855) /
802-334-6543
Candlepin Restaurant, Route 5 North (Barton 05822) / 802-525-6513

SPORTING GOODS AND GUIDE SERVICES
Orleans General Store, Main Street (Orleans 05860) / 802-754-6365 / Tackle and
current conditions on Willoughby River and other area fishing
Wright's Enterprises, Route 5 Newport/Derby Road (Newport 05855) / 802-334-1674
Northeast Kingdom Outfitters of Vermont, RR 1, Box 35A (Morgan 05853) /
802-895-4220 (day); 802-766-8013 (evening) / Francis and David Smith

MEDICAL
North Country Community Hospital, 189 Prouty Drive (Newport 05855) /
802-334-7331

FOR MORE INFORMATION
Vermont North Country Chamber of Commerce
The Causeway
Newport, VT 05855
800-635-4643 / 802-334-7782

St. Johnsbury/Lyndonville/Island Pond

St. Johnsbury Elevation–697 • Population–7,608
Lyndonville Elevation–720 • Population–5,371

ACCOMMODATIONS

Lakefront Motel, Box 448, Cross Street (Island Pond 05846) / 802-723-6507 / $–$$
Fairbanks Inn, Route 2 (St. Johnsbury 05819) / 802-748-5666 / $$$
Yankee Traveler Motel, 65 Portland (St. Johnsbury 05819) / 802-748-3156 / $$$
Days Inn of Lyndonville, Route 5 (Lyndonville 05851) / 802-626-9316 / $
The Village Inn of East Burke (East Burke 05832) / 802-626-3161 / Fishing excursions arranged / Includes breakfast / $

CAMPGROUNDS

Brighton State Park (Island Pond 05846) / 802-723-4360
Maidstone State Park, RD Box 455 (Guildhall 05905) / 802-676-3930 / South of the village of Bloomfield off Route102
Moose River Campground, RR 3, Box 197 (St. Johnsbury 05819) / 802-748-4334 / East of St. Johnsbury at the junction of Routes 2 and 18

RESTAURANTS

Cole's Filling Station-Shelly's, Route 5 (West Burke 05871) / 802-467-9808
Loon's Landing Restaurant, 135 Maine Street (Island Pond 05846) / 802-723-LOON
Lincoln Inn, 20 Hastings Street (St. Johnsbury 05819) / 802-748-5107

SPORTING GOODS AND REGIONAL INFORMATION

Caplan's Army Store, 110 Railroad Street (St. Johnsbury 05819) / 802-748-3236
The Village Sport Shop, Route 5 (Lyndonville 05851) / 800-464-4315; 802-626-8448
Mahoney's General Store & Sporting Goods, Cross Street (Island Pond 05846) / 802-723-6255

MEDICAL

Northeastern Regional Hospital, Hospital Drive (St. Johnsbury 05819) / 802-748-8141

FOR MORE INFORMATION

Northeast Kingdom Chamber of Commerce
30 Western Avenue
St. Johnsbury, VT 05819
800-639-6379 / 802-748-3678

Island Pond Chamber of Commerce
P.O. Box 255
Island Pond, VT 05846
802-723-4318

Lyndonville Chamber of Commerce
P.O. Box 886 / 51 Depot Street
Lyndonville, VT 05851
802-626-9696

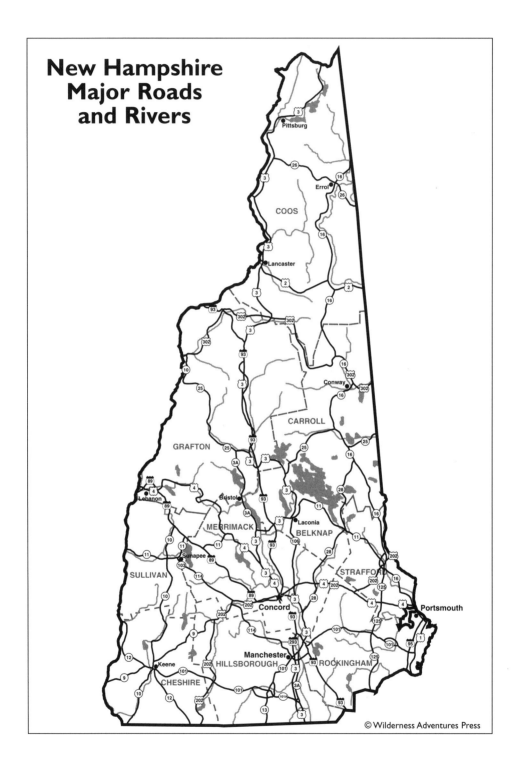

New Hampshire Major Roads and Rivers

Pittsburg

COOS

Errol

Lancaster

Conway

CARROLL

GRAFTON

Lebanon

Bristol

MERRIMACK

Laconia

BELKNAP

Sunapee

SULLIVAN

STRAFFORD

Concord

Portsmouth

Manchester

Keene

HILLSBOROUGH

ROCKINGHAM

CHESHIRE

© Wilderness Adventures Press

New Hampshire Facts

46th largest state in the union
9,351 square miles

Mean Elevation: 1,000 feet
Counties: 10
Population: 1,162,000
  39 State Parks
   6 State Forests
  14 State Natural Areas
   1 National Forest (White Mountain)

State Motto: **Live Free or Die**
State Bird: **Purple Finch**
State Tree: **White Birch**
State Flower: **Purple Lilac**
State Animal: **White-tailed Deer**
State Gem: **Smokey Quartz**
State Rock: **Granite**
State Wildflower: **Pink Ladyslipper**
State Freshwater Game Fish: **Brook Trout**
State Saltwater Game Fish: **Striped Bass**

New Hampshire Flyfishing

The Granite State offers many opportunities for fly anglers. You can fish for aggressive coastal striped bass or the more skittish sea-run brown trout of Berry Brook on New Hampshire's southeast coast. In the far north, near the border of the Province of Quebec, Canada, you'll find the hard-fighting landlocked salmon of the Connecticut Lakes Region. And in the state's center, the White Mountains, native brook trout swim in cool, crystal clear streams.

The New Hampshire Fish and Game Department manages a comprehensive fish-stocking program in the streams, lakes, and ponds of the state. Large numbers of brook trout, brown trout, rainbows, and landlocked salmon, raised in the state's several fish hatcheries, are planted each year. As a result, several rivers have flyfishing-only sections, and the state manages 31 flyfishing-only ponds. In addition, New Hampshire Fish and Game and the U.S. Fish and Wildlife Service jointly manage an Atlantic salmon broodstock fishery in the Pemigewasset and Merrimack Rivers.

The New Hampshire trout and bass fishing season generally runs from January 1 through October 15. The fishing season for landlocked salmon is from April 1 to September 30. Nonresident fishing licenses are available for 3-day, 7-day, or 15-day periods, as well as for the full season. License fees currently (1999 season) range from $18.50 to $35.50. The fee for the permit required to participate in the Atlantic salmon broodstock fishing program is $10.00.

New Hampshire's residents welcome visitors to share their state's beauty and recreational activities. Hospitality services are available in the major cities and towns, and there are full-service fly shops conveniently located throughout the state. We contacted Jim Riccardi of Riccardi's Golden Demon Fly Shop in the village of Hudson. Jim offers fly tying materials, equipment, and flies tied to order. He shared his advice for reliable fly patterns for fishing New Hampshire's streams and ponds.

Jim Riccardi's Ultimate Fly Box

Dry flies: Light olive or tan elk hair caddis #12–16; cream and light brown hairwing emerger #12–16; as well as the white or royal Wulff #10–12. Flyfish the elk hair caddis during hatches. The hairwing emerger and the Wulffs should be fished during low-light periods.

Wet flies: Soft-hackled flies, such as the partridge and green or partridge and orange (#10–14) and the little woody (#6–12). Flyfish the soft-hackled flies in moving water just under the surface as an emerger when you can't quite match the hatch. The little woody can be trolled or cast.

Nymphs: Olive hare's ear #6–12, gray nymph #10–12, and the zug bug #10–12. Nymphing, says Riccardi, is his favorite way to fish rivers and streams.

Streamers: Gray ghost #4–8, black ghost marabou #8–10, and the boulder bend #6–8, Riccardi's own pattern for salmon and trout.

As an overall choice, he also recommends the black/olive woolly bugger #6–10, adding, "Don't leave home without it."

Southern New Hampshire offers a variety of rivers and streams supplemented with hatchery brook trout, browns, and rainbows. (Photo by Elizabeth Edwards)

SOUTHERN NEW HAMPSHIRE

Southern New Hampshire is often the destination for anglers seeking coastal striped bass. However, this portion of northern New England offers several other fine opportunities. There are many rivers and stillwaters managed by the state as freshwater trout fisheries. A few of southern New Hampshire's waters offer excellent fishing for smallmouth bass and other warmwater species. And in the watershed formed by the lower Pemigewasset and Merrimack Rivers, there is a managed fishery for Atlantic salmon broodstock.

SOUTHERN NEW HAMPSHIRE MAJOR HATCHES

Insect/Bait	J	F	M	A	M	J	J	A	S	O	N	D	Patterns
Minnows and Leeches													Woolly Buggers and Muddlers #4-10; Smelt Patterns
Caddis													Black Elk Hair Caddis #16-20 (early and late season); Tan Elk Hair Caddis #14-18; Soft Hackles and Emergers #14-18; Hare's Ear Nymph and Beadhead Pupae #14-18
Blue-winged Olives													Parachute Adams #14-20; Thorax Blue-winged Olive #14-18; Pheasant Tail Nymphs #14-20
Hendricksons													Dark Hendrickson or Red Quill #12-14; Hendrickson Nymph #12-14; Rusty Spinner #14
March Brown													March Brown Dun #12; Hare's Ear Nymph
Light Cahill													Cahill Dun or Parachute #16
Sulphurs													Sulphur Duns and Hare's Ear Nymphs #16-18
Stoneflies													Black Stonefly Nymph #2-6; Yellow Stonefly Nymph #8-10; Yellow Sally #14
Leadwing Coachman *Isonychia bicolor*													Leadwing Coachman Wet Fly #10-12; Zug Bug and Prince Nymph #10-14; Gray Wulff and Adams #10-14
Tiny Mayflies *Tricorythodes stygiatus*													Trico Spinner #18-24
Terrestrials													Hoppers #6-12; Ants #14-18
Midges													Griffith's Gnat #18

New Hampshire's rocky coastline holds striped bass that will take epoxy flies, crab imitations, traditional streamers, and poppers. (Photo by Steve Hickoff)

Coastal Striped Bass Flyfishing

It was as dark as the inside of a coal bucket. The striper struck hard and gave my right wrist and hand a forceful tug. I crouched down and held the rod hard as saltwater poured around my belt-cinched chest waders.

What a fish! I squinted as the striper, an almost indiscernible shadowy movement some 30 yards out, lunged and charged around on top of the water. Lights from an offshore barge twinkled in the distance, offering brief comfort as the rapid exchange of tidal water pushed and pulled me around.

This one meant business. I worked my hightop sneakers down into a rocky crevasse for a foothold and settled in for the long haul. Finally, the striper was in plain sight. I saw a broad tail slap sea foam and smack dangerously close to the taut leader.

I eased the big fish toward me. This striper was the reward for enduring the dangerously shifting tide and loss of sleep from fishing the nighttime beachfront.

Fishing the oceanside after dark offers other rewards. New Hampshire seacoast nights are often cooler than inland summer days and generally are more pleasant to fish. Stripers also seem less wary after nightfall and haunt the shoreline to feed on baitfish, the occasional green crab, and small lobster.

The nighttime striper angler finds that the senses of hearing, smell, touch, and even taste are enhanced and enlivened to the point of creating a nighttime angling addiction. There are worse ways to spend a summer evening.

To prepare for a night of saltwater fishing along the coast, I check the weather report for the threat of approaching storm fronts and the times of tidal exchanges. Though traditional surfcasting notions suggest fishing the first hour before high tide

Upper New Hampshire Coast

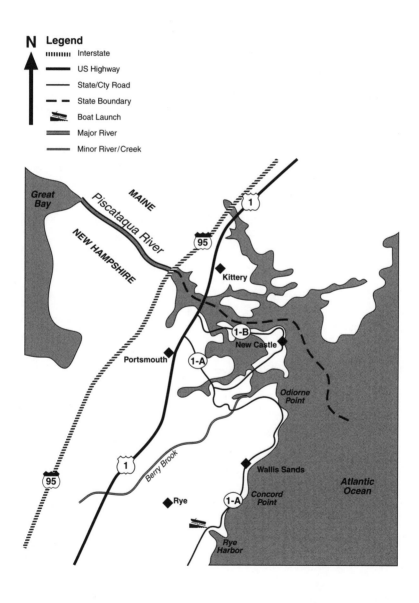

N

Legend
ⅢⅢⅢ	Interstate
▬▬▬	US Highway
────	State/Cty Road
─ ─ ─	State Boundary
⛵	Boat Launch
▬▬	Major River
▬▬	Minor River/Creek

Great Bay

MAINE

Piscataqua River

NEW HAMPSHIRE

Kittery

1

95

1-B

New Castle

Portsmouth

1-A

Odiorne Point

Berry Brook

1

95

Wallis Sands

Atlantic Ocean

Rye

1-A

Concord Point

Rye Harbor

© Wilderness Adventures Press

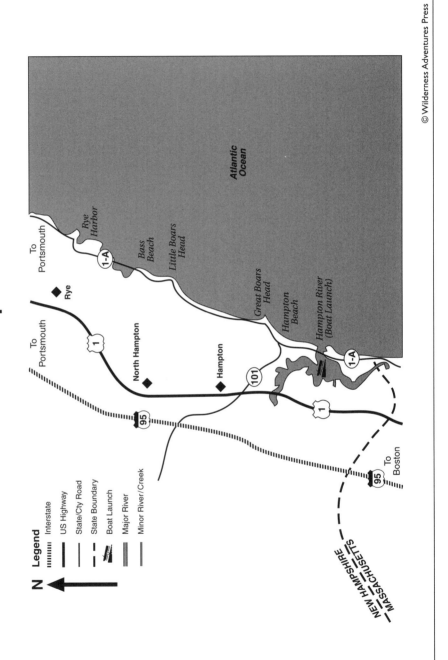

Great Bay

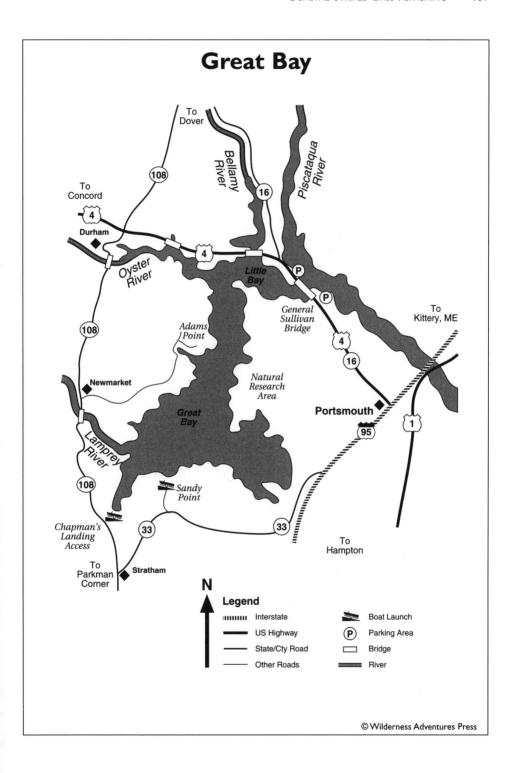

To Dover

To Concord

To Kittery, ME

To Hampton

To Parkman Corner

Bellamy River

Piscataqua River

Oyster River

Little Bay

General Sullivan Bridge

Adams Point

Natural Research Area

Great Bay

Lamprey River

Sandy Point

Chapman's Landing Access

Durham

Newmarket

Portsmouth

Stratham

108

4

16

4

P

P

4

16

1

95

108

108

108

33

33

N

Legend

⁞⁞⁞⁞⁞⁞ Interstate		🚤 Boat Launch
— US Highway		Ⓟ Parking Area
— State/Cty Road		▭ Bridge
— Other Roads		▓▓▓ River

© Wilderness Adventures Press

through the first hour after a flood tide, I often do the opposite. The bottom of the tide, particularly the dead low, holds fish as well. I've seen anglers fish until dark and then leave. That's when the good fishing is just getting started.

Flyfishing the nighttime surf involves assorted challenges. A good sense of the tidal exchange is necessary. Exchanges are often reduced to under an hour. Watch the shifting tide and fish only as long as you feel safe. Nights often require moving from one spot to another along the Atlantic Coast.

If you find someone fishing a preferred location just before dark, wait it out—he may leave. If you prefer to fish alone, move to another spot and investigate other possibilities. My wife, Elizabeth, and I once found an angler fishing a preferred haunt after dark. So we reluctantly moved. This resulted in two decent stripers well over a yard long. We had never fished this new spot before, but I can tell you we have since then.

The after-dark surf can be dangerous. Rocky outcroppings are tough to negotiate. Crawling is as important as walking in some spots. Take your time and move slowly along with a small flashlight in hand or in mouth. Avoid shining the light directly into the water. It could spook fish. Set up on areas that have been scouted out previously if possible. Some spots we fish hold dramatic dropoffs. These areas are best avoided when visual assessment is impossible.

Fish new moons and full moons and any other summer evenings you can. Some striper anglers will tell you bright nights don't provide optimum conditions. Maybe, maybe not. We've hooked fish under many a full moon. Striper outings will provide some wonderful memories. Flyfish hard, flyfish safely, and don't forget to check those flashlight batteries.

Fly Tackle for Stripers

Sheltered tidewaters can be fished with a 9-foot, 8-weight fly rod. An 8-weight line can handle small sand-eel patterns, and the light rod reduces the physical discomfort from repeated casts. Should the wind pick up, however, you may need a stouter rig.

A 9- or 9½-foot, 9-weight fly rod is a good bet for most beach casting and fishing in and around rocky outcroppings. Line weights can be increased for larger patterns and for fighting stiff breezes. Boat anglers may choose a 10- or 11-weight rod. Daytime stripers often hold in deeper water and feed on big bait. A heavier rod will handle deep sinking lines and large flies.

Basic striper reels should hold 200 yards of 20-pound test Dacron backing. Fly line choices include floating saltwater taper, intermediate sinking lines, and sinktip lines.

Leaders can be easily tied while watching TV weather reports for the evening coastal conditions. Some fly anglers prefer intricate leaders and bloodknot three sections of 40-, 30-, and 20-pound test. Others tie on a straight 8-foot section of 20-pound test monofilament. Both leader styles work well.

Traditional flies, such as deceivers and Clouser minnows, work well. Also try sand eel and crab patterns.

Steve Hickoff with a 25-pound New Hampshire striped bass. (Photo by Steve Hickoff)

Regulations

New Hampshire's striper season is open year-round. There is a 32-inch size limit, and an angler may keep one fish per day. A license is not required.

Hampton River Estuary Access

Route 1A follows the New Hampshire coastline from the Massachusetts border north to the city of Portsmouth. The highway spans the mouth of the Hampton River near the entrance to Hampton Beach State Park. From here, anglers have access to a jetty, the back portion of the estuary, and the beach itself. Fishing is not allowed from the bridge. There is a public boat launch on the north side of the bridge, and parking is available along the beach during the night and early mornings. Hampton Beach is a popular destination, and highway traffic can be heavy.

Great Bay Access

Great Bay, west of the city of Portsmouth, is a large estuary formed by four rivers: the Oyster, Bellamy, Lamprey, and Piscataqua. There is a public fishing area managed by the state of New Hampshire at the mouth of the bay at the General Sullivan Bridge off Routes 4 and 16 north of Interstate 95 in Portsmouth. Tidal rips are extremely strong at the bridge where the waters of Little Bay and the Piscataqua River mix. Fishing is best at slack tide.

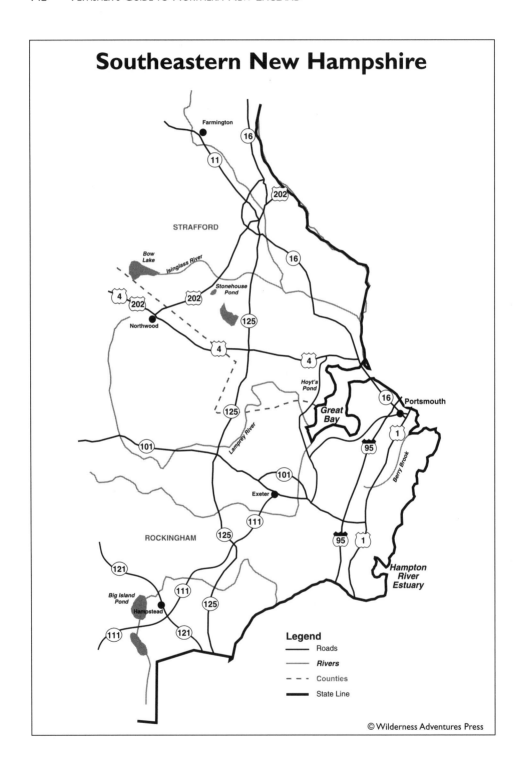

Southeastern New Hampshire

Farmington

STRAFFORD

Bow Lake

Isinglass River

Stonehouse Pond

Northwood

Hoyt's Pond

Great Bay

Portsmouth

Lamprey River

Berry Brook

101

Exeter

ROCKINGHAM

Hampton River Estuary

Big Island Pond

Hampstead

Legend

——	Roads
~~	*Rivers*
– – –	Counties
▬▬	State Line

© Wilderness Adventures Press

SOUTHEASTERN NEW HAMPSHIRE

Rockingham and Strafford Counties in southeastern New Hampshire offer two major trout rivers, the Lamprey and the Isinglass. Each holds good numbers of hatchery fish, and springtime angling is best.

With the coming of summer, many flyfishers focus their attention on the coast for migratory striped bass. Later in the season, Berry Brook, not far from the city of Portsmouth, offers angling for sea-run brown trout in the shifting tides of autumn.

The Lamprey River near Lee Hook Road. (Photo by Steve Hickoff)

Lamprey River

This 43-mile river is regularly stocked and receives heavy fishing pressure, especially in April and May. The Lamprey River, near the towns of Raymond, Lee, and Newmarket, gets a great deal of attention from local anglers. Flyfishers frequent these waters, as well, despite the fact that stocked Lamprey River trout seem to ignore their midge and early black stonefly offerings—so much for matching hatches. Maybe the fish get spoiled on juicy worms..

Don't get me wrong. The Lamprey is still one of several good rivers in the region for the trout-loving flyfisher. Expect company on springtime weekends and early evenings during the week. This river seems to see all manner of anglers, from bobber watchers to those studying strike indicators. Lamprey River trout see it all: bait, hardware, flies, the works.

Lamprey River

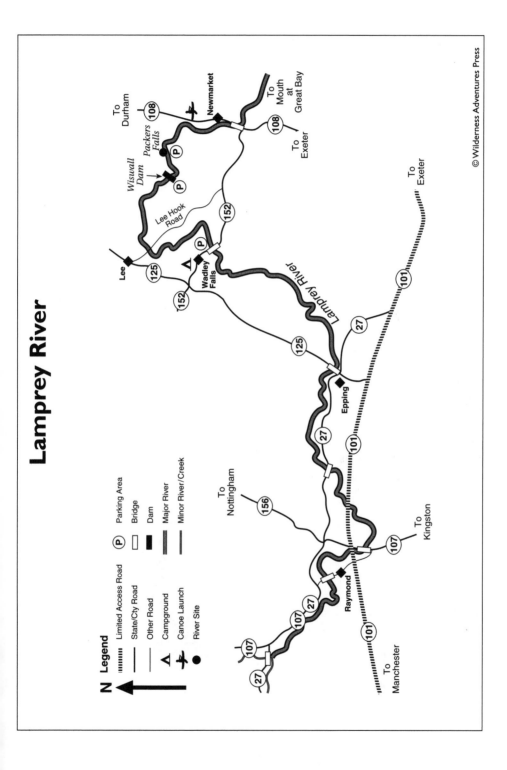

Legend

N

- Limited Access Road
- State/Cty Road
- Other Road
- ▲ Campground
- Canoe Launch
- ● River Site

- (P) Parking Area
- ▢ Bridge
- ■ Dam
- Major River
- Minor River/Creek

Isinglass River

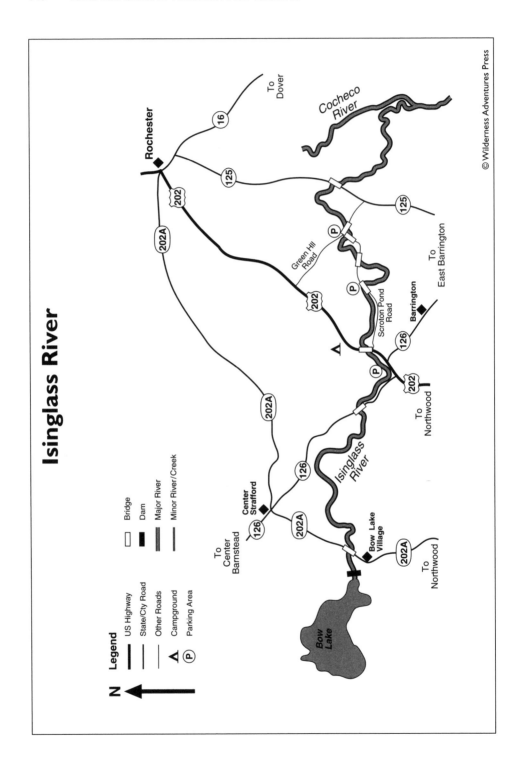

Trout fresh from holding tanks always seem to nail woolly buggers with abandon, and olive buggers work best. Stick with nymphs as you test these waters. Selections should include the Bitch Creek (#4–8), pheasant tail nymph (#12–20), or hellgrammite (#4–10). The latter dobsonfly larva imitation is a good bet on many of New Hampshire's faster flowing rivers. These nasty-looking nymphs always seem to interest both stocked and wild trout.

Water temperatures on the Lamprey get pretty warm in the summer. This can be a good time to try popping bugs for bass.

The Lamprey's trout season extends January 1 to October 15. In 1996, 1,500 brook trout, 1,050 brown trout, and 240 rainbow trout were released in the Lamprey in the town of Lee. Newmarket sections saw plantings of an additional 5,300 brown trout, while the town of Raymond received 400 brown trout and 400 rainbows. Most year-old Lamprey River trout average 10 to 12 inches.

In 1996, in an ongoing effort to establish this fishery, 27,972 Atlantic salmon fry were released in the river. According to Eric Orff of New Hampshire Fish and Game's Region 3, 550 broodstock Atlantic salmon from the Nashua Hatchery and Massachusetts were stocked in the Lamprey during the fall of 1996. Fish averaged slightly less than 15 inches. One angler flyfishing near the Lee Hook Road river access in April of 1997 told me he had released a 13-inch salmon that month. "Just a beautiful fish," he remarked with a smile.

The Lamprey River flows for 43 miles between Deerfield and Newmarket, where it empties into the Great Bay. This long, meandering river sees moderate springtime flows. There is decent riffle water and many deep pools. Springtime whitewater conditions are brief, with slow-moving flows developing by summer. The river is lined by wooded, sandy streambanks as it flows through suburban developments as well as lush, green farmland. Tidal waters flow downstream through mudflats from Route 108 to Great Bay.

In the town of Raymond, there are highway foot access points near New Hampshire Fish and Game stream stocking areas along Route 27. The Lee and Newmarket sections can be floated by canoe or waded. Popular access locations are found at Wadley Falls and Lee Hook Road in Lee, and downriver at Wiswall Dam and Packers Falls in Durham.

Isinglass River

Running 14 miles from Strafford to Barrington, the Isinglass is made up of riffles, swift runs, and flatwater pools. Silt deposits line the bottom of deepwater pools, while slick rocks in runs will find you taking your sweet time wading. Moderate springtime flows and April rains make wading difficult, but water levels drop quickly. This river falls to low levels by summer.

Like the Lamprey River, warmer spring days see local and out-of-state flyfishers gravitating to the Isinglass River. This migration commences in late April after stocking trucks have arrived. Bow Lake in Strafford is the source of this coldwater fishery. From here the Isinglass travels east to join the Cocheco River just south of Rochester.

Angler Steve Eisenhaure flyfishes the Isinglass River on an overcast April day. (Photo by Steve Hickoff)

From late April through early June, the Isinglass offers some of the best trout fishing in this corner of the Granite State. Roadside pulloffs provide ample access. The river is regularly stocked with brookies, rainbows, and browns. The availability of specific species of trout at the various New Hampshire hatcheries determines the yearly stocking schedule. Most Isinglass River trout come from the Powder Mill Hatchery in New Durham.

Sergeant Rick Jones, a New Hampshire Fish and Game conservation officer, has been active in stocking the river from Bow Lake in the town of Strafford to Route 125. Brook trout are common catches on this put-and-take fishery, as well as chunky rainbows, often weighing several pounds. Browns have been planted in the Isinglass since the early 1990s, says Jones.

Does the Isinglass contain holdover fish? "Based on my sampling experience," says Doug Grout, regional biologist, "holdovers are limited in the Isinglass." He also says there is little evidence of natural reproduction in the river. However, New

From late April through early June, the Isinglass offers some of the best trout fishing in the southeastern corner of the Granite State. (Photo by Steve Hickoff)

Hampshire Fish and Game research has shown that there are some signs of holdover fish on the nearby Cocheco and Lamprey Rivers.

The stocking program takes place during midweek, prior to the weekends. One sometimes gets the sense that phones ring all over Strafford County when stocking happens, as vehicles immediately arrive at the streams. Trout numbers are maintained at high counts through the Memorial Day weekend, making for several weeks of excellent flyfishing. Angling opportunities diminish as summer arrives and river water warms up.

Barrington sections receive the majority of stocked fish—2,500 rainbows and 1,300 brook trout were released in 1996, while 1,500 brookies and 1,500 rainbows were stocked in the Strafford region.

Fish black stonefly nymphs (#10–14) in April, but switch to black, olive, and tan woolly worms (#8–12) if you strike out. This put-and-take fishery lasts for several months. Freshly planted trout seem to strike anything from a black gnat fished wet

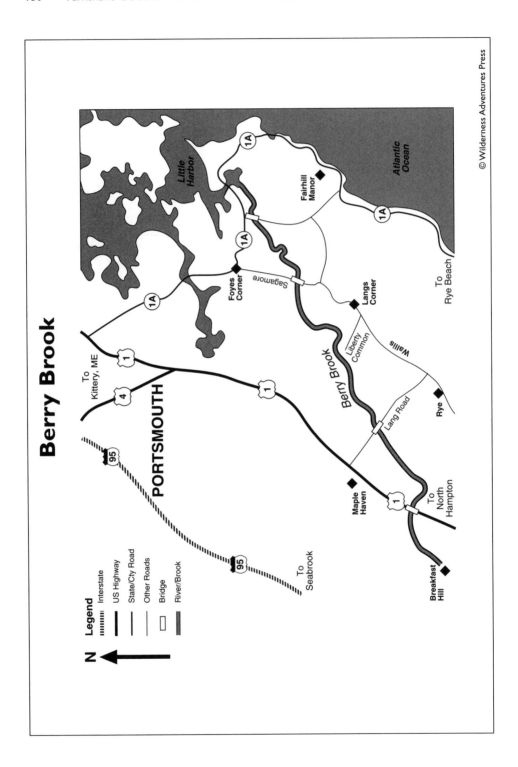

to a gold-ribbed hare's ear. Yellow, black, or olive buggers (#2–12) as well as white or black marabou muddlers (#2–10), catch fish. Rainbows will take red or maroon San Juan worms (#8–12).

Fishing season on the Isinglass extends from January 1 through October 15. The daily limit is 5 trout or 5 pounds of trout, whichever is reached first. Two fat Isinglass rainbows can fill the 5-pound limit.

Ample roadside parking is available between the intersection of Routes 126 and 202 and downriver at the highway bridge near Scruton Pond Road. Park on the river side of the highway. This section is heavily stocked. Trout are also stocked in the river near Green Hill Road in Barrington. Fish downriver from Green Hill Road to Route 125.

Berry Brook

A flyfishing experience is often measured by the difficulty of a particular quarry's acquisition, and sea-run brown trout certainly provide a challenge to flyfishers.

By October and November, most people turn their thoughts to wingshooting or deer hunting and stash the fly rod away for the winter. Not everyone, though. When autumn arrives on the New Hampshire seacoast, ardent flyfishers, eager to continue angling beyond the trout days of summer, turn to the immediate coastline, specifically Berry Brook, just a short drive south of Portsmouth. Their quarry is the sea-run brown trout.

According to Bruce W. Smith, New Hampshire Fish and Game marine biologist, the history of New Hampshire's sea-run brown trout fishery goes back to the early 1960s. Outdoor writer Dick Pinney, then a conservation officer, persuaded the chief of the Fisheries Division, Bernard "Buck" Corson, to introduce brown trout into Berry Brook in the town of Rye.

Corson agreed, and in 1964, 1,000 yearling browns from the department's Powder Mill Hatchery in New Durham were released in Berry Brook. In addition, 500 browns from the federal hatchery in Nashua were planted. Results came quickly. That spring, sea-run browns (called "salters," a liberal borrowing of the slang word used by locals for sea-run brook trout) were seen reentering tidal Berry Brook. These trout were estimated to weigh between 2 and 3 pounds. Their remarkable growth rate was attributed to the nutrient-rich qualities of coastal marine waters.

Salters return to Berry Brook in the fall. Each spring, as part of its program to establish this fishery, the state plants yearling browns.

According to biologist Smith, an increase in sea-run brown trout catches was seen in the early part of the decade. Studies in 1992 revealed the number of angler hours spent per fish caught was 14.2. In 1990 and 1991, the catch per effort was 55 and 76.8 hours, respectively. Reported catches ranged from 12 inches to 22 inches in length. The 22-inch fish weighed 4 pounds. Between 1993 and 1995, the angler-hour-per-catch figure climbed from 29 hours to 35 hours. Sightings of trout are common, but catches are few.

New Hampshire angler Pinney, the originator of this fishery, has caught several sea-run browns over the years that weighed as much as 4 pounds. Fish from 9 to 12

Berry Brook hosts ardent New Hampshire flyfishers in search of wary
sea-run browns. (Photo by Steve Hickoff)

pounds have turned up in research samples. Pinney suggests fishing the late October and late November full moon flood tides that find browns moving into Berry Brook.

Fish the half-mile section from the wooden bridge on Route 1A to Brackett Road. Most anglers agree that the two hours before dead low tide and the two hours after the turn provide the best flyfishing opportunities. Others prefer the calm lull at full flood tide and some the dead low.

Smith suggests flyfishing all stages of tides until you find fish. Angling during the low-light hours is often best. Casts are made from a crouching position, keeping your balance with your knees in the salt marsh mud. Stalk salters by keeping casts to a minimum, much as you might work a mountain stream full of skittish wild brook trout. Sea-run browns that have eluded marauding bluefish and outboard motor propellers to reach this size are true survivors.

On one particular November outing during the fall of 1996, I spoke to three fly-fishers on Berry Brook. Two were from Martha's Vineyard, the southeastern Massachusetts island. The other hailed from southern Maine. All three men knew about this special fishery. The Maine fisherman had seen a 2-pounder caught there several weeks before. "A nice fish," he whispered, as if a passerby might hear. The Bay Staters were self-professed flyfishing bums visiting this tidewater for the first time. They had heard about the place and wanted to try it out.

As Smith says, "The brown trout fishery in coastal New Hampshire streams is characterized by limited numbers of dedicated flyfishermen who enjoy the special fall season challenge in pursuit of a notoriously elusive, but highly prized quarry."

Steve Hickoff selects a fly on a southern New Hampshire river. (Photo by Elizabeth Edwards)

Fly selections here range from olive woolly buggers to the same sand-eel imitations that anglers toss at Granite State summertime stripers. Muddler minnows, crab flies, a variety of streamers, and even traditional wet flies catch salters. In addition to these choices, Pinney recommends heron patterns, hare's ear nymphs, and shrimp flies. Jim Bernstein, of Eldredge Brothers Fly Shop in Cape Neddick, Maine, offers a variety of heron patterns exclusively tied for salters.

Lack of protective cover on these tidal mudflats can torment the flyfisher and make these skittish browns tough to catch. Berry Brook salters feed on mummichog, often foraging for these baitfish nocturnally.

The season on Berry Brook runs from August 15 through December 15. Anglers must carry an all-species fishing license. There is a daily limit of 1 fish, no minimum size. Check the New Hampshire Fish and Game Department's *Saltwater Fishing Digest* for special regulation river sections.

Two small, off-road parking spots are available at the Brackett Road bridge. Park at the gravel pull-off near the wooden Route 1A bridge but leave room for small boat access to the water.

Stonehouse Pond

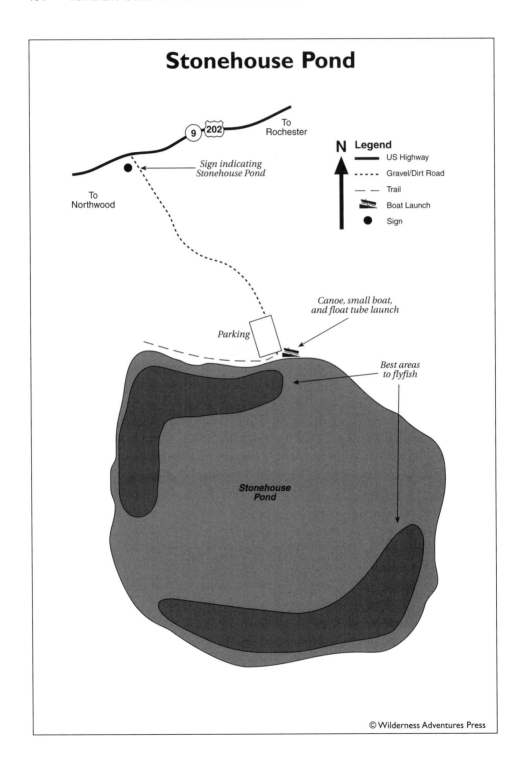

To Rochester

To Northwood

Sign indicating Stonehouse Pond

N Legend
— US Highway
---- Gravel/Dirt Road
– – Trail
Boat Launch
● Sign

Canoe, small boat, and float tube launch

Parking

Best areas to flyfish

Stonehouse Pond

© Wilderness Adventures Press

Other Southeastern New Hampshire Rivers and Streams

These rivers and streams, located in Strafford and Rockingham Counties, are stocked with trout on a regular basis. Most of these rivers are spate streams with the best angling in spring.

Salmon Falls River forms the border between the states of Maine and New Hampshire, flowing from Great East Lake into the Piscataqua River near Great Bay north of Portsmouth. The stretch of river that runs along Route 125 between the villages of Milton and Rochester is regularly stocked with rainbows, brook trout, and browns. **Branch River**, a tributary of Salmon Falls River, flows through the village of Union. It receives regular stockings of brook trout and browns.

Mad River and **Cocheco River** are both accessible from Route 11 near the Village of Farmington. The state stocks both streams with brook trout and browns. **Ela River** and **Hayes Brook** are both tributaries of the Cocheco River and are regularly stocked with brook trout.

Jones Brook is a small brook trout stream that runs out of the Jones Brook Wildlife Management Area east of the village of Union. There is an unimproved road off Kings Highway, a short distance from Middleton Corners, that will get you to the brook.

Oyster River flows into Great Bay near Durham. It is stocked with brown trout, rainbows, and brookies. **Little River** flows out of Mendums Lake, located west of Durham off Route 4. The state stocks brook trout in the stretch below the lake.

North River is another small brook trout stream in the town of Lee. It runs through the Nottingham State Forest along Route 152 near the village of Nottingham.

Bellamy River flows out of the Bellamy Reservoir and into Great Bay near the city of Dover. Access is available from Route 9. The state stocks the Bellamy with rainbows and brook trout.

Southeastern New Hampshire Stillwaters

The New Hampshire Fish and Wildlife Department manages southeastern stillwaters as flyfishing-only trout ponds. They are all located in Strafford County. Open season on flyfishing-only ponds runs from the fourth Saturday in April through October 15. The daily limit is 5 trout or 5 pounds, whichever limit is reached first.

Stonehouse Pond

This 14-acre pond receives moderate flyfishing pressure, with the heaviest coming on the New Hampshire trout pond opener, which is the fourth Saturday in April. And it's not just locals—on a recent opener, I noted license plates from Pennsylvania, New Jersey, Vermont, Massachusetts, Maine, and New Hampshire lined up along the muddy access road. Fish or not, none of these flyfishers seemed too disappointed.

"They're hitting, but sluggish," one guy told me as he got off the water. His words foreshadowed the first brook trout I'd catch that day. It was a fish that rose to a tan woolly worm fished slowly through some submerged pond-side tangle. It happened so slowly that I watched the brookie actually open its mouth to take the wet fly.

Expect good brook trout numbers at Stonehouse Pond from the late April trout pond opener through June. (Photo by Steve Hickoff)

This guy had been catching his fish on a small green ghost. As he predicted, my first trout struck sluggishly, as if the fish were chilled by the previous late April night. I was casting toward the shoreline from my little johnboat, letting the fly settle and drawing it back slowly, fishing the woolly worm the way I might an all-purpose nymph on a north country pond in summertime.

An hour later, as the sun emerged, the breeze picked up just a little. Another trout finned behind my offering and then sipped the submerged fly as if to respond to the bright break in the clouds above. Other flyfishers in float tubes and aluminum boats started to catch fish, as well.

To reach Stonehouse Pond, take Routes 9 and 202 from Northwood for roughly 3 miles, then turn right at the sign for the pond. From the village of Barrington, drive out of town until you reach the fork in the road at Routes 126 and 9. Bear left on Route 9 and take this highway until you reach Route 202. Turn left and proceed on Route 202 for about 3 miles. The sign for Stonehouse and the dirt (or muddy) road will be on your left. Four-wheel drive is suggested, and it is often the only option.

Expect abundant brook trout numbers, with fish running from 9 to 11 inches in length.

Hoyt's Pond

Roughly an acre in size, Hoyt's is stocked with brook trout in April just before the Granite State trout-pond opener. Flyfishing remains steady through early June. After the weather warms, however, angling drops off dramatically.

Action-starved flyfishers gather at this fishery in the town of Madbury on opening day for the camaraderie as much as the angling. They swap stories and catch 9- to 10-inch hatchery brookies. Some first-timers might feel hemmed in by angler numbers. If so, it's probably best to stay away. Others, however, welcome the company, viewing Hoyt's Pond as a traditional stop during their day of trout angling in southeastern New Hampshire.

Catch and release isn't necessarily protocol. The daily limit is 5 fish or 5 pounds, whichever limit is reached first. Small nymphs retrieved slowly just off the muddy and stumpy bottom work best. Scuds are great.

Access is available from Route 108 between Durham and Dover. Drive north or south from either town, then turn onto Freshet Road. Make an immediate left at the dirt road. Fish and Game signs note the location of the access area. Parking is available at the end of the dirt road. From there, walk down the trail to the pond.

Other Southeastern New Hampshire Stillwaters

Barbadoes Pond, located in Madbury, is stocked with brook trout and rainbows and receives heavy pressure. Vehicles may park along Route 9 near the access trail. This 14-acre pond fishes best in April and May.

Bow Lake has rainbows and browns, plus an assortment of warmwater game fish. It is located in the town of Strafford. This 1,160-acre pond often holds surprises —expect anything from 4-pound rainbows to lunker smallmouth bass. Bow Lake is best fished before Memorial Day and after Labor Day. Late September can be excellent for both largemouth bass and bronzebacks, especially on the rocky ledges near Bennett and Beech Islands.

Big Island Pond is a mixed warm- and coldwater fishery. It is stocked with rainbows, browns, and brookies. This 510-acre pond is located west of Hampstead and has a campground on the northeast shore off Route 121. A boat access is located at Chase's Grove near Route 111 on the south shore.

Exeter Reservoir is the 20-acre impoundment of Dearborn Brook, located in the city of Exeter. It is stocked with rainbows and brook trout.

Lucas Pond is a 52-acre impoundment located off Route 43 south of the village of Northwood. It is stocked with brown trout, rainbows, and brookies.

SOUTHEASTERN NEW HAMPSHIRE HUB CITY
Portsmouth
Elevation–Sea Level • Population–22,655

ACCOMMODATIONS
Holiday Inn of Portsmouth, 300 Woodbury Avenue (exit 6 off Route 95) / 603-431-8000 / Full-service restaurant and lounge with cable TV, nightly entertainment, an exercise room, and indoor swimming pool / Convenient to downtown Portsmouth / $$$$$

Portsmouth Inn, 383 Woodbury Avenue (exit 6 off Route 95) / 603-431-4400 / 60 AAA-approved rooms / Convenient to downtown Portsmouth / $$$$

Sise Inn, 40 Court Street / 603-433-1200 or 800-267-0525 / 34 rooms, continental breakfast included/ Located in downtown Portsmouth / $$$$$

RESTAURANTS
Buck Horn Family Restaurant, 108 Ocean Road (Greenland, west of Portsmouth) / 603-436-3636 / This local establishment serves breakfast, lunch, and dinner, 24 hours a day

Dunffey's Aboard the John Wanamaker, One Harbour Place / 603-433-3111 / This floating restaurant serves lunch and dinner and Sunday brunch

Lindbergh's Crossing, 29 Ceres Street / 603-431-0887 / Located in downtown Portsmouth, this is a country French bistro

FLY SHOPS AND SPORTING GOODS
Fox Ridge Outfitters, 400 North Main Street (Rochester 03866) / 603-335-2999 / Orvis shop

Golden Demon Fly Shop, 13 School Street (Hudson 03051) / 603-598-6518 / Jim Riccardi and Stan Fudala

Kittery Trading Post, Route 1 (Kittery, ME) / 207-439-2700 / Located just across the Piscataqua River from Portsmouth

Suds 'n' Soda Sports, 365 Portsmouth Avenue (Greenland) / 603-431-6320

Wal-Mart, 2460 Lafayette Road / 603-433-6008

HOSPITAL
Columbia Portsmouth Regional Hospital, 333-343 Borthwick Avenue (just off the Route 1 traffic circle and Interstate 95) / 603-436-5110 or 800-685-8282 / 24-hour, walk-in emergency care

AIRPORTS
Hampton Field, Route 1 North, Lafayette Road (North Hampton) / 603-964-6749

AUTO REPAIR
Baker-Wright Auto Electric Service, 202 Court Street / 603-436-2726 / Contact Terry Baker

Ben's Auto Body, Inc., 11 Mirona Road / 631-436-3115

AUTO RENTAL

Budget Rent-A-Car, 887 Route 1 Bypass South / 603-431-1986
Enterprise Rent-A-Car, 445 Route 1 Bypass / 603-433-1177

FOR MORE INFORMATION

Greater Portsmouth Chamber of Commerce
500 Market Street
P.O. Box 239
Portsmouth, NH 03802
604-436-1118

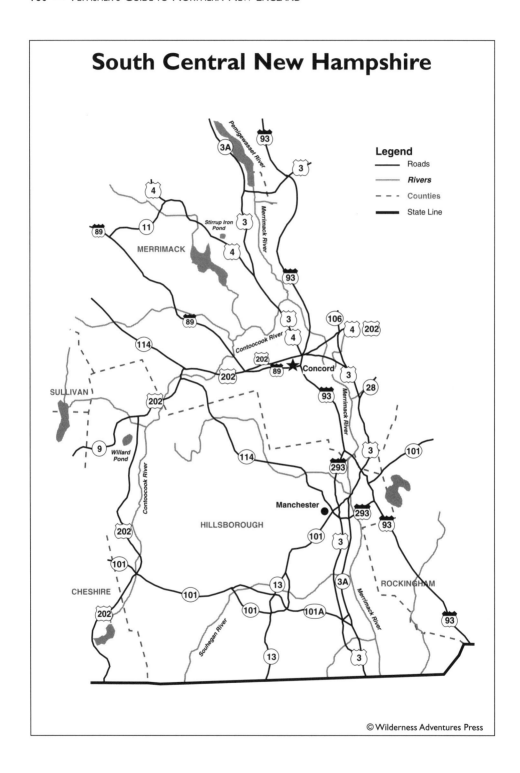

South Central New Hampshire

Legend
— Roads
~~~ *Rivers*
- - - Counties
━━ State Line

© Wilderness Adventures Press

SOUTH CENTRAL NEW HAMPSHIRE

If I told you that south central New Hampshire (Merrimack and Hillsborough Counties) has Atlantic salmon between 7 and 14 pounds swimming in the rivers of Merrimack County, you might look me in the eye, ask me what I'm drinking, and order one for yourself. But it's true. The program started in 1993 when New Hampshire Fish and Game pooled its resources with those of the U.S. Fish and Wildlife Service to create this sport-fishing opportunity. Today, approximately 3,000 broodstock Atlantic salmon are released in the Merrimack and Lower Pemigewasset Rivers annually. Such activities are certainly noticed by salmon flyfishers.

The Merrimack River Anadromous Fish Restoration Program provides the broodstock salmon and eggs for fry stocking. Credit should go to the New Hampshire Fish and Game, the U.S. Fish and Wildlife Service, the U.S. Forest Service, and conservation groups for the ongoing plan to restore salmon as well as shad and river herring to the Merrimack and Lower Pemigewasset. Three million fry are planted in the rivers and tributaries annually. According to New Hampshire Fish and Game, once there are significant returns of wild salmon, the broodstock program will be phased out.

Anglers may purchase a $10 Atlantic salmon stamp and the necessary tags from New Hampshire Fish and Game in Concord or from one of the authorized agents. In addition to the salmon stamp, participating anglers need to secure an all-species New Hampshire fishing license. Stamps must be attached to the permit form and must be with you while fishing.

The following shops and outlets sell Atlantic salmon permits:

Town	Agent
Bristol	Newfound Sales
Concord	Fish and Game Headquarters
Franklin	K&M Tobacco
Hanover	Lyme Angler
Hooksett	Steve's Sportsman's Den
Manchester	Wildlife Taxidermy Studio
New Boston	Hunter's Angling Supply
North Conway	North Country Angler
Salem	American Angling Supplies

Each permit holder is issued five numbered Atlantic salmon possession tags as part of the Atlantic salmon permit. Permit holders who wish to kill a broodstock salmon need to securely attach a possession tag to the fish by passing it through the mouth and gill openings. No person can possess an untagged Atlantic salmon nor possess a used or mutilated Atlantic salmon tag.

Only salmon marked with identification discs are legal. A Peterson-type identification tag (2 discs loosely joined by a wire) is attached to the base on each side of the dorsal fin of a salmon. Any salmon not identified by these discs must be released. ID discs must stay attached to the fish at all times.

Atlantic salmon are a limited resource. While the Merrimack and Lower Pemigewasset fishery is put and take, many practice catch and release, although there's no shame in keeping an occasional 10-pounder from this fishery.

The "Salmon Shuffle" is a common method of fishing these waters. This isn't a fashionable dance from a bygone decade but an ethical practice used on salmon waters. The salmon shuffle, better known as "fishing rotation," gives each angler an equal opportunity to fish through a salmon pool. An angler enters a pool in turn, makes a few casts, and then takes a few steps downstream, where he then is given time to switch flies and cast again. If an angler hooks an Atlantic salmon, the other anglers reel in and wait for the individual to land the fish.

Fly patterns for salmon include the rusty rat (#2–10), silver doctor (#2–8), and Mickey Finn (#4–10). Word on the river is that green or chartreuse patterns work well. Try the green highlander (#4–10), Colburn special (#2–10), or the green machine (#4–8).

The salmon season runs from April 1 to September 30.

Merrimack and Lower Pemigewasset Rivers

The Merrimack and Lower Pemigewasset Rivers create a single river system. The Pemigewasset has its beginnings near Franconia Notch in central New Hampshire. It flows south, parallel to Route 3 and Interstate 93, through the villages of Lincoln and North Woodstock to Plymouth. A dam in the village of Bristol blocks the river's flow in the lower section downstream of Plymouth. From here the Lower Pemigewasset enters a long flood plain within the Franklin Falls Dam Project. It merges with the Merrimack River at the dam north of the village of Franklin. From this point, the rivers continue south as one river, the Merrimack.

Salmon may be taken by flyfishing only on the Merrimack and Lower Pemigewasset Rivers from the Garvin Falls Dam in Bow to the Eastman Falls Dam in Franklin and in their tributaries to the first dam.

The Merrimack River from the New Hampshire/Massachusetts state line to the Garvin Falls Dam in Bow and its tributaries to the first upstream dam can be fished by flies or artificial lures that only have one hook with no more than one hook point.

Artificial lures are legal here for now, but not for long, according to the New Hampshire Fish and Game. New Hampshire's fishing laws for Atlantic salmon will soon read "by flyfishing only" to be consistent with regulations for Atlantic salmon fisheries in Canada and Maine. The daily salmon limit is one fish. The season salmon limit is 5. The minimum length limit is 15 inches.

Atlantic broodstocks range from 7 to 14 pounds. This river system also holds largemouth and smallmouth bass, chain pickerel, yellow perch, bullhead, bluegill, and carp.

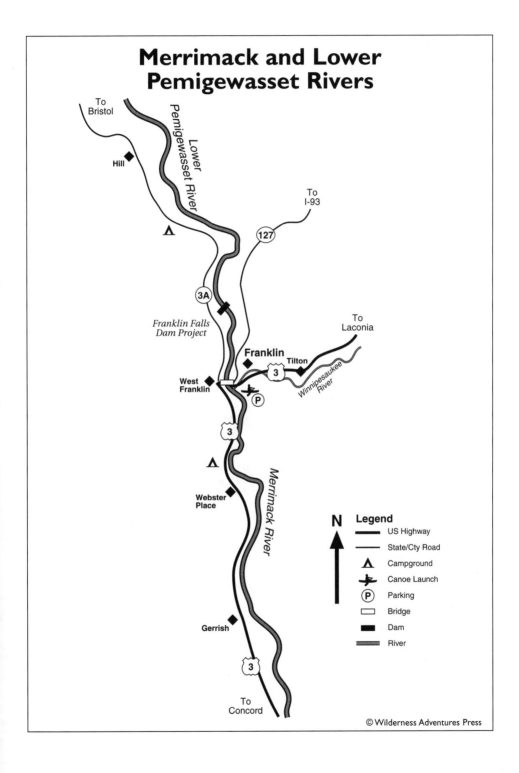

Merrimack and Lower Pemigewasset Rivers

To Bristol

Lower Pemigewasset River

Hill

To I-93

127

3A

Franklin Falls Dam Project

To Laconia

Franklin

Tilton

3

Winnipesaukee River

West Franklin

P

3

Merrimack River

Webster Place

Legend

N

▬▬▬	US Highway
────	State/Cty Road
▲	Campground
✈	Canoe Launch
Ⓟ	Parking
▭	Bridge
▬	Dam
〰〰	River

Gerrish

3

To Concord

© Wilderness Adventures Press

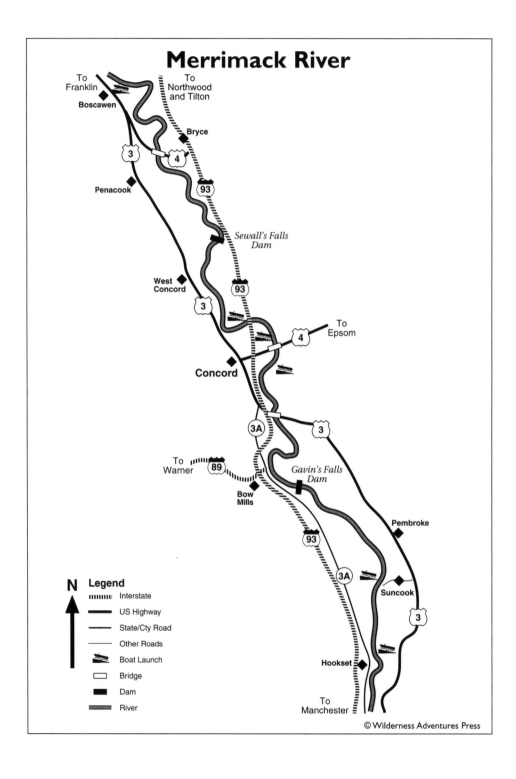

Merrimack River

To Franklin

To Northwood and Tilton

Boscawen

Bryce

3

4

93

Penacook

Sewall's Falls Dam

West Concord

93

3

To Epsom

4

Concord

3A

3

To Warner

89

Bow Mills

Gavin's Falls Dam

Pembroke

93

3A

Suncook

3

Hookset

To Manchester

© Wilderness Adventures Press

N

Legend

|||||||| Interstate

US Highway

State/Cty Road

Other Roads

Boat Launch

Bridge

Dam

River

Merrimack River

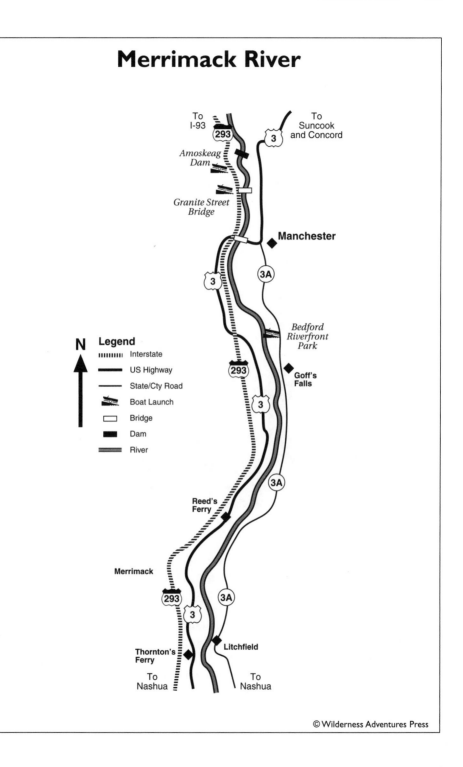

To
I-93

293

*Amoskeag
Dam*

To
Suncook
and Concord

3

*Granite Street
Bridge*

Manchester

3

3A

*Bedford
Riverfront
Park*

N

Legend

||||||| Interstate

293

**Goff's
Falls**

US Highway

State/Cty Road

Boat Launch

Bridge

Dam

River

3

3A

**Reed's
Ferry**

Merrimack

293

3A

3

**Thornton's
Ferry**

Litchfield

To
Nashua

To
Nashua

© Wilderness Adventures Press

Flyfisher Dennis Guilbeault with a Merrimack River brood-stock Atlantic salmon. (Photo courtesy of New Hampshire Fish & Game Department)

The Lower Pemigewasset River from Plymouth to Franklin is 28 miles; the Merrimack River from Franklin to Concord is 21 miles, from Concord to Manchester is 20 miles, and from Manchester to Nashua is 18.5 miles.

The river systems feature broad, flatwater sections with occasional drops, dams, and rapids running north to south through urban centers.

The Lower Pemigewasset has typical New England Class II-III rapids, with some portaging required. The Merrimack has slow-moving Class I-II rapids with some water-churning ledges and flow-restricting dams. Portaging by canoeists is necessary on some river sections. Merrimack anglers often fish by boat. The lower river from Manchester to Nashua can be fast moving early in the spring season. Use extreme caution when boating this section.

Access is available at the following:

- Eastman Falls Hydro Station, Franklin: By canoe, with parking for eight vehicles. Located off Route 3A. Owned by Public Service of New Hampshire.
- Winnipesaukee River, Franklin: Canoe access with public parking for five vehicles near Winnipesaukee River pumping station located off River Street.
- County Farm Access, Boscawen: Boat ramp available with public parking for 12 vehicles. Located off U.S. Route 3. Owned by the state, it provides access to the west side of the river.
- Sewalls Falls Multi-Use Recreation Area is north of the city of Concord and is accessible from either Route 3 or Interstate 93. A parking lot is located south of the main recreational facility at the end of 2nd Street after the Sewalls Falls Road turnoff from Route 3 on the west side of the river. This stretch of the Merrimack has a lot of good access. The current is relatively strong but the shoreline can be waded.
- Fish and Game Access Site, Concord: Canoe and cartop access with parking for eight vehicles. Located off Portsmouth Street, this state-owned property provides access to the west bank of the river.
- New Hampshire Technical Institute Ramp, Concord: Boat ramp with parking for eight vehicles located off Fort Eddy Road. This is a state-owned access on the Merrimack's west side.
- Everett Arena Access, Concord: Boat ramp with parking for 12 or more vehicles. This east shore access off Loudon Road is city owned.
- Bow Steam Plant, Bow: Boat ramp with parking for about a dozen vehicles located off River Road. Owned and operated by Public Service of New Hampshire, it provides access to the river's west side.
- Lambert Park, Hooksett: Boat ramp available with ample parking for 30 or more vehicles located off Merrimack Street. This is a state-owned access on the river's eastern shore.
- Stark's Landing, Manchester: Boat ramp available with public parking. This city-owned access site is located off Granite Street on the river's east shore.
- Bass Island, Manchester: A proposed project as of this writing. Canoe and cartop access is off Second Street. West side access owned by the city of Manchester.
- Carthegina Island, Manchester: Eastern shore fishing off Riverdale Avenue owned by the city.
- Bedford Riverfront Park: Canoe access and riverbank angling accessible from U.S. Route 3, owned by the state and operated by the town.
- Fish and Game Access Site, Litchfield: Another proposed project that will be located off Route 3A, with canoe an cartop access and parking for 15 vehicles on the Merrimack River's east side. Owned by the state.

Contoocook River

The Contoocook River flows through both Merrimack and Hillsborough Counties. It begins north of the village of Peterborough, flows through the Powder Mill Pond impoundment near the village of Bennington, and on through the villages of Hillsborough and Henniker. The Contoocook eventually joins the Merrimack River north of Concord. There are dams at West Henniker and at the Hopkinton Flood Project near the village of West Hopkinton.

The state stocks the Contoocook River with brook trout, browns, and rainbows. Near the impoundments and in downstream sections there is good smallmouth bass fishing. The most consistent trout fishing is in the trophy section in West Henniker. There is a stretch that starts about one-half mile upstream from the mill dam in West Henniker and runs upstream about a mile that is restricted to flyfishing or the use of artificial, single-hooked lures only. Brook trout need to be 12 inches in length, and the daily limit is 2 fish. This section and the access areas along Western Avenue are well marked. Other fishing and canoe access areas are clearly marked along the highways that parallel the river.

Other South Central New Hampshire Rivers and Small Streams

Bear Brook is a small brook trout stream located in Bear Brook State Park north of the city of Manchester. Camping and several hiking trails are convenient to the brook and the several ponds in the park.

Suncook River flows into the Merrimack River downstream of the Garvins Falls Dam south of the city of Concord. Route 106 follows the river and provides fishing and canoe access areas. The Suncook is stocked with brook trout, rainbows, and browns.

Blackwater River is part of a large watershed northwest of Concord. It passes through the Blackwater Dam Project south of the village of Andover and eventually joins the Contoocook River. There are regular stockings of brown trout and rainbows. Access to Blackwater River is from Routes 4 and 27.

The state lists several brook trout streams in Merrimack County: **Academy Brook** in the town of Loudon; **Burnham, Hackett, Pickard,** and **Rum Brooks** in the town of Canterbury; and **Punch Brook** in Salisbury, to name a few. A full listing of these smaller waters can be found in the pamphlet, *Fishing Waters of New Hampshire,* available from the New Hampshire Fish and Game Department in Concord.

In Hillsborough County, the **Piscataquog River** and its tributaries, the **Middle Branch** and **South Branch**, are part of a large watershed that drains the area west of Manchester. The main stem of the river starts in Perkins Pond Marsh west of Goffstown. It flows through the Lake Horace Reservoir, Everett Lake in Clough State Park, and Glen Lake before entering the Merrimack. River Road, off Route 114, follows the river and provides access. The South and Middle Branches wind through the town forests in the area that surrounds New Boston on Route 13. The New Hampshire Fish and Game Department provides regular stockings of brown trout, rainbows, and brookies in these streams.

There are several trout streams in the area surrounding the villages of Milford, Wilton, and Amherst. The **Souhegan River** follows Route 31 and 101A and is stocked with brookies, rainbows, and browns. **Spaulding Brook** holds brook trout and is accessible from Route 13 south of Milford. **Stony Brook** parallels Route 31 west of the village of Wilton. The state stocks this tributary of the Souhegan with rainbows and brook trout. **Blood Brook** follows Route 101 and enters the Souhegan south of Wilton. It holds brookies, browns, and rainbows.

South Central New Hampshire Stillwaters

Beaver Lake, in the town of Derry, covers 119 acres and is stocked with rainbows, browns, and brookies, and also holds warmwater species. A boat access is conveniently located off Route 102 north of Derry village.

Massabesic Lake, a large stillwater located east of the city of Manchester, supports a small population of brown trout. Its major attraction, though, is a smallmouth bass fishery. There are many convenient access areas located around the lake.

Flyfishing-Only Ponds

The south central region of New Hampshire offers two flyfishing-only ponds:

Stirrup Iron Pond is located in the town of Salisbury in Merrimack County. It is a 2-acre pond stocked with brook trout averaging 9 to 10 inches in length. Access is off Route 4 and 126 north of Salisbury. The road to the pond is unimproved and requires a 4-wheel drive vehicle.

Willard Pond is Hillsborough County's single flyfishing-only pond. It is reached from Route 123 north of Hancock on Willard Pond Road. There is a boat launch at the southern end of the pond. The state stocks Willard with brook trout, brown trout, rainbows, and tiger trout, a brookie-brown trout hybrid.

SOUTH CENTRAL NEW HAMPSHIRE HUB CITY
Manchester
Elevation–250 • Population–100,668

ACCOMMODATIONS

Center of New Hampshire Holiday Inn, 700 Elm Street / 603-625-1000 / Two restaurants, pool, fitness center, and airport transportation / $$$$$

Comfort Inn, 298 Queen City Avenue / 603-668-2600 / 104 rooms with a pool, fitness center, and airport transportation / $$

Econolodge, 75 West Hancock Street / 603-624-0111 / 110 rooms located along the Merrimack River in Manchester's Mill District / $$

RESTAURANTS

Blake's Family Restaurants, 353 South Main Street / 603-627-1110 / Open daily, serves breakfast

DB's Steakhouse, 20 Old Granite Street / 603-666-0000 / Reservations accepted

Richard's Bistro, 36 Lowell Street / 603-644-1180 / Reservations accepted

FLY SHOPS AND SPORTING GOODS

American Angling Supplies, 23 Main Street (Salem 03079) / 603-893-3333 / Fly tying materials, gear, and guide services

Golden Demon Fly Shop, 13 School Street (Hudson 03051) / 603-598-6518 (call for appointment) / Contact Jim Riccardi and Stan Fudala / Fly tying materials, custom-built rods, and flies tied to order / Catalog available

Hunter's Angling Supplies, Central Square (New Boston) / 800-331-8558 or 603-487-3388 / Offers a wide range of fly tying materials / Catalog available

Steve's Sportsmen's Den & Tackle Shop, 1562 Hooksett Road (Hooksett 03106) / 603-485-5085 / Contact Steve and Karen Courchesne / They offer fly tying materials, plus Atlantic salmon patterns and permits / The green Merrimack special, an Atlantic salmon pattern available at their fly shop, proved to be the hot fly during the mid- to late spring of 1997

Zyla's, Route 3 (Merrimack) / Open 7 days a week 9AM–9PM, except Sunday 9AM–5PM

Benson's Ski and Sport, 6 Martin Street (Derry 03038) / 603-432-2531

L.L. Bean Factory Outlet, 258 DW Hwy, Webster Square Mall (Nashua 03060) / 800-820-6846; 603-888-3264

L.L. Bean Factory Outlet, 55 Fort Eddie Road (Concord 03301) / 800-820-6846

Morse Sporting Goods, 85 Contoocook Falls Road (Hillsborough 03244) / 603-464-3444

AUTO RENTAL
Alamo Rent-A-Car / 603-641-1286
Avis / 603-624-4000
Budget Rent-A-Car / 603-668-3166

HOSPITAL
Optima Health-Elliot Hospital / 603-669-5300

AIRPORT
Manchester Airport, One Airport Road / 603-624-6556 /
www.flymanchester.com

FOR MORE INFORMATION
Greater Manchester Chamber of Commerce
889 Elm Street
Manchester, NH 03101-2000
603-666-6600
Website: www.Manchester-Chamber.org

Southwestern New Hampshire

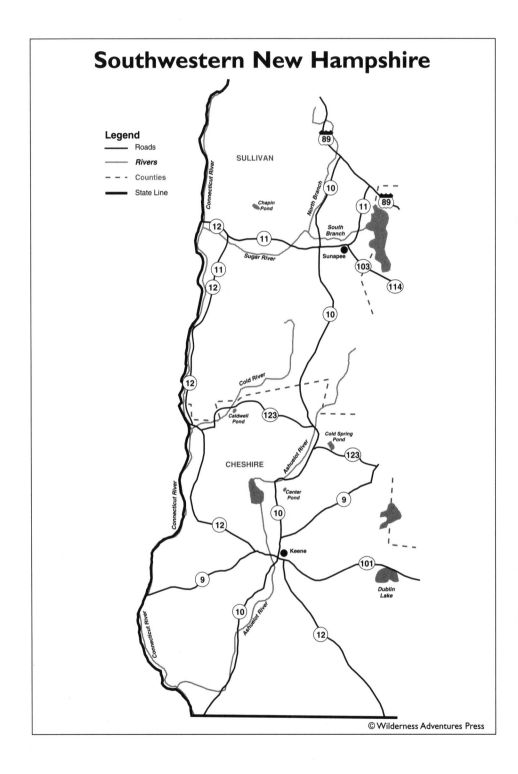

Legend
— Roads
— *Rivers*
--- Counties
— State Line

SULLIVAN

Connecticut River

North Branch

89

10

11

89

Chapin
Pond

12

11

South
Branch

Sugar River

Sunapee

103

11

12

114

10

Cold River

12

Caldwell
Pond

123

Cold Spring
Pond

CHESHIRE

Ashuelot River

123

Center
Pond

9

Connecticut River

12

10

Keene

101

9

Dublin
Lake

Connecticut River

10

Ashuelot River

12

© Wilderness Adventures Press

SOUTHWESTERN NEW HAMPSHIRE

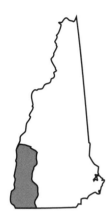

The New Hampshire Fish and Wildlife Department's southwestern trout fisheries include a long list of rivers and small streams as well as several stillwaters and one flyfishing-only pond. This region covers Cheshire and Sullivan Counties, an area rich in wildlife. Hunters should take advantage of this by scheduling some time in May, when there is the opportunity to hunt wild turkeys in the morning and flyfish for trout in the afternoon.

Steve Hickoff makes a fly selection on a southern New Hampshire river. (Photo by Elizabeth Edwards)

Ashuelot River

The Ashuelot River flows through both Cheshire and Sullivan Counties. Its source is Ashuelot Pond, a warmwater pond west of the village of Washington. It runs south, parallel to Routes 10 and 12A, and through the city of Keene. Near the village of Winchester, the river swings west along Route 119 and joins the Connecticut River near the village of Hinsdale.

The river is heavily stocked with brook trout, rainbows, and browns. Access is good at marked and unmarked roadside pull-off areas.

The **South Branch Ashuelot River** begins near the village of Troy and enters the main stem south of Keene near the village of Swanzey. There is a flyfishing-only section on the South Branch between the Iron Bridge in the village of East Swanzey and the dam at Farrar Pond in Troy. There is a 2-fish daily limit for brook trout.

Cold River

Cold River begins north of the village of Acworth in Sullivan County. The river follows Routes 123A and 123 through the villages of Alstead and Drewville and joins the Connecticut River in the village of Cold River in Cheshire County. The state of New Hampshire Fish and Game Department stocks the Cold River with brook trout, browns, and rainbows. In addition to the convenient access areas at highway pulloffs, there is a public canoe access on Route 123A near the village of South Acworth.

Other Southwestern New Hampshire Rivers and Small Streams

Otter Brook runs along Route 9 east of the city of Keene in Cheshire County. It is stocked with brookies and rainbows. To the west is **Partridge Brook** near Spofford Lake, which is stocked with brook and brown trout. Access is available from Westmoreland Road off Route 9A near the village of Spofford.

Sugar River flows west along Routes 11 and 103 near the city of Claremont in Sullivan County. It is heavily stocked with brown trout, rainbows, and brook trout. There is good roadside access. The section of river near the village of Kellyville, between the Kellyville Bridge and the Oak Street Bridge, is flyfishing only with a daily limit of 2 brook trout. This section is well marked.

The **North Branch** and **South Branch of the Sugar** hold rainbows, brown trout, and brookies as well. The South Branch is accessible from Route 10 south of the village of Newport. The North Branch follows Route 10 from the village of Grantham north of Newport.

Ashuelot River

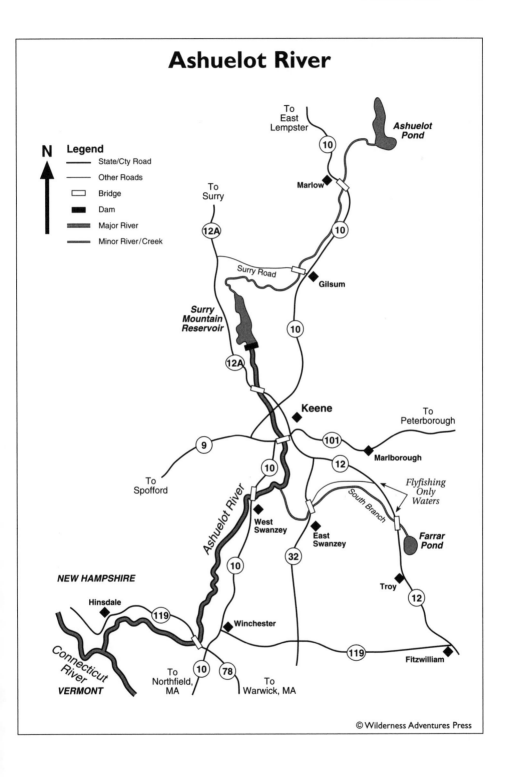

© Wilderness Adventures Press

Southwestern New Hampshire Stillwaters

Chapin Pond is a flyfishing-only pond located about 8 miles northwest of the village of Newport in Sullivan County. This remote, 12-acre pond is accessible by 4-wheel drive vehicles from an unimproved road found near the intersection of Cat Hole Road and Cornish Turnpike. The state stocks Chapin Pond with brook trout.

Caldwell Pond is a brook trout pond located in the town of Alstead. In 1996, the state stocked 890 brook trout in this 28-acre pond.

Center Pond holds brook trout and rainbows located in the town of Sullivan. Expect 9- to 10-inch brookies in this 20-acre stillwater.

Cold Spring Pond offers angling for brook trout and rainbows. Located within the town of Stoddard, this 29-acre pond was stocked with 900 brook trout in 1996.

Dublin Lake is a 239-acre trout pond located in the village of Dublin. The lake was stocked with 3,620 brook trout in 1996.

SOUTHWESTERN NEW HAMPSHIRE HUB CITY

Keene

Elevation–480 • Population–22,430

ACCOMMODATIONS

Days Inn, 175 Key Road / 603-352-7616 / Jacuzzi / Fitness Room / $$$$–$$$$$

Best Western, Winchester Street / 603-357-3038 / $$$$

RESTAURANTS

Copperfield's Steakhouse & Tavern, 401 Winchester Street / 603-357-3038 / Open 7 days a week for breakfast, lunch, and dinner

Millyard Steakhouse, Colony Mill Market Place / 603-352-3600

176 Main, at 176 Maine Street / 603-357-3100

FLY SHOPS AND SPORTING GOODS

Summers Backcountry Outfitters, West Street / 603-357-5107 / Local stream and stillwater fishing conditions and area information / Flyfishing school / Contact John Summers

MEDICAL

Cheshire Medical Center, 508 Court / 603-355-2813

FOR MORE INFORMATION

Keene Regional Chamber of Commerce
48 Central Square
Keene, NH 03431
603-352-1303

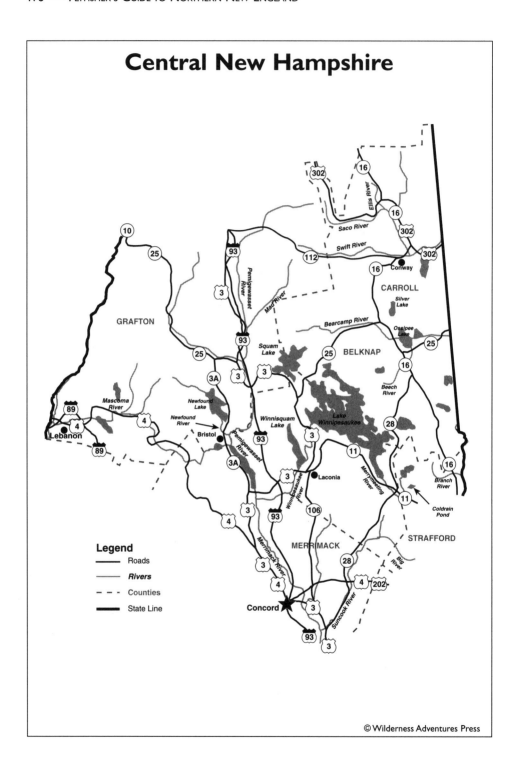

Central New Hampshire

Legend

— Roads

〰 *Rivers*

- - - Counties

— State Line

© Wilderness Adventures Press

CENTRAL NEW HAMPSHIRE

The central New Hampshire region includes Grafton, Belknap, and Carroll Counties, plus the White Mountain National Forest. Flyfishers have the opportunity to cast for native brook trout and, if you're as fortunate as Granite State angler Lance King, large-sized holdover rainbows.

Joe Conklin's Ultimate Flybox

Winter flyfishing enthusiast Joe Conklin utilizes the following patterns on Bristol's Newfound River and on the Presumpscot River in Maine's Sebago Lake Region.

"In winter, I flyfish nymphs 98 percent of the time, which includes sparsely-tied beadhead pheasant tails (#14–18). I also like to use weighted black and olive woolly buggers (#4–8), micro-egg patterns, and small San Juan worms (olive, white, burgundy)," says Conklin.

Conklin's largest Newfound River rainbows and salmon have weighed 5 pounds.

CENTRAL NEW HAMPSHIRE MAJOR HATCHES

Insect/Bait	J	F	M	A	M	J	J	A	S	O	N	D	Patterns
Minnows and Leeches	■	■	■	■					■	■			Woolly Buggers and Muddlers #4-10; Smelt Imitations #4-10
Caddis					■	■	■	■					Tan Elk Hair Caddis #14-18; Soft Hackles and Emergers #14-18; Hare's Ear Nymph and Beadhead Pupae #14-18
Blue-winged Olives					■				■				Parachute Adams #14-20; Thorax Blue-winged Olives #14-18; Pheasant Tail Nymphs #14-20
Hendricksons					■								Dark Hendrickson or Red Quill #12-14; Hendrickson Nymph #12-14; Rusty Spinner #14
Light Cahill						■							Cahill Dun or Parachute #16
Hexagenia						■							Hex Nymph, Brown #4-6; Parachute Hex #8
Sulphurs						■							Sulphur Duns and Hare's Ear Nymphs #16-18
Stoneflies					■	■							Black Stonefly Nymph #2-6; Yellow Stonefly Nymph #8-10; Yellow Sally #14
Tiny Mayflies *Tricorythodes stygiatus*							■	■					Trico Spinner #18-24
Terrestrials							■	■	■				Hoppers #6-12; Ants #14-18
Midges							■	■	■				Griffith's Gnat #18

CENTRAL NEW HAMPSHIRE RIVERS
Upper Pemigewasset River

On September 16, 1996, Lance King of Franklin landed what proved to be a New Hampshire state record, a rainbow trout weighing 15 pounds, 7.2 ounces, while fly-fishing in the Upper Pemigewasset River in the town of Bristol. His fly was a tandem Mickey Finn.

"The record fish was absolutely beautiful," says state fisheries biologist Don Miller, a flyfisher as well. "It had a big head, a bright pink stripe, and a caudal fin that was about 9 inches wide; easily one of the nicest rainbows I've ever seen." King's rainbow, according to Miller, measured 35½ inches long, with an 18¼-inch girth.

Word has it this record fish was one of a pair of late summer spawning rainbows spotted by King that day, and that the tandem streamer was the largest pattern he could find in his fly box.

The Upper Pemigewasset is a heavily stocked river, stretching 63 miles from its upper reaches in Franconia Notch south to Franklin, where it merges with the Merrimack River in the south central part of the state. Access is convenient along Interstate 93, the major connector for tourists traveling from southern New England to the White Mountains. The stretch between Lincoln and Plymouth that runs parallel to U.S. 3 and Interstate 93, is a consistent springtime trout fishery. It is heavily stocked with brook trout and rainbows. Angling pressure is high, particularly on weekends.

The Pemigewasset between Bristol and Franklin, before it joins the Merrimack, does not receive as much angling pressure. The river is accessible from Route 3A.

Several years ago, the Pemigewasset was the victim of industrial pollutants. Higher water quality standards and controls have now returned the river to a productive sport fishery. Stocking efforts by New Hampshire Fish and Game have been aggressive. Thousands of fish are stocked annually, and there are good numbers of rainbows that hold over from year to year.

According to biologist Miller, hatchery rainbows are on "a delayed photo-period program, which fools the fish." As a result, these rainbows spawn in the fall, or even in late summer. Miller adds that stocked rainbows will revert back to spring spawning behavior in most cases.

Traditional bright orange and red steelhead patterns, such as the Skyomish sunrise (#2–8), polar shrimp (#2–8), and single egg fly (#2–10) are effective. Carry a large, tandem-hooked Mickey Finn for luck.

Upper Pemigewasset River

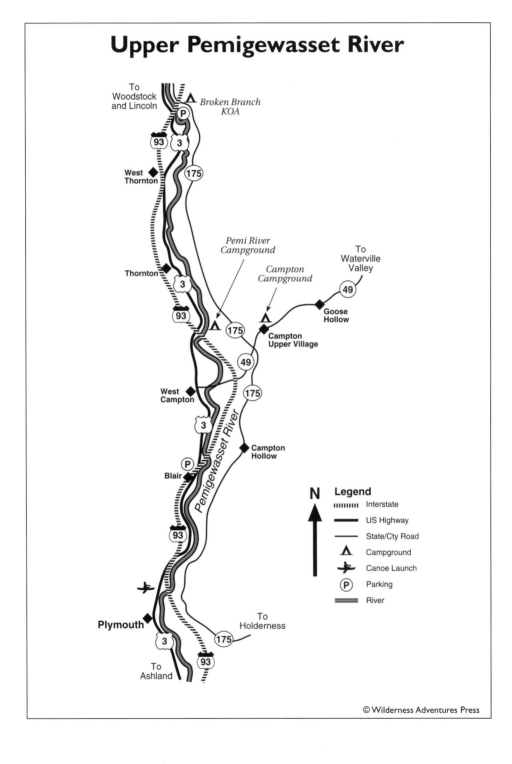

To
Woodstock
and Lincoln

Broken Branch
KOA

P

93 3

West
Thornton

175

Pemi River
Campground

Campton
Campground

To
Waterville
Valley

49

Thornton

3

93

Goose
Hollow

175

Campton
Upper Village

49

West
Campton

175

3

Campton
Hollow

P

Blair

Pemigewasset River

N

Legend

ıııııııı Interstate

—— US Highway

—— State/Cty Road

▲ Campground

Canoe Launch

Ⓟ Parking

River

93

Plymouth

3 175

To
Holderness

93

To
Ashland

© Wilderness Adventures Press

Upper Pemigewasset River

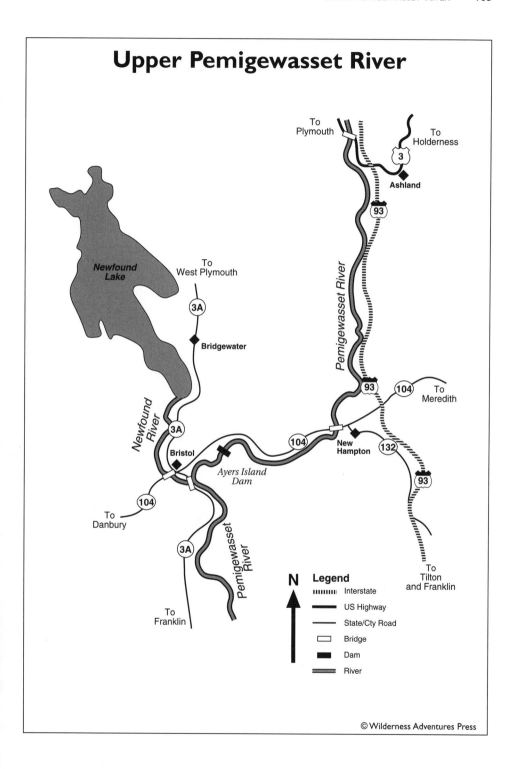

Newfound River

January 1, the traditional Granite State trout opener, finds flyfishers on the fly-fishing-only section of the Newfound River that extends from the New Hampshire Water Resources Dam at Newfound Lake downstream to the International Packing Company Dam. Access is gained at Crescent Street in the village of Bristol.

Fishing during the low-light edges of the day is best for catching rainbows that run up to 5 pounds. Landlocks will take a fly as well. Salmon must be carefully released prior to April 1, which is the opening of salmon season.

"Salmon are in the river all winter, though these fish can't be legally targeted," says biologist Miller, "but we (New Hampshire Fish and Game) keep the river open to angling since trout are in season at this time. It's a great time of the year to be fishing." Miller indicates that lakers from 3 to 4 pounds will drop down to the river from Newfound Lake.

Trout and salmon can reach 5 pounds. In 1996, New Hampshire Fish and Game stocked 3,078 brook trout and 570 rainbows, including 70 in the 3-year-old class.

Miller says he isn't that particular about the nymphs he casts to these Newfound River fish, as long as they are big stoneflies. "It's a pretty stretch of water," he enthuses, "and the dam, halfway downstream, creates a large pool, some 3 to 4 acres of impoundment water that's great for flyfishing."

According to Newfound River regulations, the area between West Shore Road and the New Hampshire Water Resources Dam is open to fishing from May 1 to September 30.

As mentioned, the river is flyfishing only from the Water Resources Dam at Newfound Lake to the International Packing Company Dam, adjacent to Crescent Street in Bristol. The daily limit for brook trout is 2 fish. New Hampshire's open-water season for trout runs from January 1 to October 15.

Nearby Newfound Lake holds angling opportunities as well. "Newfound is one of our older lakes, with crystal-clear water that stays that way throughout the season," says fisheries biologist Miller. New Hampshire Fish and Game stocks rainbows in Newfound Lake in the spring when the water temperatures reach 44 degrees. In addition to landlocked salmon and rainbow stockings, 50 three-year-old brook trout were released in 1996.

Swift River

During the Ice Age, glaciers plowed through the White Mountains of central New Hampshire, leaving behind a landscape filled with rivers, ponds, and small mountain streams. The Swift River is one of these beautiful glacial creations. It flows along the Kancamagus Highway, Route 112, off Kancamagus Mountain. From there, the river twists and turns east and joins the Saco near the village of Conway.

Several small tributaries feed the 23-mile Swift River, including the Sabbaday, Downes, and Oliverian. The "gin-clear" plunge pools and chatty riffles of these tiny streams are full of small, wild trout.

The Swift River trout fishery is easily accessible from the Kancamagus Highway. (Photo by Steve Hickoff)

Native brookie populations are found downstream in the main stem of the Swift, as well. The Swift also receives annual stockings of hatchery fish. River sections in the towns of Albany, Conway, Livermore, and Tamworth are stocked with brook trout and rainbows. A total of 6,710 fish were stocked here in 1996.

Even though the Swift is heavily stocked, angler pressure is moderate. There is plenty of room for everyone in this pleasant mountain setting, and anglers will find plenty of places to park along the Kancamagus Highway.

Early-season flyfishers may find winter runoff and fast-rising water levels that make angling difficult. Conditions improve by May, and good fishing lasts into summer.

Swift River water levels and water temperatures dictate annual trout-stocking schedules. The New Hampshire Fish and Game stocking program begins when water temperature is around 45 degrees. Water flows must be at a reasonable level for stocking to be successful. White Mountain streams such as the Swift experience tremendous winter runoffs. As a result, June is usually the best month to fish the Swift. By summer, good flyfishing is still available on the main river and in the tributaries.

Swift River

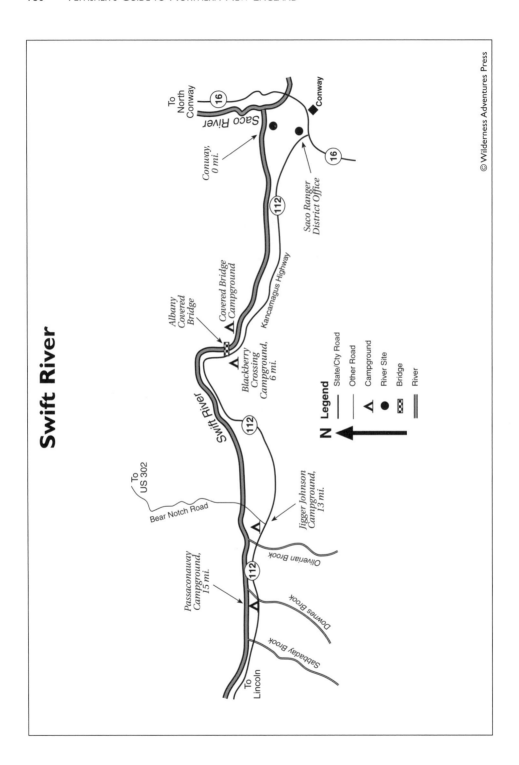

To
North
Conway

16

Conway

Saco River

Conway,
0 mi.

16

112

Saco Ranger
District Office

Albany
Covered
Bridge

Covered Bridge
Campground

Kancamagus Highway

Blackberry
Crossing
Campground,
6 mi.

Swift River

112

To
US 302

Bear Notch Road

Jigger Johnson
Campground,
13 mi.

Oliverian Brook

Passaconaway
Campground,
15 mi.

112

Downes Brook

Sabbaday Brook

To
Lincoln

N

Legend

	State/Cty Road
	Other Road
▲	Campground
●	River Site
▨	Bridge
	River

The small feeder streams that range from foot-deep trickles to deeper plunge pools, run cold and clear, and offer good angling throughout the season. Brook trout in these tributaries average 6 inches. Though small in size, these native brookies are special fish.

Since hatchery stocking numbers are high on the main river, all fly-caught native trout should be released. Use barbless hooks. Keep a main river hatchery trout or two if you like.

After liberally dousing yourself with commercial bug repellent or firing up a wonderfully foul-smelling cigar, study the stream for a moment. In June, you'll notice the ever-present Swift River mosquito. There will also be a mix of mayfly hatches, from light Cahills to March browns to blue-winged olives. The rule that Hendricksons always arrive in the North Country by mid-May is only true for some northern New England rivers. Insect hatches on the Swift can run later than expected. Flyfishing is best in June. Standard hatches are only sporadic at best.

On the other hand, Swift River tributaries are consistent throughout the season. Approach plunge pools from a downstream crouching position. Forget fancy fly-casting-clinic techniques. These wild trout are skittish enough without repeated false casts.

Carry a range of mosquito dries, sizes 12 to 20. Streamside swarms of these blood-suckers arrive in force come spring. Swift River trout sip on the natural adult or its tumbling larva. Cast upstream into slower, placid pocketwater in streamside eddies or boulder-protected pools for the best results.

Try a weighted gold-ribbed hare's ear nymph (#8–18) in the faster, more turbulent water. You should also include traditional mayfly patterns and cranefly skaters.

Swift River is full of boulder rapids, tabletop-smooth runs, steady riffles, pocketwater, and plunge pools. Study the flows and read the water. Dry flies, delicately presented on the flatwater sections behind boulders, often catch trout during mayfly and caddis hatches. Mosquito patterns almost always catch fish in June, and it's always a good idea to carry a range of adult mosquito sizes. Nymphs work in the steady riffles.

Swift's trout are skittish but not necessarily selective. Crawl on your knees to the edge of the stream and roll cast a barbless dry fly at the base of a bubbling gurgle. Let your pattern drift for a precious second. A darting wild trout may streak out for your buggy offering. This will rattle your heart, though the pretty little fish only fits in the palm of your hand.

The Swift River's season runs from January 1 to October 15, though the best fly-fishing begins in early June. New Hampshire Fish and Game's biologist, Bob Fawcett, reports that, "Winter anchor ice and the turbulent action around rocks make it difficult for hatchery trout to survive and create natural stocks." Wild fish do thrive in the tributaries, however, and a limited number will make it to the main river.

The river is 15 miles long from Passaconaway Campground to Conway. The section between Livermore and Conway rarely settles down before Memorial Day weekend. Most years you can expect whitewater rapids before the holiday. Although trout season opens January 1, flyfishing the river and its tributaries is often impossible until spring flows diminish. And then there are the mosquitoes. Factor in blackflies, and you can count on buggy outings, especially in spring.

Take Route 16 north to Conway, then turn left on Route 112, the Kancamagus Highway. Staff at the Saco Ranger District Office located on the right after the turn, can fill you in on current river conditions. Phone them at 603-447-5448.

Interstate 93 north to Lincoln will put you on this mountainous access highway as well. Route 112 runs right through Lincoln's downtown area, then eastward along the Swift River toward the village of Conway.

Recreation passports are required for parking along the Kancamagus Highway and for any other vehicles left unattended in the White Mountain National Forest. For information, write the WMNF Supervisor's Office, attention Fee Program, 719 Main Street, Laconia, NH 03246, or contact the office by phone at 603-528-8721, Monday through Friday, from 8 am to 4:30 pm.

Passports are available through the mail. A seven-day pass is $5, and a year-round pass is $20. Make your check or money order payable to USDA Forest Service. You'll need to include your name, address, phone number, and up to two license plate numbers.

The Parking Fee Program is in place through 1999. Fees are used to maintain existing trails and WMNF facilities.

Other Central New Hampshire Rivers and Streams

The **Mascoma River** runs southwest from Cummings and Reservoir Ponds, north of the village of Canaan in the Mascoma River Wildlife Management Area. From Canaan, the river follows Route 4 through Mascoma Lake and joins the Connecticut River near the village of West Lebanon. The outflow of the dam at Mascoma Lake provides good trout habitat and excellent fishing opportunities for larger-sized fish.

Early in the season, the flow is deep and fast but is easily waded. Caddis and stonefly patterns will work well. In the summer, water levels drop and fish gather in the deeper pools. Then, fishing with small emerger patterns and midges and a lot of patience are the only formula.

From the Route 4 bridge, downstream to the Packard Hill covered bridge, the Mascoma is flyfishing only. The daily limit in this regulated section is 2 brook trout. There is an unpaved road that parallels the river and provides parking and convenient access. In addition to brook trout, the state stocks the Mascoma with rainbows and browns.

The upper stretch of the Mascoma, above Canaan, offers fine fishing opportunities as well. The trout are smaller in size, but you have a chance to fish over more wild fish. There is a dirt road that parallels the river and provides parking and easy access.

Mad River is the main stem of the Waterville Valley watershed. It flows south from the village of Waterville Valley, along Route 49, to the village of Campton, where it joins the Pemigewasset River. There are several pulloffs and parking areas along the highway, providing easy access. The Mad holds brook trout and rainbows.

Mascoma River

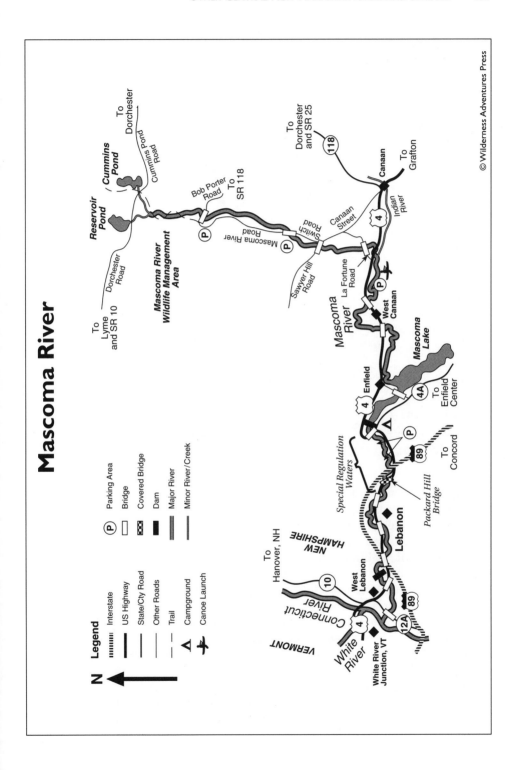

Legend

- Interstate
- US Highway
- State/Cty Road
- Other Roads
- Trail
- Campground
- Canoe Launch
- (P) Parking Area
- Bridge
- Covered Bridge
- Dam
- Major River
- Minor River/Creek

*By summer, northern
New England streams
can be waded wet.
(Photo by Steve Hickoff)*

Gale River is a fast-flowing, mountain brook trout stream that feeds the Ammonoosuc near the village of Franconia. Route 18 follows the river and access is from the main highway and secondary roads near the river. In addition to brook trout, the state regularly stocks the stream with browns.

Beaver Brook, **Coffin Brook**, **Hurd Brook**, **Post Office Brook**, and **Watson Brook** are small brook trout streams in the town of Alton.

Merrymeeting River flows into Lake Winnipesaukee at Alton Bay just north of the village of Alton. The section of river between the lower dam in Alton and the Route 11 bridge at Alton Bay is flyfishing only throughout the season. From October 1 to October 31, all fish must be released, and fishing is restricted to the use of barbless hooks. The state stocks the Merrymeeting with brook trout, browns, rainbow trout, and landlocked salmon. Access is from Route 11.

Big River is a tributary of the Suncook River and flows between the villages of Strafford and Barnstead. The state stocks Big River with brook trout. The Suncook flows south from Barnstead along Route 28 through the village of Pittsfield and joins

Mad River

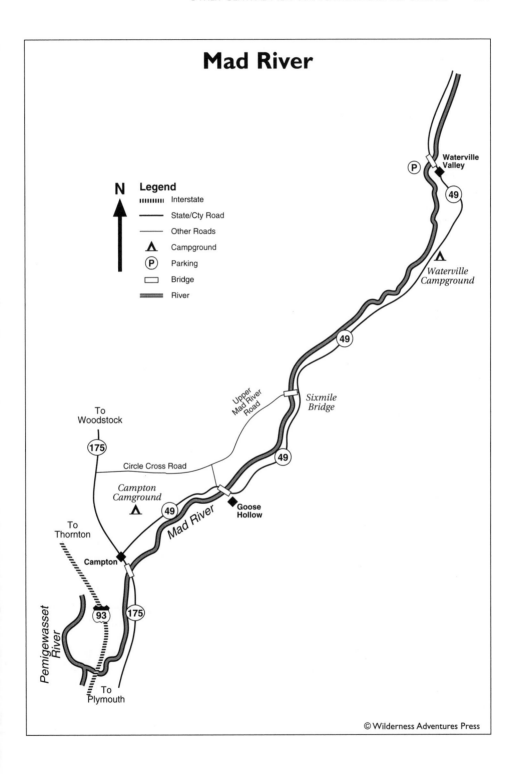

N

Legend

ⅢⅢⅢ	Interstate
▬▬▬	State/Cty Road
───	Other Roads
▲	Campground
Ⓟ	Parking
▭	Bridge
▰▰▰	River

Waterville Valley

Ⓟ

49

▲ Waterville Campground

49

Upper Mad River Road

Sixmile Bridge

To Woodstock

175

Circle Cross Road

49

Campton Camground
▲

49

◆ Goose Hollow

To Thornton

Campton

Mad River

93 175

Pemigewasset River

To Plymouth

© Wilderness Adventures Press

the Merrimack River near the village of Suncook. This river is heavily stocked with brook trout, rainbows, and brown trout.

Nighthawk Hollow Brook is a small brook trout stream that parallels Route 140 near the village of Gilmanton south of Laconia.

Gunstock Brook flows into Lake Winnipesaukee at Sanders Bay east of Laconia off Route 11. The state stocks this brook with rainbows and brookies.

Winnipesaukee River runs parallel to Routes 3 and 11 and joins the Merrimack River below the Franklin Falls Dam in the village of Franklin. The state regularly stocks this stream with brown trout, rainbows, and brookies.

Salmon Brook lies north of Franklin, near Route 127 and Exit 22 of Interstate 93. The state stocks this brook with rainbows and brook trout.

Ellis River flows from the heights of Mount Washington along Route 16 through the village of Jackson. It joins the Saco River near the village of Glen. There is a flyfishing-only section on the Ellis between the covered bridge in Jackson and the iron bridge in Glen. This section is well marked, and there is good access to the river.

The New Hampshire Fish and Game Department regularly stocks the Ellis River. The stretch of river above Jackson received 1,150 brook trout and 200 rainbows in 1996. The section downstream was stocked with 1,150 brookies as well as with 100 rainbows. Although they are raised in concrete pools, Ellis River trout quickly adapt and take on the beauty of their new surroundings.

Saco River holds brookies, rainbows, and browns and is located in the towns of Bartlett and Conway. If you're going to flyfish three rivers in Carroll County, start with the Swift along Route 112, then move over to the Saco, and then wet a line in the Ellis.

The Saco River was stocked with 1,650 brook trout, 1,600 browns, and 400 rainbows in 1996. The Conway section was stocked with 3,126 brookies, 2,200 browns, and 710 rainbows. Wild or not, big trout numbers keep flyfishers happy.

The Saco, like the Swift and Ellis, is a pretty river set in pleasant surroundings. There is ample room on the river for casting a line. A flyfishing-only section has been established from the Lucy Brook sign downstream to the confluence of Artist Falls Brook. A 2-trout limit is in place, though anglers rarely keep fish. There are plenty of put-and-take stockers elsewhere on the river.

From mid-June through the Fourth of July, there is usually a caddis hatch. This is best matched with a range of larva, pupa, wet and dry patterns. Early summer caddis hatches were spotty in some regions of the northeast in 1997. I always carry a range of mosquito adult sizes when flyfishing both the Saco and the Ellis.

At Crawford Notch State Park, angling by adults is prohibited from the dam at the Willey House Historical Site upstream to a point where the Saco River enters Willey Pond. This section is open to children under the age of 12.

Bearcamp River is stocked with brook trout, rainbows, and browns. It is located in the towns of West Ossipee, Sandwich, and Tamworth. Expect brookies and rainbows in the Ossipee river section, brook trout in the Sandwich area, and both brown and brook trout in Tamworth. Most fish run in the 9- to 11-inch range.

There is another, much smaller fishery known as **Swift River** (a tributary of the Bearcamp River) that flows in the Tamworth region. This river is south of the Kanca-

Flyfishers gravitate to the Ellis River and other Carroll County waters.
(Photo by Elizabeth Edwards)

magus Highway and is accessible from Route 113A in the town of Tamworth just southwest of Conway. Expect 9- to14-inch brookies in the 3-mile flyfishing-only stretch between the Route 113A bridge and the Route 113 bridge. The river was stocked with 485 hatchery trout in 1996.

Beech River flows through the town of Ossipee. Beech was stocked with 295 hatchery brook trout in 1996.

Branch River holds brook trout and flows through the towns of Milton and Wakefield. This river has plenty of stocked brookies. According to recent stocking reports, 1,210 fish were released in the Milton section, and 315 were stocked in the Wakefield section.

Central New Hampshire Stillwaters
Lake Winnipesaukee

Sheets of ice floated nearby as a buddy and I paddled the canoe around Lake Winnipesaukee's Alton Bay. "Did we need help or were we just crazy?" onlookers may have wondered.

For many Granite State flyfishers, open water on Lake Winnipesaukee on the first of April signals the start of the New Hampshire landlocked salmon fishing season. Alton Bay on the big lake gets some serious attention from die-hards. An open-water section the size of a football field usually appears by the April opener. At least we

Lake Winnipesaukee

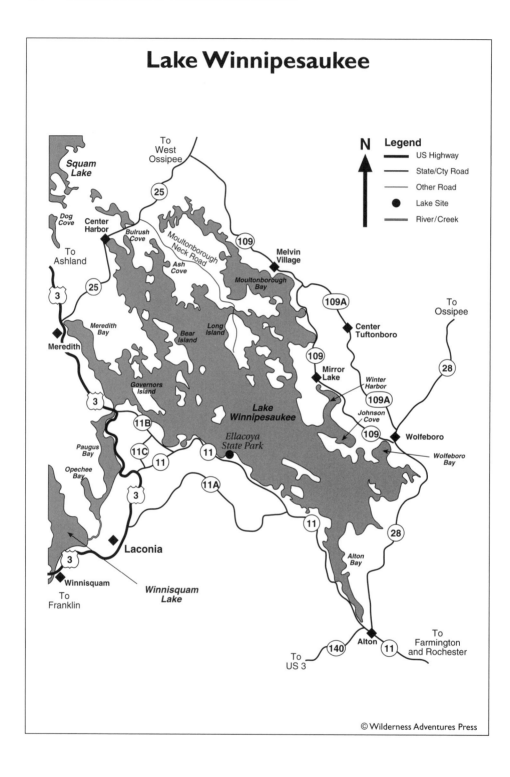

N

Legend
— US Highway
— State/Cty Road
— Other Road
● Lake Site
═ River/Creek

Squam Lake

To West Ossipee

25

Dog Cove

Center Harbor

Bulrush Cove

Moultonborough Neck Road

Ash Cove

109

Melvin Village

To Ashland

25

3

Moultonborough Bay

109A

To Ossipee

Meredith Bay

Bear Island

Long Island

Center Tuftonboro

Meredith

109

28

Governors Island

Mirror Lake

Winter Harbor

3

109A

Lake Winnipesaukee

Johnson Cove

11B

Ellacoya State Park

109

Wolfeboro

Paugus Bay

11C

11

Wolfeboro Bay

Opechee Bay

11

3

11A

11

28

11

Laconia

Alton Bay

3

Winnisquam

To Franklin

Winnisquam Lake

To Farmington and Rochester

140

Alton

11

To US 3

© Wilderness Adventures Press

Lake Winnipesaukee's Alton Bay

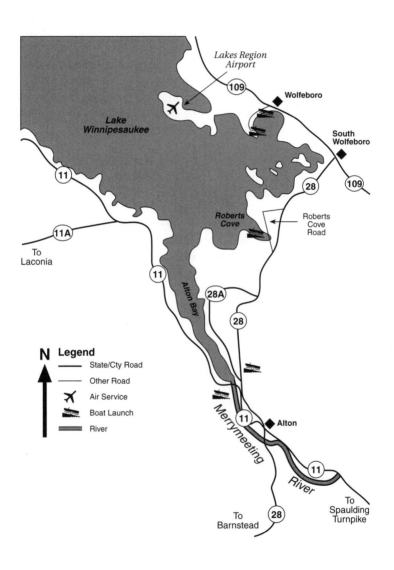

Lakes Region Airport

109

Wolfeboro

Lake Winnipesaukee

South Wolfeboro

11

109

11A

28

To Laconia

Roberts Cove

Roberts Cove Road

11

Alton Bay

28A

28

N **Legend**
— State/Cty Road
— Other Road
✈ Air Service
Boat Launch
River

Merrymeeting

11

Alton

11

River

To Spaulding Turnpike

To Barnstead

28

hope it does. Some years the ice lingers and fishing doesn't get started until a week or two later.

Lake Winnipesaukee covers 44,586 acres and has a maximum depth of 168 feet. Ice-out arrives in late April, though open water can be found in Alton Bay and near the docks and bridges around the lake by opening day. Hot spots include Weir's Beach, Long Island, and the shore near the town of Meredith. Early spring conditions can be blustery for boat anglers and canoeists trolling streamer flies. A slight chop on the water's surface, however, is often good.

As the ice leaves, smelt move into the bay and gather in the Merrymeeting River, where they eventually spawn. Salmon follow these staging smelt. Flyfishers, with vests stuffed full of smelt-imitating patterns, follow the salmon, and it's not just land-locks that get our attention—rainbows in Lake Winnipesaukee run large, and 4-pounders are not uncommon during the ice-out season.

In the summer, trout and salmon move out of the rocky shallows toward deeper water. Angling for smallmouth bass and other warmwater game fish offers good warm weather opportunities. Recreational boat traffic is heavy from Memorial Day through Labor Day. Flyfish for trout and salmon from early April through the month of May.

Alton Bay can be chilly on April Fool's Day while slowly trolling tandem streamers for salmon and rainbows. Suddenly, the sky-blue ceiling above can close up darkly and start snowing. The sudden change in the weather is typical for the Granite State, where there are two seasons—winter and the Fourth of July.

One opening day as we paddled around the bay trying to keep warm if nothing else, a half dozen boats crowded in around us. The smell of cigar smoke carried across the cold, open water. All of a sudden, a guy leisurely drifting a streamer behind his boat got a strike. His fly rod bent into a question mark that asked, "Is this a salmon, rainbow, or laker?"

Then the fish jumped a good 2 feet above the surface. It was a wild-eyed salmon. The boat began drifting toward the docks as the angler played the fish. To avoid collision, some anglers on shore pushed him back toward open water.

The Alton Bay wind seemed to blow even harder, making the fight more intense. At last, the angler leaned down over the choppy water and deftly lifted the salmon into his boat. The fish was 4 or 5 pounds. The guy's smile said it all.

So it goes on Alton Bay. Some guys get the fish, some don't. Chattering teeth or not, it is an enjoyable way to spend a day.

Though some enthusiastic flyfishers dutifully chase salmon right at ice-out, veteran Lake Winnipesaukee angler Paul Carlton likes to wait until late April. "Even though ice-out traditionalists do catch a few good fish, I find that the quality of land-locked salmon fishing usually improves two to three weeks after the start of the season. I do best when the water temperature is between 48 and 54 degrees." Good salmon fishing can last into the month of June some years, he says.

Carlton, whose largest Lake Winnipesaukee salmon was 6 pounds, prefers fishing the lake's southernmost end by boat. "I tend to target bigger fish, and many

Landlocked salmon follow staging smelt into Alton Bay every spring.
(Photo by Steve Hickoff)

salmon will go over 3 pounds these days," he says. Traditional flat-lining with tandem streamers will yield a lot of smaller-sized landlocks in the turbulent water of the lake's windward shore." As for rainbows, Carlton's biggest on the lake was 4 pounds, 2 ounces—a good trout anywhere in northern New England.

By Mother's Day weekend, angling becomes steady on the big lake. Smelt patterns and traditional salmon flies are effective at this time of the year. Sheltered coves, including Alton Bay, continue to get major attention.

Anglers flyfish Alton Bay several ways. Some cast from the wooden docks located behind Alton Bait & Tackle. Others choose to troll the southwestern side of the bay. Small-boat anglers, defying the weather, fish the Alton Bay floating bandstand area at ice-out. Many rainbows and salmon have been caught around this landmark. As veteran angler Carlton suggests, reliable and more comfortable salmon fishing comes two to three weeks later.

Carlton recommends any tandem streamer with yellow in it. "In the early days," the longtime salmon angler says, "the Governor Barrows was easily my hands-down favorite." Other patterns include the Barnes special, Magog smelt, the gray ghost (#2–12), black ghost (#2–10), black nose dace (#2–10), Mickey Finn (#6–12), and grizzly king (#6–12).

Lake Winnipesaukee's season runs from April 1 through September 30 and is closed to the taking of landlocked salmon, brook trout, browns, rainbows, and lake trout from October 1 until ice-in. Check current regulations for any changes regarding New Hampshire's designated lake trout and salmon lakes.

According to fisheries biologist Donald Miller, the 1996 fall netting program reported that salmon averaged 2½ pounds and were 18 to 20 inches in length. Some netted landlocks weighed as much as 6 pounds. In April of 1997, a 27-inch, 6½-pound landlock was landed in Alton Bay.

New Hampshire Fish and Game's 1996 stocking figures for Lake Winnipesaukee were 6,300 rainbow trout in the Gilford area on the southwestern lakeshore, 2,900 near Melvin Village, and 800 in the Moultonboro region on the lake's northern end. The fish averaged 1 pound. Lake trout average 3 pounds and run as large as 10 pounds.

Routes 11 or 28A will take you to the village of Alton Bay at the lake's southernmost tip. The Alton Bridge is just 40 miles from downtown Portsmouth via the Spaulding Turnpike.

Boat ramp access areas, both public and fee, are available around the lake on side roads. As salmon angler Carlton says, "All major points on the lake have good access. You're never really far from a launch."

The Roberts Cove boat launch, accessible near the junction of Route 28 and Roberts Cove Road, is a good put-in location for salmon angling on the lake's southern shore. The Wolfeboro town launch on Wolfeboro Bay is convenient and relatively sheltered. The Alton Bay boat access is off Routes 11 and 28A.

Other Central New Hampshire Stillwaters

The New Hampshire Fish and Game Department lists many coldwater ponds and lakes for central New Hampshire.

Located in northern Strafford County in the village of New Durham, **Coldrain Pond** offers 18 acres of flyfishing-only trout water. Not far from Alton Bay on Lake Winnipesaukee, flyfishers often stop here before heading northwest to the big lake.

The state stocked Coldrain Pond with 1,700 brook trout in 1996. Access to this pond is made off Birch Hill Road in New Durham. A boat launch is available on the pond's southernmost shore.

Club Pond holds brook trout and rainbows. It is located in the town of New Durham and covers 38 acres.

Merrymeeting Lake is stocked with rainbows, lake trout, and salmon and is located in the town of New Durham. Roughly the same size as Bow Lake in southeast New Hampshire, this clear and cold stillwater is accessible from Chesley Road near the dam. Trolled streamers work best.

Cole Pond is a flyfishing-only pond stocked with brook trout. This 17-acre stillwater is located in the town of Enfield and is accessible by foot trail from Route 4A near the village of Fish Market.

Crystal Lake is a 365-acre pond holding rainbows and smallmouth bass. It is located in the town of Enfield. The lake was stocked with 2,450 rainbows in 1996. Try bass-bugs for Crystal Lake bronzebacks in June and early autumn.

Echo Lake, located in the town of Franconia, holds brook trout and covers 28 acres. Expect fish from 9 to 16 inches in length. Most of the brook trout run a pound or less, but there are plenty of them to keep you busy.

Profile Lake is a flyfishing-only pond located in the town of Franconia. What appears to be a man's profile juts out of the granite mountainside almost 1,200 feet above the lake. Dubbed "Old Man of the Mountains," this sight attracts camera-wielding tourists from all over the world. There's another attraction, thought: Profile Lake's trout.

Brook trout in this flyfishing-only pond range from 9 to 16 inches in length. Those angling for the pan should note that there is a 2-fish limit. Profile is best fly-fished from a canoe or float tube. Highway access is convenient from Route 3 and Interstate 93. To beat the crowds, fish at daybreak. You won't be sorry.

Joe Coffin Pond is located off Route 18 north of the village of Franconia. This 10-acre pond is heavily stocked with rainbow trout. Red, orange, or burgundy colored micro-egg patterns are effective flies for these fish.

Squam Lakes, Big and Little, are stocked with rainbows, lake trout, landlocked salmon, and smallmouth bass. These small lakes are located in the town of Holderness. Big Squam is 6,765 acres and Little Squam is 408 acres in size. Expect the usual run of 9-inch trout. Holdovers can be much larger. Bass-bugging for smallmouths is excellent in the rocky shallows of these lakes, especially in the spring. Fishing is also good in early autumn after the recreational boat traffic subsides.

Streeter Pond holds rainbows and is located in the town of Sugar Hill. There is an New Hampshire Fish and Game boat access at the south end. This 68-acre pond had 2,314 trout released in it in 1996.

Hunkins Pond holds rainbows and browns and is located in the town of Sanbornton. Found not far from the lower Pemigewasset fishery, this 15-acre water is accessible from Hunkins Pond Road just northeast of the village of Sanborton. Expect fish from 9 to 11 inches.

Saltmarsh Pond is stocked with brook trout and rainbows. Located in the town of Gilford, this 34-acre stillwater is heavily stocked. In 1996, 2,030 brook trout and 1,100 rainbows were released here. Access to Saltmarsh is made from Route 11A just west of Alton Bay. Expect company.

Sky Pond contains brook trout and rainbows and is located in the town of New Hampton. Found just east of the Newfound River and the lower Pemigewasset fisheries, angling on this 13-acre pond is by flyfishing only. Sky Pond is heavily stocked.

Waukewan Lake holds rainbows as well as smallmouth bass. It is located in the town of Meredith, with highway access via Route 3. There is a boat launch for this

912-acre lake in the village of Meredith. Although 2,000 rainbows were released here in 1996, this is primarily a bass fishery by summer.

Winnisquam Lake holds rainbows and landlocked salmon. Located in the town of Laconia and close to the Lake Winnipesaukee fishery, this 4,264-acre lake was stocked with 2,000 rainbows and 1,500 landlocked salmon in 1996. Route 3 south of Meredith provides access to Winnisquam, which is a good second choice when Lake Winnipesaukee is crowded. Fishing is best during the month of May.

Upper Hall Pond is a brook trout pond located north of Squam Lake. Expect 9- to 11-inch brookies on this 24-acre flyfishing-only pond. It is accessible off Sandwich Notch Road and has a 2-trout daily limit.

Middle Hall Pond holds brook trout and is located in the town of Sandwich. It is the smallest of the Hall Ponds at only 5 acres. Middle Pond is being developed as a brook trout fishery by New Hampshire Fish and Game.

Lower Hall Pond also holds brook trout and is located in Sandwich. Again, this remote pond is a developing fishery, which should provide good flyfishing in the coming years.

Horn Pond contains brook trout, browns, rainbows, largemouth and small-mouth bass. It is located east of the village of Sanbornville on the Maine/New Hampshire border. This is one of those New Hampshire fisheries that offers both springtime angling for trout as well as bass-bugging in the summer. Fish stocked in this 435-acre pond included 4,600 brookies, 368 browns, and 1,600 rainbows in 1996.

Ossipee Lake offers rainbow, salmon, largemouth and smallmouth bass fishing. It is located in the town of Ossipee. Ossipee is 3,092 acres in size with easy access off Routes 16 and 25. The Deer Cove boat launch is located off Deer Cove Road. Ossipee Lake saw 1,000 landlocked salmon and 2,500 rainbows stocked in 1996. The lake has a 61-foot maximum depth that provides cool waters through summer. Larger-sized rainbows are often caught, especially in the early season.

Shawtown Pond is a brook trout pond located in the town of Freedom. Also known as "Shaw Pond," it is a flyfishing-only pond. This 15-acre pond is heavily fished in spring, and 1,475 brook trout were released here in 1996.

Silver Lake, located in the town of Madison, holds rainbows, lake trout, and smallmouth bass. It covers 995 acres and is managed as a rainbow fishery. Silver Lake was stocked with 3,757 fish in 1996. There is good smallmouth bass fishing in the northernmost section of the lake near Big Island. A boat launch is located off Route 41 on the lake's western side.

White Pond is stocked with brook trout and rainbows and is located in Ossipee near the Pine River State Forest. It covers a total of 47 acres, and anglers can expect 9- to 14-inch brook trout and rainbows. This flyfishing-only stillwater is accessible from White Pond Road.

A brook trout pond, **White Lake** is located within the town of Tamworth. It was stocked with 3,850 hatchery brookies in 1996. Access is available in White Lake State Park off Route 16 near Silver and Ossipee Lakes.

CENTRAL NEW HAMPSHIRE HUB CITIES
Bristol
Elevation–588 • Population–2,500

ACCOMMODATIONS

Bungalow Village, located on Newfound Lake (P.O. Box 131) / 603-744-2220 / Cottages and motel rooms and moorings available for boat access / Contact Doug and Madeline Thompson / Email: bungalo.com / Opens May 1

Lakeside Cottages at Newfound Lake, 68 Lake Street / 603-744-3075

CAMPGROUNDS

Davidson's Country Campground, RFD 2, River Road / 603-744-2403 / 130 riverfront sites, both wooded and open / Canoe rentals available / Open May 24 to October 14 / Dogs welcome but can't be left unattended

Pine's Acres, Box 379, Wulamet Road (off West Shore Road) / 603-744-3097 / Located on Newfound Lake / Owner Barbara Hayden says pets are fine so long as they're leashed or kept in a dog crate / 120 seasonals are available, including winter leases for recreational activities that include Newfound River flyfishing, lakes region ice angling, and snowmobiling

Pine Grove Campground, 14 Timberland Drive (Franklin) / 603-934-4582 / A small, family campground open May 15 through October 15 / New pool / Daily, weekly, monthly, and seasonal rates / Dogs OK if leashed

Thousand Acres Family Campground, U.S. Route 3, 1079 South Main Street (Franklin) / 603-934-4440 / 150 level, shady, wooded sites/ Dogs OK if leashed

RESTAURANTS

Bristol House of Pizza and Family Restaurant, 32 Lake Street / 603-744-3765 / Serves lunch and dinner ranging from pizzas to barbecued lamb to seafood

Cliff Lodge Country Dining, Route 3A / 603-744-8660 / Overlooks Newfound Lake

Gilly's, 101 Lake Street / 603-744-2321 / Open 6am daily for breakfast

FLY SHOPS AND SPORTING GOODS

K&M Sport Shop, 414 Central Street (Franklin) / 603-934-6170 or 800-491-6170 / Open from 6AM to 6PM seven days a week / Carries fly rods and other tackle with a huge selection of salmon and trout flies

Lyme Angler, 8 South Main Street (Hanover) / 603-643-1263 / Full service fly shop

Newfound Trading Post, 112 Lake Street / 603-744-8658 / Tackle needs, nonresident licenses, and boat registration available / Contact Lester Greenwood

AUTO REPAIR

Fuller Ford, Route 3A / 603-744-5111

Bristol Auto Care, 98 Lake Street (across from Gilly's) / 603-744-9700

MEDICAL
Closest hospitals are:
  Franklin Regional Hospital / 603-934-2060
  Speare Memorial Hospital / 603-536-1120

AIRPORT
Closest major airport is in Manchester.

FOR MORE INFORMATION
Newfound Region Chamber of Commerce
P.O. Box 454
Bristol, NH 03222
603-744-2150

Sunapee
Elevation–1,094 • Population–2,600

The town of Sunapee sits on the westernmost shore of Sunapee Lake, a fishery that holds salmon, lake trout, and bass. Flyfish before Memorial Day or after Labor Day for the best results. Ice-out arrives by mid-April. The town offers access to Sullivan County trout waters, while Cheshire County rivers and ponds might best be flyfished while staying in Brattleboro, Vermont.

ACCOMMODATIONS
The Backside Inn, Brook Road, RFD #2, Box 213 (Newport 03773) / 603-863-5161 / 10 guest rooms, most with a private bath / Located 1 mile west of both Mount Sunapee and Lake Sunapee / Contact Mackie and Bruce Hefka / Includes breakfast / $$

Best Western Sunapee Lake Lodge, 1403 Route 103 (Mount Sunapee 03255) / 800-606-5253 or 603-763-2020 / Centrally located at Mount Sunapee State Park, just a short walk to the State Park Beach on Lake Sunapee / Indoor pool, mini-gym, restaurant, and lounge / New in 1995 / Contact park officials for recreational information at 603-763-2356 / $$$$

Georges Mills Cottages & Lodging, P.O. Box 323 (Georges Mills 03751) / 603-763-2369 / Cottages and motel on Otter Lake near Lake Sunapee's northern shore / $$–$$$

CAMPGROUNDS
Northstar Campground, Inc., 27B Coonbrook Road (Newport 03773) / 603-863-4001 / Just west of Sunapee Lake

RESTAURANTS
Courtney's, Route 103, P.O. Box 636 / 603-863-2891 / Soups, salads, sandwiches, appetizers, and a full-service lounge / One-half mile west of Mount Sunapee State Park

Daniel's, Main Street, P.O. Box 839 (Henniker 03242) / 603-428-7621 / Overlooks the Contoocook River

Peter Christian's Tavern, 186 Main Street (New London 03257) / 603-526-4042

FLY SHOPS AND SPORTING GOODS
Dorr Mill Store, Routes 11 and 103, P.O. Box 88 (Guild 03754) / 800-846-3677 / Located in the Lake Sunapee region, offers men's and women's sportswear

Pelletier's Sport Shop, 105 Peterborough Street, Route 202 (Jaffrey 03452) / 603-532-7180 / Fly tying materials and tackle needs / Serves anglers in Sullivan, Cheshire, Merrimack, and Hillborough Counties

Village Sports, 140 Main Street (New London 03257) / 603-526-4948

AUTO REPAIR
Newbury Servicenter Mobil Station, Route 103 (Newbury 03255) / 603-763-5990

AIRPORT

Keene Airport, Keene 03431 / 800-272-5488 for reservations / Regularly scheduled commuter service by Colgan Air from Newark, New Jersey

Refer to the Manchester service hub for flights from Boston's Logan International Airport to Manchester Airport

MEDICAL

Closest is **Valley Regional Hospital** in Claremont, 13 miles west of Sunapee

FOR MORE INFORMATION

Lake Sunapee Business Association
P.O. Box 400
Sunapee, NH 03782
800-258-3530 / 603-763-2495

Conway

Elevation–530 • Population–8,431

Conway has heavy tourist traffic in the summer. Nearby summits range from 1,734 feet at Peaked Mountain to 2,370 feet at Black Cap.

ACCOMMODATIONS

Maple Leaf Motel, Route 16 (North Conway 03860) / 603-356-5388 / Owners Val and Bob Kempf accept pets / $$$

Sunny Brook Place Cottages, Route 16 / 603-447-3922 / 10 cottages with full kitchens / Located in a birch and pine grove on Swift Brook / $$

Tanglewood Motel & Cottages, Route 16 / 603-447-5932 / Contact Carol & Craig Koch who say, "We're a kick off your shoes and relax kind of place." They offer efficiency cottages on wooded acres, plus motel rooms. / Opens spring 1999

CAMPGROUNDS

White Mountain National Forest Campgrounds / Campsites can be reserved by calling 800-280-CAMP (2267) / All provide good Swift River access

- **Big Rock Campground**, 6 miles east of Lincoln on the Kancamagus Highway / Offers 28 campsites and trailer space near Lincoln Woods / Open year-round
- **Blackberry Crossing Campground**, 6 miles west of Conway on the Kancamagus Highway / 26 campsites
- **Covered Bridge**, 6 miles west of Conway off the Kancamagus Highway / Cross the Albany Covered Bridge to find these 49 campsites
- **Hancock**, 6 miles east of Lincoln on the Kancamagus Highway / 56 campsites / Open and plowed year-round
- **Jigger Johnson**, 13 miles west of Conway on the Kancamagus Highway / 75 campsites and flush toilets
- **Passaconaway**, 15 miles west of Conway on the Kancamagus Highway / 33 campsites at the confluence of Downes Brook and Swift River

RESTAURANTS

Mr. W's House of Pancakes, Route 112 (Lincoln 03251) / 603-745-3215 / Breakfast and lunch

Fandangle's Restaurant, Lounge, and Catering, junction of Routes 16 and 302 (North Conway 03860) / 603-356-2741 / Family dining

Gordi's Fish and Steak House, Kancamagus High (Lincoln 03251) / 603-745-6635

FLY SHOPS AND OUTFITTERS

North Country Angler, Route 16 (North Conway 03860) / 603-356-6000 / Offers flyfishing tackle, tying supplies, and expert advice on local angling / Guide services also available

L.L. Bean Factory Outlet, Route 16, P.O. Box 179 (North Conway 03860) / 800-820-6846

AUTO REPAIR

Goodie's Mobil, Route 112 (Lincoln 03251) / 603-745-3572
Wilson's Mobil Service, Main Street (North Woodstock 03262) / 603-745-8762

AIRPORTS

Best option is to fly to Manchester, then drive north to the White Mountain region in a rental car

FOR MORE INFORMATION

Conway Village Chamber of Commerce
Box 1019
Conway, NH 03818
603-447-2639

Lincoln/Woodstock Chamber of Commerce
Route 112
P.O. Box 358
Lincoln, NH 03251
Information 603-745-6621 / Reservations 800-227-4191

Mount Washington Valley Chamber of Commerce
North Conway, NH 03860
Information 603-356-3171 / Reservations 800-367-3364

Laconia

Elevation–501 • Population–33,000 (summer); 16,000 (winter)

ACCOMMODATIONS

Abakee Cottages, P.O. Box 5144 (Weirs Beach 03247-5144) / 603-366-4405 / Fully-equipped housekeeping cottages on Lake Winnipesaukee / Rents by the week: $805 per week

Black Horse Motor Court, RR 1, Box 46, Route 3 (Ashland 03217-9705) / 603-968-7116 / Housekeeping motel suites and cottages located on Little Squam Lake / Dock space available / Dogs allowed / Open year-round / $475 per week

Hi-Spot Motor Court, Route 3, Box 161 / 603-524-3281 / Housekeeping cottages and motel rooms on Lake Winnipesaukee / Open May through October / "Sorry, no pets"

Lake Shore Motel and Cottages, RR 2, Box 16-G (Center Harbor 03226) / 603-253-6244 / November through April 941-439-6625 / Located on Lake Winnipesaukee / Dogs welcome / Open May through October / $$–$$$$$

CAMPGROUNDS

Clearwater Campground, Route 104, 3 miles off Interstate 93 (Meredith 03253) / 603-279-7761 / Wooded lakeside camping area for tents and trailers, with modern restrooms, convenience store, and laundry facilities / Pets allowed

Meredith Woods Four Season Camping Area, P.O. Box 776 (Moultonboro 03254) / 603-253-6251 / Convenient to lakes region fisheries

RESTAURANTS

Fratello's Ristorante Italiano, 779 Union Avenue / 603-528-2022

Hector's Fine Food & Spirits, Beacon Street West / 603-524-1009 / Located in Laconia's mill district

Water Street Cafe, 141 Water Street, corner of Fair and Water Streets / 603-524-4144 / Open 7 days a week for breakfast and lunch

FLY SHOPS AND SPORTING GOODS

Alton Bay Bait and Tackle, just off the intersection of Routes 11 and 28A / 603-875-4978 / Primarily caters to bait anglers and boaters who may or may not troll streamers, though flyfishers traditionally cast for landlocks from the store's docks / Ask permission to do so when inquiring about recent angling conditions at Alton Bay

Paugus Bay Sporting Goods, Route 3, 135 Weirs Boulevard / 603-524-4319 / Carries fly tackle plus fly patterns for Lake Winnipesaukee and the region's other flyfisheries

Opechee Trading Post, 13 Opechee Street / 603-524-0908 / Orvis shop

Wolfeboro Bay Outfitter, 15 South Main (Wolfeboro 03894) / Located on Lake Winnipesaukee / 603-569-1114

Paquette's Sporting Goods, 645 Union Avenue / 603-524-1017

AUTO REPAIR
Globe Transmissions / 603-528-4419
Speedy Oil Change and Tune-Up / 603-528-8588

AUTO RENTAL
Affordable Car Rental, P.O. Box 1458, Route 106 / 603-524-0550 or 800-955-2746

AIRPORTS
See Manchester Hub
Laconia Municipal / 603-524-5003
Logan International, Boston, is a two-hour drive from Laconia
Lakes Region Airport / 603-569-4304 / Information on their Wolfeboro Neck
   facility

MEDICAL
Lakes Regional General Hospital, downtown off Route 3 / 603-524-3211

FOR MORE INFORMATION
Greater Laconia/Weirs Beach Chamber of Commerce
11 Veteran's Square
Laconia, NH 0324
603-524-5531 / 800-531-2347

Lakes Region Association
Center Harbor, NJ 03226
800-60-LAKES / 603-253-8555

Alton-Alton Bay Chamber of Commerce
Alton, NH 03809
603-875-5777

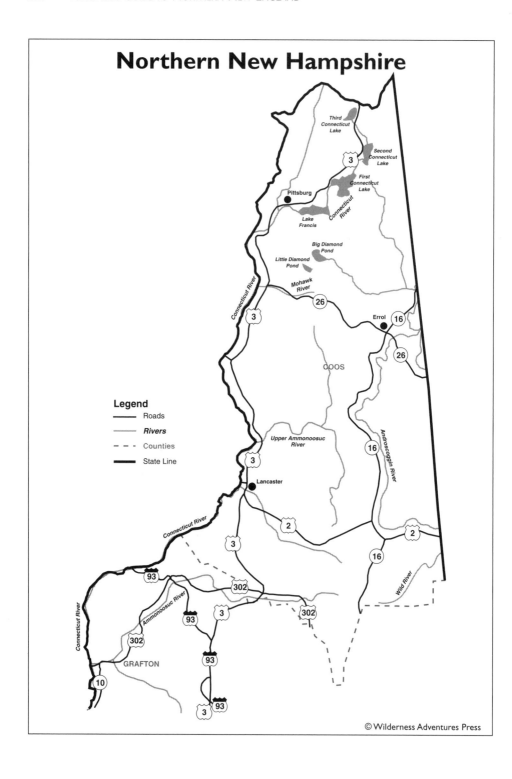

Northern New Hampshire

Third Connecticut Lake

Second Connecticut Lake

First Connecticut Lake

Pittsburg

Lake Francis

Big Diamond Pond

Little Diamond Pond

Mohawk River

Errol

COOS

Legend
— Roads
Rivers
- - - Counties
— State Line

Upper Ammonoosuc River

Androscoggin River

Lancaster

Connecticut River

Wild River

GRAFTON

Ammonoosuc River

© Wilderness Adventures Press

NORTHERN NEW HAMPSHIRE

Northern New Hampshire's Coos County offers many wonderful angling opportunities. The Androscoggin and upper Connecticut Rivers are often the main attraction for flyfishing enthusiasts. However, stillwaters, such as Diamond Ponds, Back Lake, and the Connecticut Lakes, should not be overlooked. Many of the region's small streams support wild brook trout.

At night, you'll fall asleep listening to the mournful call of loons, the North Country's most vocal bird. During daytime outings, you'll often see yearling moose lurking along roadsides.

Steve Hickoff took this New Hampshire brook trout on a #18 mosquito dry after stalking the rising fish. (Photo by Steve Hickoff)

NORTHERN NEW HAMPSHIRE MAJOR HATCHES

Insect/Bait	J	F	M	A	M	J	J	A	S	O	N	D	Patterns
Minnows and Leeches	■	■	■	■	■	■	■	■	■	■	■	■	Woolly Buggers, Streamers, and Muddlers #4-10
Caddis					■	■		■	■				Henryville Special #14-18; Tan Elk Hair Caddis #14-18; Soft Hackles and Emergers #14-18; Hare's Ear Nymph and Beadhead Pupae #14-18
Zebra Caddis (Alderfly)						■							Black Bivisible Adams or Comparacaddis #12
Blue-winged Olives					■	■			■				Parachute Adams #14-20; Thorax Blue-winged Olive #14-18; Pheasant Tail Nymphs #14-20
Hendricksons					■								Dark Hendrickson or Red Quill #12-14; Hendrickson Nymph #12-14; Rusty Spinner #14
Light Cahill						■	■						Cahill Dun or Parachute #16
Hexagenia							■						Hex Nymph, Brown #4-6; Parachute Hex #8
Stoneflies						■		■					Black Stonefly Nymph #2-6; Yellow Stonefly Nymph #8-10; Yellow Sally #14
Tiny Mayflies *Tricorythodes stygiatus*									■				Trico Spinner #18-24
Terrestrials								■	■				Hoppers #6-12; Ants #14-18
Midges								■	■				Griffith's Gnat #18; Parachute Adams #18-22

NORTHERN NEW HAMPSHIRE RIVERS
Androscoggin River

Route 16 south of Errol winds along the upper Androscoggin River. The road skirts pine woods, birch groves, and wetlands harboring the ubiquitous north country moose. The river itself supports brook trout, browns, rainbows, and landlocked salmon.

Between the town of Errol and Mollidgewock Campground, there are more than 3 miles of water easily accessible from Route 16. Clear Stream, a tributary of the Androscoggin just west of town, holds good numbers of 9- to 12-inch brook trout. Clear Stream saw 1,600 hatchery squaretails stocked in 1996. The confluence of Clear Stream and the main river just south of Errol can provide action.

Flatwater sections of the Androscoggin do not hold as many trout and salmon as the more highly oxygenated riffles. The faster runs remain cooler and offer the best flyfishing throughout the summer.

Ten miles south of Errol is the confluence of Bog Brook. This area is stocked with trout and salmon in the spring. The riffle water between Bog Brook and Pontook Dam, a 4-plus mile stretch offers great flyfishing for brookies, browns, and rainbows during the alderfly hatch from late June through mid-July.

Pontook Dam on the Androscoggin River. (Photo by Steve Hickoff)

Androscoggin River

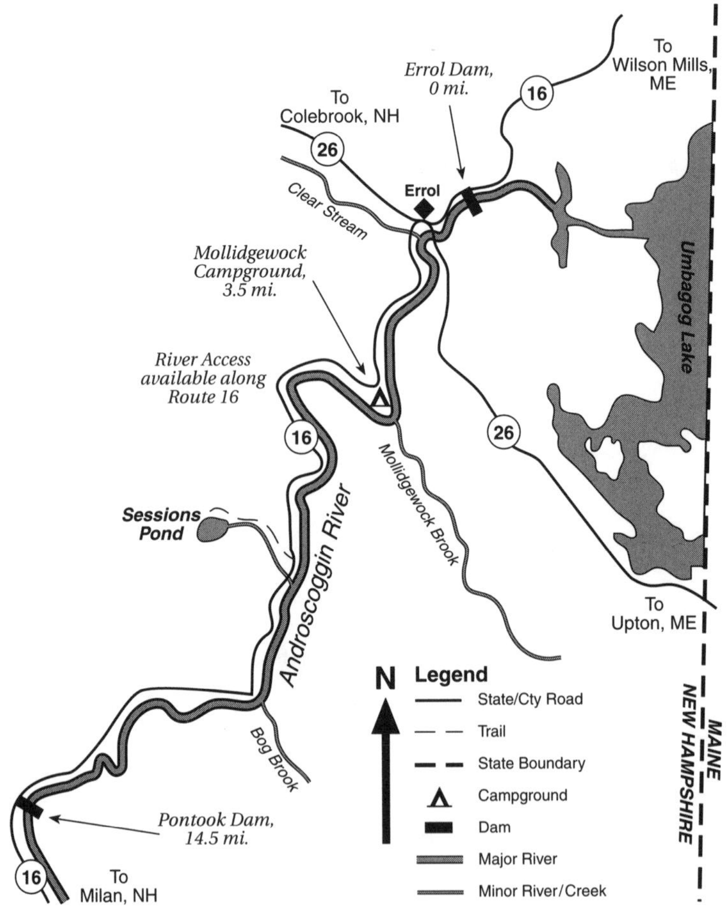

To Wilson Mills, ME

Errol Dam, 0 mi.

16

To Colebrook, NH

26

Clear Stream

Errol

Umbagog Lake

Mollidgewock Campground, 3.5 mi.

River Access available along Route 16

16

Mollidgewock Brook

26

Sessions Pond

Androscoggin River

To Upton, ME

Bog Brook

N **Legend**

— State/Cty Road

– – Trail

– ▪ – State Boundary

△ Campground

▪ Dam

▰ Major River

▰ Minor River/Creek

MAINE

NEW HAMPSHIRE

Pontook Dam, 14.5 mi.

16 To Milan, NH

© Wilderness Adventures Press

Androscoggin River.
(Photo by Steve Hickoff)

The zebra caddis, or alderfly, is abundant in the Androscoggin. The classic fly pattern, the black Palmer, is a good alderfly imitation:

Black Palmer

Hook	Dry fly, size 12
Thread	Black
Tip	Gold oval tinsel
Tag	Red wool
Body	Black floss
Hackle	Black hackle, palmered, back to front

For best results, fish the fly on a dead-drift in the current. This pattern can be successful on broken water and occasionally on stillwater flows, especially in the sections below Clear Stream, Mollidgewock Brook, and Bog Brook. Alderfly larva patterns fished slowly on the bottom using a sinking fly line can be effective, as well. Remember the alderfly at the tying bench before any trips to this region.

The Androscoggin's season runs from January 1 to October, with the section from Errol Dam to the markers at the Bragg Bay deadwater just below Route 26 designated flyfishing-only with a daily limit of 2 brook trout measuring as least 12 inches in length.

The New Hampshire Fish and Game stocks brook trout and browns downstream to the village of Berlin and brown trout in the river near the town of Milan. Errol, Cambridge, and Dummer river sections receive the majority of stocked trout. Look for brookies, rainbows, browns, and landlocked salmon from the Errol Dam downstream to Pontook Dam.

Stocked fish typically run from 9 to 11 inches. Some larger hatchery trout are stocked periodically. Brook trout, rainbows, and salmon will hold over from year to year. Browns up to 4 pounds are caught on occasion.

The river between Errol and Pontook Dams can be waded. Class III to IV rapids aren't uncommon during times of heavy flow, so use good judgement. WARNING: The portion of Androscoggin just downstream of the Pontook Dam has proven to be exceptionally dangerous to recreational users of the river.

Route 16 south through the Thirteen Mile Woods region provides easy access to the Androscoggin River between Errol and Pontook Dams. Just south of Errol on Route 16 is the Mollidgewock State Campground. This facility provides good access to the Androscoggin. Clear Stream brook trout angling is just a short drive from the camp. In addition to 35 tent sites, this remote, northern New Hampshire campground has pit toilets. You can contact the campground by calling 603-482-3373.

Upper Connecticut River

The Connecticut River flows out of Fourth Connecticut Lake, which lies near the border of the Province of Quebec, Canada. It flows through Third Connecticut Lake and meanders south following Route 3 near Deer Mountain Campground at Moose Falls. From there, it enters Second Connecticut Lake. River sections then connect the Second Connecticut Lake and First Connecticut Lake as well as First Connecticut Lake and Lake Francis.

The river sections between Second Connecticut Lake dam and First Connecticut Lake dam are very productive. The Moose Falls stretch near Deer Mountain Campground also fishes well.

The Connecticut River below Lake Francis should not be overlooked. The dam at the south end of Lake Francis not only provides the power for residents of the village, it is also the source of ice cold water for the fish in the river below. Even on the hottest days of summer, you'll find freely feeding browns, rainbows, and brook trout in this nutrient-rich water. Access is off Route 3 near the dam and as it follows the river south.

Holdover browns that weigh several pounds are not uncommon. Back in January of 1996, teenager Kevin James Rice caught a 15½-pound brown near the Canaan

Upper Connecticut River

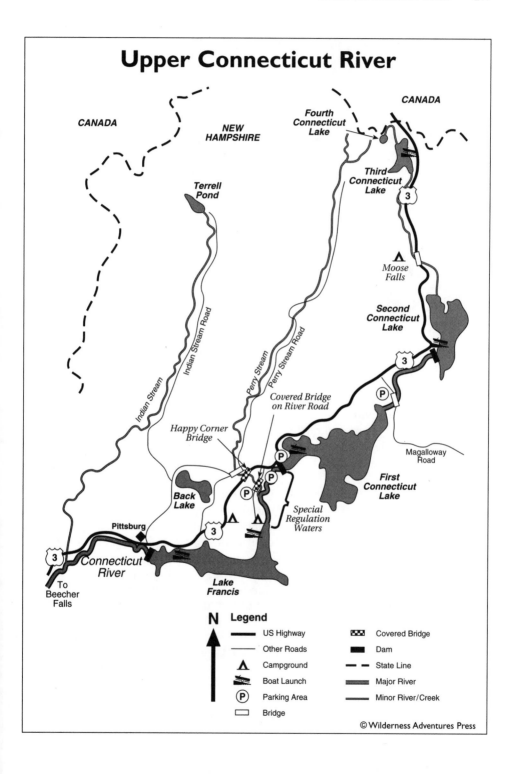

CANADA

CANADA

NEW HAMPSHIRE

Fourth Connecticut Lake

Terrell Pond

Third Connecticut Lake

Moose Falls

Second Connecticut Lake

Indian Stream Road

Perry Stream

Perry Stream Road

Covered Bridge on River Road

Indian Stream

Happy Corner Bridge

Magalloway Road

First Connecticut Lake

Back Lake

Pittsburg

Special Regulation Waters

Connecticut River

To Beecher Falls

Lake Francis

N Legend

▬▬ US Highway	▨▨ Covered Bridge
— Other Roads	▬ Dam
▲ Campground	– – State Line
⛴ Boat Launch	Major River
Ⓟ Parking Area	Minor River/Creek
▭ Bridge	

© Wilderness Adventures Press

Moose are a common sight along northern New Hampshire waters .
(Photo by Elizabeth Edwards)

Dam power station downstream of the flyfishing-only section. The monster measured 29 inches in length.

There are many stories of raising big northern New Hampshire browns to a fly. I once watched helplessly as a chunky upper Connecticut brown repeatedly nosed my dry fly the way a circus seal might nose a beach ball. Fortunately, sometimes we catch a few fish.

Stocked landlocked salmon and brown trout hold over from season to season. The upper Connecticut is also stocked with brook trout and rainbows in the 9- to 11-inch range. If you choose to kill a trout, measure your catch carefully. Brookies can fall an inch or so short of legal. Landlocked salmon average 1 to 2 pounds and 15 to 17 inches long.

Mayfly hatches can be sporadic early in the season. All-purpose flies, such as the Hornberg and brown bivisible, can be the best producers in early June. Flyfish the early summer caddis hatch with elk hair caddis patterns as well as caddis emergers. Case-making caddis are found throughout the upper Connecticut River. Woolly buggers, streamers, and bucktails can attract larger-sized holdover browns and landlocked salmon. I tend to work highly visible Mickey Finns through sweeping currents at daybreak and dusk.

The season on the Upper Connecticut runs from January 1 through October 15. From Second Connecticut Lake dam to the upstream side of the logging bridge on Magalloway Road is flyfishing only. All fish must be immediately released unharmed.

From the Magalloway Road bridge to the inlet at Green Point on First Connecticut Lake is flyfishing only. The daily limit for brook trout is 2 fish. From First Connecticut Lake Dam downstream to the signs on Lake Francis is flyfishing only with a daily limit for brook trout of 2 fish over 12 inches.

Moderate to steady flows can be expected in June when trout fishing is best. Slippery rocks underfoot demand attention while wading. Expect pocketwater, riffles, plunge pools, and calm stretches.

U.S. Route 3 provides access to all the Connecticut Lakes and the river sections between these stillwaters.

Other Northern New Hampshire Rivers and Streams

Beaver Brook is a small brook trout stream north of the village of Colebrook near Route 145. It flows out of the Beaver Brook Falls Natural Area and joins the Connecticut River just outside of Colebrook. Beaver Brook is stocked with brook trout in the spring.

Mohawk River flows down from Dixville Notch along Route 26 to Colebrook, where it meets the Connecticut. In 1996 the state stocked the Mohawk with 2,750 brook trout.

Dead Diamond River is located north of the village of Errol in the area known as the Second College Grant. Grant land is gated allowing only foot access. You can gain access to the lower section of Dead Diamond from Diamond Peaks Trail off Route 16 near the Maine border. Magalloway Road from Route 3 north of the village of Pittsburg provides access to the upper sections of Dead Diamond River by 4-wheel drive vehicle. Parking is about 12 or 13 miles in, next to the old bridge. It's well worth the journey—there are plenty of small, wild brookies eager to take your fly.

Mollidgewock Brook joins the Androscoggin south of Errol. There are unimproved access roads and foot trails off Route 26. This remote, little stream holds wild brookies.

Bishop Brook is easily accessible from Route 145 near the village of Stewartstown Hollow. The stream receives regular stockings of brook trout. In 1996, Bishop Brook was stocked with 3,125 brookies.

Indian Stream flows down from near the Canadian border and joins the Connecticut River south of Pittsburg. Jesse Young Road, off Route 3, follows Indian Stream, providing access along its full length. It is heavily stocked with brook trout, and its upper reaches and small tributaries hold wild brookies.

Perry Stream is another long stream flowing from near the Canadian border. It crosses Route 3 and meets the Connecticut in the stretch between First Connecticut Lake and Lake Francis. The portion of Perry Stream upstream from the confluence to the bridge at Happy Corner on Route 3 is flyfishing only. Both the stream and Connecticut River are heavily stocked with brook trout. Brown trout will move up into the river from Lake Francis during times of high water. There is an excellent state campground at the head of Lake Francis just a couple of miles from the covered bridge on River Road (see Upper Connecticut River map).

Lance King caught his New Hampshire state record rainbow on a tandem Mickey Finn. (Photo by Elizabeth Edwards/Steve Hickoff)

Wild River is in the southeast corner of Coos County. It flows off Mount Washington's northeast slope and enters the Androscoggin River near Gilead, Maine. Route 113 south of Gilead provides access to Highwater Trail, which brings you back into New Hampshire and follows the Wild River to its headwaters. It is regularly stocked with rainbows and brook trout.

The **Upper Ammonoosuc River** is a heavily stocked brook trout stream. It flows along Route 100 north of Berlin and meets the Connecticut River near Groveton.

Northern New Hampshire Stillwaters
Big and Little Diamond Ponds

Big Diamond Pond measures 179 surface acres, while Little Diamond Pond covers 51 acres. These Stewartstown stillwaters are heavily stocked right after ice-out in mid-May.

Early in the season, flyfishers have the opportunity to catch lake trout, particularly on Big Diamond's westernmost side. Flyfish smelt-imitating streamers, such as the gray ghost, at daybreak right after ice-out. The best angling for brook trout and rainbows usually starts around Memorial Day and last into late June.

Big Diamond was stocked with 2,800 trout in 1996. The majority of the fish were rainbows. Holdover fish do well in this Coos County pond, which has a maximum depth of 117 feet.

Little Diamond runs shallower, with a maximum depth of 15 feet. Brook trout dominate stocking lists for this put-and-take water, with 7,852 hatchery squaretails stocked in 1996. Expect fish from 9 to 14 inches. Don't hesitate to keep a few if you wish. Limits are 5 fish or 5 pounds, whichever limit is reached first. On Little Diamond, trout may by taken by flies, artificial lures, or worms.

Big and Little Diamond Ponds

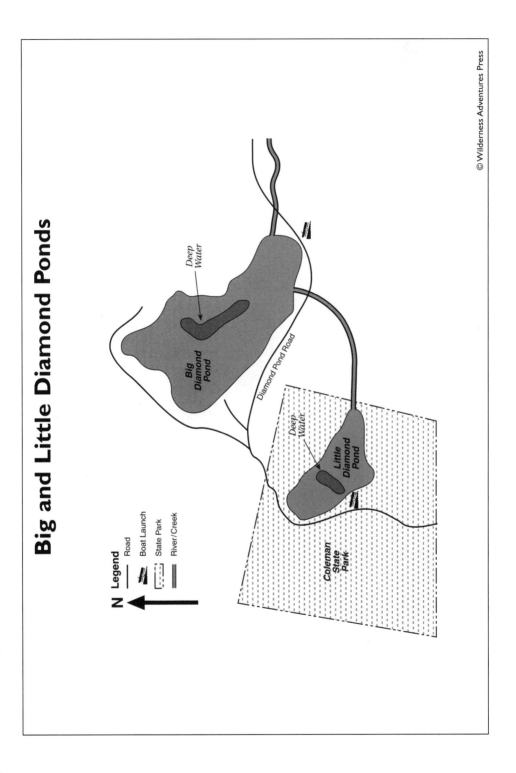

N

Legend
Road
Boat Launch
State Park
River/Creek

Big
Diamond
Pond

Deep
Water

Little
Diamond
Pond

Deep
Water

Diamond Pond Road

Coleman
State
Park

Back Lake

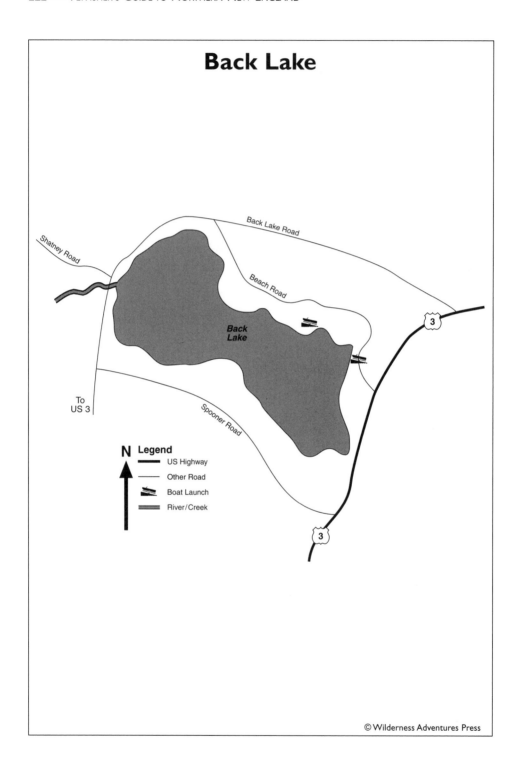

Shatney Road

Back Lake Road

Beach Road

Back
Lake

To
US 3

Spooner Road

3

3

N

Legend
US Highway
Other Road
Boat Launch
River/Creek

© Wilderness Adventures Press

Some White Mountain summits hold snow into spring.
(Photo by Elizabeth Edwards)

For access to both stillwaters, take Diamond Pond Road from the town of Kidderville on Route 26, just west of Dixville Notch. Head north to Upper Kidderville, then on to Coleman State Park and Little Diamond. Diamond Pond Road exits the park, providing access to Big Diamond. Boat launches are found off this main road.

A side trip can also include flyfishing the Mohawk River, which runs along Route 26 in Colebrook. This put-and-take trout fishery received 2,750 brookies during recent stockings.

Zug bugs, Hornbergs, dun variants, woolly worms, and pheasant tail nymphs work well on Mohawk River.

Back Lake

This 359-acre Pittsburg trout pond opens to fishing on the fourth Saturday in April. The best fishing starts in mid-May and holds through July. September can offer good fishing as well.

Stocking numbers are high—5,000 brook trout and 1,900 rainbows were released in 1996. Expect Back Lake brook trout from 9 to 14 inches and some larger rainbow trout.

The Hornberg is a Back Lake favorite. Fish early summer caddis hatches with deep sparkle pupa, emergent sparkle pupa, diving caddis, and elk hair caddis patterns. Dragonfly and damselfly nymphs, scud patterns, and midges all catch fish. Look for the Hex hatch to peak from late June through early July. This large mayfly comes off around 7 pm to dusk. Terrestrials, especially ants and moths, work well when a little breeze wrinkles the water surface in the later season.

Beach and Spooner Roads parallel this Coos County lake. Back Lake Road provides access off Route 3. Launch from the public beach off Beach Road.

Joe Silvestro with a lake trout caught from First Connecticut Lake near Timberland Lodge and Cabins. (Photo by Steve Hickoff)

Lake Francis

Depending on when you flyfish the region, Lake Francis and the Connecticut Lakes can strike you as inviting or as windswept and forbidding. Lake Francis is a 2,051-acre impoundment created to produce hydropower for the town of Pittsburg. It offers angling for brook trout, rainbows, browns, landlocked salmon, and lake trout. Chain pickerel lurk in the shallow weedbeds of the lake.

The lake was stocked by New Hampshire Fish and Game with 2,170 brook trout, 1,000 landlocked salmon, and 1,700 lake trout in 1996. Holdover fish from this stocking will reach several pounds. River Road and Route 3 both provide boat access. Trolled streamers work well in the spring and fall.

First Connecticut Lake

This lake is big and inviting. At 2,807 water surface acres, First Lake provides ample elbow room for the boating flyfisher. Three-pound lake trout are commonly taken in the spring on trolled streamers and bucktail patterns. Brook trout, rainbows, and landlocked salmon are also frequent catches.

In 1996, 1,500 landlocked salmon and 1,800 lake trout were stocked in this still-water, as well as 9,000 brookies.

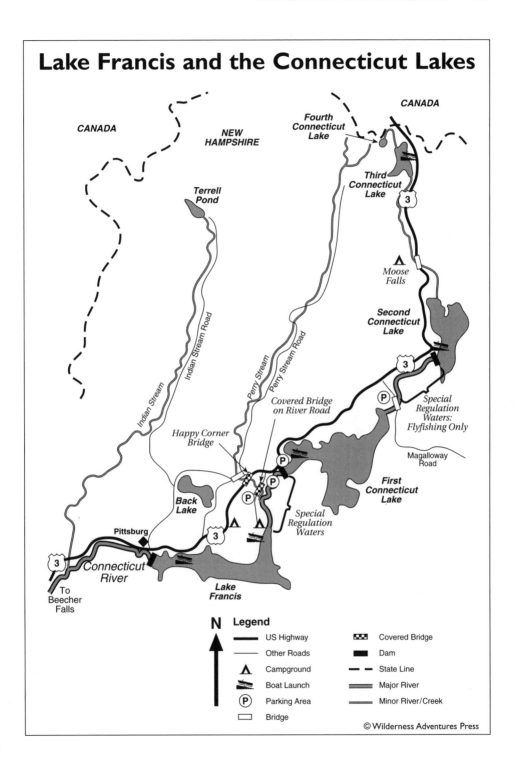

Lake Francis and the Connecticut Lakes

CANADA

CANADA

NEW HAMPSHIRE

Fourth Connecticut Lake

Third Connecticut Lake

3

Terrell Pond

Moose Falls

Second Connecticut Lake

Indian Stream Road

Perry Stream Road

Perry Stream

Indian Stream

3

Covered Bridge on River Road

P

Special Regulation Waters: Flyfishing Only

Happy Corner Bridge

P

Magalloway Road

First Connecticut Lake

P

Back Lake

P

Special Regulation Waters

Pittsburg

3

Connecticut River

3

To Beecher Falls

Lake Francis

N **Legend**

— US Highway
— Other Roads
▲ Campground
⟋ Boat Launch
Ⓟ Parking Area
▭ Bridge

▨ Covered Bridge
▬ Dam
— — State Line
▨ Major River
▤ Minor River/Creek

© Wilderness Adventures Press

Lake Francis and First Connecticut Lake

To Second Connecticut Lake

Perry Stream

Happy Corner Bridge

3

Connecticut River

First Connecticut Lake

Perry Stream Confluence

3

River Road Covered Bridge

Flyfishing Only Waters

River Road

Lake Francis

N Legend

	US Highway
	Other Road
	Boat Launch
●	River Site
	Bridge
	Dam
	Major River
	Minor River/Creek

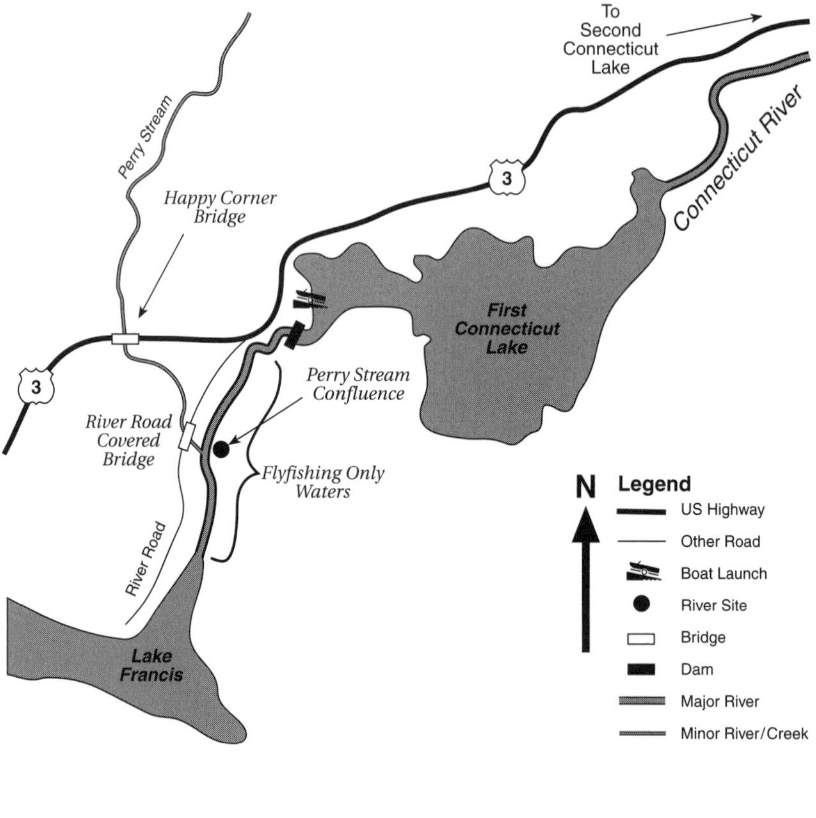

© Wilderness Adventures Press

Second and Third Connecticut Lakes

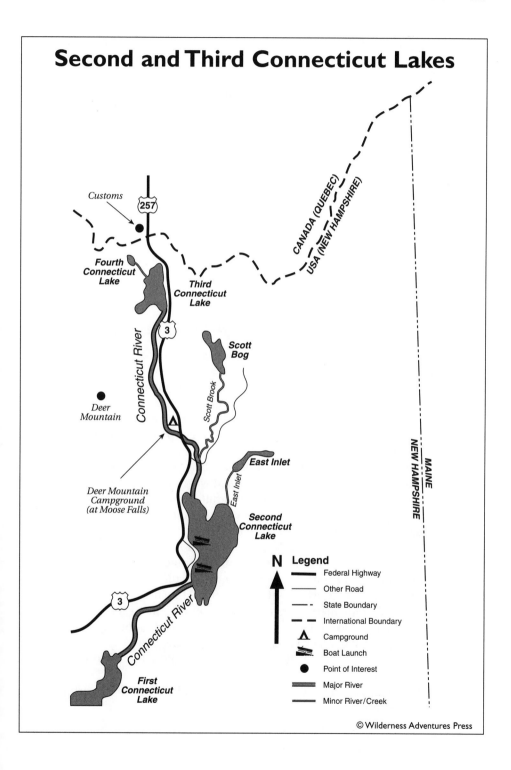

Customs

257

Fourth
Connecticut
Lake

Third
Connecticut
Lake

CANADA (QUEBEC)
USA (NEW HAMPSHIRE)

3

Scott
Bog

Connecticut River

Scott Brook

Deer
Mountain

East Inlet

East Inlet

Deer Mountain
Campground
(at Moose Falls)

Second
Connecticut
Lake

MAINE
NEW HAMPSHIRE

3

N Legend

Federal Highway

Other Road

State Boundary

International Boundary

Campground

Boat Launch

Point of Interest

Major River

Minor River/Creek

Connecticut River

First
Connecticut
Lake

© Wilderness Adventures Press

Canoeists who flyfish this big water should hug the shoreline as whitecapped waves can make for choppy going. Public access is made near the lake's westernmost tip off Route 3.

Second Connecticut Lake

The Second Connecticut Lake covers 1,286 acres. Like First Lake and Lake Francis, it was created by damming the upper Connecticut River. Common catches by streamer-trolling include lake trout and salmon, though some brook trout are also caught. There were 750 landlocked salmon stocked in this lake in 1996.

Boat access is found off Route 3 on the southwestern side of the lake. Ice-out arrives around mid-May.

Third Connecticut Lake

Third Lake boat access is off Route 3 just south of the Canadian border. This 278-acre pond produces catches of rainbows and lake trout and was stocked with 900 rainbows in 1996.

Small boats or canoes work well on this tree-lined lake.

Northern New Hampshire Flyfishing-only Stillwaters

The following waters offer flyfishing-only opportunities for brook trout:

Located in Pittsburg, **Big Brook Bog** is a 37-acre pond west of the Second Connecticut Lake. Like many other fisheries in this region, access is from Route 3. Flyfish the late June through early July caddis hatch.

Pittsburg's **Boundary Pond** is found in the northernmost tip of the state near the Quebec border. This 17-acre pond was stocked with 2,774 fingerlings in 1996.

Clarksville Pond is a 25-acre pond in Clarksville, east of Route 145.

Granite State flyfisher Dave O'Brien uses Hornberg patterns on **Coon Brook Bog**, a 6-acre flyfishing-only pond in Pittsburg. Fished wet or dry, the Hornberg is a popular imitation in northern New England for adult caddis, stoneflies, and baitfish. Colors vary from green to cinnamon to yellow to natural.

Little Bear Brook Pond can be reached by driving north from Errol and take the first left after Long Pond. Located 1mile north of Route16 after the turn. Expect somewhat selective holdover fish in the 7- to 10-inch range in this 4-acre pond.

Lime Pond holds 14 well-stocked acres located in Columbia. Holden Road south of Colebrook will give you access. Trout average 9 to 11 inches.

Little Millsfield Pond offers 37 acres of flyfishing-only water west of Errol.

Pittsburg's 10-acre **Moose Pond** is well stocked by early June. Access is gained from Shatney Road west of Black Lake, just off Jesse Young Road.

Perry Pond is 10 acres of trout water in Pittsburg near the Third Connecticut Lake. Access is by foot trail.

More pond than lake, **Saco Lake** is a 9-acre pond in the town of Carroll. It was stocked with 1,386 brookies in 1996.

Scott Bog covers 100 acres in the town of Pittsburg. It is heavily stocked with brook trout. Access is off Route 3 north of Second Connecticut Lake. Remember that wilderness road logging trucks have the right of way.

Terrell Pond or "West Branch Pond" is fed by the West Branch of Indian Stream off Jesse Young Road. This 10-acre pond was stocked with 3,800 trout in 1996. Expect 9- to 11-inch brookies that become fairly selective by midsummer. Enormous moose hoof prints are a fixture of the mud surrounding this pond that is quite close to the Canadian border.

Upper Trio Pond, located in Odell, is a remote 21-acre pond holding spunky holdover brookies.

Unknown Pond, a 6-acre pond located in the town of Pittsburg just west of the Second Connecticut Lake. Expect 7- to 10-inch brookies.

Wright Pond, another 6-acre pond in trout-rich Pittsburg can be reached via a remote access by foot trail.

NORTHERN NEW HAMPSHIRE HUB CITIES
Errol
Elevation–1,280 • Population–300

Errol provides services for Androscoggin River flyfishers and others visiting this remote New Hampshire region.

ACCOMMODATIONS

Errol Motel, Route 26 / 603-482-3256 / Jean and Robert Kenney offer housekeeping units close to the Androscoggin River fishery / Swimming pool available / $

RESTAURANTS

Bill's Seafood & Country Cookin', Route 26 / 603-482-3838 / Homemade soups, seafood, steak, sandwiches, and desserts

Lucy's North Star Cafe, 10 Main Street / 603-482-3383 / Open 7 days a week for breakfast, lunch, and dinner / Owner: Lucy Nelson

FLY SHOPS AND SPORTING GOODS

L.L. Cote Sport Shop and True Value Hardware, 290 Main Street / 603-482-7777 / Motto: "Home of Toys for Big Boys" / Offers camping equipment with a complete line of tents, camping, and backpacking gear, plus flyfishing tackle, outdoor clothing, footwear, and firearms / Wayne Underwood can fill you in on current flyfishing trends

MEDICAL

Upper Connecticut Valley Hospital / 603-237-4971 / Provides health services for the Coos County region

Pittsburg
Elevation–1,660 • Population–901

Pittsburg, New Hampshire (spelled without the ending "h" as some residents are quick to remind you) is the Granite State's northernmost town. Back in 1829, natives of this region set up an independent state separate from New Hampshire, dubbing it the "United Inhabitants of the Indian Stream Territory." Eleven years later they rejoined the Granite State, but some of that self-sufficient spirit even lingers on today.

Many Coos County flyfishers pack several coolers full of food and drinks for the duration of their trip to the north country. Provisions can also be purchased at local sporting goods stores.

ACCOMMODATIONS

Mountain View Cabin & Campgrounds, RR1, Box 30 / 603-538-6305 / Located on Route 3 across from Young's Store / Judy and Merrill Dalton have log cabins, cottages, and 60 scenic campsites for rental, some with lake or river frontage / $

Tall Timber Lodge, Back Lake / 800-835-6343; 603-538-6651 / Owned by the Caron Family, this sporting camp offers lakefront log cabins and fine food served in their main lodge / Boat rentals, fishing licenses, tackle, flies, and a flyfishing school are available, as well / $$$

Timberland Lodge & Cabins, First Connecticut Lake / 800-545-6613; 603-538-6613 / Owners Doug and Linda Feltmate offer 20 cabins ranging from 1 to 4 bedrooms with easy access to the upper Connecticut River and local stillwaters / Boat and motor rental available / Pets welcome / A selection of local fly patterns is available at the check-in desk / In early July 1997, Linda reported that "Our guests have recently caught a total of 12 salmon right off our docks." / $

RESTAURANTS

Colebrook Park Place Restaurant, Route 145 (corner of Park Street and Corliss Lane in Colebrook 03576) / 603-237-8800 / Breakfast served all day / Owners: Esther and Richard Fournier

The Wilderness Restaurant (Colebrook 03576) / 603-237-8779

FLY SHOPS AND SPORTING GOODS

JR's Mini Mart, Main Street / 603-538-6352 / Open 6am-8pm / Owner Ken Roy sells fishing licenses, tackle, gear, gas, and groceries

The Trading Post, Main Street / 603-538-6533 / Wendy and Doug Morse offer sporting goods, fishing licenses, gas, lottery tickets, beer, ice, videos—the works / Open 7 days a week

Wilderness Sporting Goods, Route 3 / 603-538-7166 / Carolyn and Buster Hutchins sell camping and boating supplies, fishing licenses, tackle, and even firewood / Canoe rentals available

Young's Store, Route 3 / 603-538-6616 / Take a right on entering the store and you'll arrive at the fishing tackle section / Sells provisions, gas, newspapers, maps, and something you'll definitely need in spring: bug repellent

Tall Timber Lodge, Back Lake / 800-835-6343; 603-538-6651 / Boat rentals, fishing licenses, tackle, flies, and a flyfishing school are available, as well / $$$

Ducret's Sporting Goods, 140 Main Street (Colebrook 03576) / 603-237-4900

Emerson & Son, 28 State (Groveton 03582) / 603-636-1220

Lopstock Outfitters and Guide Service, First Connecticut Lake / 800-538-6659 / Scott fly rods, Teton reels, wide selection of flies for Connecticut River

AUTO REPAIR

Coos Auto Supply, 2 Colby Street (Colebrook 03576) / 603-237-5504 / Located 20 minutes south of Pittsburg on Route 3 and a half-hour northwest of Errol on Route 26

Lewis and Woodward, Inc., 164 Main Street (Colebrook 03576) / 603-237-5575 / Gasoline and automotive service Monday through Saturday, 7:30am to 6:00pm

MEDICAL

Upper Connecticut Valley Hospital / 603-237-4971 / Provides health services for the Coos County region

FOR MORE INFORMATION

Connecticut Lakes Tourist Association
P.O. Box 38
Pittsburg, NH 03592
603-538-7405

Major Roads and Rivers of Maine

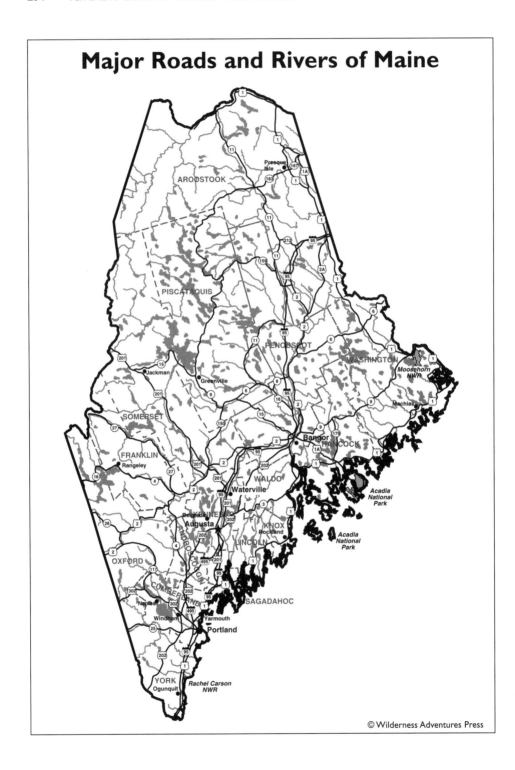

© Wilderness Adventures Press

Maine Facts

31st largest state in the union
33,215 square miles

Nickname: The Pine Tree State
Counties: 16
Population: 1.2 million
 32 State Parks
   1 National Forest (White Mountain)
   1 National Park (Acadia)
   1 National Wildlife Refuge (Moosehorn)
   1 Wilderness Waterway (Allagash)
 29 Public Reserved Lands

State Motto: **Dirigo (I Lead)**
State Bird: **Chickadee**
State Tree: **White Pine**
State Animal: **Moose**
State Gem: **Tourmaline**
State Fish: **Landlocked Salmon**

SPECIAL NOTICE

The state of Maine has closed the recreational Atlantic salmon fishing season for the 2000 season in all Maine rivers. Check the current regulations before fishing these waters.

Flyfishing in Maine

The waters of the state of Maine are made up of over 30,000 miles of rivers and streams, nearly 3,000 lakes and ponds, and a rugged, coastal shoreline that runs "Down East" for more than 300 miles. These waters offer anglers the opportunity to cast or troll flies for coastal striped bass and bluefish, sea-run Atlantic salmon and brown trout, wild and stocked brook trout and browns, landlocked salmon, lake trout or togue, as well as warmwater species, including smallmouth and largemouth bass, northern pike, and pickerel.

Inland fishing licenses are available for nonresident anglers, in person, at town clerks' offices, sporting goods stores, and some local drug stores, or by mail from the Maine Department of Inland Fisheries and Wildlife, 284 State Street, 41 State House Station, Augusta, ME 04333, phone 207-287-8000. Licenses may be purchased for a 1-day, 3-day, 7-day, or 15-day period or for a full season. There is no recreational salt-water fishing license required. A permit is required for Atlantic salmon angling. This special permit is obtained through agents or directly from the Atlantic Salmon Authority, 650 State Street, Bangor, ME 04401, phone 207-941-4449.

Many of Maine's streams and stillwaters are remote, surrounded by wilderness areas or lands owned and restricted by timber companies. To locate remote waters, the state of Maine has identified 911 of what are called "Minor Civil Divisions" on maps. Many of the roads that provide access to the more remote regions are gated and a small user fee is charged. There are also local outfitters, camps, and "fly-in" services available in outpost villages, such as Jackman, Presque Isle, and Millinocket, that can assist with access and planning. A good resource for locating individual guides, outfitters, and camps is **www.maineguides.com**.

The state of Maine is truly bountiful. Deep forests hide pristine waters filled with wild brook trout and landlocked salmon. Moose and white-tailed deer have countless, undeveloped acres of woodlands, bogs, and mountains in which to range freely. The people of Maine are down-home friendly and more than happy to offer their services and hospitality.

MAINE'S HATCHERY FISH

In 1994, the Maine Department of Inland Fisheries and Wildlife planted 1,551,373 brook trout, landlocked salmon, brown trout, lake trout (togue), and hybrid splake into inland waters. This is almost 222,036 pounds of fish. The following year, 1,086,615 salmon and trout (241,925 pounds) were stocked. In 1996, Pine Tree State waters received 1,018,440 hatchery fish. This last stocking totaled 249,792 pounds. Stockings usually take place in both spring and fall.

According to the Maine Department of Inland Fisheries and Wildlife and Christopher Short, Phillips Fish Hatchery supervisor, Maine fisheries management these days is based on enhancing genetic diversity among fish stocks in addition to tradi-

Plantings of trout in Maine traditionally take place in both spring and fall.
(Photo by Steve Hickoff)

tional measures that evaluate harvest controls, appropriate stocking numbers, and environmental attention to waterways.

During the fall of 1995, some new strains of brood fish were developed from wild fish. Broodstock strains were established from Baxter State Park's Nesowadnehunk Lake brook trout, Enfield's Cold Stream Pond togue, and brookies from the Kennebago watershed. Native trout numbers in these locations are healthy, and officials hope the new strains of brook trout, lakers, and hybrid splake will replace Maine's traditionally stocked strains. Supervisor Short stresses that genetic diversity among broodstock is the key to promoting the longevity of future hatchery operations in the state.

Maine waters, stocked by the state, occasionally lack the habitat required for wild fish production. At these locations, angling depends solely on planted trout and salmon. Many other fisheries have good habitat and support natural reproduction. Prevailing conditions for particular waters are noted in this guidebook.

DEFINING MAINE FLYFISHING

This definition is more complicated than it seems. According to the Maine Department of Inland Fisheries and Wildlife, a fly is defined as "a single pointed hook dressed with feathers, hair, thread, tinsel, or any similar material to which no additional weights, hook, spinner, spoon, or similar device is added." There are some fly patterns with which you are familiar that won't fit this definition.

For example, tandem-hooked streamers, though part of Maine's landlocked salmon fishing tradition and pictured prominently in many flyfishing publications, fall short of this specific criteria for flyfishing-only waters. However, these patterns can be used on trout and salmon waters outside flyfishing-only restrictions.

Flyfishing in Maine is defined as "casting upon water and retrieving in the usual and ordinary manner not more than 3 unbaited artificial lures individually attached to a line to which no extra weight has been added."

How about trolling? Some guys, especially northern New England landlocked salmon anglers, troll streamers. Trolling in Maine means "to fish by trailing a line rigged to catch fish through or over the water behind a watercraft being propelled by mechanical, wind, or manual power." This can be particularly tricky on flyfishing-only waters. By definition, "It is unlawful to troll a fly in waters restricted to flyfishing only." Outboards, oars, paddles, and even chilly seasonal breezes can define your fishing strategy as trolling, and wardens are paid to enforce such rules.

New Maine Trout Regulations

Historic changes have recently been enacted to protect Maine's wild trout fisheries. State biologists indicate that there has been an increase in angling pressure over the last few years, particularly on waters with wild reproduction, which include half of Maine's trout ponds. These regulations are intended to address such challenges, with the simple goal of protecting native brook trout.

For many of Maine's 474 wild trout fisheries, the new daily limit is 2 fish.

Southern Maine

Your gateway to the state of Maine is through the south. Interstate 95 and Route 1 will carry you from the cities of Portsmouth, Boston, and New York into the quiet, coastal communities and beaches of York, Ogunquit, and Biddeford and into the beautiful city of Portland. From there, if you continue down east, you'll pass the iron works and shipyards of Bath, Mount Desert Island, and eventually, to the remote coastal towns near the border with the Province of New Brunswick, Canada.

Each year, millions of vacationers seek the beaches and shopping outlets that are abundant in southern Maine. Another attraction is the fishing. Southern Maine rivers, estuaries, beaches, lakes, and ponds offer anglers almost unlimited opportunities. The waterways nearest the coast provide angling for striped bass, bluefish, sea trout, and Atlantic salmon (see notice below). Inland ponds and streams hold brook trout, lakers, landlocked salmon, and brown trout. You can cast a fly at night for large, roaming stripers or quietly drift on a remote pond looking for freely feeding brookies. Southern Maine has it all.

Maine's southwestern corner encompasses Cumberland and York Counties. Though densely populated, this area offers flyfishing for wild salmon, striped bass, and trout in waters not far from asphalt walkways. Flyfishers will also find accessible rivers, ponds, and lakes stocked with hatchery trout. These southernmost waters also support larger, late-season holdover fish. Several coastal tidewaters offer sea-run brown trout angling, as well.

Southern Maine's midcoastal area offers the opportunity to flyfish for striped bass that can reach 20 to 30 pounds as well as bluefish and even mackerel. Inland are ponds and streams that the state of Maine, with its aggressive stocking program, manage as brown, brook trout, and togue fisheries.

Southeastern Maine is referred to as "Down East." There are hundreds of streams and ponds offering angling opportunities for wild as well as stocked fish. The Down East rivers are also the native spawning waters of a remnant population of wild Atlantic salmon.

SPECIAL NOTICE

The state of Maine has closed the recreational Atlantic salmon fishing season for the 2000 season in all Maine rivers. Check the current regulations before fishing these waters.

SOUTHERN MAINE MAJOR HATCHES

Insect	J	F	M	A	M	J	J	A	S	O	N	D	Flies
Streamers			▬	▬	▬								Barnes Special #8-#10; Gray Ghost #8-#10; Kennebago Smelt #8-#10; Olive Matuka #6-#10; Black Nose Dace Bucktail #6-#10
Midges and Miniature Flies		▬	▬	▬	▬	▬	▬	▬	▬	▬	▬		Griffith's Gnat #16-#22; Parachute Adams #16-#20; Hatching Midge Pupa #12-#16; Olive Midge #16-#20; Mosquito Adult #14-#20; Midges (black and cream) #18-#22; Brassie #16-#20
Quill Gordon *Epeorus pleuralis*					▬								Quill Gordon #12-14
Hendrickson and Red Quill *Ephemerella subvaria*					▬	▬							Hendrickson #12-14; Red Quill #12-16
Caddis						▬	▬	▬					Elk Hair Caddis #6-#18; Elk-wing Parachute Caddis #12-#18; Henryville Special #12-#18; Deep Sparkle Pupa #12-#18; Brown Sparkle Pupa #6-#12; Caddis Variant #12-#18; LaFontaine's Deep Sparkle Pupa #12-#18; Beadhead Emerging Caddis #10-#14; Emergent Sparkle Pupa #12-#18
Alderfly/Zebra Caddis							▬						Black Palmer #12; Adams #12
Gray Fox *Stenonema fuscum*						▬	▬						Gray Fox #12-#16

SOUTHERN MAINE MAJOR HATCHES (cont.)

Insect	J	F	M	A	M	J	J	A	S	O	N	D	Flies
Dragonflies/Damselflies							▮						Dragonfly Nymph #4–#8; Whitlock's Dragonfly #4–#8; Damselfly Nymph #4–#8; Whitlock Spent Blue Damsel #6
Light Cahill *Stenonema canadensis*						▮	▮						Light Cahill #10–16
Hexagenia						▮							Hex Nymph #4–#6; Parachute Hex #8–#10 (carry both)
Blue-winged Olive *Ephemerella attenuata*								▮					Blue-winged Olive #14–22; Blue-winged Olive Thorax #14–20; Blue-winged Olive Nymph #16
Stoneflies				▮	▮								Early Black Stone #12–#16; Early Brown Stone #12–#16; Willow Fly #14–#16; Stimulator #8–#14; Stonefly Nymph (black or brown) #12–#16
March Brown					▮	▮							March Brown #12–#16
Leeches						▮	▮						Marabou Leech (black) #16; Woolly Bugger (olive, black, or brown) #4–#10
Terrestrials													
Ants						▮	▮						Black Fur Ant #12–20; Black Flying Ant #12–16
Beetles						▮	▮						Black Beetle #14–20
Grasshoppers						▮	▮						Parachute Hopper #8–14; Letort Hopper #8–14
Crickets						▮	▮						Cricket #8–14; Letort Cricket #8–14

Southwestern Maine

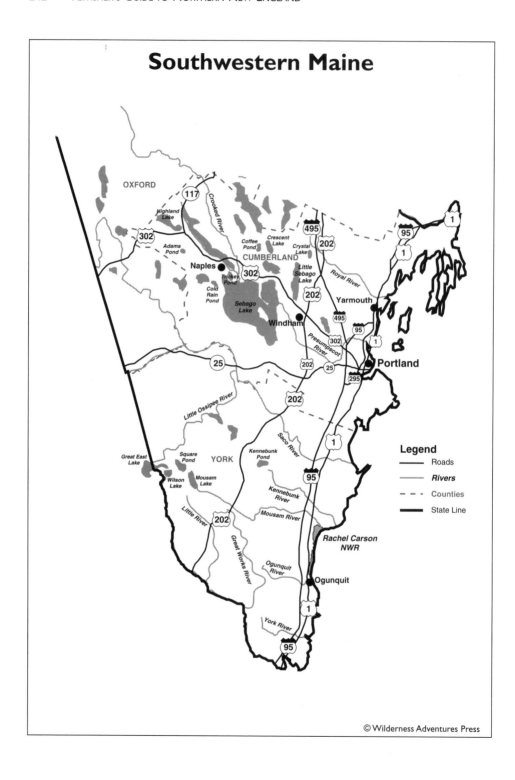

OXFORD

117

Crooked River

Highland
Lake

302

Adams
Pond

495

202

95

1

1

Coffee
Pond

Crescent
Lake

Crystal
Lake

CUMBERLAND

Naples

Trickey
Pond

302

Little
Sebago
Lake

Royal River

202

Yarmouth

Cold
Rain
Pond

Sebago
Lake

Windham

495

95

1

Presumpscot
River

302

25

202

25

Portland

295

202

Little Ossipee River

Saco River

1

Great East
Lake

Square
Pond

YORK

Kennebunk
Pond

95

Wilson
Lake

Mousam
Lake

Kennebunk
River

Little River

202

Mousam River

Great Works River

Rachel Carson
NWR

Ogunquit
River

Ogunquit

Legend

——— Roads

~~~~~ *Rivers*

– – – Counties

━━━ State Line

York River

1

95

© Wilderness Adventures Press

SOUTHWESTERN MAINE RIVERS AND STREAMS
Crooked River

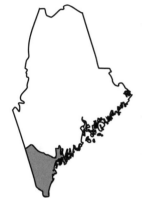

Managed as a protected resource, the Crooked River provides one of the principal wild salmon and trout fisheries here in southern Maine, according to John Boland, regional fisheries biologist for the Sebago Region.

Landlocked salmon and wild brook trout in this southern Maine fishery draw coldwater anglers from around the region during the early spring season and again in autumn. Vitally important to Sebago Lake, Crooked River's spawning grounds produce the bulk of the wild fish found in the big water.

According to Boland, springtime anglers can expect good to excellent native brook trout fishing in the Crooked River. Fish occasionally weigh as much as 3 pounds. Average wild trout will run smaller, around 6 to 12 inches. "The entire Crooked River fishery is wild," says John. "In early spring, expect good native brook trout fishing. By the first of May until the middle of the month, salmon run into the river following spawning smelt. Good fishing lasts into June for both landlocks and brook trout."

Summer months in Maine occasionally bring low water conditions. Without much rainfall, flyfishing slows down a bit. Still, there is some July and August angling available. "Some native brookies can be found in the small Crooked River tributaries by summer, and a good rain will move fish around a bit," Boland suggests.

The vagaries of weather remain an important factor on the Crooked River. Northern New England's cold September rains trigger predictable fall spawning urges in brook trout and browns as well as landlocked salmon. Landlocks enter the Crooked from Sebago Lake, then stage in pools as they negotiate upriver toward the headwaters. In September, the sky above can be as silver and gray as the landlocked salmon. Crooked River salmon flyfishers look for such skies in anticipation of the stormy weather that initiates the salmon run.

The rising water brought on by the rain moves fish—even subtly rising pools will hold staging salmon in the early autumn. Landlocks average several pounds, with larger fish occasionally caught. Boland indicates that spawning fall salmon moving up the Crooked River are influenced not only by rainfall but the changes in water temperature and the shortening photo-period. Water temperatures in the mid-50s usually trigger the spawning run. As a result, early October finds fish on the move and even sooner, given the right conditions. Local weather reports can provide clues.

The Crooked originates at Songo Pond south of the village of Bethel in Albany Township near White Mountain National Forest. The upper river is prone to substantial runoff. High flows can be expected from April through the first or second week of May, depending on the year. After mid-May, river flows taper off and are at summer levels by late June, remaining stable until September rains commence.

Crooked River runs are broken up by boulder, riffle, and rapid sections.
(Photo by Steve Hickoff)

The river moves south to Sebago Lake, snake-like, as pocketwater, followed by riffles, runs, and pools. North of Sebago, the riffles and pools near Cook Mills, Edes Falls Road, and River Road all hold fish. The section of river from Bolster's Mills Bridge in the small settlement of Bolster's Mills downstream to Route 11 in Casco provides excellent early October catch-and-release, flyfishing-only opportunities.

Boulders, riffles, and sections of rapids break up the fairly flat, sandy runs on Crooked River. Pools near the Crooked and Songo Rivers' confluence attract spring-time anglers. The river offers a low gradient with sandy sections and slow-moving pools. Riffles deepen into likely holding pools and long runs the color of iced tea.

Sebago Lake fly patterns will interest Crooked River landlocks. Fish the river through June, in the summer after a good rain, and in September. Dry-fly purists can anticipate traditional hatches. Boland fishes small nymphs or wet flies for both salmon and trout in the more gently moving water. Patterns in the 12 to 16 size range work best. Reliable wets include the light cahill (#12–14), dark Hendrickson (#12–14), quill Gordon (#12–14), and blue-winged olives (#14–16). Look for small blue-winged olive duns just as autumn leaves turn orange, red, and gold. Go smaller in September (#20–22). Soft-hackled flies and wingless wets can interest wild brook trout throughout the season. Also carry terrestrials, such as hoppers, crickets, and ants.

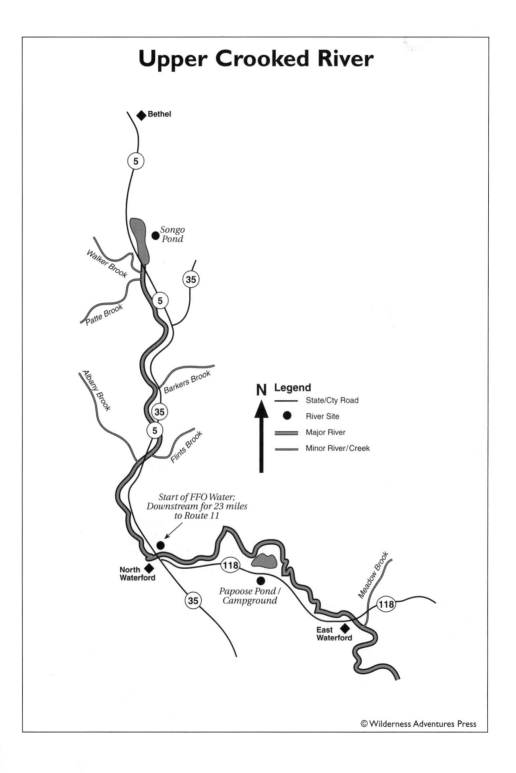

Upper Crooked River

Bethel

5

Songo Pond

Walker Brook

35

5

Patte Brook

Albany Brook

Barkers Brook

35
5

Flints Brook

N Legend

—— State/Cty Road
● River Site
▬▬ Major River
▬▬ Minor River/Creek

Start of FFO Water;
Downstream for 23 miles
to Route 11

North
Waterford

118

Papoose Pond /
Campground

35

Meadow Brook

118

East
Waterford

© Wilderness Adventures Press

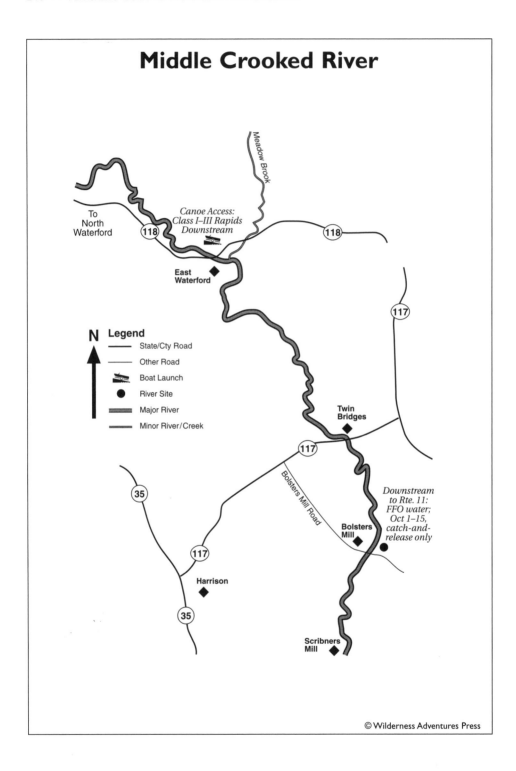

Middle Crooked River

Meadow Brook

To
North
Waterford

118

*Canoe Access:
Class I–III Rapids
Downstream*

118

East
Waterford

117

N

Legend

— State/Cty Road

— Other Road

Boat Launch

● River Site

Major River

Minor River/Creek

Twin
Bridges

117

35

Bolsters Mill Road

*Downstream
to Rte. 11:
FFO water;
Oct 1–15,
catch-and-
release only*

Bolsters
Mill

117

Harrison

35

Scribners
Mill

© Wilderness Adventures Press

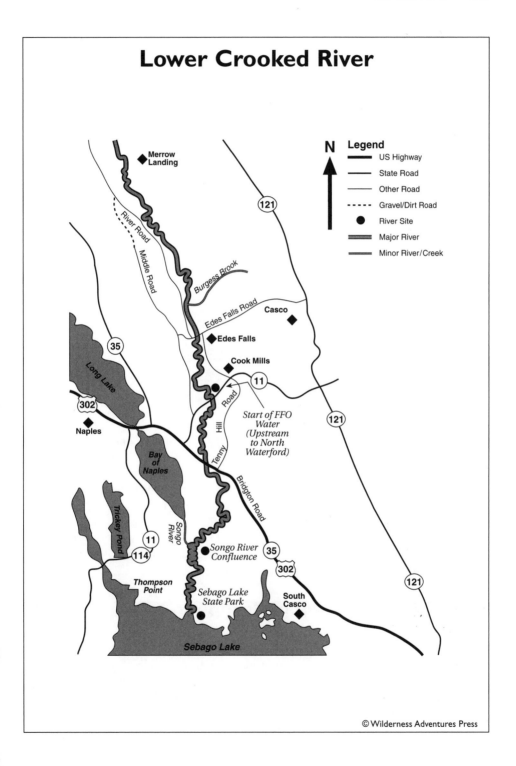

Lower Crooked River

N

Legend
- US Highway
- State Road
- Other Road
- Gravel/Dirt Road
- ● River Site
- Major River
- Minor River/Creek

Merrow Landing

River Road

Middle Road

121

Burgess Brook

Edes Falls Road

Casco

Edes Falls

Cook Mills

11

35

Long Lake

Tenny Hill Road

Start of FFO Water (Upstream to North Waterford)

302

Naples

121

Bay of Naples

Bridgton Road

Trickey Pond

Songo River

11

114

Songo River Confluence

35

302

Thompson Point

Sebago Lake State Park

121

South Casco

Sebago Lake

© Wilderness Adventures Press

A not-so-crooked section of the Crooked River. (Photo by Steve Hickoff)

Crooked River's season extends from April 1 through September 30, unless noted otherwise. The section on Route 11 near the villages of Casco and Naples to Route 35 in the village of North Waterford is flyfishing only from April 1 to September 30. All salmon caught must be released alive at once. From Bolster's Mill Road bridge downstream to Route 11 in Casco is flyfishing only from October 1 through 15, and all fish caught must be released alive at once.

Access on the Crooked is available at pull-off spots along the river. River-mouth boat ramps on Sebago Lake near Sebago Lake State Park provide downstream access as well as walk-in streambank access upstream.

Presumpscot River

While the Crooked River is managed as a wild fishery, the Presumpscot River is heavily stocked and receives a lot of fishing pressure. The many angler access points along this meandering river hold good numbers of trout. Hatchery trucks can easily stock trout and salmon near these pulloff areas.

Though springtime finds angler competition high, mild autumn and winter days will often provide flyfishers pools to themselves. Sightfishing before casting often

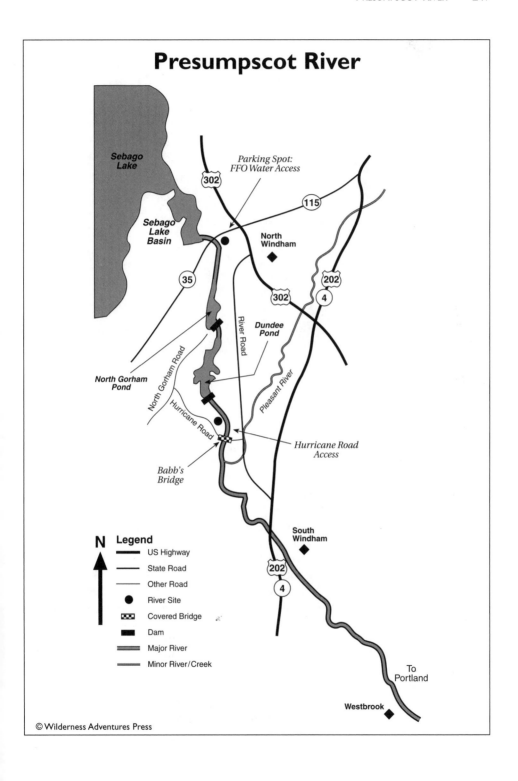

Presumpscot River

Sebago Lake

Sebago Lake Basin

Parking Spot: FFO Water Access

302

115

North Windham

35

202

North Gorham Pond

River Road

302

4

Dundee Pond

North Gorham Road

Hurricane Road

Pleasant River

Hurricane Road Access

Babb's Bridge

South Windham

N Legend
— US Highway
— State Road
— Other Road
● River Site
▦ Covered Bridge
■ Dam
━ Major River
━ Minor River/Creek

202

4

To Portland

Westbrook

© Wilderness Adventures Press

Presumpscot River pools are heavily stocked and heavily fished.
(Photo by Elizabeth Edwards)

helps find fish. The nearby Pleasant River, a Presumpscot tributary, also holds brook and brown trout and is heavily stocked. Stillwaters connected by the Presumpscot include North Gorham and Dundee Ponds. North Gorham saw a handful of 26- to 28-inch browns planted in 1996. Keep a few woolly bugger or matuka patterns handy and you may run into one of these 5- to 7-pound fish.

The Presumpscot is open year-round for fishing. There is a flyfishing-only section from the Outlet Dam at Sebago Lake to North Gorham Pond. The daily limit on trout during the open-water season, April 1 through September 30, is 1 fish. Catch and release all salmon. The area approximately 100 feet from Sebago Lake outlet dam downstream to designated red markers is closed to fishing. Also closed is the area approximately 100 feet from the emergency spillway at the Eel Weir Dam downstream to designated red markers.

Carry midge patterns year-round. Early black and early brown stonefly nymphs (#12–16) fished slowly work in the flyfishing-only section from April through May. Hatchery trout and salmon adapt quickly, so delicate presentations can help. Fish traditional dry-fly patterns, such as Adams (#12–18) or blue-winged olives (#14–18), in spring and early summer. Late September blue-winged olives are the predominant hatch—go with #20–22 in early fall. Terrestrials will also work. Fish midge patterns

Flyfisher Steve Eisenhaure works a Presumpscot River pool in early spring.
(Photo by Steve Hickoff)

during the woodstove months, and if winter daytime temperatures climb into the mid-40s, call in sick, mumbling something about "bugs," and find your fly tackle.

Holdover salmon range from a pound to several pounds, and all salmon must be immediately released. Stocked salmon average 12 to 15 inches in length. Hatchery browns stocked in 1996 ranged from 8 to 28 inches, while stocked brookies ranged from 8 to 18 inches.

While fishing the Presumpscot on April 1997's first Saturday, I glanced at a handful of angler survey cards. One flyfisher wrote, "Didn't catch a damn thing, so I'm going back to Wyoming!" while another scratched out, "No fish, but I almost stepped on a brown that would've gone 16 to 20 inches." Another angler noted catching brook trout while other folks were flat-out skunked. Moral: Watch where you wade or do your flyfishing out West, where I once lost a steelhead that still haunts me.

The flyfishing-only section between the Sebago Lake Outlet dam and North Gorham Pond has flow readings of 75 cfs from April through June. These stabilize at 50 cfs during July and August. In September and October, this section returns to springtime readings of 75 cfs. This is a popular river section for anglers from April through October.

The Presumpscot has everything from runs, pocketwater, and pools to riffles and holding lies. A wading staff is helpful, particularly in the early spring when flows can buckle your knees.

Access on the Presumpscot River is available off Route 35 via Route 302 near the eastern shore of Sebago Lake. The river winds south through rolling farmland from North Windham to South Windham, then on toward the city of Portland and Casco Bay. Where Route 35 crosses the river, anglers can either park along the main highway or drive their rigs down onto the flat, sometimes muddy area near the highway bridge. This section gets hit hard. Work downstream under the far pine-shaded riverbank to avoid the crowds.

Route 35 also provides good parking and access to the flyfishing-only section. Hurricane Road crosses the river downstream at Babb's Bridge. Both Hurricane and North Gorham Roads provide good side-road access.

Royal River

Try Cumberland County's Royal River in suburban Yarmouth for sea-run browns. Dead-drift weighted beadhead nymphs and woolly buggers to these fish, typically called "salters" by locals. Historically, this term was reserved for sea-run brook trout and now is used in reference to both species. Salters average several pounds, though some that can be as wily as feral cats will go larger. Smaller stocked browns of 6 to 8 inches and brookies of 10 to 12 inches are also present and will take a range of wet flies and nymphs.

An all-tide boat launch provides saltwater access to the river mouth, where anglers target their efforts near the Interstate 95 overpass. The section between East Elm Street and Bridge Street has access by foot. Also fish the water between Bridge Street and the Interstate.

As part of an ongoing Maine Department of Inland Fisheries and Wildlife management program, 2,600 browns from 6 to 8 inches were stocked in October of 1996. In June of the same year, brook trout of 10 to 12 inches in length were released in Yarmouth. The previous year several hundred 8- to 10-inch brookies were stocked in this section.

Upriver in New Gloucester, the Royal receives annual springtime stockings of brook trout 8 to 12 inches in length. Fish the New Gloucester sections from April through June. Stevens Brook, a small tributary of the upper Royal River, is stocked with brook trout of the same size. All manner of traditional wet flies, including black, brown, olive, or yellow woolly worms in small sizes, work well during spring.

Royal River regulations restrict angling to artificial lures only from Elm Street downstream to tidewater. The minimum length for trout is 12 inches. Daily limits on the Royal are no more than 2 browns and 1 brook trout. The extended season runs until the end of November. So forget about all that Thanksgiving Day hoopla—the TV football and the inconsequential parades. Think brown trout instead of turkey—the leftovers will wait.

Royal River

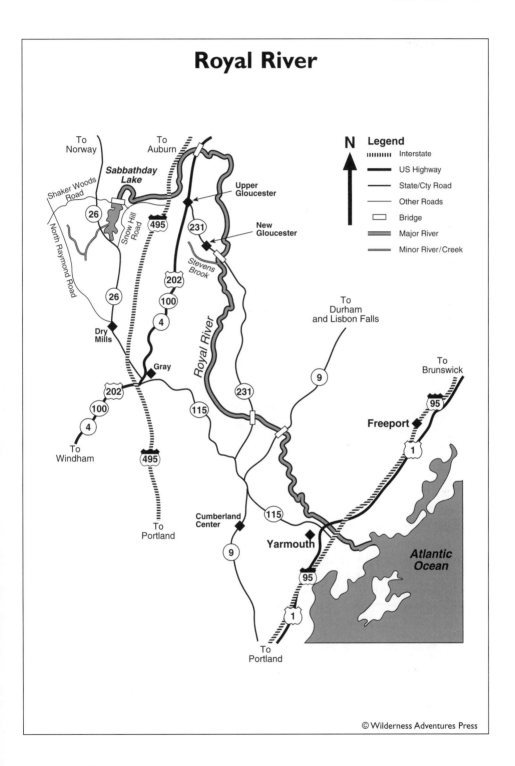

N

Legend

‖‖‖‖‖‖	Interstate
▬▬▬	US Highway
───	State/Cty Road
───	Other Roads
▭	Bridge
▬▬▬	Major River
▬▬▬	Minor River/Creek

To Norway

To Auburn

Sabbathday Lake

Shaker Woods Road

Upper Gloucester

New Gloucester

North Raymond Road

Snow Hill Road

26

495

231

Stevens Brook

202

100

4

26

Dry Mills

Royal River

To Durham and Lisbon Falls

To Brunswick

Gray

231

9

95

202

115

Freeport

100

1

4

To Windham

495

To Portland

Cumberland Center

To Portland

115

9

Yarmouth

9

95

Atlantic Ocean

1

To Portland

© Wilderness Adventures Press

Maine tidewaters, such as the Ogunquit River and others, offer flyfishing for sea-run browns. (Photo by Steve Hickoff)

Ogunquit River

With the coming of autumn, a tight-knit group of fly anglers target York County's Ogunquit River for sea-run browns. Some die-hards even continue fishing tidal water into the woodstove months, as southern Maine is often blessed by the occasional mild winter day. Serious fly anglers know the first three months of the year can offer excellent tidewater opportunities here. The area between Beach Street, toward the beachfront just northeast of Route 1, and the Atlantic Ocean is a good place to start.

After following Route 1 to the Ogunquit, pause to survey the situation by reading the river for staging salters. Work the water above and below the Beach Street bridge. This area provides the best shoreline access. This is also a good summertime striper holding area.

Target rising tidal flows, especially the last hour of the incoming tide, since salters and striped bass move with shifting water. Other flyfishers concentrate their efforts during low tide phases, since browns are occasionally contained by the dropping tide and can be sightfished. "Fish the Ogunquit just after the low tide has

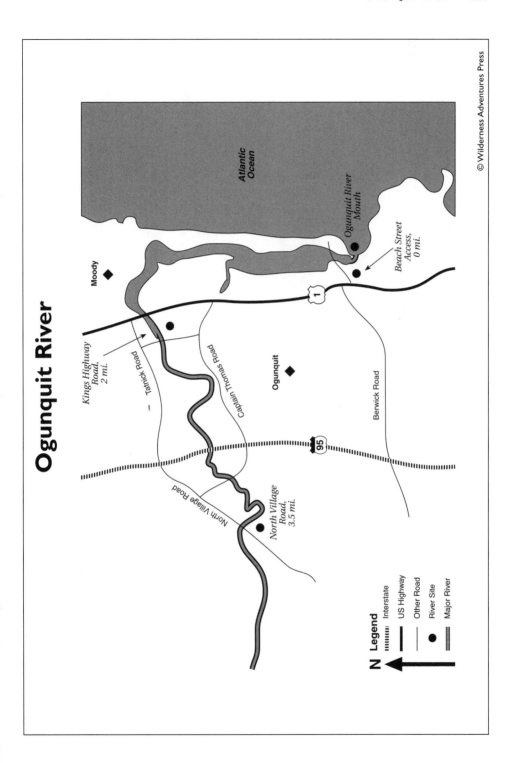

Ogunquit River

Atlantic Ocean

Ogunquit River Mouth

Beach Street Access, 0 mi.

Moody

Kings Highway Road, 2 mi.

Tatnick Road

Captain Thomas Road

Ogunquit

Berwick Road

North Village Road

North Village Road, 3.5 mi.

95

1

N

Legend
|||||||| Interstate
— US Highway
— Other Road
● River Site
— Major River

© Wilderness Adventures Press

Bird dog pups are often selected for their ability to make reliable fly pattern choices. (Photo by Steve Hickoff)

turned," says avid fly angler Joe Conklin, "and you'll sometimes see big browns holding in pools." Pinch yourself—though this isn't New Zealand or Patagonia, these elusive trout run just as large.

Conservation issues are important here on the southern Maine coast. Jim Bernstein, manager of the Eldredge Brothers Fly Shop, stresses this when it comes to Ogunquit River fishing: "Anglers should know how fragile this fishery is and that conservation should be kept in mind, especially here. Some guys who fish strictly by catch and release elsewhere are sometimes inclined to keep these big browns. To preserve this resource, fish need to be released."

Tactics here involve a good deal of patience as well. If you want to flyfish the Ogunquit well, Jim suggests that you think more about reading the river than actually casting into it. "One guy came into the fly shop recently and said he had studied the river most of the day, and when the time was right, he cast just once to a fish and caught it." Indeed, the Ogunquit River's allure is the possibility of catching robust autumn sea-run browns in shifting tidal water. The attitude here is akin to the Atlantic salmon angler's wish for fish: fly casting with the reliable expectation of intangible pleasures beyond big numbers.

Trout nuts, sipping coffee from thermoses, wearing fleece and fingerless gloves, seek Ogunquit browns that run from 14 inches in length to several pounds. Sightfishing anglers report seeing, but failing to interest, cagey salters in the 5- to 6-pound range. Those who fish in the low-light hours are often rewarded.

Coastal Maine anglers report success fishing marabou muddlers (#2–10), gold-ribbed hare's ears (#8–16), matuka sculpins (#2–6), rabbit streamers (#2–10), bead-head pheasant tails (#12–18), and the meat fly of choice in these parts, the woolly bugger (#2–8). Make the first cast count—it may be the only one you get or need. Sand eel patterns and black deceivers work well for stripers.

The Ogunquit River's season is year-round in tidewaters, with these special regulations: From April 1 to August 15, the section between Interstate 95 and U.S. Route 1 is artificial lure only, with a daily limit of 2 trout over 12 inches. Restrictions are the same from August 16 to 31, with a daily limit of 1 trout. Speaking as an insider, you should know that this sea-run fishery is special to coastal anglers. Though the law allows for the taking of these salters—one source told me how delicious these fish are —many Ogunquit River fly anglers advocate catch and release, some defiantly.

The season for striped bass is June 10 through October 15. There is a slot limit for stripers of 1 fish per day between 20 and 26 inches in length or over 40 inches. All others must be released unharmed. Expect striped bass by summer. Best times to flyfish are the tidal exchanges after dark and at daybreak.

The Ogunquit features moderate tidal flows between slack and flood tides. Downstream, this saltwater river is dominated by Atlantic Ocean conditions. Dead-low and full-flood tides stabilize water, and fish move on transitional rips created by the push and pull of tides. Study the river before making your move.

The best access to shoreline locations near the river's mouth are on Beach Street, where it crosses the Ogunquit by bridge.

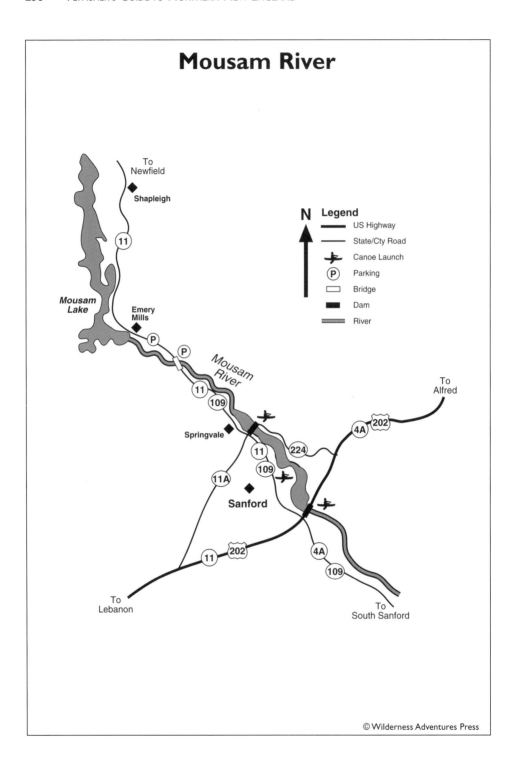

Mousam River

N

Legend

— US Highway
— State/Cty Road
Canoe Launch
(P) Parking
Bridge
Dam
River

To Newfield

Shapleigh

11

Mousam Lake

Emery Mills

(P)

(P)

Mousam River

11

109

Springvale

11

109

11A

Sanford

224

4A 202

To Alfred

11 202

To Lebanon

4A

109

To South Sanford

© Wilderness Adventures Press

Mousam River

The Mousam River begins its journey at the outflow of Mousam Lake near the village of Emery Mills. The river passes through several ponds and dams between the villages of Springvale, Sanford, and West Kennebunk. From Kennebunk, the Mousam makes a 5-mile run to the Atlantic Ocean near Parsons Beach.

There are three distinct fisheries: the upper, the midsections, and the estuary. The Mousam's upper section, between Emery Mills and the dam in Springvale, offers flyfishing opportunities for brook trout and browns. Routes 11 and 109 parallel the river and provide canoe and fishing access. The river runs more slowly and is considerably warmer through the dams and ponds of its midsection. Smallmouth bass, perch, and pickerel are abundant, and there are several canoe and boat accesses.

Striped bass fishing in the estuary of the Mousam River has drawn flyfishers from all over New England in recent years. There are areas of flats for those who enjoy wading and stalking stripers by night. Boat access is available for fly casters who chase stripers during the day. Two miles east of the village of Wells, Route 9 leads to Parsons Beach and the mouth of the Mousam River.

Saco River

The Saco River enters Maine at its border with the state of New Hampshire near the village of Fryeburg. The section of river between Hiram Falls, about a mile downstream from the village of Hiram, to the village of East Limington offers the most productive trout fishing on the Maine portion of the Saco. It is primarily a put-and-take fishery with good numbers of brown trout averaging 8 to 10 inches in length. There are some larger-sized browns that will hold over from year to year. This section of the Saco is also one of the most popular canoeing areas in the state of Maine.

The estuary of the Saco near the city of Biddeford is a popular area for flyfishing to stripers. The best access is by boat, although shore casting is available on the north side from the jetty at Camp Ellis. On the south side of the river mouth is Biddeford Pool, where there is good current at the pond's entrance.

North of Camp Ellis, Old Orchard Beach stretches for almost 6 miles along Route 9. There is plenty of access, and in addition to stripers, bluefish chase bait close to the beach. Plan to fish at night to avoid the crowds.

Saco River

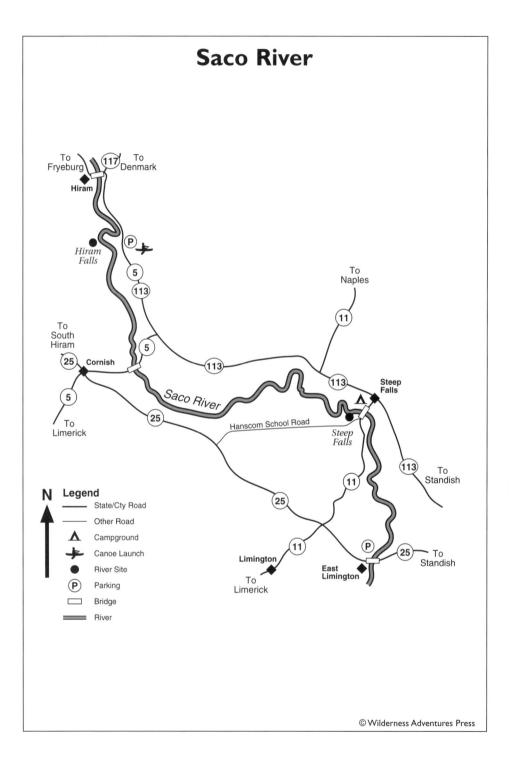

Other Southwestern Maine Rivers and Streams

Little Ossipee River is a small put-and-take stream that flows east through the village of Newfield. The state manages this fishery with annual stockings of brown trout that average 8 to 10 inches in length. The river stretch between the dam west of the village of North Shapleigh and the bridge in Newfield is special regulation water: Fishing is restricted to flies and artificial lures, and all trout must be released. There is access to this section of the Little Ossipee from Mann Road.

The river from Newfield to the village of Ossipee Mills also fishes well. Fishing is best in May and June before high water temperatures make the fish uncomfortable. Caddisfly and early season mayfly patterns are effective, as well as attractor patterns, such as Hornbergs and small Wulffs.

The river can be floated in the early season from North Shapleigh to Ossipee Mills. Access is found on Mann Road and the take-out near the Route 5 bridge in Ossipee Mills.

Little River is a tributary of Salmon Falls River on the New Hampshire border north of the village of Berwick and Route 9. The state stocks brook trout and browns annually and manages a catch-and-release section between Hubbard Road and Long Swamp Road. From Long Swamp Road upstream, access to the river is from Little River Road.

Great Works River flows through the village of North Berwick west of Route 4. This put-and-take stream is stocked with large numbers of brook trout in the spring and fall.

The upstream section of the **Kennebunk River**, north of the city of Kennebunk-port, is a heavily stocked put-and-take brookie and brown trout fishery. The river mouth offers fishing for stripers and blues. Access is limited to boat fishing.

There is also some striper fishing available near the mouth of the **York River** near York Beach.

York County Region

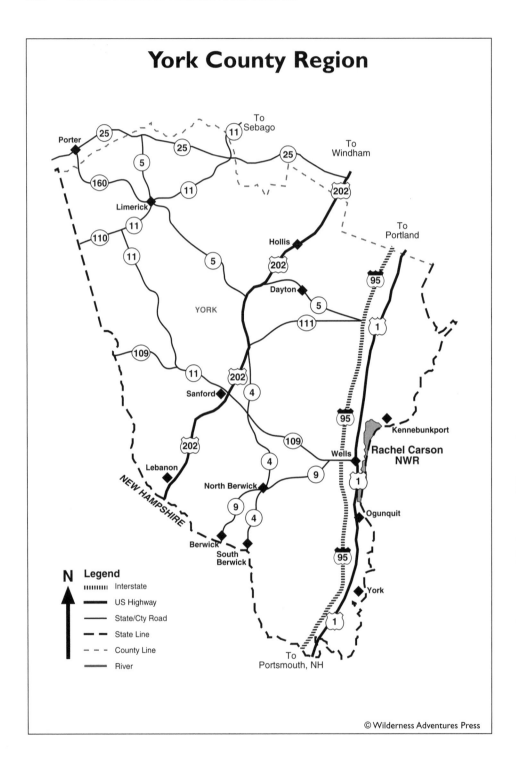

N

Legend

ⅢⅢⅢ	Interstate
▬▬	US Highway
—	State/Cty Road
– –	State Line
- - -	County Line
═══	River

© Wilderness Adventures Press

Other Fishing Opportunities in York County

River	Town	Fish
Batson River	Kennebunkport	Brown trout
Branch Brook/Merriland River confluence	Wells	Sea-run brook trout
Cape Neddick River	York	Brook trout
Cooks Brook	Dayton and Hollis	Brook trout
Great Brook	Lebanon	Brook trout
Josias Brook	York	Brook trout
Keay Brook	Berwick	Brook trout
Lovers Brook	South Berwick	Brook trout
Merriland River	Wells	Brown trout
Neoutaquet River	North Berwick	Brook trout
Ossipee River	Porter	Brown trout
Pendexter Brook	Limerick	Brookies and browns
Smelt Brook	York	Brook trout
Smith Brook	Kennebunkport	Brook trout
Swan Pond Brook	Dayton	Brook trout
Webhannet River	York	Brook trout
Worster Brook	Berwick	Brook trout
York River		Brook trout (200 in 1996); also striped bass opportunities at the mouth near York Beach

Sebago Lake

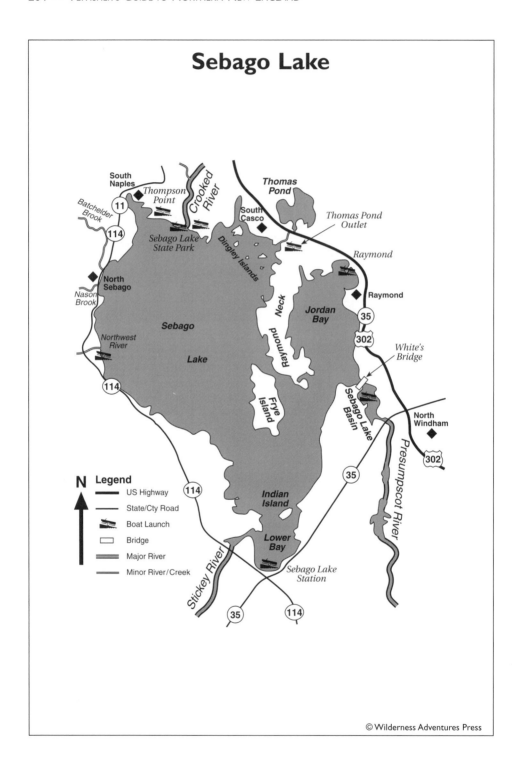

© Wilderness Adventures Press

Winds can whip up fast on Maine's big lakes. Keep your eyes on the sky
for developing weather, especially when canoeing such waters.
(Photo courtesy Maine Office of Tourism)

SOUTHWESTERN MAINE STILLWATERS
Sebago Lake

Sebago Lake, derived from the Native American description for "big water," spans 28,771 acres, with a maximum depth of 316 feet—the greatest in any New England lake. Springtime promises ice-out, which, translated into flyfisher language, means landlocked salmon, Maine's official state fish. Angling by fly is practiced on the edges of shoreline shallows along Sebago's sandy beaches and quite often near tributary inlets and outlets.

According to John Boland, Maine Department of Inland Fisheries and Wildlife regional fisheries biologist for the Sebago Region, ice-out will typically start on the "Big Bay" sometime during the first 10 days of April, though dates can vary. Often, the entire lake won't be free of ice until the end of the month. "Big Bay" is the area of Sebago extending from the mouth of the Songo and Crooked Rivers to Frye Island near the middle of Sebago Lake and the bay area along the entire western shore. Coinciding with ice-out, smelt and flyfishers begin to stage at specific Sebago Lake river and brook mouths. These include the Crooked and Songo Rivers near Sebago Lake State Park and Batchelder and Nason Brooks on the western side.

Good landlocked salmon flyfishing can also be found at the mouth of the Northwest River, just south of both Nason and Batchelder Brooks. Hundreds of hatchery brook trout (10 to 12 inches) and landlocked salmon fry are stocked in the Northwest River annually.

The shoal just offshore from this spot holds good numbers of spring fish. In fact, the entire western shore of the lake qualifies as a general location worth targeting. Stickey River on the lake's southern end offers shoreline access and good flyfishing opportunities.

Smelt move up Sebago Lake tributaries to spawn and are followed by feeding landlocked salmon. Boland indicates that the biggest concentration of smelt usually occurs near the mouth of the Songo River in April, often toward the end of the month. Access is good for boat anglers at the nearby Sebago Lake State Park public boat ramp. Other salmon flyfishing opportunities include autumn angling at Sebago Lake Station, a catch-and-release area for spawning fall landlocks. Sandy beaches and offshore deepwater areas ring Sebago, as well.

For landlocks, Boland, an avid flyfisher himself, suggests casting a Joe's smelt. He adds that any other salmon angler's favorite fly will work, including the gray ghost, a standard offering in this part of the country. Traditional patterns, which include the green ghost, Kennebago smelt, Mickey Finn, and supervisor, can be trolled or retrieved with short, fast jerks.

One early-season technique, and perhaps unheard of outside the northern New England region, involves trolling a streamer just outside the wash of the boat's propeller. Another method finds one angler slowly paddling while the other retrieves a smelt pattern behind the drifting canoe. Both strategies, as well as casting from shoreline spots near tributaries, work for ice-out landlocks. Whether trolling or casting from shore, some of the more successful Sebago Lake anglers make a point of arriving at daybreak, fly rods rigged, and ready for action.

In addition to this exceptional springtime landlocked salmon fishery, anglers will find abundant numbers of lake trout in Sebago Lake. Maine lake trout are also dubbed "togue," the Canadian French word derived from the MicMac Indian word atoghwaasu. High numbers of these fish in Sebago have reduced their size from an average weight of 6 pounds down to just 2½ pounds. To benefit both lakers and salmon, the Maine Department of Inland Fisheries and Wildlife is engaged in an ongoing effort to better manage this fishery.

Despite this average size, Sebago yields a respectable number of togue every year, 10- to 20-pound fish are not uncommon, and average-sized Sebago lakers can be good sport on a fly rod. Flyfish early, from ice-out through May, for the best springtime results on shallows-staging togue. Fish go deep in the summer—just after ice-out remains the best time to get one on a fly.

What about browns and brookies? Maine Department of Inland Fisheries and Wildlife records show that although Sebago produced a 19-pound, 7-ounce brown trout in the late 1950s, these waters now offer negligible brown trout fishing. Brook trout numbers here are also spotty. Look to nearby rivers and creeks for brookies and to local stillwaters for browns. Salmon in the spring and fall and ice-out togue offer flyfishers the best opportunities on Sebago Lake.

Flies for salmon include streamers, such as the black nose dace (#6–12), golden darter (#4–10), green ghost (#2–12), gray ghost (#2–12), grizzly king (#6–12), Joe's smelt (#4–10), Mickey Finn (#6–12), silver darter (#4–10), and matuka patterns (#2–10). Beadhead nymphs, traditional wets, and woolly buggers work when fishing the river outlets.

Sebago Lake has an open-water fishing season from April 1 through September 30. It is unlawful to fish into inland waters while standing on ice. Waters must be naturally free of ice. From October 1 through October 31, the area designated by red markers at Sebago Lake Station is flyfishing only with barbless hooks. Fishing is from shore and dock only, and all fish caught must be released alive at once.

Sebago's daily limit for togue is 3 fish. The 7½-pound weight limit in the aggregate of salmon, trout, and togue is waived here. The minimum length limit on salmon is 16 inches; for all other species read the General Law in the state's regulations. The daily limit for salmon is 1 fish. No fishing is allowed within 100 feet of White's Bridge near the village of North Windham.

Sebago Lake holds salmon (*Salmo salar*) from 2 to 4 pounds. The state record landlocked salmon, caught in 1907, weighed 22 pounds, 8 ounces. In 1996, 4,000 6- to 8-inch landlocks were stocked in Sebago Lake. The average lake trout runs 2½ pounds. Annual catches of togue from 10 to 20 pounds are not uncommon. On June 3, 1996, Kezar Falls angler William Day landed a 27½-pound Sebago Lake togue.

Several routes provide access to this renowned body of water. Look for the sign reading "Sebago Lake West Shore" from I-95. Take Exit 6 off the Interstate. From Exit 6, follow Route 114 to the west shore. Route 302 follows Sebago's northern shore; Route 114 will get anglers to the westernmost tributaries; and Route 35 parallels the southeastern end.

Boat ramps consist of Northwest River (western shore), Raymond (northern shore on Jordan Bay), Sebago Lake Basin (eastern shore), Sebago Lake Station (southern shore), Sebago Lake State Park (two ramps on the northern shore), Thompson Point (northern shore near park), and Thompson Pond Outlet (northern shore near Dingley Islands).

Cumberland County Stillwaters

The minimum length limit of brook trout in Cumberland County lakes and ponds is 8 inches, with a daily limit of 2 fish. Many flyfishers practice catch and release in these well-stocked fisheries. You'll find reliable angling at the following stillwaters:

Adams Pond, a small Bridgton stillwater off Route 107, holds 10- to 12-inch brookies. Flyfish through the month of May and into June for the best results. This is good canoeing water, and a hand-carried boat launch is available. An "artificial lure only" regulation prevails from April through June 20. Carry a nymph box full of zug bugs, pheasant tails, gold-ribbed hare's ears, and Prince nymphs in sizes 10 to 14.

Coffee Pond, located just off Route 11 in Casco, holds 10- to 12-inch hatchery brookies from late April into June, when the water begins to warm. Smallish woolly buggers catch Coffee Pond trout. The Wade State Fish Hatchery, located in Casco, raises landlocks for annual plantings. The public can visit the rearing station by request.

Cold Rain Pond lies off Tiger Hill Road in Naples and has a launch for canoes or small boats. Expect springtime brook trout from 10 to 12 inches. Fish all-purpose nymphs on this water.

Crescent Lake (Rattlesnake Pond) in the town of Raymond is currently being managed as a landlocked salmon fishery. Salmon of 8 to 10 inches are planted here annually. Access is available at the south shore boat launch just off Route 85. Keep an eye on this developing fishery.

Maine Department of Inland Fisheries and Wildlife stocking records report that brown trout from 10 to 28 inches in length were planted in **Crystal Lake** (Dry Pond) in 1996, as well as brook trout from 10 to 16 inches. To reach this water, take Route 26 north out of downtown Gray and then left on North Raymond Road. A boat launch is available on Crystal Lake's western shore. Fish leech patterns, damselfly and dragonfly nymphs, as well as traditional streamer patterns.

At **Highland Lake** (Duck Lake), which is open from spring through September's end and during a special extended catch-and-release season, anglers can expect 12- to 16-inch browns, brookies, and splake. Fish are stocked in Highland Lake in both spring and fall. A handful of 26- to 28-inch browns was released in 1996. Route 320 in Falmouth and Windham provides public access. The lake's southern end offers a hand-carried boat launch.

Browns from 10 to 28 inches are planted in **Little Sebago Lake**, located in the Gray and Windham Minor Civil Divisions. Look for trout along the shallow water shoreline just after ice-out, especially during the low-light hours of the day. A western shore boat launch provides access to this 1,898-acre fishery.

Ice-out typically arrives by late April. Fish woolly buggers, streamers, and large stonefly nymphs and expect catches of both trout and bass. Smallmouth and largemouth bass spawn in the shallows in late spring. Fly anglers can anticipate catching more bass than browns as summer commences, since trout move into the depths by Independence Day. Return here in early fall to flyfish during the extended October 1 to November 30 catch-and-release season.

Trickey Pond brookies run 10 to 16 inches in length, and the minimum legal togue length here is 16 inches. Fish just after ice-out through May.

This pond also holds "splake" (a word developed when Canadian biologists combined the term speckled trout with lake trout), which can reach a weight of 3 pounds. These brookie/laker hybrids can be identified by the togue's telltale yellow spotting on the sides and a somewhat forked tail. The state record currently stands at 10 pounds, 3 ounces.

Lake House Road off Route 302 or off Routes 11/114 in South Naples provides public access to this fishery.

Effective Patterns for Cumberland County Stillwaters

Fish *Hexagenia* nymphs (#4–8) with a sinking line and a slow retrieve on northern New England stillwaters (late June into July). Carry parachute *Hex* patterns, as well. A midge-imitating Griffith's gnat (#16–20) cast to fussy trout will often get a look, as will other midge patterns (pupa and adult) tied in varying color combinations. In fact, make a point of carrying such flies throughout the region on stillwaters and streams. Go smaller and smaller until you get results—size 22 flies aren't out of the question. Work the Griffith's gnat by holding the fly line in one hand while gently shaking your rod hand the way you do involuntarily while sightfishing a big trout. Slowly retrieve the tiny offering and allow it to rest at intervals. Think slow—many anglers just allow the fly to rest on the water without movement since the natural hardly moves at all. My father ties his Griffith's gnats in three sizes, #16–20, flyfishing this pattern on his Pennsylvania home waters starting in April and using a 6X or 7X leader. This approach works in Maine, as well.

York County Stillwaters

Though Cumberland County's Sebago Lake and nearby stillwaters and streams get major attention, fisheries located in Maine's southernmost tip are also worth noting. Except where listed otherwise, the minimum length limit on brook trout in York County lakes and ponds is 8 inches, and the daily limit is 2 fish.

Robert Hodsdon's all-state brown trout record of 23½ pounds was caught in **Square Pond** in 1995. "That fish was a real butterball," says the Maine Department of Inland Fisheries and Wildlife's Peter Bourque. "Hodsdon's catch clearly indicates the health of Square Pond brown trout. In fact, this entire region of the state, which includes Mousam Lake and Great East Lake, provides tremendous brown trout fishing." Maine Department of Inland Fisheries and Wildlife biologist John Boland agrees, "Square Pond is probably the best brown trout pond in Maine."

Square Pond is about 9 miles northwest of the Sanford-Springvale area off Route 11. There is a hand-carried boat launch and public access area on West Shore Drive at the southwest corner of the pond. The Maine Department of Inland Fisheries and Wildlife is currently working to improve this access. Other access is available off Route 11 and Town Farm Road on the northern end of the lake.

Want more big browns? Try **Mousam Lake**. "We (the Maine Department of Inland Fisheries and Wildlife) had received several comments from Maine anglers regarding the slow fishing at Mousam Lake," says regional biologist Boland, "but were puzzled by this since the water is actively managed for browns. As a result, one of my assistants used a set net in one particular Mousam Lake location in early August (1996). His daytime catch during this study yielded healthy browns from 2 to 4 pounds." Make no mistake about it—the fish are here.

Primarily managed for browns with landlocked alewives stocked as forage, Mousam trout numbers are healthy. In 1996, 700 brown trout (14 to 16 inches) were released, along with 10 trophy broodstock browns from 26 to 28 inches in length. A limited smelt population provides additional food for these fish, and holdover trout numbers are good. The broodstocks average a hefty 5 to 7 pounds.

In addition to browns, recent brook trout stocking reports show that 1,000 fish of 10 to 12 inches, 163 fish of 14 to 16 inches, and 57 fish of 16+ inches were planted in Mousam Lake.

Two easily accessible Mousam Lake boat launches are found on the water's southern end off Route 11 and Route 109. The Mousam River, running southeast from the big water along the main highway toward Sanford, is heavily stocked with browns and brookies. Fish this location and the lake itself April through early June.

Located in the village of Acton, **Great East Lake** shoreline locations are best fished just after ice-out. Browns, salmon, and lakers roam these shores early for smelt. Togue averaging 2 to 3 pounds are common and are good sport on the fly rod. Just ask any ice anglers who fish this shallow water during the winter months—many of their catches match this size.

Great East Lake is a 1,768-acre coldwater lake. It is easily accessible from Route 109 northwest of Wilson Lake. Check special regulations for Maine and New Hampshire border waters regarding limits, open seasons, and tackle restrictions. A license from either state is valid for fishing on Great East Lake.

Kennebunk Pond, just west of the village of Saco and Biddeford, offers fishing for holdover brookies and browns from 2 to 5 pounds, with some 8-pounders caught on occasion. Browns run larger than brookies. There is a good population of landlocked alewives providing forage. The state annually stocks trout from 10 to 18 inches.

Access is made off route 111 on Kennebunk Pond Road. Fish late April through May during low-light margins of the day. All-purpose nymphs, marabou muddlers, leech patterns, and wet flies will catch these fish.

Wilson Lake near the village of Acton is regularly stocked with browns and brook trout in both spring and fall. In 1996, a few whopper broodstock brown trout were released in late April, ranging from 26 to 28 inches in length. Browns and brookies from 14 to 16 inches were planted that October. Boat access is available off Garvin Road.

SOUTHWESTERN MAINE HUB CITIES
Ogunquit
Elevation–Sea Level • Population–30,000 to 50,000 (summer)

ACCOMMODATIONS
The Beachmere Inn, 12 Beachmere Place (P.O. Box 2340) / 207-646-2021; 800-336-3983 / Open late March to mid-December / $$$$$

Garnsey Bros. Rentals, corner of Webhannet Drive and Ocean Avenue / 207-646-8031 / Housekeeping cottages available on beach / Call for seasonal rates / Open year-round

Norseman Motor Inn, Ogunquit Beach / 207-646-7024; 800-822-7024 / Open April through November

RESTAURANTS
Egg & I Pancake and Waffle House, Route 1 / 207-646-8777 / Serves pancakes, waffles, and omelettes / Breakfast from 6AM-2PM / Daily luncheon specials, including crab sandwiches

Motion Pizza, 125 South Main Street / 207-646-2080 / Pizza, subs, salads, calzones, and more

Ogunquit Lobster Pound, Route 1 North / 207-646-2516 / Specialties include boiled lobsters and steamed clams, plus steak, chicken, and seafood

Poor Richard's Tavern, Shore Road / 207-646-4722 / Fine dining in a 1780 colonial building that once served as a coach stop between Boston and Portland / Reservations advised

FLY SHOPS AND SPORTING GOODS
Eldredge Brothers Fly Shop, Route 1 (located above Eldredge Lumber Company in Cape Neddick) / 206-363-2004 / "We're open from 8 to 5, 7 days a week except Sundays," manager Jim Bernstein jokes, implying things get pretty busy here; ask him about the wood duck heron fly pattern they sell, an Ogunquit River favorite/ Guides Dan Bonville and R.J. Mere operate out of the shop as well / Well stocked with flies and tackle

Kittery Trading Post, Route 1 (Kittery, 10 miles south of Cape Neddick) / 207-439-2700 / Located just off southern Maine's first three Interstate 95 exits (before the tolls), the KTP's fishing department caters to saltwater and freshwater anglers from around the region, including flyfishers, some of whom fish the Ogunquit / From Windham (Sebago region), drive just over one hour south to reach KTP / From New Hampshire, cross the I-95 bridge that spans the Piscataqua River and exit accordingly

Northeast Angler, 176B Port Road (Kennebunk 04043) / 207-967-5889 / Orvis shop

AUTO REPAIR
Alexandre's Mobil Garage, 8 Main Street (Ogunquit Square) / 207-646-5438 / Full service / AAA road service

Hutchins Garage, Inc., 116 Main Street (next to Post Office) / 207-646-5656

PUBLIC TRANSPORTATION

Brewster's Taxi & Micro-Mall / 207-646-2141 / Local and long distance service

AIRPORT

Portland International Jetport, near Fore River and just off I-95 / Taxi and van service available / Airlines: Business Express 800-345-3400; Continental 800-525-0280; Delta 800-221-1212; USAir 800-428-4322; United 800-241-6522 / A metro bus runs downtown from the airport

MEDICAL

York Hospital, 15 Hospital Drive (York 03909) / 207-363-4321

FOR MORE INFORMATION

Ogunquit Chamber of Commerce
P.O. Box 2289
Route 1
Ogunquit, ME 03907-2289
207-646-2939

Windham

Elevation–Near Sea Level • Population–13,800

ACCOMMODATIONS

Round Table Lodge, HC 75, Box 736 (North Sebago 04029) / 207-787-2780 / Western side of Sebago Lake near Batchelder and Nason Brooks / Light housekeeping cabins with fully equipped kitchens / Private beach / Contact Steve Sloan / $360 per week

Sebago Lake Cottages, HC 75, Box 905 (North Sebago 04029) / 800-535-3211 (outside Maine); 207-787-3211 / Owners Ray and Fran Nelson / 16 housekeeping cottages located at Nason's Beach (Routes 11 and 114) / Open year-round

Sebago Lake Lodge & Cottages, White Bridges Road, P.O. Box 110 (North Windham 04062) / 207-892-2698 / Waterfront bed and breakfast and housekeeping cottages / Registered guide, fishing licenses, continental breakfast, picnic tables, and grills / Free use of canoes and rowboats / Off-season rentals / Cottage / $500–$1000 per week / $200 per night, 3 night minimum

Windham Way Motel, P.O. Box 1574 (Windham 04062) / 207-892-4762 / Owners Phil and Peg Wescott / Located on Route 302 / Efficiency suites, handicapped unit, swimming pool, antique shop, cable TV, air conditioning, and phones / Open year-round / $–$$$$

RESTAURANTS

Barnhouse Tavern, junction of Routes 302, 114, and 35 (Windham 04062) / 207-892-2221 / Steak and seafood restaurant / Hours: 11:30AM–10PM (dining); 11:30AM–12:30AM (tavern)

Charlie Biegg's, Route 302 (North Windham 04062) / 207-892-8595 / Open daily for lunch, dinner, and cocktails

Miller's Diner, Route 302 / 207-892-1705 or 892-3630 / Seafood, steaks, and 28 sandwiches / Breakfast, lunch, and dinner

FLY SHOPS AND SPORTING GOODS

Yankee Sports, Route 302 (Windham Mall) / 207-892-5137

Bibeau's Fly Shop, 302 North Windham (North Windham 04062) / 207-892-4206

Wal-Mart, 788 Roosevelt Trail (Windham 04062) / 207-893-0603

AUTO REPAIR

Century Tire Co., Route 302 / 207-892-7528

Genuine Auto Parts (NAPA), Route 302 / 207-892-3221

North Windham Exxon, 746 Roosevelt Trail / 207-892-7290

Ray's Auto Parts, 483 Gray Road / 207-892-2264

AUTO RENTAL

See Portland International Jetport or through Quest Travel

AIRPORT

Portland International Jetport, near Fore River and just off I-295 / Taxi and van service available / Airlines: Business Express 800-345-3400; Continental 800-525-0280; Delta 800-221-1212; USAir 800-428-4322; United 800-241-6522 / A metro bus runs downtown from the airport

Quest Travel of Windham, Windham Shopping Center, Route 302 (next to the Post Office) / 800-947-2246 (out-of-state); 207-892-2246 / Handles air travel arrangements to the Sebago Lake Region

MEDICAL

Nearest hospitals are in Bridgton (15 miles northwest of downtown Windham on Route 302), Portland, and Westbrook (10 miles southeast of downtown Windham on Route 302)

Brighton Medical Center, 335 Brighton Avenue (Portland 04102) / 207-879-8111

Maine Medical Center (Portland) / 207-871-0111

Mercy Hospital, 144 State Street (Portland 04101) / 207-879-3000

Northern Cumberland Memorial Hospital, South High Street (Bridgton) / 207-647-8841 / 24-hour emergency medical services

Westbrook Community Hospital, 40 Park Road (Westbrook 04092) / 207-854-8464

FOR MORE INFORMATION

Windham Chamber of Commerce
P.O. Box 1015
Windham, ME 04062
207-892-8265

Note: The town of Windham lies on the eastern side of Sebago Lake, while Naples, located on Route 302 near the northern end of the big water, is closer to Crooked River angling.

Naples

Elevation–Near Sea Level • Population–10,000 to 15,000 (summer); 3,500 (winter)

ACCOMMODATIONS

Inn at Long Lake, Lake House Road / 207-693-6226 / $$$$–$$$$$

Romah Motor Inn, Route 302 / 207-693-6690 / $$

West Shore Motel, Route 302 / 207-693-9277 / $$–$$$$

Songo Locks Bed and Breakfast, Box 120, Songo Locks Road / 207-693-6955 / Continental breakfast arrangements available / Located near the confluence of the Songo and Crooked Rivers / Smoke-free accommodations

CAMPGROUNDS

Colonial Mast Campground, P.O. Box 95Y / 207-693-6652 / Located on Long Lake / Trailer and boat rentals are also available

Four Seasons Camping Area, Route 302 (P.O. Box 927) / 207-693-6797 / 115 sites in tall pines, birch groves, and on Long Lake / 11 full hookups, 104 water and electric sites / Reservations recommended

K's Family Circle Campground, Box 557N, Route 114 / 207-693-6881 / Over 100 large, wooded, and open sites on Trickey Pond / Lakefront sites available / Boat and canoe rentals

RESTAURANTS

The Black Horse Tavern, Route 302 (Bridgton 04009) / 207-647-5300 / Steak, ribs, chicken, fresh seafood, Cajun fare, homemade soups and desserts / Open daily from 11AM

Bray's Brewpub and Eatery, at the light on Routes 302 and 35 / 207-693-6806 / Lunch and dinner specials served daily in a 150-year-old Victorian farmhouse / Menu ranges from filet mignon to seafood, ribs, and burgers / Outdoor beer garden (I repeat: outdoor beer garden)

Charlie's on the Causeway, Route 302 / 207-693-3286 / Steaks, lobsters, seafood, and ice cream / Ample parking

Sandy's at the Flight Deck, on Long Lake / 207-693-3508 / Fresh seafood (broiled or fried), steak, chicken, prime rib, pasta, desserts, and cocktails / Lakeside deck or large air-conditioned rooms / Take-out service available

FLY SHOPS AND OUTFITTERS

Naples Bait & Tackle, Route 35 / 207-693-3638 / Contact Dave Garcia, who suggests fishing the marabou black ghost, needle smelt, and red gray ghost on local salmon waters / Drop by his place for the latest flyfishing information

AUTO REPAIR

Naples Small Engine & Appliance, Route 302 / 207-693-6793

AIRPORTS

Portland International Jetport, near Fore River and just off I-95 / Taxi and van service available / Airlines: Business Express 800-345-3400; Continental 800-525-0280; Delta 800-221-1212; USAir 800-428-4322; United 800-241-6522 / A metro bus runs downtown from the airport

Western Maine Flying Service, Inc., Route 302, Box V / 207-693-6162

FOR MORE INFORMATION

Naples Business Association
P.O. Box 412
Naples, ME 04055
207-693-3285 (summer) / 207-693-6817 (winter)

Yarmouth
Elevation–Sea Level • Population–8,600

Situated on the coast, Yarmouth puts you close to Royal River angling in addition to many other southern Maine fishing haunts, including the Sebago Lake region streams and stillwaters.

ACCOMMODATIONS
Brookside Motel, 3 U.S. Route 1 / 207-846-5512 / $$$
Freeport Inn & Cafe, U.S. Route 1 (Freeport 04032) / 207-865-3106 / Freeport borders Yarmouth and is accessible to the north via Route 1 or Interstate 95 / $$$

RESTAURANTS
Down East Village Restaurant, 31 U.S. Route 1 / 207-846-5161
Moonlight Roasters at Westcustogo Inn, Route 88 / 207-846-5797
Pat's Pizza, 43 U.S. Route 1 / 207-846-3701
The Cannery Restaurant, Lower Falls Landing / 207-846-1226

FLY SHOPS AND SPORTING GOODS
Barnes Outfitters, Inc., 184 U.S. Route 1 (Freeport) / 207-865-1113
L.L. Bean, Inc., Casco Street (Freeport 04033) / 800-341-4341 / Open 24 hours a day, 365 days a year / Located just north of Yarmouth off Interstate 95 or Route 1 / Also offers Outdoor Discovery Schools, which includes beginner, intermediate, and advanced fly tying workshops

AUTO REPAIR
Yarmouth Auto Servicenter, U.S. Route 1 / 207-846-5593
Yarmouth Exxon, U.S. Route 1 / 207-846-3316

MEDICAL
Harbourside Family Practice, Lower Falls Landing / 207-846-2229
Village Family Physicians, 2 School Street / 207-846-6211

FOR MORE INFORMATION
Yarmouth Chamber of Commerce
16 U.S. Route 1
Yarmouth, ME 04096
207-846-3984

Midcoastal Maine

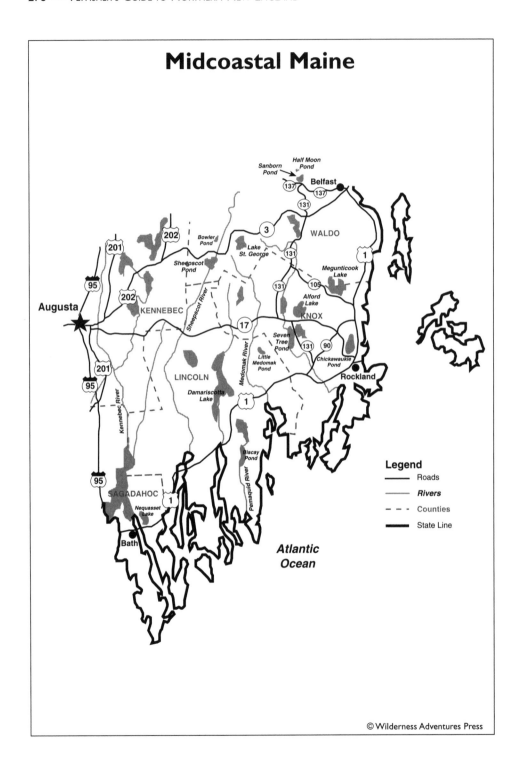

Legend
— Roads
— *Rivers*
- - - Counties
— State Line

Atlantic
Ocean

© Wilderness Adventures Press

MIDCOASTAL MAINE RIVERS AND STREAMS

Midcoastal Maine encompasses Sagadahoc, Lincoln, Waldo, and Knox Counties. The lakes, ponds, and streams of this region hold limited flyfishing opportunities for stocked brook trout, browns, and landlocked salmon. The rivers adjacent to the coast offer angling for sea-run browns, stripers, and even Atlantic salmon.

SPECIAL NOTICE

The state of Maine has closed the recreational Atlantic salmon fishing season for the 2000 season in all Maine rivers. Check the current regulations before fishing these waters.

Kennebec River

The huge area that is the mouth of the Kennebec River runs from the dam in Augusta to Popham Beach and the Atlantic Ocean. It encompasses Merrymeeting Bay northeast of Brunswick, the river itself as it flows past the shipyards of Bath, Morse River, and Popham Beach.

The river below the Augusta dam is tidal, and a fishing license is not required. Regulations that cover saltwater species apply. For stripers, the season is from June 10 through October 15. There is a slot limit allowing you to keep 1 fish between 20 and 26 inches, and/or 1 fish greater than 40 inches daily. There is no closed season for bluefish, no size limit, and the kill limit is 3 fish per day. The best fishing is during the months of June and July, when stripers up to 20 pounds migrate upriver to the dam. There is a public parking area in Augusta off 1-95 (exit 30) and Route 27 near the dam on Bond Street.

Merrymeeting Bay is a treasure of tidal marshes teeming with wildlife. School-sized stripers are in abundance during June and July. There is a good launch for boats and canoes in the village of Richmond.

The Kennebec's strong currents below Bath require boats with strong engines. This river has a reputation for large-sized stripers and bluefish closer to the mouth. There is a boat launch in the village of North Bath upriver from Route 1. It is advisable to use the services of one of the many excellent area guides for your first trip.

Popham Beach is about 18 miles south of Bath on Route 209, where there is plenty of parking at the state park and at least 2 miles of beautiful beach to fish. Morse River is on the back side of Popham Beach. You can reach the river's estuary by a foot trail from the state park parking area. Stripers enter these shallows at night and can provide the stalking angler good sport.

Lower Kennebec River

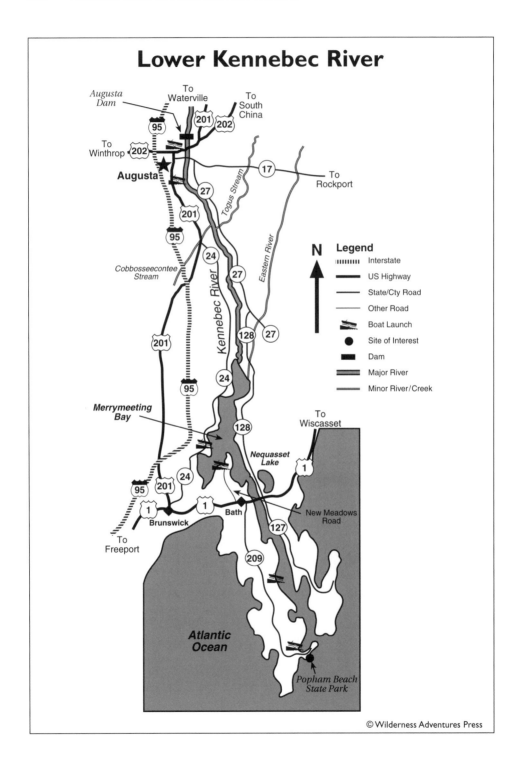

© Wilderness Adventures Press

Other Midcoastal Rivers

The **Sheepscot River** begins as a small stream before it flows out of a dam at Sheepscot Pond north of the village of Somerville on Route 105. Its waters run cold all summer long and support brook trout, brown trout, and small landlocked salmon. Casting is done in tight quarters on this heavily overgrown stream, but the effort can be worthwhile, especially from mid-May through June during the strong mayfly hatches. The state manages the river stretch from 150 feet below the dam to the upstream side of the Route 105 bridge in Somerville as catch and release and limits angling to artificial lures only. Access can be gained from Turner Ridge Road.

The river section downstream from Somerville to the dam at Head Tide, south of the village of Whitefield on Route 218, is popular among canoeists. There is a put-in access area off Route 126 near the village of North Whitefield and a take-out area at the dam. This part of the Sheepscot also holds wild brook trout and browns. Good caddis hatches help the fishing, especially in May and June.

There is a small but significant run of Atlantic salmon in the Sheepscot in the stretch below the dam at Head Tide. The pools below the natural "reversing falls" in the village of Sheepscot offer lies for migrating fish as well as upstream at the corner pools near the bridge in the village of Alna. In Sheepscot, river access is available along the east shore from the bridge and in Alna near the bridge and downstream. June and September are the best times for Atlantics (season is currently closed, check current regulations). The months of July and August are good months to fish for feeding stripers.

Medomak River is easily accessible from Route 32 north of the village of Waldoboro. The state stocks the river with brown trout and manages the stretch of river from the bridge in the village of Winslow Mills to tidewater in Waldoboro as flyfishing only between August 16 and October 31.

To the south, the **Pemaquid River** also offers angling for sea-run brown trout. Access is limited to a boat access off Route 130 north of the village of Bristol.

Sheepscot River

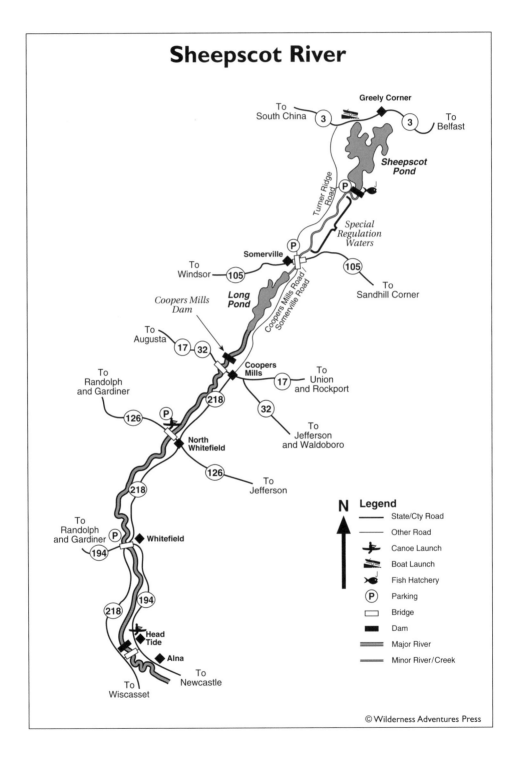

Greely Corner

To South China — (3)

(3) — To Belfast

Sheepscot Pond

(P)

Special Regulation Waters

Turner Ridge Road

Somerville

(P)

To Windsor — (105)

(105) — To Sandhill Corner

Coopers Mills Dam

Long Pond

Coopers Mills Road / Somerville Road

To Augusta — (17)—(32)

Coopers Mills

To Union and Rockport — (17)

To Randolph and Gardiner

(126)

(218)

(32)

To Jefferson and Waldoboro

(P)

North Whitefield

(218)

(126) — To Jefferson

To Randolph and Gardiner — (P)

(194)

Whitefield

(194)

(218)

Head Tide

Alna

To Wiscasset

To Newcastle

N

Legend

———— State/Cty Road

——— Other Road

✈ Canoe Launch

Boat Launch

Fish Hatchery

(P) Parking

▭ Bridge

▬ Dam

Major River

Minor River/Creek

© Wilderness Adventures Press

Midcoastal Stillwaters

Nequasset Lake is north of the village of Woolwich and the city of Bath off Route 1. The Maine Department of Inland Fisheries and Wildlife stocks this 430-acre, mixed cold and warmwater fishery with brown trout and limits the use of motorboats to 10 horsepower. There is a public boat launch at the north end of Nequasset on Old Stage Road and an access on the south shore near Route 1.

Damariscotta Lake is a 4,625-acre impoundment located south of the village of Jefferson on Route 213. The lake is a mixed warm and coldwater fishery supporting togue, landlocked salmon, and brown trout in the colder and deeper north basin, and smallmouth bass and other warmwater species in the southern section. There are several public boat launches, a public beach at the state park on the lake's northern end, and camping available nearby.

Biscay Pond is part of the Pemaquid River chain of lakes and lies north of the village of Bristol near Route 130. It has a good reputation as a brown trout fishery, especially in the spring after ice-out. There is a public boat access at the pond's northern end off Damariscotta Road.

Little Medomak Pond, also known as Storer Pond, is a small brown trout fishery located north of the village of North Waldoboro. There is a hand-carried boat access on Storer Pond Road off Route 32.

St. George Lake is an inviting piece of water located amid hills and forests off Route 3 west of the village of Belfast. The lake covers about 1000 acres and has a maximum depth of 65 feet. It is a mixed cold and warmwater fishery holding landlocked salmon and brown trout as well as smallmouth bass and chain pickerel. There are camping facilities, boat rentals, and a boat launch at the state park on the lake's northern shore.

Sheepscot Pond, due west of St. George Lake, is a 1,200-acre impoundment that provides the coldwater flow for the Sheepscot River from the dam at the pond's south end. The pond itself supports both cold and warmwater species. In its colder depths, it holds brook trout, togue, and splake. There is a boat launch just off Route 3 at Greely Corner on the north shore.

Bowler Pond is accessible from Level Hill Road off Route 3 west of St. George Lake. It is managed by the state as a brook trout fishery with a 16-inch minimum length limit.

Sanborn Pond holds brook trout and lies northwest of the village of Belfast on Route 137. There is a boat launch at the pond's southern end. **Half Moon Pond**, another small brook trout pond, is just north of Sanborn off Route 203.

There are several stillwaters in Knox County east of the villages of Camden and Rockport that offer angling for brown trout and brookies. **Alford Lake** is located off Route 235 with a public boat launch on the west shore. **Megunticook Lake**, north of Camden, offers boat access off Route 52. There is a boat access for **Chickawaukie Pond** off Route 17 north of Rockland village. **Seven Tree Pond** is located south of the village of Union off Route 235.

Effective Approaches for Midcoastal Stillwaters

Angling in stillwater shallows often requires that you retrieve nymph and larva patterns slowly—patience catches fish. Ever see one pond angler in a float tube catching one fish after another while others flail and thrash the same water trying to replicate this miraculous feat? Chances are the successful stillwater flyfisher was paying attention to the depth of the fly and matching the speed of retrieve to the speed of the natural bait.

Fish nymphs slowly and retrieve leech patterns to pulsate like small snakes. Dragonfly and damselfly nymphs can be crawled along the pond bottoms. Fish midge imitations (#14–20) in the surface film with slow retrieves.

Relax. Remember that you're flyfishing, not sampling seafood at an all-you-can-eat buffet.

MIDCOASTAL HUB CITY
Rockland

Elevation–Sea Level • Population–7,960

ACCOMMODATIONS

Navigator Motor Inn, 520 Main Street / 207-594-2131 / 80 rooms / Breakfast, lunch, and dinner served / Open year-round / $$–$$$

Samoset Resort, on the ocean / 207-594-2511/ 800-341-1650 (outside Maine) / 150 rooms / Breakfast, lunch, and dinner/ Heated indoor and outdoor pools / Open year-round / $$$$$

Trade Winds Motor Inn, 2 Park View Drive / 207-596-6661; 800-834-3130 / 142 rooms / Breakfast and dinner served / Dogs welcome / Heated indoor pool / Open year-round / $$–$$$$$

CAMPGROUNDS

Megunticook by the Sea, P.O. Box 375, U.S. Route 1 (Rockport) / 207-594-2428 / 85 camping sites / Water view / Dogs welcome

RESTAURANTS

Grapes Restaurant, 227 Park Street / 207-594-9050 / Pasta, seafood, steaks, salads, and pizza / Lunch and dinner served / Open year-round

Landings Restaurant & Marina, 1 Commercial Street / 207-596-6563 / Seafood, steak, and chicken / Breakfast, lunch, and dinner / Open May to October

Schooner Fare Restaurant, 421 Main Street / 207-596-0012 / Sandwiches, chowders, seafood, and steaks / Lunch and dinner served

Waterworks Pub & Restaurant, 5 Lindsey Street / 207-596-7950 / Pub-style fare and brews / Lunch, dinner, and late-night hours / Open year-round

FLY SHOPS AND SPORTING GOODS

Maine Sport Outfitters, Route 1, Main Street (Rockport 04846) / 207-236-7120

AUTO REPAIR

Bragg's, 643 Main Street / 207-594-8443

Prompto, 74 Camden Street / 207-594-8884

AUTO RENTAL

National Car Rental / 207-594-8424

U-Save Auto Rental (Smith's Garage), 211 Union Street / 207-236-2320

AIRPORT

Colgan Air, P.O. Box 1594 / 207-596-7604; 800-272-5488 / Daily commercial air service is available from Boston to Knox County Airport in Owls Head, 2 miles south of Rockland / Taxi and van services available / Call for information

FOR MORE INFORMATION

Rockland-Thomaston Area Chamber of Commerce
Harbor Park, P.O. Box 508
Rockland, ME 04841
207-596-0376

Southeastern Maine

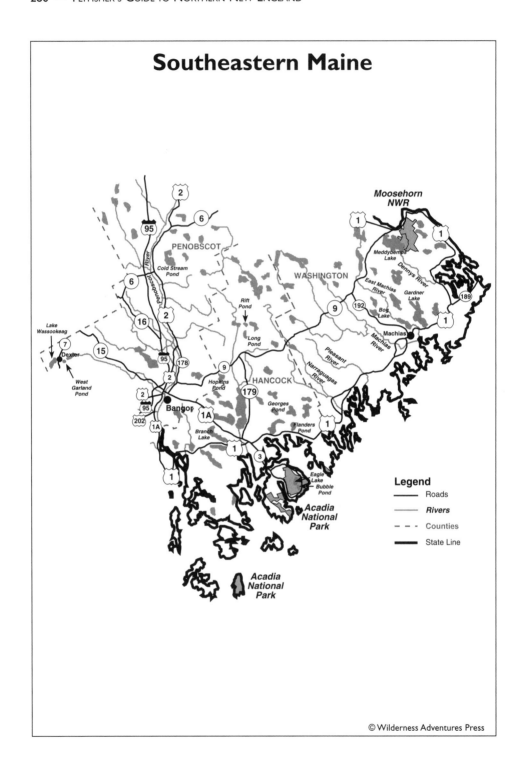

Legend

— Roads

— *Rivers*

- - - Counties

— State Line

© Wilderness Adventures Press

SOUTHEASTERN MAINE RIVERS AND STREAMS

Atlantic Salmon Fishing

For a small group of anglers, Atlantic salmon fishing is the ultimate fly rod challenge. This is not so much because they are hard to catch by all sorts of methods. The question of why they allow themselves to be caught on a fly has created the obsession. In fact, it is because the fish are so vulnerable that Atlantic salmon rivers are tightly regulated and access is usually very restricted (see notice below).

For over 200 years the mystery of Atlantic salmon angling has created volumes of works suggesting "how to" and "why," and in all cases, offering almost-holy praise for this fish. Kings and lords and clubs of wealthy men owned salmon rivers. Atlantic salmon fishing was not for the common person. This was the early tradition.

By the latter part of the mid-1900s, Atlantic salmon rivers in North America began to be more and more accessible to the public. The government of Canada was ending club leases and taking control of rivers. Lee Wulff, the adventurer, was exploring the rivers of Newfoundland and Labrador and promoting Atlantic salmon fishing to sporting groups in the United States.

In Maine, the problem was not public access but diminishing runs of salmon because of pollution and dams. The famous Penobscot River run of Atlantic salmon that started the tradition of presenting the President of the United States the season's first catch all but disappeared 50 years ago. Downstate the other salmon rivers, the Dennys, the Machias, and the Narraguagus were barely sustaining their meager stocks. In 1948, the Atlantic Sea-run Salmon Commission was created, and a major effort to restore the wild Atlantic salmon in Maine began.

SPECIAL NOTICE

The state of Maine has closed the recreational Atlantic salmon fishing season for the 2000 season in all Maine rivers. Check the current regulations before fishing these waters.

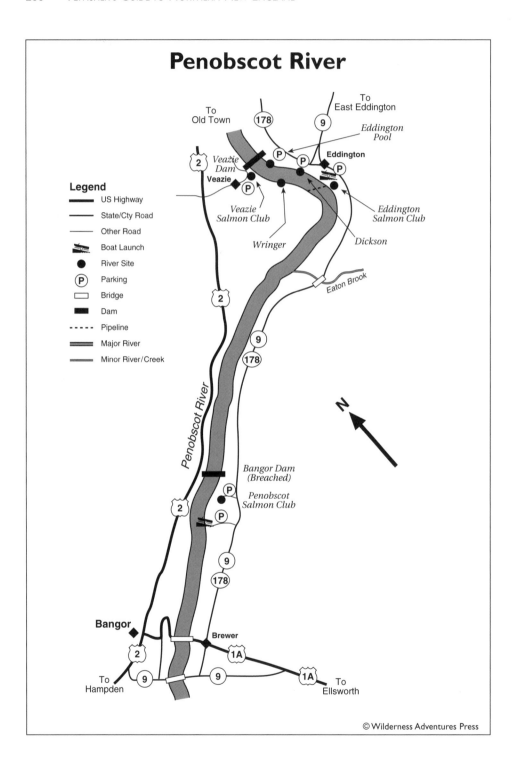

Penobscot River

Legend
- US Highway
- State/Cty Road
- Other Road
- Boat Launch
- River Site
- P Parking
- Bridge
- Dam
- Pipeline
- Major River
- Minor River/Creek

To Old Town

To East Eddington

178

9

Eddington Pool

2

Veazie Dam

Eddington

P

P

P

P

Veazie

P

Veazie Salmon Club

Eddington Salmon Club

Wringer

Dickson

Eaton Brook

2

9

178

Penobscot River

N

Bangor Dam (Breached)

P

Penobscot Salmon Club

P

2

9

178

Bangor

2

9

Brewer

1A

9

1A

To Hampden

To Ellsworth

© Wilderness Adventures Press

Donna Fleming with a nice, 12-pound Atlantic salmon from the Penobscot River.
(Photo by Braden Fleming)

Penobscot River

Traditionally, the first Atlantic salmon caught from the Penobscot River each season is presented to the President of the United States. However, in keeping with catch-and-release regulations, the first Penobscot salmon caught in 1997 was set free by angler Gayland Hachey, owner of Hachey's Fly Shop in the village of Veazie. In Hachey's words, "I caught the salmon at 6:30 am on opening morning. It was 30 inches long and weighed around 10½ pounds—a bright, fresh-run fish." As a token for releasing the salmon, Hachey received a 22-pound, farm-raised salmon and a trophy to commemorate his catch.

Flyfishing for Atlantics can be good on the traditional opening day, May 1, as Hachey will testify. However, Penobscot River angling is often best from around Memorial Day to mid-June. "Water levels are high in May," says Hachey, "but by the holiday, fish start coming regularly."

Local fly patterns seem to rule, especially those invented at the local tying bench. Traditional salmon flies, such as the Cosseboom (#2–10), the nighthawk, rusty rat,

Bill Weber fishing for Atlantic salmon on the Dennys River.
(Photo by Charley Lovelette)

hairy Mary, silver downeaster, and undertaker all catch fish. Hachey's 1997 opening–day Atlantic struck a gremlin, a local pattern, available at his fly shop.

Anglers concentrate at the pools in the river section below the Veazie Dam between the cities of Bangor and Veazie. Popular pools include the Eddington Pool, Dickson, the Wringer, and Pipeline. You'll find a sense of order and fairness as anglers practice fishing through pools in rotation. Flyfishers wait their turn on a bench. Each angler moves through the pool casting and taking steps so that everyone gets a chance to fish.

Between hydroelectric projects obstructing spawning access and effluent from paper mills causing salmon decline, the subject of management is as political as fly-fishing ever gets. As of this writing, new regulations are being considered. Proposals include measures banning nets to closing fishing altogether. Contact Maine salmon biologist Ed Baum at 207-941-4452 for current Atlantic salmon angling laws and management information.

More Down East Atlantic Salmon Rivers

According to biologist Ed Baum, Maine's Atlantic salmon rivers generally saw an increase in 1996 salmon runs. The good news is that flyfishers caught and released 60 fish from the Dennys River alone. The bad news is that no salmon were reported to have been hooked on the Pleasant River.

*Fish the Machias River,
an Atlantic salmon
fishery, from the summer
solstice on through July,
especially if the summer
holds consistent rainfall.
(Photo by Steve Hickoff)*

Some of these salmon are wild, but others, according to Baum, may be released broodstock fish. An air of secrecy has always surrounded Atlantic salmon fishing and, accurate or not, Maine survey estimates are based on participating angler information. It goes without saying that not every Atlantic salmon flyfisher is willing to part with hard-won secrets related to anadromous fish movements and annual catches. Managers are optimistic though, despite the fact that regulations are being over-hauled. It remains a difficult task as the interests of industrialists, lawmakers, salmon anglers, and conservationists are as divergent as the rivers where these fish swim.

The **Dennys River**, an Atlantic salmon river, is best flyfished in late June. As of this writing, regulations state that the 200-foot portion of the Dennys River in the

The Narraguagus River holds estimated annual Atlantic salmon catches of roughly 30 fish. (Photo by Steve Hickoff)

town of Dennyville and Plantation 14 from the red markers 100 feet either side of the Batson Meadow Spring mouth is closed to fishing.

The Dennys, in addition to being a significant Atlantic salmon river, provides good brook trout fishing, especially in the river's upper reaches. The Dennys begins at the dam in the southwest corner of Meddybemps Lake near the small village of Meddybemps on Route 191. The upper Dennys flows through a wilderness area and is accessible by unimproved logging roads and foot trails. There are hand-carried canoe accesses and primitive campsites available.

The **East Machias** and **Machias Rivers'** self-sustaining but limited runs resulted in an estimated 30 Atlantics caught in 1996.

Located some 50 miles east of Bangor, the **Narraguagus River** offers flyfishing opportunities for Atlantic salmon. Popular pools below the Cherryfield Dam are Stillwater, Maples, and Cable Pool, which is probably the best of the three. This fishery consists of Class I to Class II rapids, with some sudden Class III sections—let experience rule if you canoe this salmon water. Water levels drop by late July most years. An estimated 30 Narraguagus Atlantics were caught in 1996.

Angler surveys said no Atlantics were caught in the **Pleasant River** in 1996. However, biologists found active spawning redds in the river.

SOUTHEASTERN (DOWN EAST) MAINE STILLWATERS
Penobscot County Stillwaters

Cold Stream Pond, located in the town of Enfield, holds brook trout, togue, and landlocked salmon. The daily limit is 3 fish, to include no more than 1 salmon, 2 trout, and 2 togue. The length limit on lake trout stipulates that 1 togue must be over 18 inches and the other between 14 and 18 inches. Brook trout run from 8 to 12 inches in length. Fish beadhead pheasant tails, small woolly buggers, and dries, such as elk hair caddis and blue-winged olives. A boat launch is available off Route 188, which runs through the village of Enfield.

West Garland Pond is a brook trout pond located about 4½ miles east of the village of Dexter on Route 94. There is a 2-fish limit, with a minimum length of 8 inches. Brookies typically run from 8 to 10 inches. Fish stonefly, damselfly, and dragonfly nymph imitations. A hand-carried boat launch off Valley Avenue Road at the east end of the pond will put you on this small fishery.

Wassookeag Lake, in the town of Dexter, holds brookies, lake trout, and landlocked salmon. According to the Maine Department of Inland Fisheries and Wildlife, this 1,062-acre impoundment is highly oxygenated, and the cold depths (to 86 feet) produce some good trout. Salmon angling is limited, despite the ongoing salmon stocking program. Lake trout angling is particularly good. The 20-inch length, 1-fish limit on togue sees 4-pounders caught with regularity. Streamers catch many fish right after ice-out on the lake's rocky shallows. Two boat launches are available off Crockett and North Dexter Roads not far from downtown Dexter.

This spunky little Maine brown smacked a beadhead pheasant tail.
(Photo by Steve Hickoff)

Hancock County Stillwaters

Hancock County lakes and ponds provide flyfishing opportunities for a mixed bag of brown trout, brookies, togue, salmon, and some warmwater species. Tributaries to some of these waters hold game fish, as well.

Brown trout and landlocked salmon can be found in **Branch Lake** in the town of Ellsworth. This 1,728-acre lake supports browns in the 4- to 8-pound range. Fish are often caught during the low-light margins of the day. Expect opportunities for decent 2- to 3-pound landlocks, as well. The Maine Department of Inland Fisheries and Wildlife manages this lake for salmon with an aggressive stocking program.

The minimum length limit on brown trout is 18 inches. Big Branch Lake browns favor woolly buggers (#2–8 brown, olive, and black), stonefly nymphs (including the Kaufmann's brown stone #2–10), Montana (#6–14), and black swimming stones (#6–14). Damselfly and dragonfly nymphs (#10–14) will also catch Maine's stillwater browns. Boat launch access is found off Winkumpaugh Road.

Bubble Pond is a brook trout pond located near Bar Harbor on Mount Desert Island. The daily bag limit on brook trout is 2 fish with a maximum length of 8 inches. Fish from 6 to 12 inches and will take all-purpose nymphs. Access is off Park Loop Road just south of Eagle Lake.

Eagle Lake, which holds brook trout and togue, is located near Bar Harbor within Acadia National Park. Brookies run from 10 to 12 inches in length, and lakers average several pounds. The length limit on togue is 20 inches. Motorboats over 10 horsepower are prohibited. Access is available at the boat launch off Route 233 on Mount Desert Island (pronounced "dessert," as in hot apple pie).

Flanders Pond is located in the town of Sullivan and holds brookies and browns. The minimum brown trout length is 14 inches. When flyfishing streamers, you can expect the V-wake strikes of chain pickerel in the shallows. Thorne Road from Route 183 ("Lake Road") provides access.

Georges Pond holds brook trout and is located in the town of Franklin. Brownies average from 12 to 14 inches in length; minimum length limit for browns is 14 inches. Bass will take a popping bug or streamer in the summer. Boat access is available off Georges Pond Road just northwest of Flanders Pond.

Hopkins Pond holds brookies and togue and is located in the town of Mariaville. Trout range from 4 to 10 inches, with lake trout reaching several pounds. There is a hand-carried boat launch available on the pond's eastern side.

Long Pond is a brook and brown trout fishery located in the town of Aurora near Great Pond. The minimum brook trout length is 14 inches, and the minimum brown trout length is 20 inches. There is an artificial lure-only restriction. Boat launches are found off Great Pond Road on the pond's southernmost shore and near King Pond to the north.

Located in the Great Pond Plantation, **Rift Pond** is stocked with brookies and browns. There is an artificial lure-only restriction. Minimum length on brook trout is 16 inches. The minimum length on brown trout is 20 inches. Fish damselfly and dragonfly nymphs (#4–8).

Washington County Stillwaters

Meddybemps Lake covers well over 6,000 acres and supports both cold and warmwater species. In addition to holding some brook trout and landlocked salmon, the lake has a reputation as a fine smallmouth bass fishery. There is a boat launch near the dam at Meddybemps on Route 191.

Gardner Lake is a mixed warm and coldwater lake east of the village of East Machias. The best angling for landlocks is after ice-out in the spring. There is a boat launch near the lake's outlet at Chase Mills off Route 1.

Bog Lake holds brown trout and landlocked salmon. It lies north of the village of Machias on Route 192, where there is a hand-carried boat access.

SOUTHEASTERN (DOWN EAST) MAINE HUB CITIES
Bangor
Elevation–Near Sea Level • Population–33,189

ACCOMMODATIONS

Bangor Motor Inn, off Interstate 95 at Exit 49, 701 Hogan Road / 800-244-0355 or 207-947-0355 / Breakfast buffet included / Nonsmoking, waterbed, and VCR rooms available / Free hors d'oeuvres nightly in Fireside Lounge / 103 rooms / 6 miles from airport; shuttle available / $–$$

Days Inn, Exit 45B off Interstate 95, 250 Odlin Road / 800-835-4667 or 207-942-8272 / Free shuttle to and from the airport; continental breakfast bar, and cable TV included / 101 rooms / 3 miles from airport / Dogs OK / $$$

EconoLodge, Exit 45B off Interstate 95, 327 Odlin Road / 800-55-ECONO or 207-945-0111 / Remote control TVs, guest laundry on premises, vending area, and free morning coffee / 98 rooms / 2 miles from airport with shuttle available / Dogs OK / $$

CAMPGROUNDS

Barcadia Campground, RR 1, Box 2165 (Bar Harbor 04609) / 207-288-3250 / Minutes from Acadia National Park and Eagle Lake / 200 wooded and open sites, with picnic tables and hot showers available / Reservations accepted year-round / Dogs allowed

Branch Lake Camping Area, Route 1A (Ellsworth 04605) / 207-667-5174 / 55 sites with full hook-ups, hot showers, and boat launch / Open May to October / Reservations accepted / Dogs allowed

Paul Bunyan Campground, 1862 Union Street / 207-941-1177 / 52 sites / Dogs allowed / Open April 1 to November 30 / Access off Interstate 95 (Exit 47), take Route 222 west for 2.8 miles

Pleasant Hill Campground, RFD 3, Box 180C, Union Street / 207-848-5127 / 105 sites / Dogs allowed / Open May 1 to October 15 / Access off Interstate 95, take Route 222 west 3.8 miles past airport / Reservations recommended

RESTAURANTS

Coffee Express, 308 State Street and 500 Main Street / 207-942-5779 (State Street); 207-945-6399 (Main Street) / Open 6AM–8PM, Monday through Friday; 7am-7pm Saturday and Sunday / Sandwiches, bagels, coffee, and pastries

Governor's, 643 Broadway / 207-947-3133 / Open Monday through Thursday 6:30PM–11PM; Friday and Saturday 7AM–12AM; Sunday 7AM–11PM / Fresh Maine seafood, steak, Pizza, and sandwiches / Take-out available

Paul's Restaurant & Speakeasy, 605 Hogan Road / 207-942-6726 / Open Monday through Saturday 11AM–12:30AM; Sunday 11AM–10PM / Steak and seafood

FLY SHOPS AND SPORTING GOODS

Eddie's Flies and Tackle, 303 Broadway / 207-947-1648 / Fly tying materials and tackle

Gayland Hachey's Fly Shop, 1076 Main Street (Veazie 04401—same Zip code as Bangor) / 207-945-9648 / Hachey's is a "full-blown fly shop" as he says, with many of the local patterns favored by Penobscot River salmon anglers / Guide recommendations are available on request, including those for handicapped anglers who wish to fish the river from a boat

L.L. Bean Factory Outlet, 150 High Street (Ellsworth 04605) / 800-820-6846

Mike's Pro Shop, 46 Pine Grove Avenue (Glenburn Center 04401) / 207-947-4818

Van Raymond Outfitters, 388 South Main (Brewer 04412) / 207-989-6001 / Orvis shop

AUTO REPAIR

Frost's Garage, 46 Western Avenue (Hampden 04444) / 207-862-3210

Rawcliffe's Garage, 651 Main Road North (Hampden 04444) / 207-945-2916

AUTO RENTAL

Bangor International Airport, 287 Godfrey Boulevard / 207-947-0824 / Avis, Budget, Hertz, and National / Call for reservations

AIRPORTS

Bangor International Airport, 287 Godfrey Boulevard / 207-942-0384 / Served by Business Express, Continental, Delta, Northwest Airlink, Downeast Express, and international charter flights

MEDICAL

Eastern Maine Medical Center, 489 State Street / 207-973-7000 / Comprehensive health services

FOR MORE INFORMATION

Greater Bangor Chamber of Commerce
519 Main Street
Bangor, ME 04401
207-947-0307

Machias

Elevation–Sea Level • Population–2,550

ACCOMMODATIONS

Bluebird Motel, Route 1 / 207-255-3332 / $
Machias Motor Inn, 26 East Main Street / 207-255-4861 or 255-4862 / $–$$

CAMPGROUNDS

Greenland Cove Campground, Greenland Cove Road (Danforth 04424) /
207-448-2863 / 37 sites open from May 1 to October 1 / Located in northern-most Washington County / Dogs allowed
Hilltop Campground, Ridge Road (Robbinston 04671) / 207-454-3985 / 84 sites /
Open May 15 through October 15 / Close to the Dennys River / Dogs allowed
Pleasant Lake Camping Area, 371 Davis Road (Calais 04619) / 207-454-7467 /
120 sites / Open from Memorial Day to Columbus Day / Located near
Meddybemps Lake / Dogs allowed
Sunset Acres Campground, Route 9 (Woodland 04694) / 207-454-1440 / 15 sites
open from May to November 1 / Near the New Brunswick border / Dogs
allowed

RESTAURANTS

Blue Bird Ranch Restaurant, Route 1 / 207-255-3351 / Breakfast opens Monday
through Saturday at 5AM; Sundays at 6AM / Lunch and dinner also served
Helen's Restaurant, 28 East Main Street / 207-255-8423
Joyce's Lobster House, Route 1 / 207-255-3015

FLY SHOPS AND SPORTING GOODS

Pine Tree Store, 1 Water Street (Grand Lake Stream 04637) / 207-796-5027

FOR MORE INFORMATION

Machias Bay Area Chamber of Commerce
23 East Main Street
Machias, ME 04654
207-255-4402

Central Maine

Central Maine is where it all began. The great, old fishing lodges of central Maine hosted flyfishers from all over the country: Colonel Joseph D. Bates, Jr., flyfisher and author; Carrie Gertrude Stevens, housewife-turned-fly-dresser, who designed the gray ghost streamer; and Herb Welch, one of the first fly tiers to fashion smelt patterns on long-shanked hooks, are part of the long list of flyfishing pioneers who sought the large brook trout and landlocked salmon of central Maine.

Many of the lodges are gone but not the fly anglers. Covering about two-thirds of the state, this vast area stretches from Oxford, Franklin, and Androscoggin Counties near the New Hampshire border to the west, through Somerset, Kennebec, and Piscataquis Counties and on to Penobscot and Washington Counties to the east and the border with the Province of New Brunswick, Canada. The east-west division is made at Maine's largest inland body of water, Moosehead Lake. The west central region encompasses the Rangeley Lakes area, Kennebago, Androscoggin, and Kennebec Rivers in Oxford, Androscoggin, Kennebec, Franklin, and Somerset Counties. The east central region covers Moosehead River, Grand Lake, Grand Lakes Stream, and the west branch of the Penobscot, and includes Piscataquis County and the northern portions of Penobscot and Washington Counties.

SPECIAL NOTICE

The state of Maine has closed the recreational
Atlantic salmon fishing season for the 2000 season
in all Maine rivers. Check the current regulations
before fishing these waters.

CENTRAL MAINE MAJOR HATCHES

Insect	J	F	M	A	M	J	J	A	S	O	N	D	Flies
Streamers													Barnes Special #8–10; Gray Ghost #8–10; Kennebago Smelt #8–10; Olive Matuka #6–10; Black Nose Dace Bucktail #6–10
Midges and Miniature Flies													Griffith's Gnat #16–22; Parachute Adams #16–20; Hatching Midge Pupa #12–16; Olive Midge #16–20; Mosquito Adult #14–20; Midges (black and cream) #18–22; Brassie #16–20
Hendrickson and Red Quill *Ephemerella subvaria*													Hendrickson #10–14; Red Quill #12–16
Caddis													Elk Hair Caddis #6–18; Elk-wing Parachute Caddis #12–18; Henryville Special #12–18; Deep Sparkle Pupa #12–18; Brown Sparkle Pupa #6–12; Caddis Variant #12–18; LaFontaine's Deep Sparkle Pupa #12–18; Beadhead Emerging Caddis #10–14; Emergent Sparkle Pupa #12–18
Alderfly, Zebra Caddis													Alderfly Larva (on the bottom) #10–12; Black Palmer (as an emerger) #12; Alderfly Adult (as a drowned alderfly) #12
Gray Fox *Stenonema fuscum*													Gray Fox #12–16
Dragonflies/Damselflies													Dragonfly Nymph #4–8; Whitlock's Dragonfly #4–8; Damselfly Nymph #4–8; Whitlock Spent Blue Damsel #6
Light Cahill *Stenonema canadensis*													Light Cahill #10–16

CENTRAL MAINE MAJOR HATCHES (cont.)

Insect	J	F	M	A	M	J	J	A	S	O	N	D	Flies
Hexagenia						X	X						Hex Nymph #4–6; Parachute Hex #8–10 (carry both)
Blue-winged Olive *Ephemerella attenuata*				X	X	X	X	X	X	X			Blue-winged Olive #12–22; Blue-winged Olive Thorax #14–20; Blue-winged Olive Nymph #12
Stoneflies				X	X	X							Early Black Stone #12–16; Early Brown Stone #12–16; Willow Fly #14–16; Stimulator #8–14; Stonefly Nymph (black or brown) #12–16
March Brown					X	X							March Brown #12–16
Leeches				X	X	X	X	X	X				Marabou Leech (black) #16; Woolly Bugger (olive, black, or brown) #4–#10
Terrestrials Ants							X	X	X				Black Ant #14–18; Black Gnat(wet) #14–18; Black Fur Ant #12–20; Black Flying Ant #12–16; Black Deer Hair Ant #12–16
Beetles						X	X	X	X				Black Beetle #14–20; Dave's Black Beetle #14–18
Grasshoppers								X	X				Parachute Hopper #8–14; Letort Hopper #8–14
Crickets								X	X				Cricket #8–14; Letort Cricket #8–14

West Central Maine

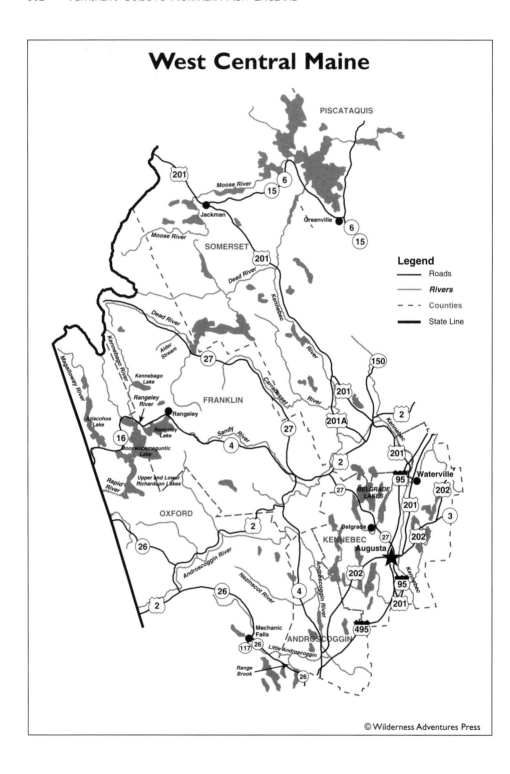

PISCATAQUIS

201

Moose River

6

15

Jackman

Greenville

6

15

Moose River

SOMERSET

201

Dead River

Kennebec River

Legend
— Roads
— *Rivers*
- - - Counties
— State Line

Dead River

Alder Stream

27

Kennebago Lake

Rangeley River

Magalloway River

Kennebago River

FRANKLIN

Carrabassett River

150

Aziscohos Lake

Rangeley

Rangeley Lake

16

Mooselookmeguntic Lake

Sandy River

4

201

Kennebec

2

201A

27

201

2

Waterville

95

202

Upper and Lower Richardson Lakes

Rapid River

OXFORD

2

27

BELGRADE LAKES

201

202

3

26

Androscoggin River

Belgrade

KENNEBEC

Augusta

27

202

95

201

Nezinscot River

4

202

Androscoggin River

Kennebec

26

495

2

26

Mechanic Falls

ANDROSCOGGIN

117

26

Little Androscoggin

Range Brook

26

© Wilderness Adventures Press

WEST CENTRAL MAINE RIVERS AND STREAMS
Kennebago River

"First off," says Chris Aylesworth, manager of the Fly Box, a Rangeley region sport shop in the village of Rangeley, "the Kennebago's excellent reputation as a trout and salmon fishery is definitely deserved. Whether year-round fishing is available, however, can vary from summer to summer. As a fall spawning-run river, it's exceptional."

Chris stresses that the river will hold fish throughout the year, but in summer, only with more than average rainfall and accompanying cool temperatures. "By the end of June some locals give up on the river, which at that time can be low and warm, and they don't fish it again until it rains," Chris continues. "A heavy shot of rain will afford good fishing, and I'm talking about a major weather event with four or five days of rain."

In spring, water levels are steady, then decline toward late June. Summer rains revive good flyfishing, but the dog days keep locals off this water. Fish terrestrials in July and August while stalking trout. September with its accompanying cool rains provides good flyfishing until the season closes.

The Kennebago River descends from Big Island Pond (2,149 feet) to Little Kennebago Lake (1,782 feet), and then downstream to the Mooselookmeguntic confluence (1,467 feet). The gravel and slippery rock bottom on some pools is best waded with caution early in the season. There is excellent spawning habitat for Mooselookmeguntic Lake salmonids.

The upper stretch near Kennebago Lake is full of native brookies, and small pools hold browns and landlocks as well. Upstream areas are best flyfished by wading. Start with an Adams in pocketwater but also mix offerings up with soft-hackled flies and streamers, such as the Hornberg and Joe's smelt. Fish low-light hours for browns.

The middle section doesn't get much pressure, though the fish are definitely there. September salmon runs find flyfishers targeting the Steep Bank Pool on the lower section. The Kennebago River is Mooselookmeguntic Lake's primary salmon and brook trout spawning tributary. Nearby tributaries, such as the Cupsuptic River running north of Cupsuptic Lake, also produce wild fish.

Streamers work well on the Kennebago—some anglers fish brightly-colored offerings and catch fish; some fish dull-colored patterns with success. Both parties swear by their personal favorites, which often include the traditional gray ghost.

During cool summers with consistent rainfall, Hex patterns can be effective as dries (especially from late June into July), but Aylesworth admits that the Kennebago, at times is "a difficult river to figure out." Hatches, in other words, can be sporadic and tough to call, however, terrestrials consistently catch summertime fish.

In season (mid-May to September), fish midge patterns for trout. Streamers will catch salmon in pools, while light cahill dries (#12–16) interest July trout. In the fall,

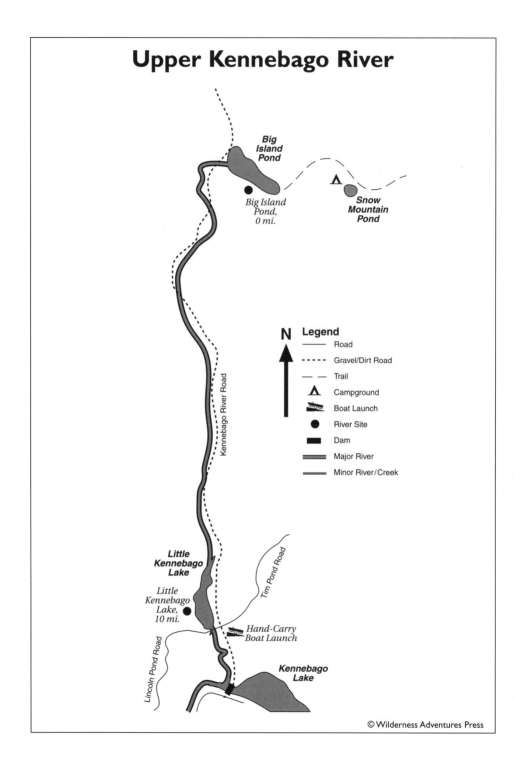

Upper Kennebago River

Big
Island
Pond

Big Island
Pond,
0 mi.

Snow
Mountain
Pond

N

Legend
——— Road
‑ ‑ ‑ ‑ Gravel/Dirt Road
— — Trail
A Campground
Boat Launch
● River Site
■ Dam
Major River
Minor River/Creek

Kennebago River Road

Tim Pond Road

**Little
Kennebago
Lake**

Little
Kennebago
Lake,
10 mi.

Hand-Carry
Boat Launch

**Kennebago
Lake**

Lincoln Pond Road

© Wilderness Adventures Press

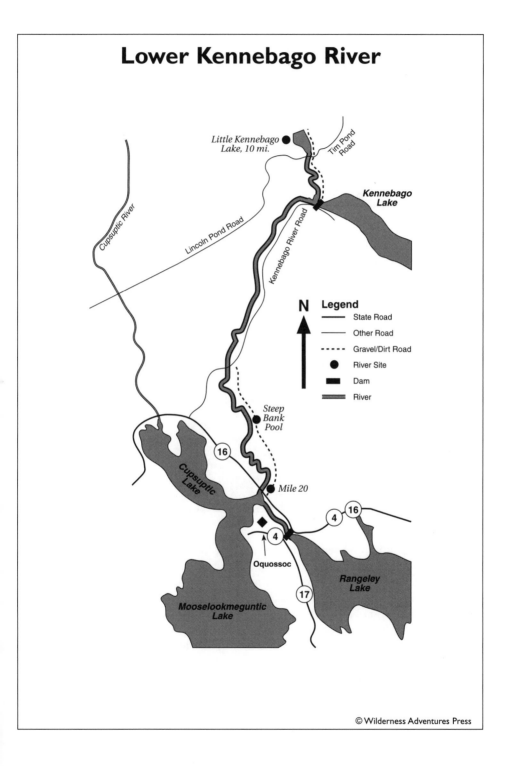

Lower Kennebago River

Little Kennebago Lake, 10 mi.

Tim Pond Road

Kennebago Lake

Cupsuptic River

Lincoln Pond Road

Kennebago River Road

N

Legend
— State Road
— Other Road
--- Gravel/Dirt Road
● River Site
▬ Dam
▬ River

Steep Bank Pool

16

Cupsuptic Lake

Mile 20

4 16

4

Oquossoc

Rangeley Lake

17

Mooselookmeguntic Lake

© Wilderness Adventures Press

Wade with caution on west central Maine's rivers. Serious white-water flows can make the going tough. (Photo by Steve Hickoff)

flyfish the sporadic blue-winged olive hatches for native squaretails in upstream areas. We're talking small, eye-squinting fly sizes here (#20–22; sometimes 18). Try soft-hackled wet flies as well. Stoneflies can be fished effectively throughout the river from late June to season's end. Terrestrials are especially good from midsummer on. Hopper, cricket, and beetle patterns get a look from wild brookies.

Kennebago's season runs from April 1 through September, unless otherwise noted. The section from the confluence with Cupsuptic Lake to Big Island Pond is fly-fishing only, and all tributaries are closed to fishing. One fish in the aggregate is allowed from the Cupsuptic Lake confluence to the first dam, but between August 16 and September 30, all fish must be released alive at once. All trout less than 10 inches and between 14 and 18 inches must be immediately released alive.

From the first dam to Little Kennebago Lake, including the Logans, the daily limit on brook trout is 2 fish with a minimum length of 10 inches and only 1 may exceed 12 inches. The section of river known as the spawning beds (approximately 200 yards long between red markers) is closed to fishing after September 15. Check current laws for any updated measures.

Salmon average a few ounces shy of 2 pounds, while brook trout run in the 8- to 12-inch range and occasionally larger.

Access is not a problem, with numerous unimproved roads that parallel the 20 miles of river. Public access is available by gravel road off Route 16.

Franklin County Rivers and Streams

Access to **Alder Stream**, a wild brook trout stream is made northwest of Eustis off Route 27 in Alder Stream Township. June offers the best flyfishing when water levels begin to drop. Barbless hooks and a gentle release are recommended. During the consistent mayfly hatches, you'll find fly anglers stalking the holding lies in hipboots.

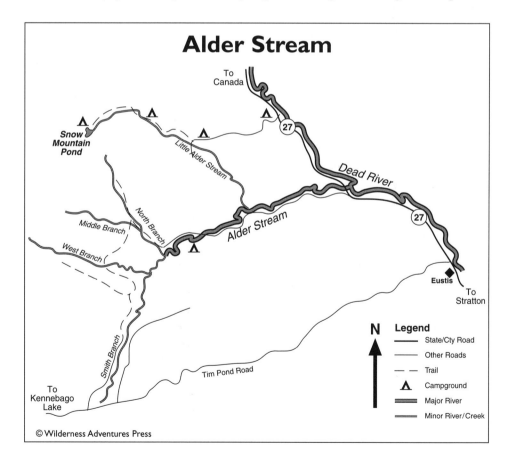

Other Franklin County rivers, such as the Carrabassett pictured here, offer flyfishing-only sections. (Photo courtesy Maine Office of Tourism)

Special Maine Department of Inland Fisheries and Wildlife regulations permit youngsters under 16 years of age to fish with single-point artificial lures in the section of Alder Stream from the confluence of Alder and Little Alder Streams downstream to the Indian territorial boundary. Anglers 16 and older are restricted to flyfishing only with a daily limit of 5 fish in this section. For all other Alder Stream sections and tributaries, anglers are restricted to flyfishing only from April 1 to August 15 and a bag limit of 5 fish (though many release these wild trout). From August 16 through September 30, all angling is by flyfishing only with a daily limit of 1 fish.

The **Carrabassett River**, near the village of Kingfield, is a brook trout fishery. There is a flyfishing-only section from the river's source in the Carrabassett Valley to where Route 146 crosses the river at East New Portland. The best canoe access along this water is made from Route 16.

The **Dead River's** north branch holds brook trout and some landlocks and is located in Alder Stream Township. This river section is composed of whitewater stretches and glass-flat pools. Its trout average 10 to 12 inches.

The south branch, flowing through the town of Dallas, also holds brook trout. Route 16 provides access to this water, where brookies run from 7 to 10 inches. This branch's good riffle sections seem to call out for soft-hackled flies.

Rangeley River is another good brook trout stream. The portion of Rangeley Lake and the Rangeley River from the two red posts set 300 feet above the fish screen downstream to the confluence of the Rangeley and Kennebago Rivers is designated flyfishing only with a daily limit of 1 fish.

Offering brown trout, **Sandy River** is flyfishing only from October 1 through 31 from the Route 145 bridge in the village of Strong, where there is a good access point, downstream to the Kennebec River confluence. Holdovers suffer the rigors of winter runoff, with planted hatchery fish supplementing surviving stocks. Still, ample access off Route 149 makes this trout water worth trying at least once.

Androscoggin and Oxford Counties Rivers and Streams

Androscoggin and Little Androscoggin Rivers

The Androscoggin River enters Maine from the White Mountains of New Hampshire near the small village of Gilead. It flows east through the pulp mill villages of Rumford and Mexico, south through the cities of Lewiston and Auburn, and on to the city of Brunswick, where it enters Merrymeeting Bay. Just 25 years ago, the Androscoggin River was almost written off as a dead river. Pollution from the discharge of pulp mills and dams pushed this river to a fatal limit. Restoration efforts were started, however, and now the state of Maine can once again be proud of this river.

The best trout fishing on the Androscoggin is in the section from the New Hampshire border to just west of the dam in Rumford. Route 2 runs along the river and provides good access for fishing and canoeing.

The Little Androscoggin flows south and east from the village of West Paris, twisting and turning until it joins the Androscoggin in Auburn/Lewiston. Trout fishing is best upriver, above the dam near the village of Oxford. Route 26 parallels the Little Androscoggin and offers good fishing and canoeing access.

The Maine Department of Inland Fisheries and Wildlife aggressively stocks both the Androscoggin and Little Androscoggin. In 1996, the rivers were stocked with a total of 16,538 brookies and browns.

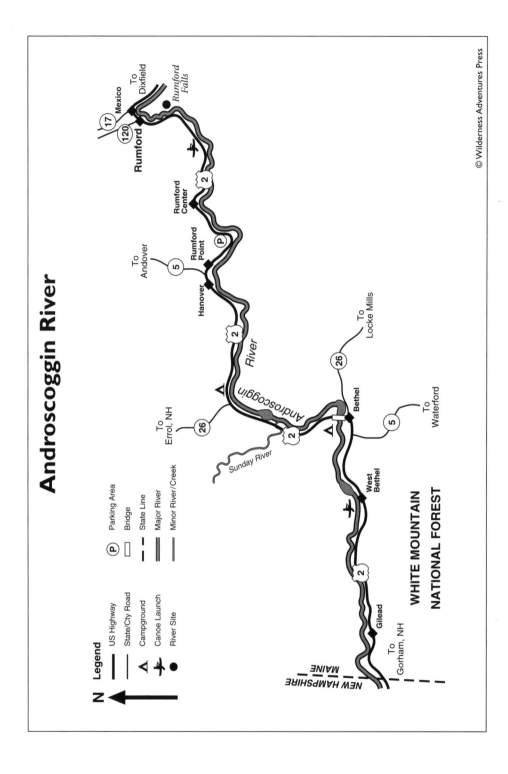

Androscoggin River

Legend

N

US Highway
State/City Road
State Line
Major River
Minor River/Creek

(P) Parking Area
☐ Bridge
△ Campground
✈ Canoe Launch
● River Site

© Wilderness Adventures Press

Little Androscoggin River

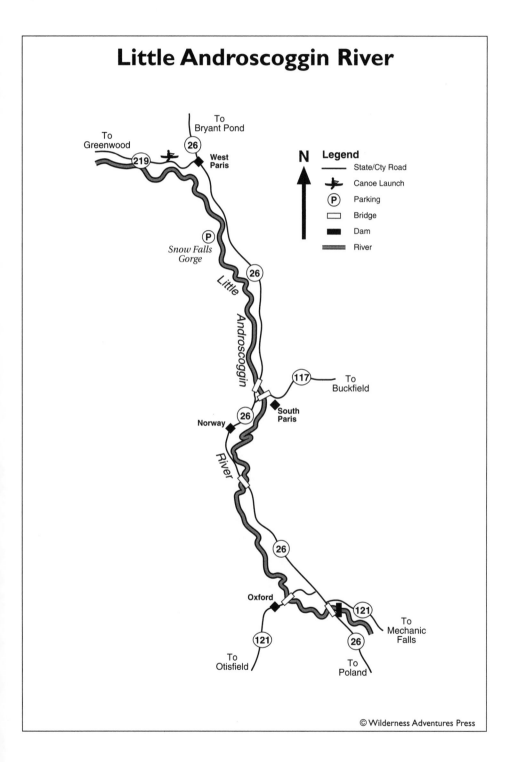

To Bryant Pond

To Greenwood

West Paris

N

Legend
— State/Cty Road
Canoe Launch
P Parking
Bridge
Dam
River

Snow Falls Gorge

Little Androscoggin

To Buckfield

South Paris

Norway

River

Oxford

To Mechanic Falls

To Otisfield

To Poland

© Wilderness Adventures Press

Rapid River

Rapid River, the outflow of Lower Richardson Lake, passes through the "Pond in the River" and into Umbagog Lake on the New Hampshire border. This flyfishing-only river holds landlocked salmon and brook trout. Brook trout fishing is restricted to catch and release throughout the season, and from August 16 to September 30, all salmon must be released.

Gated logging roads restrict access to the Rapid River. There is a boat launch near the camping area at the South Arm of Lower Richardson Lake that can be reached via South Arm Road north of the village of Andover and Route 120. It is about 5 miles by water to Middle Dam and Rapid River. Once there, you'll find a dirt road and well-worn footpaths leading to the river's pools and runs. There are several primitive campsites near the river mouth at Lake Umbagog.

Other Androscoggin and Oxford Counties Rivers and Streams

Magalloway River, where it flows between Lake Parmachenee and Aziscohos Lake, is another hard-to-get-at, flyfishing-only brook trout stream near the New Hampshire border. Access can be made by water from the boat launch off Route 16 at the south end of Aziscohos Lake.

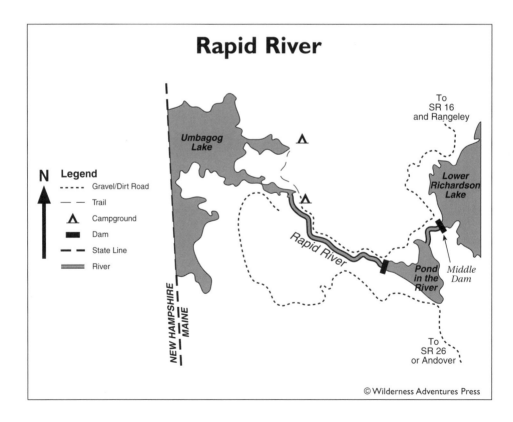

Range Brook is a small tributary of the Androscoggin River that flows near the village of Mechanics Falls. Access to this brook trout stream is off Routes 11 and 26.

Nezinscot River and its two branches, the East and West, flow south from the town of Sumner through the villages of Buckfield and Turner, joining the Androscoggin near Turner Center. The state stocks the Nezinscot system with brown trout. There is convenient access to these streams along Routes 117 and 140 and their side roads.

Somerset County Rivers and Streams

Kennebec River

According to Scott Davis, fisheries technician for the Maine Department of Inland Fisheries and Wildlife, "The Kennebec is one great trout and salmon river, and fishing here just seems to be getting better and better." It flows from the east and west outlets of Moosehead Lake, carving a long, deep valley through the center of Maine to the Atlantic Ocean south of the city of Bath. The upper Kennebec offers good springtime landlocked salmon and brook trout fishing. The cold outflow of the Wyman Dam in the river's middle stretch holds larger-sized rainbows and landlocks. There are warmwater species (smallmouth bass and perch) downstream and in the slower flows above the dams.

The Kennebec's passage south is interrupted by a series of dams that have, for years, prevented the migration of spawning fish in the lower river. On November 25, 1997, the Federal Energy Regulatory Commission (FERC), in a landmark decision, ordered the removal of Edwards Dam, located on the lower Kennebec in the city of Augusta. The removal of this dam opens up a 15-mile section of river between Augusta and the village of Waterville to spawning sea-run fish. Wild Atlantic salmon, striped bass, sturgeon, shad, and rainbow smelt once again will be able to return to their native spawning areas.

Both the West and East Outlets of the Kennebec as they flow out of Moosehead Lake offer good landlocked salmon fishing in the spring. The West Outlet river stretch is about 8 miles long. Route 15 north from the village of Greenville will take you to the headwaters, where there is a campground and hand-carried canoe put-in area. West Outlet flows through a series of ponds and pools and is floatable only at high water. There is a gravel road that parallels the river on the west bank and offers easy access for wading.

Kennebec's East Outlet is only 3 miles long but maintains a greater flow than West Outlet. A road parallels the river's west bank for about 1½ miles before it turns into a foot trail. East Outlet is restricted to flyfishing only throughout the season. Both river stretches offer an extended catch-and-release season during the month of October. Landlocked fishing is best in the spring during May and June, when the fish are actively feeding on smelt and caddisflies.

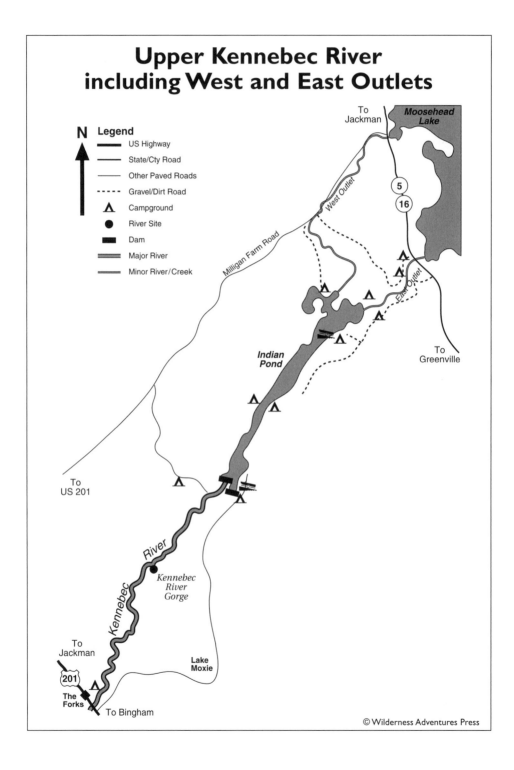

Upper Kennebec River including West and East Outlets

N

Legend

━━━ US Highway
─── State/Cty Road
─── Other Paved Roads
- - - Gravel/Dirt Road
▲ Campground
● River Site
▬ Dam
━━━ Major River
━━━ Minor River/Creek

To Jackman

Moosehead Lake

West Outlet

Milligan Farm Road

⑤
⑯

East Outlet

Indian Pond

To Greenville

To US 201

River

● *Kennebec River Gorge*

Kennebec

To Jackman

Lake Moxie

(201)

The Forks

To Bingham

© Wilderness Adventures Press

West Outlet of the Kennebec

While fly casting the Kennebec River West Outlet, anglers can anticipate 8- to 10-inch stocked brook trout along with the occasional wild fish. This river section is stocked annually by the state and is managed as a put-and-take fishery.

The slower-flowing West Outlet affords canoeing opportunities between the connected ponds—Long Pond, Round Pond, and Indian Pond. Smallmouth bass thrive in this section of river. Some Maine flyfishers regard bronzebacks as "trash fish," undeserving of the respect reserved for their native squaretails. Others view the abundant smallmouth as providing yet another fine flyfishing opportunity.

Pools, riffles, ample stillwater, and moderate flows provide a mixed bag of conditions as well as game fish. Navigable river flows are maintained by the Kennebec Water Power Company through its West Outlet dam. This water can be flyfished by canoe or on foot. An added attraction is the wildlife viewing opportunities—moose and deer are common sights throughout the region. Bring a camera but park vehicles off main roads to avoid conflicts with logging trucks.

Soft-hackled flies popularized by writers Sylvester Nemes and Dave Hughes are effective in addition to traditional winged wets. Nymphs, such as the gold-ribbed hare's ear (#12–16), zug bug (#10–14), and pheasant tail (#14–18), interest hatchery trout. Fish popping bugs and streamers for stillwater smallmouth.

Kennebec's West Outlet season opens to fishing on May 1and has a 2-trout limit. Expect hatchery brook trout from 8 to 10 inches with the occasional wild fish. Smallmouth bass can be found in Long, Round, and Indian Ponds.

This beautiful float-trip water has moderate flows with stillwater opportunities. Its flows can vary seasonally, and wet summers produce higher flows between the three connected ponds. Access is available from Indian Pond, and river access is available near the Route 15 bridge.

East Outlet of the Kennebec

"In 1996, East Outlet brook trout caught between May and September average 14.1 inches," says Paul Johnson, Maine Department of Inland Fisheries and Wildlife biologist, "and angler surveys indicated that 90 percent of these fish were released." In October of that year, during the mandatory catch-and-release season, Johnson indicated brookies ran just a little larger, averaging 15 inches. "These statistics," he explains, "are based on legal trout over 12 inches. Some trout may indeed run smaller."

Salmon catches in 1996 averaged 16.6 inches between May and September, when fish were kept, and 16 inches when released. In October, landlock lengths dropped slightly to 15.8 inches during the fall catch-and-release season. Again, these fly angler survey figures are based on the size of legal fish caught, specifically landlocks over 14 inches.

Moosehead Lake, Kennebec's headwater, influences East Outlet fishing. "The size of East Outlet salmon is a direct reflection of Moosehead Lake landlocks," says biologist Johnson, "since fish routinely move out of Moosehead and spend time in the East Outlet."

Commencing at the Moosehead Lake dam, the East Outlet provides reliable landlocked salmon fishing between the railroad bridge and the main highway. River flows in this section can vary. A pull-off spot along Route 15 provides ample vehicle parking. The nearby voluntary survey booth, one of four on the East Outlet, allows fly anglers to record their daily catches. The Maine Department of Inland Fisheries and Wildlife uses this information to manage the resource. From here, an unimproved road runs along the East Outlet's north bank, providing angler access. Primitive campsites, located along lower river sections and near Indian Pond, require fire permits.

Reading the water in this section of river requires discipline and the patience of a heron stalking fish. Steady and sometimes steep, East Outlet's boulder-filled runs hold salmon and brook trout. A streamer or nymph drifted in front of finning fish will often draw strikes. Cover river sections by adjusting casts according to current speed. Holding, feeding, and sheltering lies can be worked in this manner, blanketing water until the fly swings and settles the way you wish. Stick with it. Hooked fish will dictate your best approach, which can sometimes be a game of inches.

East Outlet trips are best planned for June, when river flows have dropped, and for the last two weeks in October, during the special extended catch-and-release season. Recently, commercial paddle and drift boat trips have become available through local outfitters.

Streamers worth trying on the East Outlet include the gray ghost (#2–12), grizzly king (#6–12), black nose dace (#2–8), Mickey Finn (#2–12), marabou muddlers (#2–10, matukas (#2–10), and of course, the "meat fly" of choice in these parts, olive or brown woolly buggers (#2–12). Stonefly nymphs will interest both trout and salmon.

May 1 to September 30 is flyfishing only on the East Outlet from Moosehead Lake to Indian Pond. There is also a flyfishing-only, catch-and-release season from October 1 through 31. Trout, togue, and salmon limits are modest: 1 fish per day with a 12-inch minimum trout length, a 14-inch minimum on salmon, and an 18-inch minimum for lake trout. Optional or not, 90 percent of fly anglers chose to release fish here in 1996.

Salmon typically run from 14 to 18 inches in length. My largest East Outlet landlock, which smacked a tumbling woolly bugger, measured just shy of 19 inches. Trout run from 9 to 19 inches in length, and many average 14 to 15 inches.

The East Outlet features moderate to heavy water, and tailwater flows near the East Outlet dam can make wading tough. A growing drift boat fishery finds floating flyfishers working river runs with nymphs and streamers. Wade with caution in June and late October to fish riffles and flats when flows diminish.

High, cold water can be expected in May, with flows in excess of 2,000 cubic feet per second, which can be tough to wade. Flows drop in June and average summer flows fall to 1,000 cfs. Wet July and August rains can again cause flows to rise over 2,000 cfs, however. Moosehead Lake, which provides regulated storage for downstream hydropower operations, is drawn down in September, raising East Outlet flows to over 2,000 cfs through mid-October. River flows during the last two weeks of

October are generally in the 1,000 to 1,500 cfs range, when "cast and blast" opportunities abound for game fish and grouse.

A boat ramp is available at Indian Pond, 4 miles south of the East Outlet Dam.

Middle Kennebec River

From the outlets, the Kennebec flows through Indian Pond to a dam at the pond's southern end. The flow rates and water levels throughout the Kennebec River can change rapidly, and the state warns canoeists and kayakers to use extreme caution, particularly in the river below the dam at Indian Pond. Anglers are advised to fish from shore and be mindful of flow changes.

Dead River joins the Kennebec at The Forks near Route 201. During the summer months when water levels are down, this is a good area to hike into, following the river north. There are some nice runs and brook trout pools near the confluence of Cold Stream and Moxie Falls.

The Kennebec continues south through the Wyman Lake impoundment. Wyman Dam in the village of Moscow has a coldwater release and provides good fishing downstream throughout the season. There is a well-marked access to the dam from Route 201 in Moscow. Downstream, there are access points near the Route 16 bridge in the village of Bingham and the Route 201A bridge in the village of Solon as well. This river stretch holds larger-sized landlocks and rainbow trout, and there are good caddis hatches in June. Again, wading anglers are cautioned to watch flow levels.

The flatwater section of the Kennebec below the city of Skowhegan offers excellent smallmouth bass fishing and a put-and-take fishery for brown trout and salmon. Most of this river stretch is fished from boats or canoes. It is possible to wade the faster flowing stretch upstream from a boat launch located off Route 2.

Biologist Scott Davis is an avid fly angler. On the Skowhegan river section, he recommends blue-winged olives—both dries and nymphs will work. Fish nymphs slowly along the stream's bottom. Olive-bodied dry fly patterns with smoky-gray wings are hard to beat for Kennebec River trout because they can imitate a variety of species. "Go from #14 to 18 as the season progresses," he adds.

He speculates that, "Better Kennebec River water quality finds blue-winged olive hatches lasting longer, often from one in the afternoon to sunset, when the caddis start up." Fish June and July for the best results. Blue-winged olives are also active on the Shawmut area of the river where access makes bank fishing popular. "Basic elk hair caddis offerings will also catch fish here," says Davis. "Go with #14 in June, then switch to #18 in July."

Scott Davis' blue-winged olives and elk hair caddis catch fish all season. Try a range of caddis dries, from the Henryville special to the elk-wing parachute caddis. Fish stonefly nymphs, which include the early black and early brown, as well as traditional wet flies. Streamers are effective for September bass and salmon.

The area from Skowhegan to Shawmut Dam has open fishing year-round. The minimum salmon, trout, and togue length is 12 inches, with a daily bag limit of 2 fish in the aggregate. Shawmut Dam to the upstream side of the new Donald Carter

Middle Kennebec River

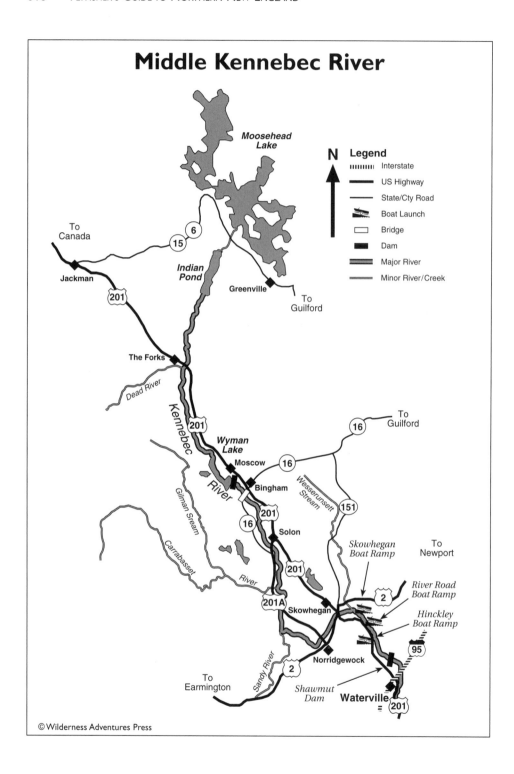

Moosehead Lake

N

Legend

IIIIIIII	Interstate
▬▬▬	US Highway
———	State/Cty Road
🚤	Boat Launch
☐	Bridge
■	Dam
▬▬▬	Major River
∼∼∼	Minor River/Creek

To Canada

Jackman

Indian Pond

6
15

201

Greenville

To Guilford

The Forks

Dead River

Kennebec River

201

Wyman Lake

Moscow

16

Bingham

16

To Guilford

Wesserunsett Stream

201

16

151

Gilman Stream

Solon

Skowhegan Boat Ramp

To Newport

201

Carrabassett River

201A

Skowhegan

River Road Boat Ramp

2

Hinckley Boat Ramp

95

Norridgewock

Sandy River

2

To Earmington

Shawmut Dam

Waterville

201

© Wilderness Adventures Press

Bridge in Waterville/Winslow is artificial lures only with a minimum length for salmon, rainbow trout, and brown trout of 16 inches. The total daily limit for salmon, trout, and togue is 1 fish. Check current fishing laws for the entire river section.

Heavily stocked, the river holds hatchery brown trout from 8 to 10 inches when first planted, and holdovers grow larger. Landlocked salmon average 1 to 2 pounds. Smallmouth bass mix with browns between Skowhegan and Shawmut Dam.

Note: Trace amounts of dioxin have been detected in fish tissue from certain sections of the Kennebec. The Maine Department of Inland Fisheries and Wildlife and Department of Human Services suggest that the general public should not eat more than 2 fish meals per month from the Kennebec River. A "fish meal" is considered to be one 8-ounce portion. For further information, contact the Maine Department of Human Services at 207-287-5378.

The Kennebec is subject to rapid fluctuations in water level, which has resulted in loss of life. Riverbank or boat fishing is the best way to go. The river between Skowhegan and Shawmut Dam consists of flat but steady runs.

Boat launches for Kennebec include the Skowhegan Boat Launch on Canaan Road, River Road Boat Launch, and the Hinckley Boat Launch on U.S. Route 201.

Moose River

Moose River begins near the state of Maine's western border with the Province of Quebec, Canada, west of the village of Jackman, and flows through several ponds and lakes before it enters Moosehead Lake. West of Jackman and Route 206, the river passes through a remote wilderness area that is accessible only by air or water from Jackman. Local sporting goods stores, flying services, and guides will be able to assist you with your plans. The river offers a true wilderness experience with brook trout and landlocked salmon fishing.

The section of river that connects Long Pond and Little Brassua Lake, as well as the section between Brassua Lake and Moosehead Lake, holds some of the most beautiful landlocked salmon and brook trout pools in central Maine. The river is much more accessible through this river stretch since it runs parallel to Routes 6 and 15 and the Canadian-American Railroad tracks.

Between Long Pond and Little Brassua, the Moose is big water with huge boulders, riffles, and long runs. Access is from a side road, off Routes 6 and 15, that crosses the river midway through this portion of the river.

The Moose finishes its journey from the dam in Brassua Lake with a 3-mile run to its mouth at Moosehead Lake near the village of Rockwood. Moderately moving currents, tumbling riffles, and deep pools create prime brook trout and salmon lies in this stretch. The dam's cold water outflow offers good angling throughout the season in the upper mile of this section. A camp road on the river's' north bank provides access, as well as the driveway owned by the Kennebec Water Power Company off Route 15.

The lower 2 miles of the river flow at lake level throughout the summer. Anglers trolling with flies take togue in this flatwater section at ice-out. In the fall, landlocked salmon run up the river from Moosehead. Route 15 parallels the river on the south bank, and there is a boat launch and parking available near the highway.

Moose River is open to fishing from May 1 to September 30 with a number of special regulations: From the confluence of Holeb Stream to Attean Falls is artificial lures only. From Attean Falls downstream to the red markers at the outlet of Big Wood Pond, the daily bag limit on brook trout is 2 fish (including splake), a minimum length of 12 inches, and only one may exceed 14 inches. From the red markers at the outlet of Big Wood Pond to Brassua Lake, there is a 2-trout daily bag limit.

The river and its tributaries from Brassua Lake Dam to the red markers at the Rock Pile Pool has a 12-inch minimum trout length restriction. Minimum length for togue is 18 inches. May 1 to August 15 is an artificial-lures-only season with a total daily bag limit on salmon, trout, and togue of 1 fish. From August 16 to September 30 is flyfishing only with a total bag limit for salmon, trout, and togue of 1 fish.

In addition, the regulations for the section from Brassua Lake Dam to the red markers at Rock Pile Pool also apply to the section from the red markers at Rock Pile Pool to Moosehead Lake but without the artificial lure restriction between May 1 and August 15. Check current laws carefully for any changes on this highly regulated water.

Anglers can expect salmon to several pounds, with brook trout averaging about a pound and the occasional larger brookie. My time on this river has yielded brookies in the 10- to 14-inch range. Many were caught on stonefly nymphs.

River flows near the Brassua Lake Dam retain cold, fast water throughout the season, while the lower river section near Moosehead is flatwater best fished in June and September. The section from Brassua Lake to Moosehead Lake holds pools and rapids just below the dam, then settles into steady flatwater that is often trolled by boat. Moderate to heavy flows can be expected between Long Pond and Little Brassua Lake, and rock-strewn fastwater and deep holding lies define this stretch.

To troll the lower river's flatwater section, use the Rockwood Boat Launch. Route 15 provides access for both Moose River sections.

West Central Maine Stillwaters
Rangeley Lake

Rangeley, a 6,000-acre lake, draws flyfishers pursuing landlocks, especially after ice-out in early May. Originally called Oquossoc Lake (a town here still bears the name), this Franklin County lake offers springtime flyfishing opportunities, particularly in its many coves. Target these sheltered bays near Rangeley Lake tributaries where smelt stage during their annual spawning ritual. Springtime salmon-holding locations include Greenvale Cove (at the southeastern end of the lake), Town Cove, Hunter Cove, Smith Cove (northern shore), and South Bog Cove (southwestern end of Rangeley).

Flyfish near Greenvale Cove tributary mouths, specifically Nile Brook and Long Pond Stream. Town Cove tributaries (Hatchery and Haley Pond Brooks) draw smelt

Late September is a good time to fish Rangeley Lake.
(Photo courtesy Maine Office of Tourism)

as does Hunter Cove, where Quimby Brook and Dodge Pond Stream feed into the bigger water. South Bog Cove's shoals around the South Bog Islands and near the South Bog Stream shoreline offer flyfishing opportunities as well. Salmon angling is sustained by holdover fish and annual plantings—3,000 salmon, 8 to 10 inches in length, were stocked in 1996.

Forrest Bonney, Rangeley Lake Region fisheries biologist for the Maine Department of Inland Fisheries and Wildlife, says, "There is some brook trout fishing here, but Rangeley is primarily managed for salmon. Wonderful trout fishing can be found on nearby Mooselookmeguntic Lake, a wild brookie fishery with excellent habitat consisting of rocky shoals."

Rangeley is stocked with 6- to 8-inch salmon (legal at 14 inches). Bonney reports that salmon plantings have decreased from 4,000 spring yearlings in 1993 to 3,000 fish in 1996 due to an indication of decreased growth rates. Still, 1996 voluntary surveys reflect a 66 percent success rate for anglers targeting legal landlocked salmon, with the average length of these fish measuring 17.2 inches. The good news is that catch-and-release anglers returned a lofty 70.2 percent of all legal salmon caught.

Landlocks range from 1 to several pounds with occasional 5-pounders. Fish recently sampled during fall Maine Department of Inland Fisheries and Wildlife

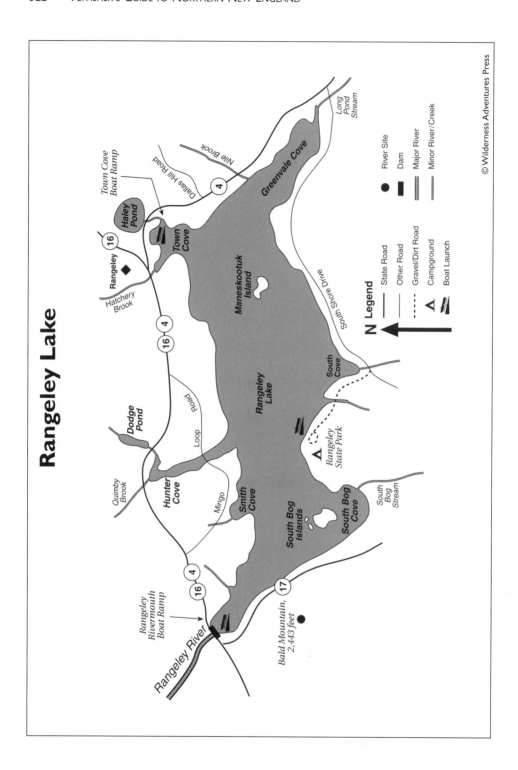

Rangeley Lake

© Wilderness Adventures Press

N

Legend

	State Road
	Other Road
	Gravel/Dirt Road
△	Campground
	Boat Launch

●	River Site
■	Dam
	Major River
	Minor River/Creek

Long Pond Stream

Nile Brook

Greenvale Cove

Town Cove Boat Ramp

Dallas Hill Road

Haley Pond

Rangeley

Town Cove

Hatchery Brook

Maneskootuk Island

South Shore Drive

South Cove

Rangeley Lake

Rangeley State Park

Dodge Pond

Loop Road

Quimby Brook

Hunter Cove

Mingo

Smith Cove

South Bog Islands

South Bog Cove

South Bog Stream

Rangeley Rivermouth Boat Ramp

Bald Mountain, 2,443 feet

Rangeley River

trapnetting efforts at Rangeley Outlet average 16.9 inches and 1 pound, 1 ounce. The largest salmon recorded during this study was 22.4 inches in length and weighed 3 pounds, 8 ounces. Biologists indicate landlocked salmon were first introduced to Rangeley Lake in 1873. The biggest ever recorded here weighed a shade over 18 pounds.

Bonney says that the abundance of older salmon reported from trapnet surveys can be attributed to the single salmon limits imposed back in 1996, and because many Rangeley Lake anglers are voluntarily releasing legal fish. He relates that, "Given the increase in the number of wild salmon and the decrease in the growth rate, the stocking rate was lowered in 1996 from 3,000 (0.5 per acre) to 2,500 (0.4 per acre) spring yearlings to prevent overpredation of the smelt population."

And what of Rangeley Lake brook trout? Rangeley Lake holds planted brook trout from 10 to 12 inches with some holdover fish. Bonney says, "Although growth rates are good, catch rates by anglers remain low despite annual stockings of approximately 10,000 fall fingerlings per year. Accordingly, 1,000 spring yearling trout, which average 10 inches in length, are scheduled to be stocked annually beginning in 1998." Growth rates influence Maine Department of Inland Fisheries and Wildlife decisions, since yearly planted spring trout eat smelt, too.

"Although fewer trout will be stocked, the spring yearlings are expect to provide higher returns to the angler because of their larger size at stocking," Bonney concludes. Salmon continue to dominate attention for the moment.

And how do you catch Rangeley's landlocks? Chris Aylesworth, manager of the Fly Box and Rangeley Region Sport Shop, says this in regard to Rangeley Lake Region salmon angling, "Most people fish salmon by trolling, which is the most productive form of angling here. Some local salmon die-hards, eager to wet a line, paddle a canoe around and fish open water near remaining ice, casting streamers to potential fish."

Ice-out can arrive between May 1 and 15, depending on the year. Just after ice clears, Chris suggests fishing tandem streamers using high-density, sinking fly lines, down 10 to 15 feet, or trolling a streamer using lightweight, lead-core line at a distance of 70 feet or so behind the boat. Try trolling a streamer just outside the propeller wash or sometimes right in it.

What smelt patterns does Chris recommend? "That can depend on the year, too," he says. "Over the last five or six years, pattern choices have changed, occasionally veering toward the unorthodox. The black ghost marabou, though more effective when cast, has taken salmon recently when trolled. Of course, old standbys, such as the green ghost, routinely catch fish, as well as the pearl smelt and forest blue smelt, good local patterns that have earned reputations as productive flies." As Chris says, "We at the fly shop wait to see what folks are using, and we keep up to date with trends."

Some anglers prefer hardware and sewn bait when fishing Rangeley Lake for salmon. But the undulating smelt-like movements of Carrie Stevens' gray ghost are still hard to beat for aesthetics.

Western Maine's Rangeley Chain of Lakes offer flyfishing for trout and salmon. (Photo courtesy Maine Office of Tourism)

Rangeley Lake's season is April 1 to September 30 with these special regulations: A daily limit on brook trout (including splake) of 2 fish and a minimum length limit of 10 inches (only 1 may exceed 12 inches); minimum length for trout in tributaries is 8 inches; and a daily bag limit on salmon is 1 fish at least 14 inches. In addition to lake angling, October flyfishing-only, catch-and-release opportunities exist downstream from the Rangeley Lake outlet dam near the big water's westernmost side to the confluence of the Rangeley and Kennebago Rivers.

This 6,000-acre lake has a maximum depth of 149 feet with fish shoals near previously noted coves and tributaries. Chilly springtime afternoons can be accompanied by occasional gusty winds, snow squalls, and choppy water conditions. Dress warmly and think with your head not your heart. The scenery here and the desire for fish can easily distract you from dangerous conditions.

Bald Mountain, situated on Maine Public Reserve Land near the western shore, rises to 2,443 feet. Here in Maine's western mountains, the town of Rangeley sits at 1,800 feet on the lake's northeastern shore. It's a classic place to flyfish—cold springtime storms or not.

Route 4 will take you to the town of Rangeley, while South Shore Drive provides Rangeley Lake State Park access. Route 17 skirts the westernmost shore. Boat ramps can be found at Town Cove off Route 4 on the northeastern shore, the mouth of Rangeley River off Routes 4 and 16 on the northwestern shore, and Rangeley State Park off South Shore Drive on the southern shore.

Mooselookmeguntic Lake

"Mooselookmeguntic Lake is a wonderful wild brook trout fishery, where fish can run as large as 5 pounds," according to Forrest Bonney, Maine Department of Inland Fisheries and Wildlife fisheries biologist.

If you want traditional Maine squaretails, this is the place to go. The largest of the Rangeley Chain of Lakes, Mooselookmeguntic offers exceptional trout and salmon fishing, drawing anglers from all over the country. According to the Maine Department of Inland Fisheries and Wildlife's David Boucher, "Fishing pressure at Mooselookmeguntic remained stable from 1981 to 1995 at about 10,000 angler trips per year. This level of use is within the normal range for large Maine lakes."

Catch and release is increasingly more popular on the lake and elsewhere in the Rangeley Lakes region. In fact, Boucher suggests that anglers released 65 percent of their legal 1995 salmon catches. This statistic shows a marked increase when compared to 27 percent released in 1986, and 11 percent in 1981. Recent years have seen an increase in the harvest of salmon over 20 inches in length as well. The average size of Mooselookmeguntic landlocks taken by anglers has increased from 16.2 inches in 1986 to 17.1 inches during the period of 1991–1995.

As Boucher says, "Growth rates and conditions of salmon remained stable from 1981 to 1995. Only minor fluctuations were noted. It is presumed that the changes are related to year-to-year variations in salmon density arising from variations in spawning success. The percent of sublegal fish in the catch, an indirect measure of spawning success, ranged from 50 percent in 1986 to 71 percent in 1991 but exhibited no upward or downward trend."

Anglers are also applying catch-and-release standards on this wild brook trout fishery. In 1981, released legal brook trout were at a lowly 5 percent. But by the mid-1990s, roughly 35 percent of fish were being returned to Mooselookmeguntic. Boucher indicates that a decline in trout exceeding 15 inches in length occurred between 1986 and 1991 but reversed itself in 1995. He speculates that, "It was possible that a real increase in numbers of large, older trout in the population occurred as a result of higher release rates practiced by anglers.

"However, it was also possible," he concludes, "that anglers have become more selective in their choice of which fish to harvest, and more chose to kill larger, older fish." As biologist Bonney indicates, some of these wild brookies go 5 pounds—beautiful fish indeed.

Mooselookmeguntic Lake

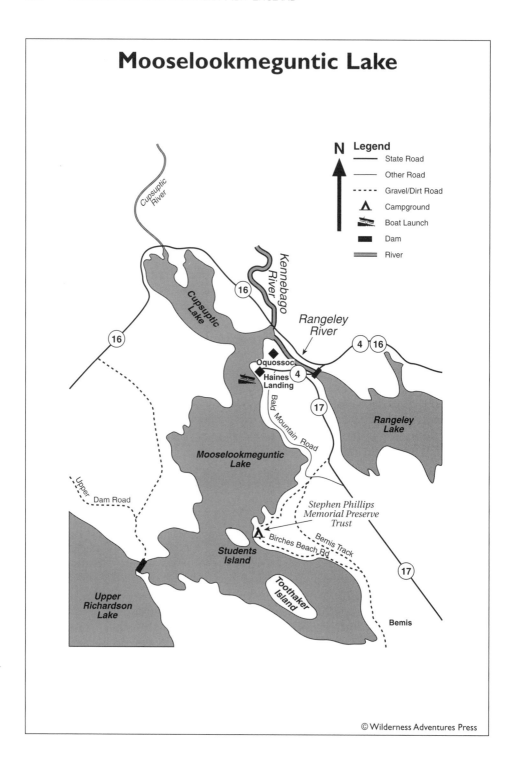

N

Legend

—— State Road

—— Other Road

---- Gravel/Dirt Road

⋀ Campground

Boat Launch

▬ Dam

River

Cupsuptic River

Kennebago River

Cupsuptic Lake

16

16

16

Rangeley River

4 16

Oquossoc

Haines Landing

4

Bald Mountain Road

17

Rangeley Lake

Mooselookmeguntic Lake

Upper Dam Road

Stephen Phillips Memorial Preserve Trust

Bemis Track

Birches Beach Rd

17

Students Island

Toothaker Island

Upper Richardson Lake

Bemis

© Wilderness Adventures Press

The lake's open water fishing season starts April 1 and goes through September 30. The daily bag limit for brook trout (including splake) is 2 fish with a minimum length of 10 inches and only one exceeding 12 inches. Mooselookmeguntic is closed to ice fishing.

Expect to find wild brook trout and landlocked salmon from several pounds to several more. Neither species has been stocked here since 1984.

The lake's surface area is 16,300 acres, having a mean depth of 60 feet and a maximum depth of 139 feet. Mooselookmeguntic has ideal summer water temperatures and habitat for trout and salmon. While southeast coves have seen some development, much of the shoreline remains untouched. It is always important to pay attention to weather conditions on the lake, as they can change in an instant.

Access to the lake includes the Haines Landing boat launch, which provides trailered access on the easternmost shore off Route 4 and fishing from nearby rocky shoals after the mid-May ice-out. Roads providing access include Bald Mountain Road on the eastern shore, Birches Beach Road on the southeastern shore, and Upper Dam Road on the southwestern shore.

Upper and Lower Richardson Lakes

For now, the area surrounding Richardson Lakes is sparsely developed. The Mooselookmeguntic Dam ("Upper Dam") area is a favored flyfishing-only site. Since fish are prevented from moving upstream into Mooselookmeguntic Lake via Upper Dam, mature salmonids congregate, providing a tremendous fishery. Though ample angling opportunities exist, fishing pressure on Richardson Lakes has actually been decreasing.

Maine Department of Inland Fisheries and Wildlife biologist Bonney indicates that, "The number of anglers fishing the Richardsons has recently declined by 30 percent from an estimated 9,962 in 1991 to 7,090 in 1996. The estimated harvest of salmon and brook trout declined by similar proportion—lake trout catches dropped by 64 percent." What happened? According to Bonney, "The salmon growth rate was stable from 1986–1991 but declined in succeeding years as the percentage of released sublegal fish increased. In 1994, in response to this decline in growth rate, we (the Maine Department of Inland Fisheries and Wildlife) lowered the salmon stocking rate from 3,500 to 2,000 spring yearlings per year, and the growth rate has stabilized since then. We requested that Mill and Metallak Brooks be closed to the dipping of smelts effective in 1996 to increase the lakes' forage base, but that request was denied. We will therefore continue to stock salmon at the reduced rate of 2,000 per year."

The average salmon length for Richardson Lakes is 16.9 inches and 1 pound, 9 ounces in weight. Hatchery-reared landlocks accounted for 62 percent of the 1996 harvest.

Other concerns affect management thinking as well. Lake trout numbers have grown since the illegal introduction of this species in the mid-1970s. Maine Department of Inland Fisheries and Wildlife studies now suggest these togue are reproducing naturally. Subsequent to unauthorized stocking, lakers have been

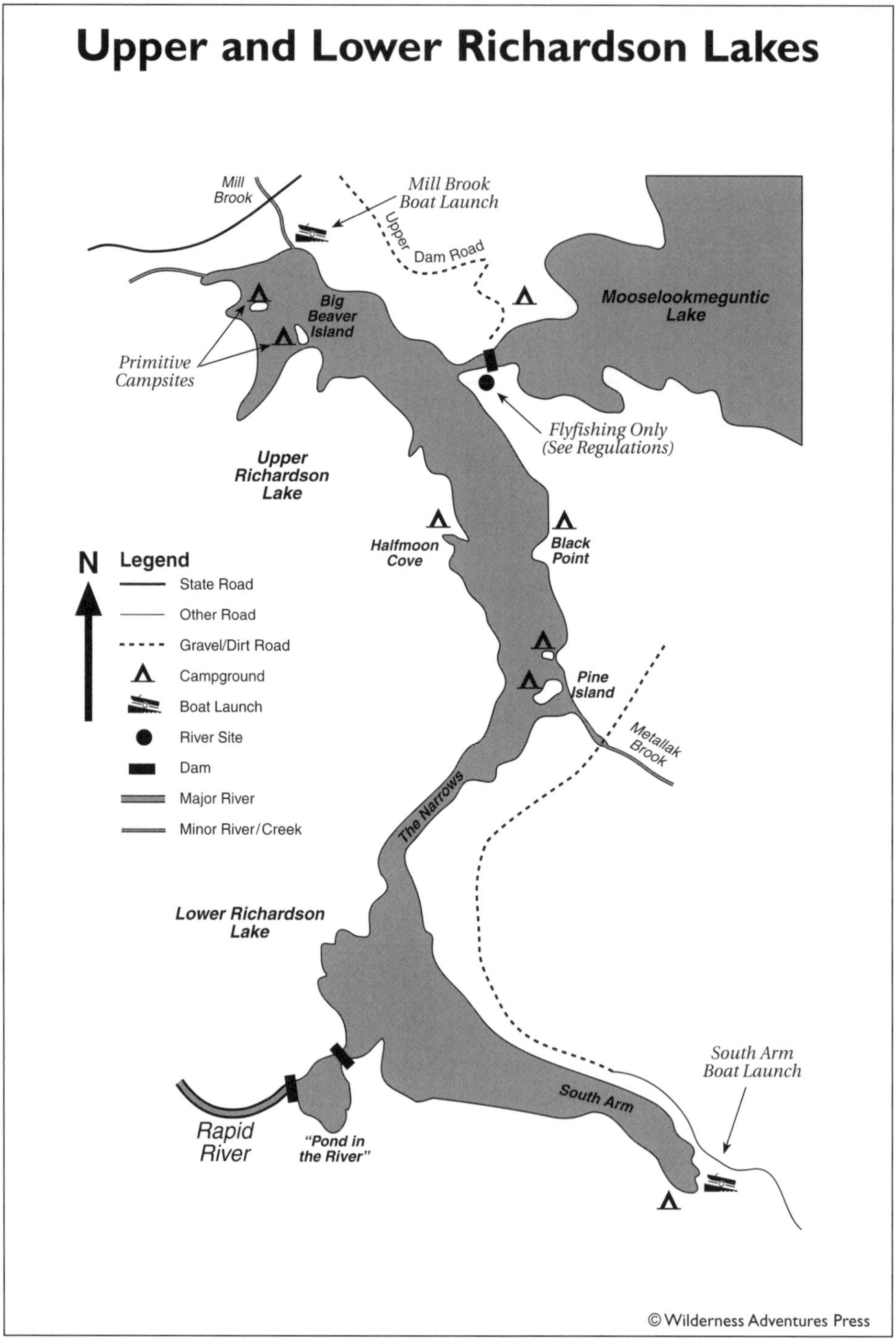

Upper and Lower Richardson Lakes

Mill Brook

Mill Brook Boat Launch

Upper Dam Road

Mooselookmeguntic Lake

Big Beaver Island

Primitive Campsites

Flyfishing Only
(See Regulations)

Upper Richardson Lake

N

Legend

—— State Road

—— Other Road

- - - Gravel/Dirt Road

Δ Campground

Boat Launch

● River Site

Dam

Major River

Minor River/Creek

Halfmoon Cove

Black Point

Pine Island

Metallak Brook

The Narrows

Lower Richardson Lake

South Arm Boat Launch

South Arm

Rapid River

"Pond in the River"

© Wilderness Adventures Press

legally planted by the state every third or fourth year in an effort to manage this natural reproduction. As Bonney says, "It was our intent to sustain a small lake trout population by stocking and to rely on the fall drawdown of the lake level to destroy the lake trout eggs that had been deposited."

According to Bonney, the Maine Department of Inland Fisheries and Wildlife felt this strategy would prevent excessive predator numbers for which the forage base might prove inadequate. Despite the yearly autumn drawdown, however, lake trout egg deposition continues to yield wild fish. Consequently, lake trout stocking will be suspended.

All stocked lake trout are identified by fin excision. In 1996, the department confirmed the presence of wild togue. Lakers studied recently ranged from 5.2 inches to 25.6 inches in length. Biologist Forrest Bonney reports that a "reliable diary keeper" caught two unmarked (wild) lake trout in 1996. One measured 14 inches while the other went 22 inches in length and weighed 4 pounds, 12 ounces.

As brook trout go, growth remains good, though catches are low despite Maine Department of Inland Fisheries and Wildlife stocking efforts. New 1996 regulations should benefit this species, but future years will tell. Average brook trout length is 12.6 inches and weight is 13.4 ounces.

Richardson Lakes' season extends from April 1 through September 30, and the daily bag limit on brook trout (including splake) is 2 fish with a minimum length of 10 inches and only 1 can exceed 12 inches. On the Upper Dam Pool, the area between the Mooselookmeguntic Lake Dam and a line drawn between the two cribwork piers approximately 800 yards west of the dam is flyfishing only. The minimum length for trout is 12 inches and for salmon is 18 inches. The daily limit is 1 fish. No motorboats are allowed from the dam gates downstream or westerly for 150 yards.

Upper Richardson covers 4,200 acres, while Lower Richardson has 2,900 acres of angling. Connected by the bottlenecking stretch of water dubbed "The Narrows," both lakes are each roughly 100 feet deep. Maximum and mean depths range from 108 feet to 44 feet. The Union Water Power Company draws water from the Richardson Lakes in the fall, lowering lake levels by several feet.

Summer storms arrive unannounced, so it pays to watch the sky for thunderheads. If whitecaps appear, get off the water. Because Richardson Lakes are oligotrophic waters, they lack plant nutrients and have large amounts of dissolved oxygen throughout. The Upper and Lower lakes are actually one lake distinguished by two basins.

Public boat launch sites are available on either extreme of the lakes. Mill Brook offers access on the northern shore, while South Arm does on the southern end. Unrestricted vehicular access via Upper Dam Road is available to within a mile of Upper Dam Pool, the main tributary to the lakes. For those interested in flyfishing history, Carrie Stevens, inventor of the gray ghost, is reputed to have first cast her now-famous streamer in this flow.

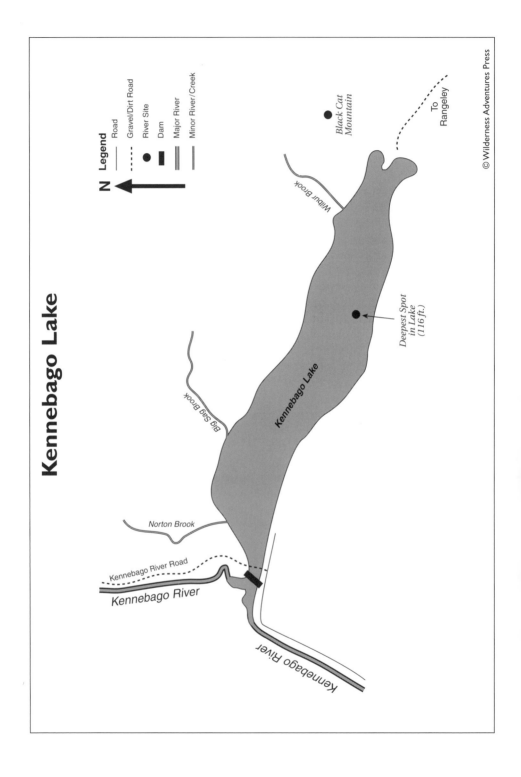

Kennebago Lake

N

Legend

— Road
····· Gravel/Dirt Road
● River Site
▮ Dam
 Major River
 Minor River/Creek

Black Cat Mountain

To Rangeley

Wilbur Brook

Deepest Spot in Lake (116 ft.)

Kennebago Lake

Big Sag Brook

Norton Brook

Kennebago River Road

Kennebago River

Kennebago River

© Wilderness Adventures Press

Kennebago Lake

Believe it or not, only brook trout, browns, salmon, and a forage base of smelt swim in this flyfishing-only water. There are none of the prolific perch that plague fisheries managers in other locations of the state. Ice-out arrives by mid-May on this large lake.

John Blunt, owner of Grant's Kennebago Camps, services this water, opening operations on May 23 most years. He indicates fish can be just a little sluggish after ice-out. Blunt puts clients into flyfishing through September's end. Though salmon and brook trout are the primary catches, a few browns are caught as well.

His suggested traditional salmon pattern is the nine three, a classic Maine streamer, which owes its name to the 9-pound, 3-ounce salmon this fly first caught.

Dry-fly purists take note: the red quill (#12–18) and dark Hendrickson (#12–18) interest trout in early June after several weeks of ice-out salmon angling with streamers. The brown drake spinner (#10–12) and the brown drake thorax (#8–12) will catch brookies from mid-June through the week after Independence Day. Think *Hexagenia* duns by summer, a stillwater, dry-fly favorite in this state. Fish the parachute *Hex* (#8–10) but don't forget about the nymph (#4–6). It pays to scrutinize the water closely. By September, the nine three, gray ghost, and Kennebago smelt, among other streamers, will catch salmon. Fish black gnat patterns after Labor Day in sizes 14–20. A *Hex* dry will catch brookies toward season's end (September 30). Count on mid- to late September for blue-winged olives—size 18 flies work well. Carry a few tiny Adams dries in your fly wallet this time of year as they work when the going gets tough.

Kennebago Lake's season is April 1 to September 30 and is flyfishing only. Tributaries, which include Norton Brook, Big Sag Brook, and Wilbur Brook, are closed to fishing. The exception is the Kennebago River. The daily bag limit for brook trout is 2 fish with a minimum length of 10 inches and only 1 can exceed 12 inches.

The 1,700-acre lake has a maximum depth of 116 feet and holds brookies, browns, and landlocks from one to several pounds. There is little shoreline development to disrupt the beauty of this fishery, which rests at 1,779 feet above sea level.

Public access is available via the Kennebago River or by private road open to guests at Grant's Kennebago Camps.

Franklin County Stillwaters

Many flyfishing-only waters are best fished by float tube or from a canoe, since a fair share of Maine's trout ponds have shoreline silt. Test the water with a wading staff or an available stick before wading. When flyfishing these waters, look for springholes in both deeper and shallower water—trout hold in these places. Expect to shoulder float tubes or portage canoes to some waters.

Black bear sows with cubs may cross your path and should be avoided. Biting bugs are to be expected, but brook trout fishing is worth braving the bug swarms in any of the following 21 flyfishing-only ponds. Some fishers retaliate with cheap cigars. Remember German philosopher Nietzsche's dictum: "What does not kill me makes me stronger." Did old Friedrich flyfish? Beats me, but if his attitude doesn't work, try a head net.

The wilderness area north and west of the village of Eustis holds a number of fly-fishing-only stillwaters. This region is reached by Route 16 from the village of Rangeley to Route 27.

Arnold Pond, **Caribou Pond**, **South Boundary Pond**, and **Horseshoe Pond** are four flyfishing-only stillwaters located on the border of the Province of Quebec near Coburn Gore and Massachusetts Gore off Route 27. The ponds are accessible from foot trails off the highway. There are primitive campsites in the area.

Blanchard Pond and **Round Mountain Pond** are located in Alder Stream Township. The access road just north of Alder Stream Bridge is gated, and the ponds can be reached by foot trail. From Eustis, Tim Pond Road provides access for the trails to **Little Kennebago Lake** in Stetsontown Township, **Secret Pond** in Seven Ponds Township, **Tim Pond** and **Tea Pond** in Jim Pond Township. About 4,000 acres of this area are privately owned by the Calden families who operate Tim Pond Wilderness Camps. They can be contacted in Eustis, ME 04936, 207-897-2100. **Little Jim Pond** is easily accessible via King and Bartlett Road north of Eustis and Route 27. There is a primitive campsite near the trail.

In the Rangeley Region, **Kamankeag Pond**, **Quimby Pond**, **Ross Pond**, and **Round Pond** are found north of Rangeley Lake. Access to Kamankeag and Round is from Dodge Pond Road about 3 miles west of Rangeley village off Routes 16 and 4. The access road to Quimby Pond is about a mile east, and there is a hand-carried boat launch near the pond's outlet. The road and trail to Ross Pond is in Rangeley.

Moxie Pond and another stillwater named **Round Pond** are located in Maine Public Reserve Lands east of Mooselookmeguntic Lake. They are accessible from the Appalachian Trail near Route 17 north of the city of Rumford. **Spencer Pond** is a short distance south of the trail and is accessible from Route 17. **Beal Pond** can be reached from Route 4 south of Rangeley. There is an access road near the small village of Madrid.

On the eastern edge of Franklin County is **Shiloh Pond**. This flyfishing-only stillwater is accessible from Tufts Pond Road off Routes 16 and 27 north of the village of Kingfield. **McIntire Pond** is located in the southernmost corner of Franklin County near the village of New Sharon on Routes 2 and 27 east of the city of Farmington. Access to McIntire Pond is from Route 27 about 4 miles south of Sharon.

Other Franklin County Stillwater Options

The Maine Department of Inland Fisheries and Wildlife stocks several other Franklin County lakes and ponds with brook trout, togue, and brown trout. General fishing regulations for the majority of these stillwaters restrict the use of live bait and limit creels to 2 fish at least 8 inches in length.

There are three easily accessible brook trout ponds in the northwest corner of Franklin County. **Bug Eye Pond** and **Otter Pond** are located near the border of Quebec off Route 27 north of Eustis. Gold Brook Road off Route 27, just north of Bug Eye Pond, provides access to **Hurricane Pond** in Kibby Township.

Big Indian Pond is a more remote stillwater that lies north of Route 27 and is accessible from unimproved roads and foot trails off Gold Brook Road near Bug Eye Pond.

Barnard Pond, east of Eustis, is accessible by foot trail from Tim Pond Road. There is a primitive campsite at the pond.

Four brook trout ponds are located east of Rangeley Lake in Dallas Plantation. **Little Greely Pond** and **Gull Pond** are north of Rangeley and accessible from Route 16. **Loon Lake** is north of Rangeley as well and can be reached from Kennebago Road. **Saddleback Lake** is accessible from Dallas Hill Road off Route 4 south of Rangeley. Boats with motors are prohibited on both Loon and Saddleback Lakes.

Located in Sandy River Plantation in the Saddleback Mountain region, **South Pond**, also called **Pine Tree Pond**, and **Ledge Pond** can be reached by the Appalachian Trail off Route 4 north of the village of Madrid. **Midway Pond** and **Rock Pond** are farther north on the Trail or can be reached from a secondary trail off Dallas Hill Road south of Rangeley. **Perry Pond** is easily accessible from an unimproved road off Route 4 north of Madrid.

Stetson Pond and **Lufkin Pond** are in the town of Phillips and can be reached from a foot trail off Route 4 near Madrid. Both ponds offer hand-carried boat launches.

Swift River Pond, Little Swift River Pond, and **Long Pond** are located in Township E north of the city of Rumford. These brook trout ponds are accessible from the Appalachian Trail off Route 17. **Beaver Pond** lies in Township D and has convenient access off Route 17.

Varnum Pond and **Wilson Pond** are easily reached from Routes 156 and 2 near the village of Wilton. **Podunk Pond** in the town of Carthage is accessible from an unimproved road and trail off Route 2 west of Wilton. Also in this region, west of the city of Farmington, are **Webb Lake** and **Staples Pond**, two stillwaters stocked with brown trout. Webb Lake, the larger of the two, is located near the village of Weld off Route 142 north of the village of Dixville. Staples Pond is found north of the village of Temple off Route 43. **Tumbledown Pond** is a brook trout pond located north of Weld and can be reached from Little Jackson Trail off Route 142. **Hills Pond** is accessible from Route 156 south of Weld.

North of Farmington, in the town of Avon, you will find **Mount Blue Pond** and **Schoolhouse Pond**. Both stillwaters can be easily reached from unimproved roads off Route 4 between the villages of Strong and Phillips. **Pinnacle Pond** and **Grindstone Pond** are located near the village of Kingfield north of Strong off Routes 145 and 142.

Porter Lake and **Clearwater Lake** are larger stillwaters that hold brook trout and togue. Porter is reached from Route 234 west of the village of New Vineyard. Clearwater is northeast of Farmington off Route 43.

South of Farmington are **Norcross Pond** and **Egypt Pond** near the village of Chesterfield.

Oxford County Stillwaters

Aziscohos Lake

Created after the 1910 damming of the Magalloway River, Aziscohos is a man-made, 6,700-acre lake in the Rangeley Region. It holds landlocks and brook trout, and ice-out salmon are eagerly sought by flyfishers trolling streamers. Water opens fully around the first week of May most years. Good fishing follows directly. Summertime angling for trout is best in the feeder streams running into Aziscohos Lake.

"Most of the fish here are wild," says biologist Forrest Bonney. "Although salmon were stocked annually until 1993, they accounted for only 23 percent of the total salmon catch."

Bonney continues, "Anglers were interviewed at Aziscohos Lake during the summer of 1996 to gather biological information on the quality of the salmon and brook trout fishery. This information was compared with that collected in a similar manner in 1986, 1991, and 1993, and showed a 12 percent increase in the number of anglers who fished the lake from 1986 to 1996. Despite the increase in the number of anglers fishing Aziscohos Lake, use is among the lowest of the Rangeley Lakes."

From 1991 to 1993, trout and salmon catch rates increased, while growth rates fell. However, from 1993 to 1996, angler catches remained high and growth rates improved. Smelt tell the story here. Biologist Bonney says that, "The improved growth rates resulted from an increase in the number of smelt in the lake, which, in turn, is attributed to a two-year salmon stocking moratorium. We have resumed salmon stocking in anticipation of adequate smelt abundance resulting from the closure of the west shore tributaries to smelt dipping. There were also more older brook trout sampled in 1996, suggesting that the more restrictive regulations are effective in protecting these fish." Do check current regulations—twice.

Restrictive Maine brook trout regulations have been imposed recently in a statewide effort to protect wild brook trout populations from overharvest. The good news is that a higher proportion of older brook trout were sampled here during Maine Department of Inland Fisheries and Wildlife studies in 1996. Average brookies weighed 1 pound, 2 ounces in 1993 and 1 pound, 6 ounces in 1996.

According to the Maine Department of Inland Fisheries and Wildlife, the average growth rate for landlocked salmon has increased from 1 pound, 3 ounces in 1993 to 1 pound, 10 ounces in 1996. An abundance of smelt in the forage base influenced these positive changes.

The season for Aziscohos Lake is April 1 to September 30. Flyfishing-only opportunities are available in that part of Aziscohos Lake north of a straight line between the red post by the Brown Company Landing and the red post at the point where the Big and Little Magalloway Rivers join, and also the area of water north of a straight line between the two red posts at each end of Wheeler Dam on the Magalloway Arm of Aziscohos Lake.

Close to the New Hampshire border in western Maine, Aziscohos is one of the headwaters of the Androscoggin River drainage. This narrow lake is 18 miles long, with a mean depth of 31 feet. The Maine Department of Inland Fisheries and Wildlife

Aziscohos Lake

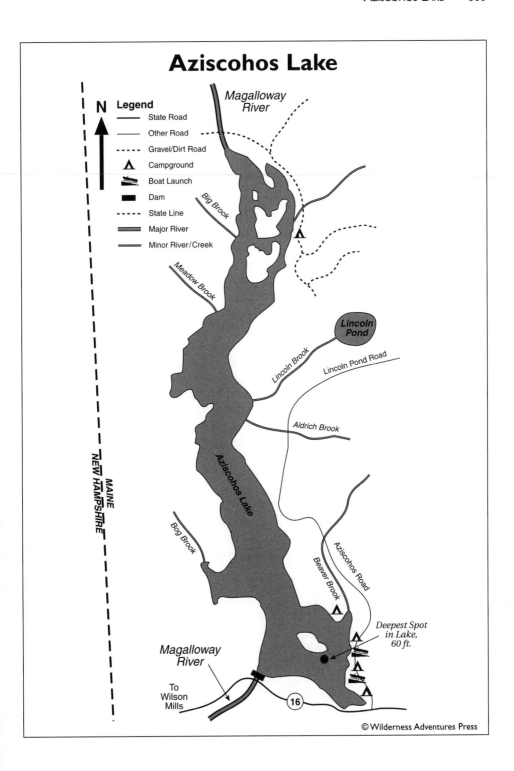

Legend

State Road
Other Road
Gravel/Dirt Road
Campground
Boat Launch
Dam
State Line
Major River
Minor River/Creek

Magalloway River

Big Brook

Meadow Brook

Lincoln Pond

Lincoln Brook

Lincoln Pond Road

Aldrich Brook

Aziscohos Lake

Bog Brook

Beaver Brook

Aziscohos Road

MAINE
NEW HAMPSHIRE

Deepest Spot in Lake, 60 ft.

Magalloway River

To Wilson Mills

16

© Wilderness Adventures Press

reports that water below 30 feet is deficient in oxygen by summer. As Bonney suggests, "For this reason, and because it is drawn for power generation, Aziscohos Lake provides only fair landlocked salmon habitat. Water quality is ideal for brook trout, however, and the lake and its tributaries support good populations of this species." This fishery primarily depends on natural trout and salmon reproduction.

A public launch site and commercial campground near the southern lakeshore are accessible off Route 16, which, along with Aziscohos Road, provide the best access to the lake.

Other Oxford County Stillwaters

North of Aziscohos Lake is **Parmachene Lake**. This remote stillwater holds brook trout, landlocked salmon, and togue. Angling is restricted to flyfishing only, casting or trolling. The roads in this region are private and gated. Access to Parmachene Lake is by air or by water through Lake Aziscohos. Contact Bosebuck Mountain Camps at the north end of Aziscohos, 207-243-2925, for services and access information. **Wells Pond** is a small, flyfishing-only pond located just north of Parmachene Lake.

Big Beaver Pond, **Little Beaver Pond**, and **Long Pond** are located in Magalloway Plantation. Long Pond is a wide stretch of the Little Magalloway River and is restricted to flyfishing only. Access to this area is on an unimproved road off Route 16 south of the boat access located at the southern end of Lake Aziscohos.

Surplus Pond is a flyfishing-only stillwater located off the Appalachian Trail north of the village of Andover and Route 5. The Trail can be reached from East B Hill Road. **Speck Pond** lies west of Surplus Pond on the Appalachian Trail near Grafton Notch State Park off Route 26.

Little Ellis Pond, also called **Garland Pond**, lies west of the village of Byron and Route 17. It is accessible by a trail off Andover Road.

East of the city of Rumford is **Howard Pond** in the town of Hanover. Access is from Routes 2 and 5 west of the village of Rumford Point.

Worthley Pond and **Canton Lake**, also known as **Lake Anasagunticook**, are larger stillwaters located southeast of Rumford off Route 108 near the village of Canton. Canton Lake is an excellent smallmouth bass fishery with a limited number of brown trout in the deeper areas. West of Worthley Pond are **Abbott Pond**, **Little Concord Pond**, **Shagg Pond**, and **Washburn Pond**, in the towns of Woodstock and Sumner. Concord Pond is flyfishing only. These ponds are accessible from Route 232 and Shagg Pond Road south of Rumford.

North Pond lies north of the village of Buckfield off Route 140, and its access road is gated.

Round Pond and **South Pond** are located near the village of Locke Mills off Route 26 east of the village of Bethel. **Bryant Pond**, also called **Lake Christopher**, holds brook trout as well as landlocked salmon. It is located east of Locke Mills off Route 26 and east of the village of Bethel. **Broken Bridge Pond** and **Crocker Pond** are located south of Bethel off an access road from Route 5. **Trout Pond** lies in Mason Township west of Bethel. There is an access road and trail off Route 2 in West Bethel.

Hall Pond holds both brookies and brown trout and is easily reached from Route 199 and Hall Pond Road east of the village of South Paris. West of this region, in the town of Norway, are **Big Pennesseewassee Lake**, also called **Norway Lake**, and **Little Pennesseewassee Pond**, known locally as **Hobbs Pond**. These stillwaters are accessible from Route 118 west of Norway.

West of Norway are **Trout Pond** and **Virginia Lake** in the town of Stoneham. Virginia Lake lies north of Route 5 near the village of East Stoneham. Trout Pond is south of Route 5 on a gated road. **Cushman Pond**, just south of Trout Pond, is more easily accessible. Take Route 5 to Slab City Road and Cushman Pond Road. **Bradley Pond** is reached from an unimproved road off Route 5 near the village of North Lowell. Motorboats are prohibited on Bradley Pond.

Keoka Lake and **Bear Pond** are accessible from Route 37 near the village of Waterford. Bear Pond holds brookies, landlocks, and togue. Keoka holds brook trout. **Stearns Pond** is a brown trout fishery located in the town of Sweden and can be reached off the Waterford-Sweden Road.

There are several stillwaters found in the southwest corner of Oxford County west of Sebago Lake. **Clay Pond** lies south of the village of Fryeburg and is accessible via Porter Road. Motorboats are prohibited on Clay Pond. **Hancock Pond** is a brown trout fishery located in the town of Denmark. Swamp Road and Hancock Pond Road are off Route 107 south of the village of Bridgton. **Burnt Meadow Pond** holds brook trout and browns. It is easily reached from Route 160 south of the village of Brownfield. **Stone Pond** is a brook trout pond and is also found in Brownfield via Dugway Road.

Little Clemons Pond and **Stanley Pond** are located off Route 160 north of the village of South Hiram. Stanley Pond is a mixed warm and coldwater fishery that supports brookies and landlocks, as well as smallmouth bass. **Chapman Pond** can be reached from a trail off Spee Pond Road north of South Hiram. **Colcord Pond** and **Bickford Pond** are both reached from Route 25 north of the village of Porter.

Androscoggin County Stillwaters

Upper Range Pond, **Middle Range Pond**, **Lower Range Pond**, and **Worthley Pond** are located southwest of the city of Auburn in the town of Poland. The "Range" Ponds, as they are known to locals, support brookies, browns, landlocked salmon, and togue, as well as warmwater species. Range Ponds State Park, off Route 26 south of Poland, offers camping and boat launch facilities. Motorboats with motors over 10 horsepower are prohibited on Lower Range Pond. Worthley Pond is accessible from Route 122 near the village of Poland Spring. This stillwater holds browns and brookies.

Auburn Lake is a public water supply covering 2,260 acres north of the city of Auburn. This impoundment supports brookies, brown trout, landlocks, and larger-sized togue, as well as warmwater species. The lake's southern end, south of a line from the Route 4 boat launch to Pine Point on the west shore, is closed to fishing and all other water related activities. Between April 1 and June 20, from the Route 4 bridge downstream to the dam in East Auburn, fishing is restricted to anglers under 16 years of age. **Gulf Island Pond** is the upstream stillwater formed by the Androscoggin River dam north of Auburn. The "pond" holds brown trout as well as warmwater species.

Pleasant Pond and **Crystal Pond**, also known as **Beals Pond**, are located north of the village of Turner. Crystal is stocked with brown trout and is accessible from Route 4. Pleasant Pond supports brook trout and is found north of Turner Center off Route 117.

Allen Pond holds brookies and brown trout. It lies east of the Androscoggin River in the town of Greene off Routes 100, 11, and 202, and Allen Pond Road. There is camping available on the pond's west shore.

Kennebec County Stillwaters

The seven lakes and ponds that make up the Belgrade Lakes lie west of the city of Waterville. These major stillwaters offer angling for trout, salmon, smallmouth bass, and northern pike.

Great Pond, the largest of the lakes, covers 8,000 acres. It receives annual stockings of brook trout, brown trout, and landlocked salmon. Larger fish are occasionally taken in the marshy, shallow area near Bog Brook at the pond's southern end. **North Pond**, located on Route 137 near the village of Smithfield, is an excellent largemouth bass fishery. It also supports limited numbers of brown trout and northern pike.

East Pond is primarily a warmwater fishery with limited numbers of brown trout. It lies east of Smithfield and is accessible from Route 137. **Salmon Lake**, also called **Ellis Pond** and **McGrath Pond**, is actually one body of water joined by a narrows. This 1,000-acre stillwater is located east of Great Pond off Route 8 near the village of North Belgrade. It is a mixed warm and coldwater fishery that offers good brown trout and limited landlocked salmon fishing in the early and late seasons. **Messalonskee Lake** offers good fishing for landlocked salmon and warmwater species. It is located southwest of the village of Oakland with access areas along Routes 23 and 11.

Long Pond is located west of the village of Belgrade Lakes off Route 27. This stillwater has a maximum depth of over 100 feet and is managed by the Maine Department of Inland Fisheries and Wildlife as a landlocked salmon fishery. It is heavily stocked and fishes very well after ice-out in April and into June. Salmon fishing picks up again during September and through the special catch-and-release season in October. **Androscoggin Lake**, located off Route 106 north of Lewiston, has an excellent reputation as a largemouth and smallmouth bass fishery.

Basin Pond supports brook trout and splake. It is located north of Androscoggin Lake in the town of Fayette and is accessible from a trail off Route 41 and Sandy River Road near the village of West Mount Vernon. **Echo Lake**, also called **Crotched Pond**, lies south of West Mount Vernon. It supports landlocked salmon, lake trout, and warmwater species. **Kimball Pond**, a small brook trout pond, is found in the northern section of this region near the village of Vienna off Route 41. Access is from Berry Hill Road.

Cobbosseecontee Lake, sometimes called **Cobbossee Lake**, is a large stillwater covering nearly 5,000 acres located east of the city of Augusta. It is best known as a largemouth and smallmouth bass fishery. However, the lake is heavily stocked with browns, and larger holdover brown trout up to 5 pounds are commonly caught.

Cochnewagon Pond is a brown trout fishery located near the village of Monmouth on Route 132 north of Lewiston. The pond also offers good bass fishing in the warmer months through October.

China Lake and **Threemile Pond** are located in eastern Kennebec County near the village of South China. They are mixed warm and coldwater fisheries supporting bass and stocked brown trout. Both stillwaters have convenient access and boat launch facilities off Routes 3 and 9.

Somerset County Flyfishing-only Stillwaters

The Somerset County region of central Maine holds dozens of brook trout ponds managed by the Maine Department of Inland Fisheries and Wildlife as flyfishing-only waters. Many of these stillwaters are remote and are only accessible by all-terrain vehicles, water, air, or by foot trail. The village of Jackman on Route 201 is the outpost for services and the access to several of the ponds located in the county's northwest corner.

The **Three Dingley Ponds, Upper, Little**, and **Dingley** are remote stillwaters located northwest of Penobscot Lake. **Wounded Deer Pond** and **Cape Horn Pond** are in Prentiss Township south of Penobscot Lake. Old Kelly Dam Road, from Routes 201 and 6 about 5 miles east of the Quebec border, provides access to the logging roads and trails to these ponds. As this road runs parallel to the South Branch of the Penobscot River, it also provides access to the trail leading to **Little Fish Pond** in Alder Brook Township.

Daymond Pond lies north of Jackman, just east of Routes 201 and 6 in Moose River Plantation. On the west side of Routes 201 and 6, there is an unimproved access road and trail to **Rancourt Pond** in Dennistown Plantation. **Big Fish Pond** is a remote pond in Holeb Township. The pond lies within the jurisdiction of the Maine Indian Tribal-State Commission that regulates the fishery. Motors greater than 10 horsepower are prohibited. Access to Big Fish Pond can be made by air or by water as part of the Moose River Bow Trip from Jackman.

Baker Pond is found west of Moosehead Lake in Tomhegan Township about 6 miles from the village of Rockwood. There is an access road off Routes 6 and 15, where a trail to the pond can be found.

Hardscrabble Road, west from Route 201, near the village of Lake Parlin south of Jackman, provides access to the trails leading to **Iron Pond** in Hobbstown Township, **Blakeslee Lake** in T5 R6 BKP WKR west of Hobbstown Township, and **Little**

Enchanted Pond in Upper Enchanted Township. There is a primitive campsite at Little Enchanted Pond.

Big Berry Pond, Little Berry Pond, Snake Pond, and **Durgin Pond** lie in Johnson Mountain Township east of the village of Lake Parlin. Boats with motors are prohibited on Durgin Pond and Little Berry Pond. There are unimproved roads that provide access to the ponds and adjacent primitive campsites. **Cold Stream Pond** lies east of Lake Parlin, as well. However, the best access to this pond is south on the road that intersects Routes 6 and 15 near the east end of Long Pond on the Moose River. The access road to **Markham Pond**, also located in Johnson Mountain Township, is south of Lake Parlin on the west side of Route 201. Capitol Road, south of the Markham Pond access road off Route 201, provides access to the trails for **Tobey Pond** and **Little Wilson Hill Pond** in Johnson Mountain Township, **Ellis Pond** and **Horseshoe Pond** in Chase Stream Township, and **Dead Stream Pond** in West Forks Plantation.

Frypan Pond is located in Squaretown Township east of the village of Forks on Route 201. The access road to Frypan, east of Lake Moxie, is gated.

Everett Pond is located in the King and Bartlett Township. The access road to this region and Everett Pond is off Route 27 north of Eustis.

Kilgore Pond, Split Rock Pond, Dixon Pond, and **Fish Pond** are flyfishing-only stillwaters located in the remote Pierce Pond Township northwest of the village of Moscow on Route 201. There is a road that runs north along the west side of the Kennebec River north of Moscow that provides access to logging roads and trails in this region. **Bean Pond, Clear Pond** (also known as Mill Pond), and **Lost Pond** are located in Pleasant Ridge Plantation and are accessible from Rowe Pond Road west of Moscow.

Heald Pond is located in the town of Caratunk north of Moscow. Take Stream Road off Route 201 in Moscow to reach the pond and a nearby primitive campsite.

Spruce Pond lies north of the village of North New Portland in Lexington Township. The east fork of Long Falls Dam Road will put you on the trail to the pond.

WEST CENTRAL MAINE HUB CITIES
Rangeley
Elevation–1,546 • Population–1,300

Regarded as a well-established resort and sport fishing town since the early 1900s, Rangeley hospitality will keep you comfortable between outings.

ACCOMMODATIONS

Rangeley Inn & Motor Lodge, Box 160, Route 4 / 800-666-3687 or 207-864-3341 / Restored turn-of-the-century inn and motel lodgings / Kitchens, fireplace woodstoves, and private two-person whirlpool baths available / Moderately priced off-season rates apply before Memorial Day and after Labor Day / Open year-round / Hot tubs, fireplaces, and kitchenettes available / On the web: **rangeleyinn.com** / $$$-$$$$

Saddleback Inn, Route 4, P.O. Box 377 / 207-864-3434 / Modern motel rooms with a dining room and lounge (open peak season) / Housekeeping units / Cable TV and full baths / Open year-round / $–$$

Town & Lake Motel, P.O. Box 47, Main Street / 207-864-3755 / Two-bedroom shorefront cottages with kitchens, cable TV, fireplaces, and oil furnaces / Boats and motors for rent / Dogs welcome / $$

CAMPGROUNDS

Black Brook Cove Campground, P.O. Box 319 (Oquossoc 04964) / 207-486-3828 / Located on Aziscohos Lake / Offers wilderness island campsites and others (shorefront and wooded) / Complete general store / Boat and canoe rentals with loading ramp and dock

Rangeley Lake State Park, located on the lake's south shore / 207-864-3858 / 50 campsites with tables and fireplaces / Boat ramp and loading dock / Open mid-May to October 1

Stephen Phillips Memorial Preserve Trust, Box 21 (Oquossoc 04964) / 207-864-2003 / Wilderness campsites located on Student's Island / Sites on Mooselookmeguntic Lake / Obtain reservations and permit by mail or phone

RESTAURANTS

Gingerbread House, downtown Oquossoc / 207-864-3602 / Homemade soups, chowders, and desserts / Breakfast available

The Oquossoc House Restaurant, Routes 4 and 17 in Oquossoc / 207-864-3881 / Dinner every day (summer and fall) / Specialties: seafood and prime rib

The People's Choice Restaurant and Lounge, Main Street / 207-864-5220 / Breakfast, lunch, and dinner specials served 6AM–9PM, including beef, prime rib, and fresh seafood / Lounge features a game room

Red Onion Restaurant, Center Main Street / 207-864-5022 / Homemade soup, sandwiches, and fresh-dough pizza / Open year-round

FLY SHOPS AND SPORTING GOODS

Dockside Sports Center, Town Cove / 207-864-2424 or 800-941-2424 / Boat rentals and dock slips available

The Fly Box & Rangeley Region Sport Shop, 85 Main Street (across from the boat launch) / 207-864-5615 / Chris and Gayle Aylesworth, owners and operators / Also offers guide referrals for interested flyfishers

Haines Landing Marina, P.O. Box 868 / 207-864-5836 or 864-5956 (Winter 203-663-1695) / Located on Mooselookmeguntic Lake / Tackle, fly patterns, rental boats, moorings, gas, oil, ice, soft drinks, and snacks available

Rangeley Rod Company, Route 4 at Dallas Hill Road / 207-864-3898

River's Edge Sports, Route 4 at Rangeley Lake Outlet (Oquossoc 04964) / 207-864-5582 / Contact Rusty and Carol Harvey / Canoe rentals, licenses, etc.

King & Bartlett Fish and Game Club, P.O. Box 4 (Eustis 04936) / 207-243-2956 / Orvis shop

Rapid River Fly Fishing, Box 404 Middle Dam (Andover 04126) / 207-392-3333 / Orvis shop

AUTO REPAIR

Koob's Garage, Route 4 (Oquossoc 04964) / 207-864-3737 / 24-hour road service and towing / Complete auto repairs

AIRPORT

Mountain Air Service, Main Street / 207-864-5307 / Complete charter service, including fishing trips

MEDICAL

Rangeley Region Health Center, Dallas Hill Road / 207-864-3303 (after hours 800-398-6031 / Primary care and health services

FOR MORE INFORMATION

Rangeley Lakes Chamber of Commerce
P.O. Box 317
Rangeley, ME 04970
800-MT-LAKES (685-2537)

Belgrade

Elevation–234 • Population–2,375

ACCOMMODATIONS
Abenakis Camps, Route 27 / 207-495-2294 / Opens in June
Woodrest Cottages, RFD 2, Box 4690 / Contact Tom and Jan Barton

CAMPGROUNDS
Great Pond Campground, Route 27 / 207-495-2116 / 45 sites

RESTAURANTS
The Sunset Grille, 4 West Road (Belgrade Lakes 04918) / 207-495-2439 / Sunday breakfast buffet 8–11AM / Outdoor dining / Daily specials
The Korner Store & Deli, 26 Oak Street (Oakland 04963) / 207-465-3293 / Pizza and sandwiches
Village Inn Restaurant, Route 27 (Belgrade Lakes 04918) / 207-495-3553 / Steak, seafood, pasta, and prime rib

FLY SHOPS AND SPORTING GOODS
Charlie's Log Cabin, 22 Dunn Street (Oakland 04918) / 800-465-2454 or 207-465-2451 / Located near Messalonskee Lake / Guide service also available
Belgrade Boats, Canoes & Trailers, Foster Point Road / 207-495-3415
Rob's Fly Shop, Route 4, P.O. Box 116 (North Jay 04262) / 207-645-4508

AIRPORT
Robert LaFleur/Waterville Municipal Airport, Exit 33 from Interstate 95 (Waterville 04901)

MEDICAL
Belgrade Regional Health Center, School Street (Belgrade Lakes 04918) / 207-495-3323
Also see Waterville

FOR MORE INFORMATION
Belgrade Lakes Region, Inc.
P.O. Box 72-B
Belgrade, ME 04917
207-495-2744 (seasonal)
An information booth is also found on Route 27 in Belgrade

Waterville
Elevation–140 • Population–17,173

ACCOMMODATIONS
Best Western, 356 Main Street / 207-873-3335 / Exit 34 off Interstate 95 / Restaurant, cable TV, swimming pool / $$$

Budget Host Airport Inn, 400 Kennedy Memorial Drive / 800-876-2463 / Room rate includes a continental breakfast / Restaurant on premises / Pets allowed / $$

Holiday Inn, 375 Main Street / 800-785-0111 or 207-873-0111 / Exit 34 off Interstate 95 / 138 rooms with a full-service restaurant and pub / Indoor heated pool, hot tub, fitness room, and sauna

CAMPGROUND
Countryside Camping, West River Road / 207-873-4603

RESTAURANTS
Best Western, 356 Main Street / 207-873-3335

Budget Host Airport Inn, 400 Kennedy Memorial Drive / 800-876-2463

Holiday Inn, 375 Main Street / 207-873-0111

AIRPORT
Robert LaFleur/Waterville Municipal, Exit 33 from Interstate 95

Waterville Travel Service, 135 Main Street / 207-873-0692 / Air travel and car rental arrangements to south central Maine region

MEDICAL
Mid-Maine Medical Center, Seton Unit, downtown Waterville on Chase Avenue

Mid-Maine Medical Center, Thayer Unit, downtown Waterville on North Street (off Exit 34, Interstate 95)

FOR MORE INFORMATION
Mid-Maine Chamber of Commerce
One P.O. Square
Waterville, ME 04901
207-973-3315

Jackman
Elevation–1,000 • Population–920

ACCOMMODATIONS

Cozy Cove Cabins, P.O. Box 370 MS / 207-668-5931 / Contact Dianne and Leroy Baker / Registered Maine guide available / 5 cabins on lake / Weekly and nightly rates available; $300 per week / $

Moose River Lodge & Motel, Main Street, P.O. Box 641 / 207-668-5311 / Contact Frank and Linda Dubois / Open year-round / Registered Maine guide, home-cooked meals, and color TV available / $

CAMPGROUNDS

Jackman Landing Campground, Route 201, P.O. Box 567-VG / 207-668-3301 / Located on Moose River at Big Wood Lake / Waterfront RV and tent sites / Canoe rentals

Moose River Campground, Heald Stream Pond / 207-668-3341

Riverview Campground, Moose River Road / 207-668-5601

RESTAURANTS

Loon's Lookout Restaurant at Tuckaway Shores, HCR 64, Box 44-VG / 207-668-3351 / Contact Phil and Paulette Thomas / Specializing in Italian cuisine, steak, and daily "American specials" / Open Friday to Sunday, 5–9PM

Moose Point Tavern & Restaurant, Big Wood Lake, HCR 76, Box 1200 / 207-668-4012 / Contact Lisa Hall / Open for dinner Wednesday through Sunday, 5–9PM

Truck Stop Restaurant, Route 201, 2 miles north of Jackman / 207-668-4025 / Open Monday through Saturday, 4AM–8PM, Sunday, 8AM–4PM / Gas, beer, soda, and snacks also available

FLY SHOPS AND SPORTING GOODS

Bishop's Store, Main Street, P.O. Box 369 / 207-668-3411 / Fishing supplies, nonresident licenses, gas, pizza, subs, and groceries available / Open daily from 7AM-9PM / Motto: "If we don't have it, you don't need it"

Fly Fishing Only, 230 Main Street (Fairfield 04937) / 207-453-6242 / Contact Mike Holt / Caters to flyfishers in southernmost Somerset County

Jackman True Value Hardware, Main Street / 207-668-5151 or 800-287-SNOW (Maine only) / Complete line of sporting goods with canoe and rentals available / Nonresident licenses

AUTO REPAIR

Moose River Tire, Main Street / 207-668-4158 / Contact Razor and Brenda Smith / Auto repair and tire service

AIRPORT

Coleman's Flying & Guide Service, HCR 76, Box 102 / 207-668-4436 or 668-7777 / Fishing, local charter flights, scenic float plane rides, and sightseeing

Wally's Flying Service / 207-668-3421

MEDICAL

Closest hospital services available in Rangeley or Greenville

FOR MORE INFORMATION

Jackman/Moose River Chamber of Commerce
Route 201
Jackman, ME 04945
207-668-4171

West Central Maine Guides

John Baillargeon
Jackman, ME
207-668-7683

Hal Blood
Jackman, ME
207-668-4169

Tim Casey
Jackman, ME
207-668-5091

Steve Coleman
Jackman, ME
207-668-4436

Fred Haigis
Jackman, ME
207-668-4139

Robert and Raymond Miller
Waterville, ME
207-474-3730

Mike Stevens
Jackman, ME
207-668-4025

Rodney Small
Jackman, ME
207-487-5704

West Central Maine Sporting Camps

Bald Mountain Camps
P.O. Box 332
Oquossoc, ME 04964
207-864-3671 or 684-3788
Contact: Stephen Philbrick
Sporting camp services on
Mooselookmeguntic Lake

Bosebuck Mt. Camps
Wilson's Mills, ME 03579
207-243-2925 (May-December);
207-486-3238 (December–May)
Sporting camp services on the north
end of Aziscohos Lake

Clearwater Camps & Guide Service
P.O. Box 270
Oquossoc, ME 04964
207-864-5424
Contact: Michael Warren
Regional Maine guide specializing in
flyfishing instruction, trips, salmon
and trout angling

Cy Eastlack
Box 284, Route 17
Oquossoc, ME 04964
207-864-3416
Regional Maine guide

Grant's Kennebago Camps
Box 786
Rangeley, ME 04970
207-864-3608; 800-633-4815
Contact: John Blunt, owner
Sporting camp services between the
twin Kennebago Mountains; services
Kennebago Lake and Kennebago
River

Lakewood Camps
Middledam
Andover, ME 04216
207-243-2959 (summer); 207-392-1581
or 486-3200 (winter)
Sporting camp services on the Rapid
River

West Central Maine Sporting Camps (cont.)

Westwind Charters and Guide Service
P.O. Box 1092
Rangeley, ME 04970
207-864-5437
Contact: Larry Guile, registered Maine
  guide
Salmon fishing

Sporting Camps
The Last Resort
Box 777VG (on Long Pond)
Jackman, ME 04945
207-668-5091 or 800-441-5091
Time and Ellen Casey
Brook trout and salmon fishing avail-
  able out of remote yet accessible
  wilderness camps

Red Buck Sporting Camps
Box 114
Jackman, ME 04945
207-668-5361
Sandra and Thomas Doughty
Flyfishing available on remote ponds

East Central Maine

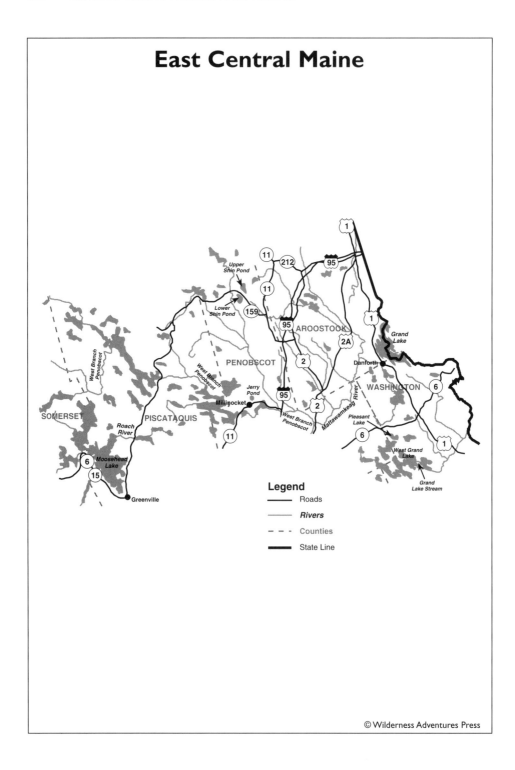

Legend

—————— Roads

··········· *Rivers*

— — — Counties

██████ State Line

© Wilderness Adventures Press

EAST CENTRAL MAINE
RIVERS AND STILLWATERS

Moosehead Lake Region,
Piscataquis County

Piscataquis County's Moosehead Lake is Maine's largest lake. It is a massive body of water, covering 74,890 acres. More than the big water itself, Moosehead Lake tributaries and nearby stillwaters offer some of the best flyfishing in the northeast. The village of Greenville, the major business center in the area, though sparsely populated, provides an abundance of comfortable accommodations. Flyfishers visiting the region can feel at ease here, as this town caters to outdoor enthusiasts.

Located on the eastern side of the lake, the Roach River, a flyfishing hot spot between First Roach Pond and Moosehead Lake, holds landlocked salmon that weigh several pounds. The Roach also supports some larger-sized brook trout. Not

View of Moosehead Lake from the Lily Bay side.
(Photo courtesy Maine Office of Tourism)

View of Mt. Kineo on Moosehead Lake. (Photo courtesy Maine Office of Tourism)

far from Moosehead Lake's northern shore, the West Branch of the Penobscot River offers excellent salmon and brook trout flyfishing.

North central Maine outfitters and guides can provide excellent introductions to these trout and salmon waters. Over time, flyfishers can revisit their favorite salmon pools and trout runs with or without the angling wisdom of the natives who acquainted them with this area. Dan Legere of the Maine Fly Shop & Guide Service in Greenville probably knows as much about flyfishing the Moosehead region as anyone. Give him a call if you visit the area.

Moosehead Lake itself, though wide and deep, challenges Maine Department of Inland Fisheries and Wildlife fisheries managers as they work to decrease flourishing togue numbers and to increase smelt, the baitfish on which both landlocks and lake trout forage. Despite inherent competition for food, Moosehead togue can run from 10 to 15 pounds, while brookies go 2 to 3 pounds at best. Salmon average 14 to 16 inches in length.

Twenty miles wide and 30 miles long, Moosehead serves as the headwater of the Kennebec River. As previously mentioned, the East and West Outlets of this river have fine angling opportunities, as does the Moose River.

Roach River

In addition to being an expert on southern Maine's trout and salmon fisheries, John Boland, Maine Department of Inland Fisheries and Wildlife biologist, has this to suggest about fishing the Roach River: Initially search the Roach with a woolly bugger

Roach River

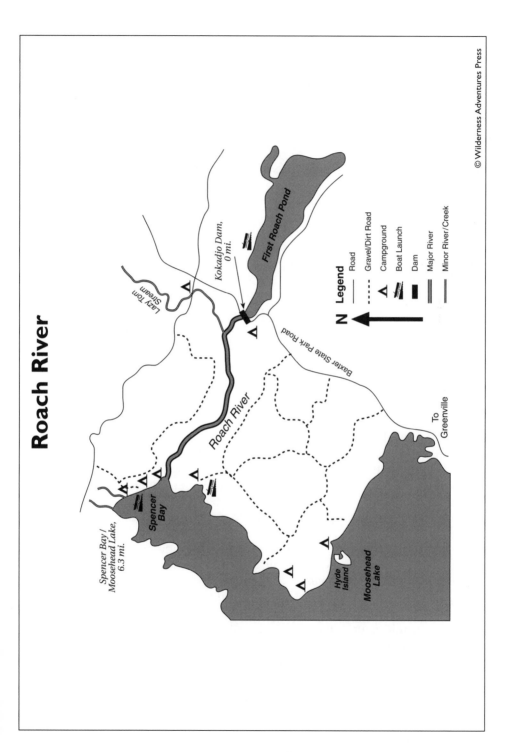

First Roach Pond

Kokadjo Dam,
0 mi.

Lazy Tom
Stream

Baxter State Park Road

Roach River

Spencer
Bay

Spencer Bay /
Moosehead Lake,
6.3 mi.

Hyde
Island

Moosehead
Lake

To
Greenville

N

Legend
— Road
--- Gravel/Dirt Road
△ Campground
Boat Launch
■ Dam
— Major River
— Minor River/Creek

Boulder riffles make for difficult angling on the Roach River between
First Roach Pond and Moosehead Lake. (Photo by Elizabeth Edwards)

to locate fish down where they are holding. Such prospecting for Roach River trout
and salmon often draws results.

Some anglers concentrate their efforts in the stretch just downstream from the
First Roach Pond dam to the Lazy Tom Stream confluence. Others target the last half-
mile of river before it enters Moosehead Lake. Boulder riffles make for difficult
springtime angling on 90 percent of the water between the dam and river mouth.
Decreased summer and early fall flows offer more typical fish holding areas.

In the midsection, the Roach's fast runs may frustrate you, but remember that
split-shot attached to a leader is illegal on Maine flyfishing-only waters, even if the
hellbent devil on your shoulder begs for it. Concentrate on flyfishing the previous
river section or the one that follows.

Reliable late-season angling associated with cooler water temperatures and
attendant salmon make this a classic place to flyfish the last two weeks of September.
Expect opportunities for salmon in the 2- to 4-pound range, with brook trout running to several pounds.

Effective patterns below the Kokadjo Dam to the Lazy Tom Stream confluence
include traditional streamers, such as the black nose dace (#6–10), gray or black
ghost (#4–10), muddler minnow (#4–10), and stonefly nymphs in sizes 4 to 8, from
Kaufmann's brown stone to the giant black stone. Though the literary flyfishing intel-

ligentsia sometimes snub the woolly bugger, it remains a reliable North Country meat fly. Salmon routinely nail it with passionate strikes. I vote for fish over fashion.

In the last half-mile before Moosehead Lake, fish nymphs, including the hare's ear (#8–16) and pheasant tail (#10–16). Hornberg wets (#8–14) will catch fish in holding lies. Quick-draw short, several-second drifts through riffle corners to interest trout and salmon. Stay ready with your finger on the trigger. Streamers remain effective on this river section. If you can flyfish here the last two weeks of September, do it.

May 1 to September 30 is the season for the Roach River, and it is restricted to catch-and-release angling by flyfishing only. Brook trout to several pounds can be caught here, as well as landlocked salmon from 2 to 4 pounds.

Roach River consists of riffle water with good holding pools just below the dam and near Moosehead Lake. Springtime and early fall water temperatures make for the best angling, although fish are in the river all season. There are Class II and some Class III waters, with strong currents running from the dam to the lake. Canoe all 6-plus miles of it, but let experience be your guide.

The Maine Department of Inland Fisheries and Wildlife owns corridors on either riverbank, excluding several hundred yards of land immediately below First Roach Pond. Easements are provided by the state at six access sites—three on either side of the river—that provide right-of-way foot access from Scott Paper Company logging roads. NOTE: When parking at trailheads, pull off main roads—active logging operations require open passage.

West Branch Penobscot River

Two river sections of the West Branch Penobscot are of interest to flyfishers. The first commences at Seboomook Dam flowing northward to Chesuncook Lake. Anglers tend to target two spots within this area: the water just below the dam and the 2 miles of river southwest of Hannibal's Crossing on Golden Road. Stonefly nymphs catch salmon as readily as traditional streamers. Medium to heavy fly rod outfits are the norm for casting big flies for these river landlocks that average several pounds. These fish could push a 4- or 5-weight rod. Once hooked, one of these lively jumpers can make an entire fishing trip worthwhile.

The other river section worth noting might challenge the easily daunted. Beyond the Ripogenus Dam on Ripogenus Lake, heavy water muscles its way downstream, channeled first through the vertical granite walls of Ripogenus Gorge. The river then emerges as a lengthy downstream glide before reaching the Nesowadnehunk Deadwater. Some manage this challenge with a controlled intensity only rivaled by the river itself.

Dan Legere, owner of the Maine Guide Fly Shop & Guide Service in Greenville, rafts the gorge and opts for a drift boat on the lower river section. The Class I to Class IV rapids make this water best traveled by experts. There are also whitewater falls, heavy rapids, turbulent glides, and powerful flatwater. Legere can put you on the river with his guide service. Bordered by foot trails, West Branch Penobscot flyfishing is possible from either riverbank, as well.

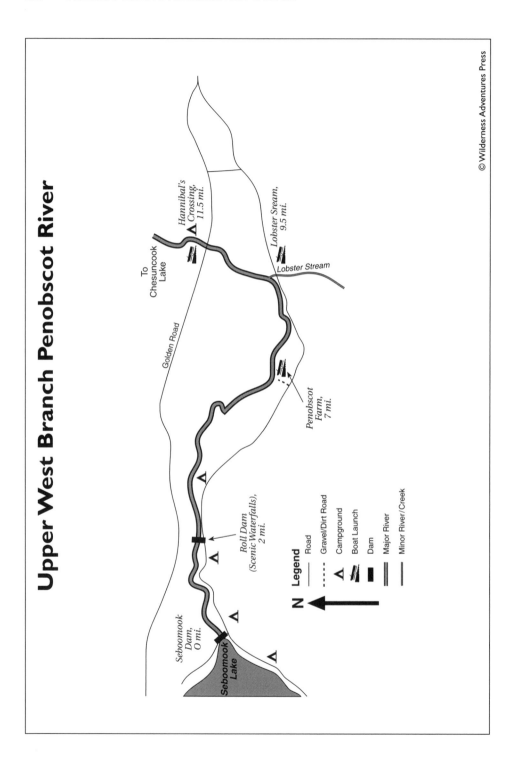

Upper West Branch Penobscot River

Lower West Branch Penobscot River

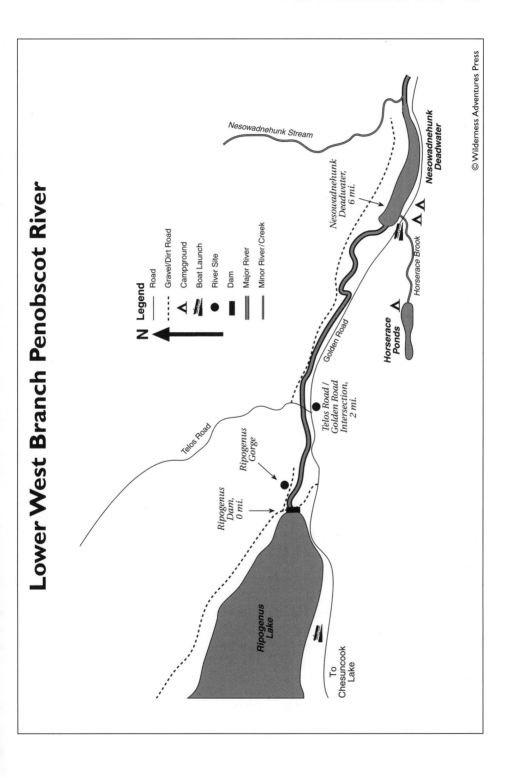

Legend

	Road
	Gravel/Dirt Road
▲	Campground
	Boat Launch
●	River Site
▮	Dam
	Major River
	Minor River/Creek

N

Nesowadnehunk Stream

Nesowadnehunk Deadwater, 6 mi.

Nesowadnehunk Deadwater

Horserace Brook

Horserace Ponds

Golden Road

Telos Road / Golden Road Intersection, 2 mi.

Telos Road

Ripogenus Gorge

Ripogenus Dam, 0 mi.

Ripogenus Lake

To Chesuncook Lake

© Wilderness Adventures Press

Legere recommends the following patterns for use on the West Branch Penobscot River and the previously mentioned Moose River, Kennebec River East Outlet, and Roach River:

As dry flies go, fish the dark Hendrickson (#12–14)in June, the olive elk wing caddis (#14–16) in July, and stimulators, including olive, yellow, and royal (#8–10) in August.

When nymphing, Legere chooses the giant black stone (#6), beadhead hare's ear (#12), and the beadhead caddis pupa (olive).

Legere's favorite streamers include the marabou black ghost (#4–10), Mitchell Creek marabou (#4–10), and the contractor (#4–10). He fishes woolly buggers, both olive and black, and brown muddlers on these waters as well.

The West Branch Penobscot opens for fishing on April and finishes September 30. From the Seboomook Dam to the red posts on the shores of Chesuncook Lake, April 1 through August 15 is artificial lures only with a daily limit for salmon of 1 fish, flyfishing only from August 16 to September 30 with a 1-fish limit for both salmon and trout.

The section from Ripogenus Dam downstream to the Telos Road Bridge is flyfishing only from April 1 to September 30 with a minimum length for salmon of 26 inches.

From Telos Road Bridge downstream to the red posts at the head of Debsconeag Falls, a one-hook, artificial-lure-only (single-pointed or treble hook allowed) season runs from April 1 to August 15 with a daily limit for salmon of 1 fish, minimum length of 18 inches. From August 16 to September, this section is flyfishing only and a daily limit of 1 salmon or 1 trout, minimum salmon length of 18 inches.

Salmon average 2 pounds with 4- to 5-pounders caught on occasion. Rumor has it that a "9-pounder" was caught here recently—translation: The landlock weighed 4 or 5 pounds wet, which, I might add, is still a good fish.

Piscataquis County Flyfishing-only Waters

The Golden Road, north from the village of Millinocket and about 9 miles west of Interstate 95, is the gateway to the remote stillwaters and streams of northern Piscataquis County. There is a gate and toll booth at the entrance to Golden Road. A modest fee is charged for recreational use of the area. To locate particular waters, the nearest roads have been identified and locations of ponds in regional land parcel divisions are listed in descending order, T10 through T1, north to south. DeLorme's *Maine Atlas and Gazetteer* is a good reference.

Mooseleuk Stream, the outflow of Mooseleuk Lake in T10 R9 WELS, is a tributary of the Aroostoock River. This stream is flyfishing only and restricted to catch and release for landlocks. Chase Road and Mooseleuk Dam Road follow the river north from Pinkham Road. **Little Pleasant Pond**, in T10 R11 WELS, is west of Mooseleuk Lake and accessible from an extension of Jack Mountain Road.

Brown Brook Pond lies in T9 R9 WELS and is reached from an access road located near the ranger station off Pinkham Road. **Ragged Pond** is accessible off Pell

Float-tubing a North Country pond. Piscataquis County offers many flyfishing-only stillwaters. (Photo by Steve Hickoff)

& Pell Road and Island Pond Road in T9 R10 WELS. The six stillwaters known as **Currier Ponds** are found off Pell & Pell Road in T9 R11 WELS.

Near the western border of Piscataquis County are **Allagash Pond**, located in T9 R15 WELS, and **Desolation Pond**, found just across the county line in T8 R16 WELS.

Spring Pond is located in T7 R10 WELS and can be reached from an extension of Huber Road northwest of the village of Shin Pond and Route 159.

Coffelos Pond is a flyfishing stillwater located in the Allagash Wilderness in T6 R11 WELS. Access is available from Telos Road, running north from Golden Road near Big Eddy Pool and the West Branch Penobscot River. South of Coffelos Pond are **Nesowadnehunk Lake**, also known as **Sourdnahunk Lake**, and **Little Nesowadnehunk Lake** in T5 R11 WELS. Access is from East Road and Telos Road east of the Telos Checkpoint. Boats with motors are prohibited on Little Nesowadnehunk. **Nesowadnehunk**, or **Sourdnahunk Stream**, the outflow of the lakes, is a flyfishing-only tributary of the West Branch Penobscot River.

There are several beautiful flyfishing-only ponds located on the western slope of Mount Katahdin that can be reached from side trails off Telos Road and the Appalachian Trail. The trail joins the Golden Road near a bend in the West Branch of the Penobscot at Abol Falls. The trail follows the river back upstream before turning north toward the ponds. This area is about a one-half hour drive from the village of Millinocket. **Windy Pitch**, **Daicey Pond**, **Lily Pad Pond**, and **Celia Pond** are located in T3 R10 WELS. **Jordan Pond**, also called **Jackson Pond**, **Polly Pond**, **McKenna Pond**, **Harrington Pond** and another stillwater called **Jackson Pond** are found in T3 R11 WELS.

Blood Pond, also known as **Duck Pond**, is located west of this region off Golden Road and Greenville Road in T2 R13 WELS.

The stillwaters found east of Moosehead Lake are best reached from Route 11 southwest of Millinocket. **Little Pleasant Pond** and its tributary waters, the three **Birch Ridge Ponds**, and **Fox Pond** are located not far from the Appalachian Trail off Johnston Road and J-Mary Road in TA R11 WELS. **East Chairback Pond** and **West Chairback Pond** are located in T7 R9 NWP. They can be reached from the Appalachian Trail a short distance from where it crosses the Katahdin Ironworks Road northwest of the village of Brownville Junction.

The four **West Branch Ponds**, **Trout Pond**, and **Big Lyford Pond** are located in TA R12 WELS, east of First Roach Pond. Lily Bay Road, north from Greenville, offers easy access to this region.

East of Greenville in the Bowdoin College Grant East and West are **First Little Lyford Pond**, **Second Little Lyford Pond**, **Notch Pond**, two stillwaters that make up **Pearl Pond**, **Grassy Pond**, **Fogg Pond**, and **Baker Pond**. **Notch Pond** is restricted to catch and release. Greenville Road provides access to the roads and trails in this region. **Mountain Pond** is found a short distance north in the Beaver Cove district and is best reached from Lily Bay Road north of Greenville.

Washington County Region

West Grand Lake and Grand Lake Stream are the major fisheries in the Washington County region, and these waters are known specifically for their landlocked salmon angling. The lower section of the St. Croix River that forms the border of Maine and the Province of New Brunswick, holds limited Atlantic salmon flyfishing opportunities. Salmon fishing in the St. Croix is regulated by New Brunswick.

West Grand Lake

"Ice-out arrives in early May most years," says Jo-Anne Cannell of Indian Rock Camps in Grand Lake Stream, "and fishing usually picks up toward the end of the month."

Indeed, cold, blustery weather often pervades available flyfishing early on. Nevertheless, a small number of die-hard West Grand Lake traditionalists hook up on ice-out salmon. They feed line through frozen fingertips until the warmer Memorial Day weekend. Usually, that is when angler activity begins to flourish. A word of caution

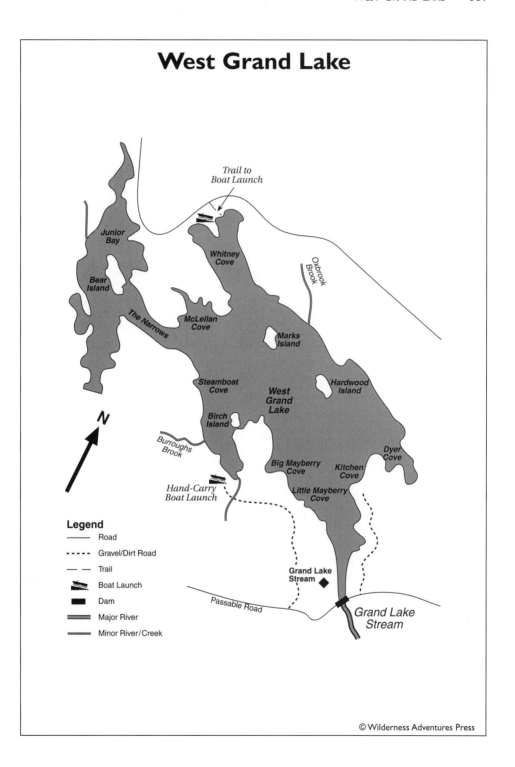

West Grand Lake

Trail to
Boat Launch

Junior
Bay

Whitney
Cove

Oxbrook
Brook

Bear
Island

The Narrows

McLellan
Cove

Marks
Island

Steamboat
Cove

West
Grand
Lake

Hardwood
Island

Birch
Island

N

Burroughs
Brook

Dyer
Cove

Big Mayberry
Cove

Kitchen
Cove

Hand-Carry
Boat Launch

Little Mayberry
Cove

Legend

———	Road
- - - -	Gravel/Dirt Road
— —	Trail
	Boat Launch
▬	Dam
	Major River
———	Minor River/Creek

Grand Lake
Stream ◆

Passable Road

Grand Lake
Stream

© Wilderness Adventures Press

Most West Grand Lake flyfishers will tell you their sole objective is to catch one of these lively landlocked salmon. (Photo by Steve Hickoff)

to ice-out flyfishers: Some early May days find West Grand Lake whitecaps charging boats and canoes like NFL linebackers. Keep your eyes on the sky, though, since a manageable chop on the water can make for excellent salmon fishing conditions. Otherwise, get off the lake.

West Grand Lake is half the size of Cumberland County's Sebago Lake. Angling pressure is rarely a problem on this 14,340-acre fishery, which is still large by Maine standards. According to the Maine Department of Inland Fisheries and Wildlife, this Grand Lake Stream headwater is primarily managed for landlocks, as well as togue. Both game fish target smelt as a food source. Smallmouth bass, chain pickerel, white and yellow perch, plus several other species swim here, too. Like Sebago, a healthy forage base helps keep game fish populations thriving, and feeder streams, including Oxbrook and Burroughs Brooks, hold spawning smelt come spring.

Coves around the lake contain staging smelt. Whitney Cove, Dyer Cove, Kitchen Cove, Big and Little Mayberry Coves, Farm Cove, Steamboat Cove, and McLellan Cove all provide reliable salmon angling. Landlocks gather in these sheltered bays to feed on schools of forage fish. Many flyfishers lose their share of sleep chasing landlocks during this time period. And it's true enough that salmon get all the glory.

Most West Grand Lake flyfishers will tell you their sole objective is to catch one of the lively landlocks. However, lake trout are also targeted by a few streamer-wielding anglers, especially early on, from the first two weeks after ice-out to the end of May.

Smelt-imitating streamers rule on the big lake for both landlocks and lake trout, though big stonefly nymphs and woolly buggers work, as well.

West Grand Lake's season is April 1 through September 30, although ice-out arrives a month after the opening date. From October 1 to 15, fishing is by artificial lure only, and all fish caught must be released at once.

Lake trout average 2 to 10 pounds, while salmon typically weigh 1 to 3 pounds, occasionally more.

The lake has a maximum depth of 128 feet. Anglers can expect passing squalls early on and choppy water conditions throughout the spring season. Violent wind-storms are to be taken seriously, though moderate blows can make for some excellent fishing. In 1997, ice-out arrived on May 5. As one regional source told me then, "There was a foot and a half of ice on the lake, but in a day or so it was suddenly gone." Die-hards fished for salmon that Monday.

A passable road skirts the northwestern lakeshore that will take you to Whitney Cove. There is an unimproved road access to Farm Cove. Boat launches are found at Whitney Cove (trails to boat launch and the northwestern lakeshore) and Farm Cove (unimproved road access to the western lakeshore).

Grand Lake Stream

Grand Lake Stream flows for 2 miles from the dam at the outflow of West Grand Lake down to Big Lake. Flyfishing for salmon, brook trout, and togue is best from late May, right after the Memorial Day weekend, through the middle of June. Good angling picks up again in September and is especially good in the first two weeks of October. Just below the dam is a good spot to haunt, where salmon and, occasionally, lake trout are picked up on streamers.

The stream holds brook trout from 1 pound to several pounds; lake trout from 2 to 5 pounds, occasionally larger; and salmon from 1 to 3 pounds. A 4-pound leaping landlock is always possible. In 1996, there were 1,200 salmon fry and 400 brook trout of 8 to 10 inches stocked in Grand Lakes Stream.

According to Eddie Reif of Eddie's Flies and Tackle in Bangor, effective Grand Lake Stream patterns tend to run on the small size. Beadhead caddis, brassies, and small pheasant tail nymphs catch a lot of fish. "The river has the normal run of hatches," says Reif, "and caddis dries are often effective."

As streamers go, the Barnes special (#8–10) is a reliable searching pattern. Other traditional bets include the gray ghost (#8–10), Kennebago smelt (#8–10), nine three (#8–10), olive matuka (#6–10), and the black nose dace bucktail (#6–10). Reif's choices are rock-solid standards. Late May through mid-July caddis hatches should be fished with a range of selections (nymphs and dries), including LaFontaine's deep sparkle pupa (#10–16) in dark gray and ginger.

Grand Lake Stream's season runs from April 1 to September 30 and has an extended catch-and-release season that is flyfishing only from October 1 to 15, including that portion of the stream adjacent to the hatchery pools. It is closed to all fishing within 150 feet of Grand Lake Stream dam. Daily bag limits are as follows: From April 1 to August 15, 2 trout and 1 salmon; from August 16 to September 30,

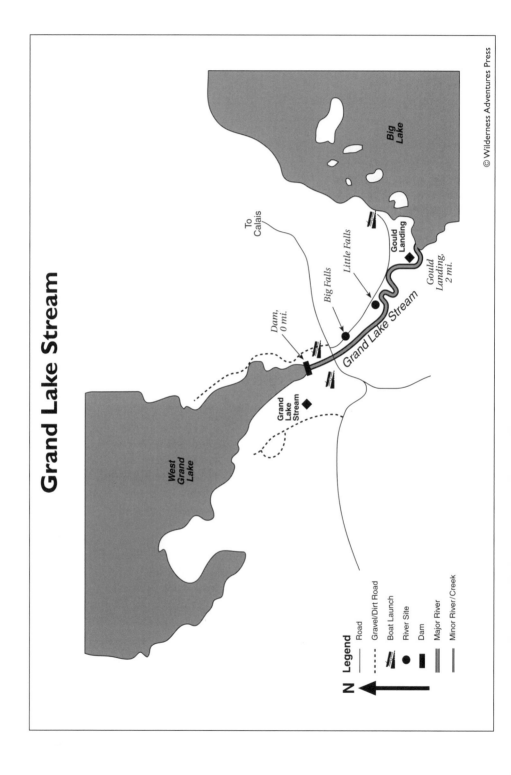

Grand Lake Stream

Big Lake

West Grand Lake

To Calais

Little Falls

Big Falls

Dam, 0 mi.

Gould Landing

Gould Landing, 2 mi.

Grand Lake Stream

Grand Lake Stream

© Wilderness Adventures Press

Legend

N

— Road
---- Gravel/Dirt Road
Boat Launch
● River Site
■ Dam
Major River
Minor River/Creek

1 fish total of salmon, trout, or togue; from October 1 to 15, all fish must be caught and released at once.

Anglers can expect a gravel and rock bottom with wading opportunities available. Flyfish the pool below the dam according to regulations. Downstream sections to Gould Landing are good, though the Big Falls to Little Falls section holds the best angling. Big Lake has salmon, also. Expect a strong current in the early season. Like West Grand Lake, this river gets hammered by gusty springtime winds. Class III rapids can be found on several river sections.

There is a passable road on the northern riverbank that affords access to anglers.

Pleasant Lake

Located south of the village of Danforth near Route 6, Pleasant Lake has good smallmouth bass fishing throughout the season as well as ice-out landlocked salmon fishing. There is camping and a boat launch at the lake's north end.

East Grand Lake

This lake is considered one of the best landlocked salmon lakes in the state of Maine. The lake, located near Danforth, is shared with the Province of New Brunswick and covers more than 16,000 acres. Its Canadian name is Chiputneticook Lakes. The East Grand Lake region offers several lodges, camps, and services.

Penobscot County Region

The **Mattawamkeag River** is a major tributary of the West Branch of the Penobscot River. The river section between the villages of Kingman and Mattawamkeag is the most accessible and offers good fishing for brook trout and landlocked salmon. There is an unimproved road off Route 2 in Mattawamkeag that follows the river on the south side. This leads to the Mattawamkeag Wilderness Park where campsites are available. The river has dangerous rapids in the spring and should only be canoed by experts.

From July 1 to September 30, the river is flyfishing only from the red posts on both shores, 100 yards above Big Gordon Brook junction to the red posts located 100 yards below the Little Gordon Brook junction. It is also flyfishing only from the red posts located on both shores 100 yards above the Mattakeunk Stream junction. From August 16 to September 30, the total daily bag limit for salmon, trout, and togue is 1 fish. Pattern choices include the marabou leech (#4–6 black or olive), beadhead pheasant tail (#12–18), stonefly nymphs (#4–12), and woolly buggers (#2–8 in black or olive).

Jerry Pond is a convenient little brook trout pond located on the outskirts of Millinocket village. The October 1 to October 31 season is catch and release by artificial lure only; motorboats are prohibited. Trout range from 6 to 12 inches. Scuds (#4–10 cream or olive) will catch these brookies in this primarily put-and-take fishery.

Lower Shin Pond is a brook trout pond located south of Shin Pond village at the termination of State Route 159. Expect fish from 6 to 10 inches. In 1996, 1,800 trout

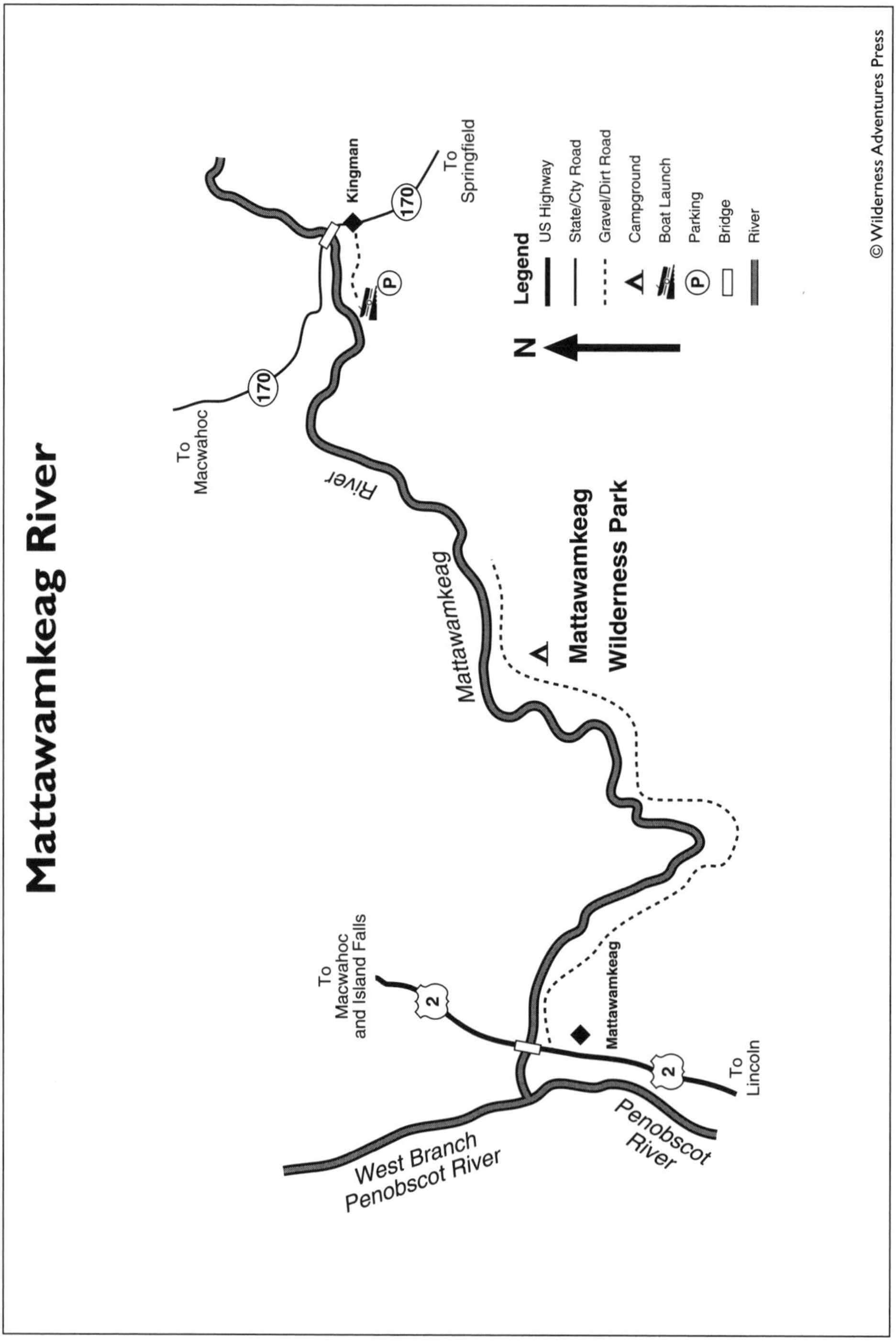

Mattawamkeag River

Legend

——	US Highway
—	State/Cty Road
- - -	Gravel/Dirt Road
▲	Campground
⌇	Boat Launch
Ⓟ	Parking
▢	Bridge
——	River

N

To Springfield

Kingman

170

To Macwahoc

170

Ⓟ

Mattawamkeag River

Mattawamkeag Wilderness Park

To Macwahoc and Island Falls

2

Mattawamkeag

2

To Lincoln

Penobscot River

West Branch Penobscot River

© Wilderness Adventures Press

were stocked in Lower Shin Pond. It is managed as a put-and-take fishery. Light, medium, and dark all-purpose nymphs will catch these stockers.

Upper Shin Pond also hosts brook trout and is located at Mount Chase Plantation north of Shin Pond village. The Maine Department of Inland Fisheries and Wildlife stocked 1,078 brookies here in 1996. The fish are from 10 to 12 inches in length. These brookies aren't too selective. Flyfish stonefly, damselfly, and dragonfly nymphs, as well as traditional wet flies.

East Central Maine Hub Cities
Greenville
Elevation–1,028 • Population–1,884

Accommodations

Allagash Gateway Cottage and Campsite, Ripogenus Lake / 207-723-9215 / Close to West Branch Penobscot River

The Birches Resort, P.O. Box 81M1 (Rockwood 04478) / 800-825-9453 / This 11,000-acre wilderness resort on Moosehead Lake offers remote cabins and lakeside dining / Open July and August / $845 per week

Evergreen Lodge Bed & Breakfast, Route 15 (6miles south of Greenville) / 207-695-3241 / Contact Sonda and Bruce Hamilton, who describe their accommodations as "casual but elegant" / Lodging includes the Caribou Room, Coyote Room, Moose Room, Deer Room, Bear Room, and Bobcat Room / Full breakfast and dinner packages available / On the web: **mainlodge.com** / $$$–$$$$

Greenwood Motel, Greenville Junction (southern end of Moosehead Lake 04442) / 800-477-4386 / Air-conditioned units, direct dial telephones, morning wake-up calls, continental breakfast, daily newspapers, individual heat controls, cable TV, guide service, and freezer for fish / 16 units / Open year-round / $$

Campgrounds

Baxter State Park, 64 Balsam Drive (Millinocket 04462) / 207-723-5140 / This 201,000-acre wilderness state park offers 8 drive-in campgrounds / Reservations may be mailed or made in person (no phone calls), sites go fast / The Katahdin Area Chamber of Commerce (1029 Central Street, Millinocket) can provide additional lodging information for this remote location

Casey's Spencer Bay Campground, P.O. Box 1161 / 207-695-2801 / Season: May 15 to October 15 / 65 sites / Fee for dogs

Moosehead Family Campground & Camp Rental Agency, P.O. Box 1244, Route 15 / 207-695-2210 / Season: May 1 to February 28 / 35 sites / Dogs welcome

Restaurants

Flatlander's, Pritham Avenue / 207-695-3373 / Steaks, ribs, burgers, and broasted chicken

Greenville Inn, Norris Street / 207-695-2206 / Maine seafood, duckling, veal, and lamb / Also offers lodging (7 rooms, 6 cottages)

Lost Lobster, North Main Street / 207-695-3900 / Seafood, ribs, chicken / Lobster boat bar serves beer and wine

Road Kill Cafe, Greenville Junction / 207-695-2230 / Serves breakfast, lunch, and dinner / I recently survived the "Cheesy Weasel Burger" / Mottos: "Not your normal restaurant" and "Never assume it's a raisin"

Fly Shops and Sporting Goods

Maine Guide Fly Shop & Guide Service, P.O. Box 1202, Main Street / 207-695-2266 / Contact Dan and Penny Legere / Caters to the Moosehead and Allagash regions / Offers drift boat and remote pond float-tubing services / Their fly selection includes over 400 patterns / Inquire here for current local flyfishing trends / email: flyshop@moosehead.net

Moose River Country Store, Route 15 (Rockwood 04478) / 207-534-7352 / Fishing supplies, nonresident licenses, beer, wine, and grocery needs / Open 7 days a week

West Branch Fly & Supply, corner of Massachusetts Avenue and New Jersey (Millinocket 04462) / 207-723-5989 / On east side of Millinocket Lake

Auto Repair

Fred's Body Shop, Greenville / 207-695-3352

Airport

Currier's Flying Service, Inc., Moosehead Lake (Greenville Junction 04442) / 207-695-2778 / Located on Route 15 near the railroad trestles / Serves all wilderness flying needs

Jack's Air Service, Box 584 (Greenville) / 207-695-3030 / Located on Moosehead Lake

Medical

Charles A. Dean Memorial Hospital, Greenville / 207-695-2223
Hospital services also available in Rangeley

Danforth/Weston/Forest City

ACCOMMODATIONS

Cowger's Lakeside Cabins, Greenland Cove (Danforth) / 207-448-2455

Davis Cottage, c/o North Woods Tours, Route 1 (Weston 04424) / 207-448-2300 / $360 per week

First Settler's Lodge, Route 1 (Weston 04424) / 207-448-3000 / $$–$$$

Greenland Cove Camps, Greenland Cove (Danforth) / 207-448-7739 / 2 night minimum / $

The Village Camps (Forest City 04413) / 207-448-7726 / On lake / $340 per week

Twin Rivers Cabin, c/o North Woods Tour, Route 1 (Weston 04424) / 207-448-2300 / $360 per week

Danforth Bed 'n' Breakfast, Depot Street (Danforth) / 207-448-2031 or 207-448-7390

Faulkner Cottage, c/o North Woods Tour, Route 2 (Weston 04424) / 207-448-2300 / On water / $450 per week

CAMPING

Greenland Cove Campground, Greenland Cove (Danforth) / 207-448-2863

RESTAURANTS

Central Street Restaurant, Central Street (Danforth) / 207-448-2863

Cornerstone Inn, Depot Street (Danforth) / 207-448-2028

FLY SHOPS AND MARINAS

Bob's Bait & Tackle, Route 169 (Danforth) / 207-448-3161

Brookton Bait & Tackle, Route 1 (Brookton 04413) / 207-448-2812

Dickinson's Sunset Park Marina, East Grand Lake (Orient 04471) / 207-448-2294

Gilpatrick Marina, Route 1 (Weston 04424) / 207-448-2648

MEDICAL

East Grand Health Center, Houlton Road (Danforth) / 207-448-2347

FOR MORE INFORMATION

East Grand Lake Area Chamber of Commerce
P.O. Box 159
Danforth, ME
207-448-3000

East Central Maine Sporting Camps

Beaver Cove Camps
Greenville, ME
800-577-3717 or 207-695-3717
Allows dogs but leash required

Brassua Lake Sporting Camps
Rockwood, ME
207-654-3412 or 534-7328
Dogs welcome

Casey's Spencer Bay Camps
Greenville, ME
207-695-2801
Allows dogs (fee required)

Indian Rock Camps
P.O. Box 117-SC
Grand Lake Stream, ME 04637
800-498-2821 or 207-796-2822
Offers guide services out of camp and a flyfishing school, which runs all summer by appointment (800-558-7658). Fishing on West Grand Lake, Big Lake, and Grand Lake Stream available.

Leen's Lodge
Box 40
Grand Lake Stream, ME
800-99-LEENS
Dick and E.J. Beaulieu
Sporting camp services a 20-mile radius around Grand Lake Stream. Dick recommends flyfishing traditional gray ghost and supervisor streamer patterns in this region. Cast-and-blast practitioners take note: "October bird hunting is fantastic," he says. "Dogs definitely allowed!"

The Pines
Box 158-SC
Grand Lake Stream, ME
207-796-5006
Open May through September, with flyfishing trips, guide service, boat and canoe rentals available.

Weatherby's
P.O. Box 69-SC
Grand Lake Stream, ME
207-796-5558
Open May through October with flyfishing trips available.

Foster's Maine Bush Sporting Camps
Greenville, ME
207-695-2845

Frost Pond Camps
Greenville, ME
207-695-2821
Allows dogs

Kokadjo Camps
Roach River
Greenville, ME
207-695-3993
Allows dogs

Little Lyford Pond Camps
Greenville, ME
207-695-2821

Medawisla
Greenville, ME
Second Road Pond
207-695-2560
Allows dogs (leash and fee required)

Raymond's Northeast Carry
Greenville, ME
207-695-2821

Spencer Pond Camps
Greenville, ME
207-695-2821
Allows dogs

Wilson's on Moosehead Lake
Greenville, ME
8000-817-2549 or 207-695-2549
Dogs welcome

Wilson Pond Camps
Greenville, ME
3.5 miles on Pleasant Street from downtown Greenville
207-695-2860
Allows dogs

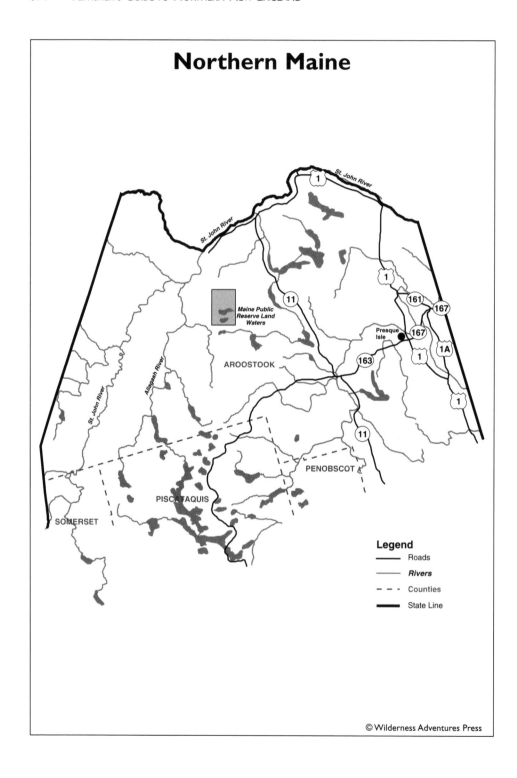

Northern Maine

Legend
— Roads
— *Rivers*
- - - Counties
— State Line

© Wilderness Adventures Press

NORTHERN MAINE

Bordering Canada are the so-called "unorganized town-ships" of Aroostook County. This remote country, owned primarily by timber companies, is scarred by clearcuts and private, unmapped logging roads that crisscross through low hills and bogs. That buzzing in your ear could be the noise of a far–off chainsaw or one of the North Country's famous biting bugs trying to make a meal of you. Mud-splattered logging trucks, shiny sport utility vehicles, and rusty 4x4 pickups rule the roads. Moose, deer, coyote, bear, and bobcat are in abundance in this vast wilderness that surrounds the Allagash and St. John Rivers.

NORTHERN MAINE MAJOR HATCHES

Insect	J	F	M	A	M	J	J	A	S	O	N	D	Flies
Streamers				■	■	■	■	■	■	■			Barnes Special #8–#10; Gray Ghost #8–#10; Kennebago Smelt #8–#10; Olive Matuka #6–#10; Black Nose Dace Bucktail #6–#10
Midges and Miniature Flies				■	■	■	■	■	■	■			Griffith's Gnat #16–#22; Parachute Adams #16–#20; Hatching Midge Pupa #12–#16; Olive Midge #16–#20; Mosquito Adult #14–#20; Midges (black and cream) #18–#22; Brassie #16–#20
Caddis						■	■						Elk Hair Caddis #6–#18; Elk-wing Parachute Caddis #12–#18; Henryville Special #12–#18; Deep Sparkle Pupa #12–#18; Brown Sparkle Pupa #6–#12; Caddis Variant #12–#18; LaFontaine's Deep Sparkle Pupa #12–#18; Beadhead Emerging Caddis #10–#14; Emergent Sparkle Pupa #12–#18
Dragonflies/Damselflies						■	■						Dragonfly Nymph #4–#8; Whitlock's Dragonfly #4–#8; Damselfly Nymph #4–#8; Whitlock Spent Blue Damsel #6
Light Cahill Stenonema canadensis						■							Light Cahill #10–16
Hexagenia						■							Hex Nymph #4–#6; Parachute Hex #8–#10 (carry both)

NORTHERN MAINE MAJOR HATCHES (cont.)

Insect	J	F	M	A	M	J	J	A	S	O	N	D	Flies
Blue-winged Olive *Ephemerella attenuata*						▓	▓	▓					Blue-winged Olive #12–#22; Blue-winged Olive Thorax #14–20; Blue-winged Olive Nymph #12
Stoneflies				▓	▓	▓							Early Black Stone #12–#16; Early Brown Stone #12–#16; Willow Fly #14–#16; Stimulator #8–#14; Stonefly Nymph (black or brown) #12–#16
Leeches						▓	▓	▓					Marabou Leech (black) #16; Woolly Bugger (olive, black, or brown) #4–#10
Terrestrials													
Ants						▓	▓	▓					Black Fur Ant #12–20; Black Flying Ant #12–16
Beetles							▓	▓					Black Beetle #14–20
Grasshoppers							▓	▓					Parachute Hopper #8–14; Letort Hopper #8–14
Crickets							▓	▓					Cricket #8–14; Letort Cricket #8–14

Allagash River

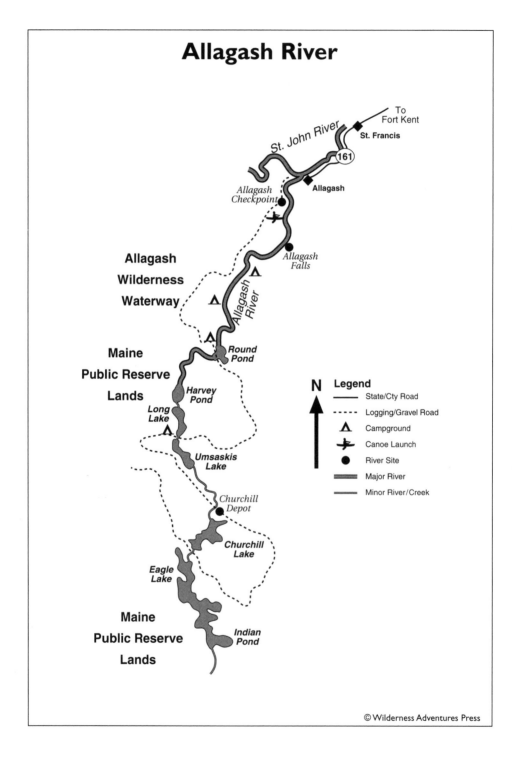

© Wilderness Adventures Press

Allagash River

In the wilds of far northern Maine, the Allagash River is best reached by canoe. It offers angling for brook trout and an opportunity to experience one of the great wilderness areas of America. The river flows through harvested timberlands and bogs. Strips of trees, intended to lessen the visual shock of clearcuts, preserve forested views. Look no further than this waterway for the wilderness brook trout fishing you crave.

Flyfishers with canoes and bug dope in tow target river sections in June and September, which typically prove to be the best months. June rates the best for biting bugs, too. As with many Maine river systems, trout gravitate toward cooler brook mouths come midsummer.

Expect prolific numbers of brook trout on the smaller side, from 6 to 10 inches, with the average brookie running 8 to 12 inches. Good trout run in the 2-pound size range.

Dry-fly purists carry a range of standard patterns into the Allagash's wilderness waters, including the mosquito (#2–20), blue-winged olive (#14–20), March brown (#12–16), light cahill (#12–20), and black gnat (#12–18). Fish generally aren't all that selective. Caddis hatches are to be relished in June. Olive woolly buggers catch some of the bigger Allagash River trout and also work in many of the region's lakes. Fish grasshopper patterns in July and August. Other terrestrial choices include foam or cork beetles and ants.

April 1 to September 30 comprises the Allagash River's season. Current angling laws, which are lengthy (like the river), are found in the Piscataquis County section of the Maine Department of Inland Fisheries and Wildlife's open water fishing regulations. For a complete copy of regulations and reservation information for the use of the Allagash Wilderness Waterway, write to the Bureau of Parks and Recreation, #22, Augusta, ME 04333, 207-287-3821.

The Allagash waterway is best covered by canoe. Plan on several days to a week or more to flyfish this river thoroughly. The river runs 90 miles from Telos Lake to Allagash and features Class I and II water with falls, gentle runs, and mixed lake sections. Portaging is necessary at times. You'll sleep better at night with the exercise. (Note: This is a wilderness fishery—services you may be accustomed to are not available along this river—no cigarettes, coffee, beer, candy. Plan ahead.) Flows are moderate to gentle and strong winds can be expected on the lakes.

Study the maps—there is good flyfishing access most anywhere along these 90 miles.

St. John River

The St. John is a tremendous river flowing from the most remote areas of northern Maine, forming a good portion of the Maine/New Brunswick border, then flowing through New Brunswick and eventually into the Bay of Fundy. The river stretch of over 130 miles through northern Maine between the village of Allagash and the

St. John River

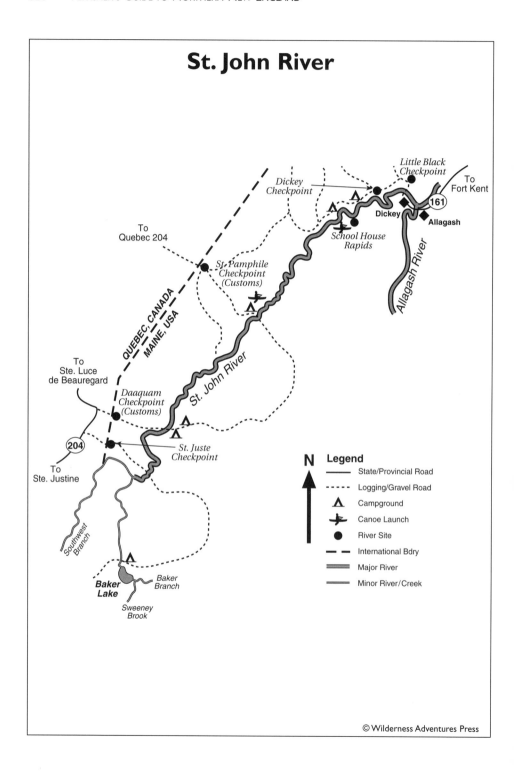

To Fort Kent

Little Black Checkpoint

Dickey Checkpoint

161

Dickey

Allagash

School House Rapids

To Quebec 204

St. Pamphile Checkpoint (Customs)

QUEBEC, CANADA

MAINE, USA

Allagash River

St. John River

To Ste. Luce de Beauregard

Daaquam Checkpoint (Customs)

204

To Ste. Justine

St. Juste Checkpoint

N

Legend

State/Provincial Road

Logging/Gravel Road

Campground

Canoe Launch

River Site

International Bdry

Major River

Minor River/Creek

Southwest Branch

Baker Lake

Baker Branch

Sweeney Brook

© Wilderness Adventures Press

headwater ponds offers the adventurer and flyfisher an opportunity to canoe and fish in a truly wild area.

This area, if it is at all possible, is wilder than the Allagash Wilderness. The St. John is what is called a "flashy" river, or river of extremes. In the spring at ice-out, blocks of ice 30 feet tall on the flood crash through the trees and river channel. In contrast, on a hot summer's day, the river turns shallow and "bony," making it possible to cross by wading at almost any point. For canoeists, this means a narrow window of opportunity.

In general, with the permission of the lumber companies, access is good, although some of the roads run in and out of Canada. North Maine Woods, an organization of the lumber companies, controls the gated roads and manages the primitive campsites and "carry only" canoe accesses in the St. John River Wilderness Area. Their headquarters are in Ashland, Maine 05732, where they can be reached by mail. The phone number is 207-435-6213. You can contact them for reservations into the area and for information about river conditions.

The St. John's season runs from April 1 to September 30, and anglers are advised to refer to the Maine Department of Inland Fisheries and Wildlife regulations. The river supports great numbers of wild brook trout in the 6- to 10-inch length range. Caddis and attractor patterns work well.

Maine Public Reserve Land Waters
Deboule Mountain Region

The minimum legal length for trout on the following Aroostook County fisheries is 8 inches, and only 1 fish may exceed 12 inches. The bag limit is 2 trout per day, unless otherwise noted. These stillwaters are located in T15 R9 WELS and offer maintained, wilderness campsites nearby. When planning a trip to this wild, remote area, refer to DeLorme's *Maine Atlas and Gazetteer*.

Sitting at 1,225 feet, **Black Pond** is an artificial-lure-only fishery and is stocked with brook trout. There is flyfishing only on **North Little Black Pond** and **South Little Black Pond** and a hand-carried boat launch on Black Pond. Access is by foot trail. Damselfly and dragonfly nymphs are especially good, as well as black leech-imitating streamers (#8–10).

Crater Pond is an artificial-lure-only pond with a hand-carried boat launch. Flyfish the mosquito emerger (#14–20), brown and tan woolly worms (#6–12), and a range of caddis pupa and larva patterns.

Deboule Pond, called "Deboullie Lake" on some regional maps, sits at 1,128 feet and has a hand-carried boat launch. Caddis pupa and larva patterns, damselfly nymphs, and terrestrials, such as beetles, ants, inchworms, and hoppers, will all catch trout.

Denny Pond is flyfishing only and also has a hand-carried boat launch. A 25-acre springhole pond that is 35 feet deep, it is full of 8- to 12-inch brook trout. An elk hair caddis will do the job, though terrestrials, especially hoppers, catch trout in the summer. A well-maintained forest campsite is located on the eastern shore. Access is by foot trail.

On **Fifth Pelletier Brook Lake**, flyfish olive, black, and brown sedges (#12–16), terrestrials, such as beetles and inchworms, damselfly and dragonfly nymphs, as well as cream or olive scuds (#4–10).

Fish scuds, leech patterns, damselfly and dragonfly nymphs on **Gardner Lake**, listed as "Gardner Pond" on some maps. Its elevation is 1,134 feet.

On **Galilee Pond**, a flyfishing-only water, use midges, dragonfly and damselfly nymphs, and scuds to catch trout. Stop here on your way to and from Gardner.

Cast from a canoe along the western shore of **Island Pond**, which is flyfishing only. The entire pond holds trout, and caddis dries, pupa, and larva patterns, along with damselfly and dragonfly nymphs are effective patterns here.

On **Mud Pond**, fish traditional mayfly and caddisfly patterns; scuds fished along the pond's bottom also catch trout.

Small flies work on **Perch Pond**, including scuds, foam or cork beetles, and mosquito dries (#18–22). Flyfish scuds slowly with sinking lines. Access is by foot trail, and there is a hand-carried boat launch.

Fish scuds, damselfly and dragonfly nymphs on **Pushineer Pond**, which also has a hand-carried boat launch.

Stink Pond, a 16-acre float-tube water, is 5 feet deep at most and flyfishing only. The limited access to this fishery diminishes angling pressure.

On **Togue Pond**, the daily bag limit on salmon, trout, and togue is 3 fish in the aggregate, not to include more than 2 salmon, 2 trout, or 2 togue. There is a trailered boat launch, and several maintained wilderness campsites are located on the pond's northern shore with unimproved road access available. Search this water with sinking line and a black or olive marabou leech (#4–6).

Upper Pond is flyfishing only and has a hand-carried boat launch and is accessible by foot trail.

Northern Maine Hub City
Presque Isle
Population–10,550

Accommodation
Budget Traveler Motor Lodge, 71 Main Street / 207-769-0111 or 800-958-0111 / $
Keddy's Motor Inn and Convention Center, 116 South Main Street / 207-764-3321 or 800-561-7666 / $$
Northeastland Hotel, 436 Main Street / 207-768-5321 / $$
Rum Rapids Inn Bed & Breakfast, Route 164 (Crouseville, 5 miles from Presque Isle) / 207-455-8096
The Old Iron Inn Bed & Breakfast, 155 Main Street (Caribou) / 207-492-4766 / On the web: **www.mainerec.com/ironinn** / $

Campgrounds
Arndt's Aroostook River Lodge and Campground, 15 Wilson Street / 207-764-8677
Neil E. Michaud Campground, 164 Houlton Road / 207-760-1951

Restaurants
Riverside Inn Restaurant, 399 Main Street / 207-764-1447
Governor's Restaurant, 360 Main Street / 207-769-2274
Winnie's Restaurant & Dairy Bar, 79 Parsons Street / 207-769-4971

Fly Shops and Guides
Roy's Army and Navy, 710 Main Street / 207-768-3181 / Dana Packard is the proprietor as well as a local guide / A full service fly shop and guide referral service
Brown's Trading Post, Box 337, RFD #1, Ludlow Road (Houlton 04730) / 207-532-2534 / Mary Brown is the proprietor / A full service fly shop that offers a referral service for area guides
Scott Arndt / 207-764-0730
Libby Camps, P.O. Box V (Millinocket Lake, Ashland 04732) / 207-435-8274

Airport
Northern Maine Regional Airport / U.S. Airways Express, 207-764-4724

Medical
Aroostook Medical Center / 207-768-4000

For More Information
Presque Isle Chamber of Commerce
3 Houlton Road
Presque Isle, ME 04769
207-764-6561

Northern New England Game Fish

Brook Trout Identification
Salvelinus fontinalis

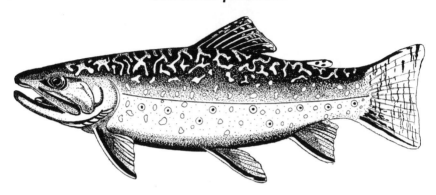

Regional Names: squaretail, brookie, speckled trout, native. Sea-run brook trout are called salters.

Technically a char, planted and wild brook trout sport gunmetal-blue, blue-green, or olive-colored backs, depending on the fishery and origin of the fish. Worm-like markings cover their upper sides with a spray of red dots, each encircled by a blue halo splashed across their sides. Color variations are many. Bellies are typically cream-colored and orange-hued. Native northern New England brookies are more brightly colored than their stocked cousins, with variations in brilliance.

Brown Trout Identification
Salmo trutta

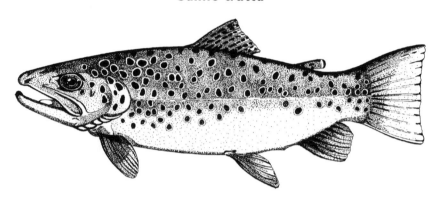

Regional Names: brown, brownie, German brown, Loch Leven trout. Sea-run browns are also called salters.

Brown trout exhibit bronze, gold, and bright yellow washes of color, with predominantly black or brown spots covering their sides. A few red or orange dots may appear there, too, each encircled by a halo of blue. Bellies are yellow. Sea-run brown trout in the Ogunquit River and Berry Brook fisheries are colored a light silvery brown or tan with black spots surrounded by halo-like markings.

Pale-colored brown trout caught on northern New England's bigger lakes may resemble landlocked salmon at first glance. Obvious differences are found in the mouths and tails. Jawbones on browns extend well beyond the rear edge of the eye and usually just to the rear edge of the eye on salmon. Vomerine teeth inside the upper jaws of browns are zigzagged, while salmon sport a single row. Brown trout caudal fins are square. The tails of landlocked salmon are slightly forked.

Rainbow Trout Identification
Oncorhynchus mykiss

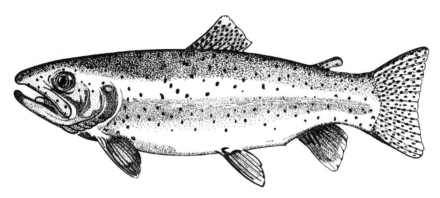

Regional Names: used here, the word "steelhead" denotes lake-run Vermont rainbows.

The rainbow has prominent black spots on its head, flanks, back, dorsal and caudal fins, with a distinctive pink band running along each side. Displaying vibrant red to cotton-candy pink gill covers, the rainbow's sides flash silvery on the inevitable jump.

Lake Trout Identification
Salvelinus namaycush

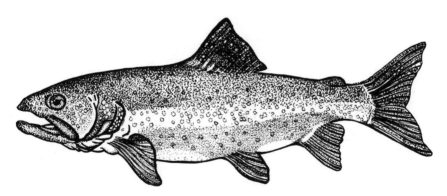

Regional Names: togue, laker, mackinaw, forktail.

Colors can vary between specimens: some have gray-green to dark olive backs with blue-gray to bronze-green sides. All are fork-tailed and marked with many pale yellow spots. Splake, the laker/brook trout hybrids, have the same appearance but with squarer tails.

Landlocked Salmon/Atlantic Salmon Identification
Salmo salar

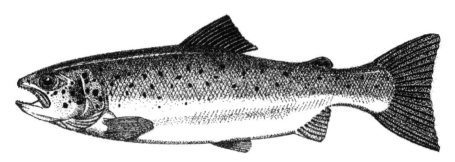

Regional Names: landlock, Sebago salmon, ouananiche (landlocked salmon), salmon (Atlantics).

Ice Age salmon survivors that were sealed off from the Atlantic Ocean became landlocked. Atlantic salmon are anadromous.

These fish are primarily silver-colored with well-spaced black spots across the sides and gill plates and black (dark gray to gray-green) above. Merrimack River broodstock salmon are pale green in color with the same markings. Sea-run Atlantics and landlocks sometimes exhibit x-shaped black spots across their silvery sides.

Largemouth Bass Identification
Micropterus salmoides

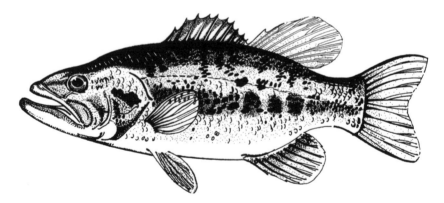

Regional Names: black bass, bucketmouth, bigmouth bass.

Dark green, even black, on the back and upper sides with a horizontal (sometimes broken) band running from behind the gill plate to the tail. On big bass, this band is sometimes blotchy as ink stains or as subtly jagged as a seismograph line. Dark olive, silvery-green, or dusky bronze-green sides fade to a white belly. Colors vary from water to water.

Smallmouth Bass Identification
Micropterus dolomieui

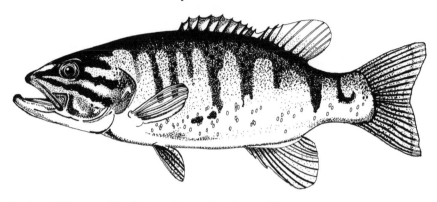

Regional Names: black bass, bronzeback, smallie.

Olive-colored, bronze-toned or brownish-tinged back and sides. Sides are marked with dark vertical bars running from back to belly and across the gill plates. They are white under the jaw and have reddish eyes.

Striped Bass
Morone saxatilis

Regional Names: striper, lineside, rockfish, greenhead, schoolie (small striper)

Identified by the six to eight longitudinal black strips running along its silvery sides. The upper side and back are typically olive-gray and nearly black on top. Heads are pale green above and white below. A bronze tinge washes over the silvery tone of some fish, while others seem silvery-blue with a slight, shimmering hint of purple. The have a pearl-white belly and golden, glowing eyes. Cows grow larger than bulls.

Catch and Release

I eat fish but release plenty, too. Moderation yields long-term results in almost all walks of life. The following will help ensure a successful release:

1. Land and release game fish as quickly as possible. Stressing trout, salmon, black bass, and stripers can make release difficult. Enjoy the fight but match your fly-fishing tackle with your quarry.

2. Fish obviously do their breathing in water—keep them there as much as possible. Stage photographs quickly, then take your time reviving fish in the water.

3. Handle fish gently.

4. Remove hooks carefully. Use barbless hooks to expedite easy release. Never touch the gills.

5. If hook retrieval is impossible, cut the leader and leave the hook in the fish. Hook extractors work as long as you proceed as cautiously as a surgeon.

6. Hold the fish upright in the water to revive it. Gently move the fish back and forth to force water through its gills. Continue to do so until the fish fins off under its own power.

—Steve Hickoff

Getting There

Depending on your taste for adventure, prop planes service much of the northern New England region with connecting flights northward from Boston's Logan Airport (617-973-5500) to Bangor and Portland, Maine; Manchester, New Hampshire; and Burlington, Vermont. Major carriers include USAir (800-247-8786), Delta (800-221-1212), Continental (800-525-0280), Colgan (800-272-5488), and American (800-433-7300). Car rental chains are also established at these airports.

Flyfishers can also just drive to the region and either prospect for angling opportunities or hire a guide. Both methods can be effective. Sometimes, just booking a room near a reliable fishery is productive.

Outdoor sports are a dominant factor of North Country haunts. As a result, you can usually bet that many owners of lodges, hotels, motels, cottages, and cabins know what they're talking about when it comes to local angling. After all, many of them also fish, and many flyfishers pass through their main office. These people tend to hear about current angling conditions and can often recommend flies, specific approaches, and even locations to fish during your visit.

—Steve Hickoff

What To Take

An 8½- to 9-foot, 4-, 5-, or 6-weight fly rod is recommended for most freshwater North Country situations. You'll need to be armed with stouter tackle for saltwater stripers (see "Coastal Striped Bass Flyfishing" on page 136 of the New Hampshire section). Waters harboring outsized trout, salmon, and black bass beg for 7- to 9-weight rod and line considerations. Many passionate flyfishers carry an assortment.

What about reels? Ubiquitous single-action reels store line efficiently with few moving parts to gum up the works. High quality disc drags can help fight bigger trout and salmon. Essentially, your reel of choice should hold the appropriate fly line and the requisite amount of backing in the event your landlock salmon decides to make for the next county—dacron is best. Trout require roughly 100 yards of the stuff, while salmon and saltwater stripers require 100 additional yards.

As fly lines go, floating options prove to be the most useful, enabling the flyfisher to work all manner of dries, wet, smelt-imitating streamers, and even weighted woolly buggers through riffles and runs. Intermediate lines can work well on big salmon lakes, such as New Hampshire's Winnipesaukee and Maine's Sebago, nullifying (somewhat) the influence of water-surface winds. Slow- and fast-sinking lines can be useful on a conditional basis where stillwater and river situations dictate a deeper delivery. Specialists often flyfish lead-core lines in the depths of lakes and deeper ponds with good results. Select tapers according to your personal preference.

Knotless commercial leaders stacked an inch thick in your nearest fly vest pocket will save you valuable time after raising a good fish or while standing in the midst of a monster caddis hatch. I can never have enough and grow nervous on outings when I'm down to just a few. Carry a range of leaders from 3X for chucking woolly buggers to 7X for dinky midges. Leaders in 5X or 6X leaders are as essential as sandwiches and cold drinks in the cooler. Tippet spools should fill yet another pocket. And then we have the matter of flies.

You can never have too many flies, and you can never have too many sizes of the same fly pattern. Well stocked vests, though adding considerable weight to the fly-fisher, are essential when angling northern New England waters. Carry a range of mayfly, caddis, and stonefly options, plus terrestrials and streamers. Fly shop owners can often provide valuable insight where a local water is concerned.

As waders go, neoprene is seen as often as old-school rubber in northern New England. Hipboots are good for small stream angling, and anglers can wade wet in many locations by summer. Felt soles improve traction as you negotiate slippery rocks, while aluminum-studded felts bolster gripping ability. Archaic or not, some guys even carry wading staffs.

You can opt to go it alone or flyfish with a reliable guide. If you choose the latter, reward his or her efforts with something stronger than your grateful words: money. Tips compensate individuals who put you into good flyfishing, provide extra wood for your cabin, or cook you wonderful meals. Sometimes it's the same person. Generally, tips average 15 to 20 percent of your bill relating to service, excluding taxes, licenses, and so on.

Some sporting camps factor tips into the final bill. Some places have all tips put into a "tip pool" to be divided among the employees. Often, it's best to give your tip to the person directly. If they politely decline to accept, smile and stuff the money in their front shirt pocket.

—Steve Hickoff

Dangers and Distractions

If you don't like biting bugs, stay home or stay inside when you visit, because springtime in northern New England means blackflies. Jokingly dubbed Maine's "state bird" (or New Hampshire's or Vermont's, depending on where you are), this annually biting bug flurry can make wading flyfishers lurch out of productive waters and waddle clownlike to their nearby vehicles.

Unfortunately, depending on your mental toughness, some of the best flyfishing occurs during this time frame, which falls between early May and the heart of summer, depending on the region.

I've been mildly surprised at times to encounter backwoods blackflies on the Canadian border in August.

Blackflies and mosquitoes will definitely pester you, although repellent and cheap cigars do an adequate job of keeping them away. Many convenience stores carry both. Image be damned, some folks wear head nets during the worst of it. All in all, though, biting bugs are only distracting, while moose straddling the yellow lines of a highway are just plain dangerous.

Moose love muddy roadside bogs and are dangerous at any speed when you're behind the wheel of an automobile at dusk, after dark, or at dawn. Gruesome annual accounts of North Country motorists plowing into these massive animals serve as reminders to drive slowly even when under the influence of the flyfishing addiction.

Black bears, native residents of these northern woods, are reclusive by nature, although a meeting with a protective sow with young cubs should be taken seriously. My personal encounters with solitary black bears while flyfishing can be counted on one hand. In each case, the animal moved off upstream, and in one case, ran away.

Northern New England weather provides far more drama than most black bear encounters. When fishing from a boat or canoe, keep an eye on the sky. Storms can blow in quickly, turning stillwater to whitecaps. Be especially careful when flyfishing mountainous regions on foot.

—Steve Hickoff

General Index

*Bold page numbers indicate the primary listing for that entry.

Vermont Index

New Hampshire Index

Maine Index

NOTES

NOTES

NOTES

NOTES

NOTES

WILDERNESS ADVENTURES GUIDE SERIES

If you would like to order additional copies of this book or our other Wilderness Adventures Press guidebooks, please fill out the order form below or call **1-800-925-3339** or **fax 800-390-7558.** Visit our website for a listing of over 2000 sporting books—the largest online: **www.wildadv.com**

Mail to: Wilderness Adventures Press, 45 Buckskin Road
Belgrade, MT 59714

☐ **Please send me your quarterly catalog on hunting and flyfishing books.**

Ship to:
Name _____

Address _____

City _____ State _____ Zip _____

Home Phone _____ Work Phone _____

Payment: ☐ Check ☐ Visa ☐ Mastercard ☐ Discover ☐ American Express

Card Number _____ Expiration Date _____

Signature _____

Qty	Title of Book and Author	Price	Total
	Flyfisher's Guide to Colorado	$26.95	
	Flyfisher's Guide to Idaho	$26.95	
	Flyfisher's Guide to Montana	$26.95	
	Flyfisher's Guide to Northern California	$26.95	
	Flyfisher's Guide to Wyoming	$26.95	
	Flyfisher's Guide to Oregon	$26.95	
	Flyfisher's Guide to Washington	$26.95	
	Flyfisher's Guide to Northern New England	$26.95	
	Flyfisher's Guide to Pennsylvania	$26.95	
	Flyfisher's Guide to Michigan	$26.95	
	Total Order + shipping & handling		

Shipping and handling: $4.00 for first book,
$2.50 per additional book, up to $11.50 maximum